Low Intensity Cognitive Behaviour Therapy

Low Intensity Cognitive Behaviour Therapy

A Practitioner's Guide

Mark Papworth, Theresa Marrinan and
Brad Martin with Dominique Keegan
and Anna Chaddock

Los Angeles | London | New Delhi
Singapore | Washington DC

SAGE

Los Angeles | London | New Delhi
Singapore | Washington DC

SAGE Publications Ltd
1 Oliver's Yard
55 City Road
London EC1Y 1SP

SAGE Publications Inc.
2455 Teller Road
Thousand Oaks, California 91320

SAGE Publications India Pvt Ltd
B 1/I 1 Mohan Cooperative Industrial Area
Mathura Road
New Delhi 110 044

SAGE Publications Asia-Pacific Pte Ltd
3 Church Street
#10-04 Samsung Hub
Singapore 049483

Editor: Susan Worsey
Assistant editor: Emma Millman
Production editor: Rachel Burrows
Copyeditor: Wendy Pillar
Proofreader: Derek Markham
Marketing manager: Tamara Navaratnam
Cover design: Wendy Scott
Typeset by: C&M Digitals (P) Ltd, Chennai, India
Printed in Great Britain by MPG Printgroup, UK

MIX
Paper from
responsible sources
FSC
www.fsc.org   FSC® C018575

Library of Congress Control Number: 2012947324

British Library Cataloguing in Publication data

A catalogue record for this book is available from the British Library

ISBN 978-1-4462-0919-6
ISBN 978-1-4462-0920-2 (pbk)

Contents

List of Figures, Tables and Exercises

Figures

Tables

Exercises

About the Authors

Dr Mark Papworth is the course director of Newcastle University's PGCert in Low Intensity Psychological Therapies and also works as a consultant clinical psychologist within the National Health Service in the northeast of England.

Theresa Marrinan is a clinical psychologist and was formerly the assistant course director of Newcastle University's PGCert in Low Intensity Psychological Therapies. Currently she is a clinical tutor and senior academic tutor on the Doctorate in Clinical Psychology programme at Newcastle University.

Dr Brad Martin was previously a clinical lecturer at Newcastle University and the clinical lead for the Sunderland Primary Care and Improving Access to Psychological Therapies Service. He is currently a consultant clinical psychologist and cognitive therapist in Wellington, New Zealand.

Dr Dominique Keegan is a principal clinical psychologist and cognitive therapist working for the National Health Service in the northeast of England. She also works as a trainer, supervisor and tutor on the Cognitive Behaviour Therapy Diploma and has contributed as a clinical lecturer to the Low Intensity Cognitive Behaviour Therapy, High Intensity PGDip and Clinical Psychology Doctoral programmes at Newcastle University.

Dr Anna Chaddock is a clinical psychologist and cognitive behaviour therapist. She trained as a high intensity cognitive behaviour therapist in the first wave of Improving Access to Psychological Therapies services and now tutors on Newcastle University's PGDip in High Intensity Psychological Therapies.

Acknowledgements

Thank you to the PGCert trainees from Newcastle University for helping us to develop our understanding of low intensity cognitive behaviour therapy. We are indebted to Professor Mark Freeston and a number of anonymous reviewers for feedback over the planning and final stages of the book.

MP: Thank you Danna for your great patience, support and proof-reading skills.

TM: Many thanks to all those who provided feedback on drafts, particularly to Kate Aitchison, David Barker, Terri Hollinghurst, Denise Mangan, John Moiser and Stephen Short. Thanks also to my family and friends who have been so supportive, particularly to Janet and my parents who are a constant and much appreciated source of encouragement.

BM: Thanks to Michael LeBow, Ian James, Theresa Marrinan and Mark Freeston for their patience and generosity; to Jen Cottam, Natalie Dickens, Ashley Cave, Darren Liddle, Anna Dunwoodie and Gemma Finch for their various contributions to this work; and to Chelsea, Jack, Frankie and Amelie for everything else.

DK: To Mark and Theresa for their help, advice and the opportunity. To Phil and Freddie for their patience and support.

AC: I would like to thank Theresa Marrinan, Anna Hodgson, Michelle Bowen, Kelly Oliver and Dominique Keegan for their help and support with the chapter; as well as Richard Thwaites and James Bennett-Levy who have been so influential in forming my understanding of empathy and the therapeutic relationship.

Introduction

Mark Papworth

Learning objectives

- To understand the fundamental principles of CBT and LICBT.
- To know the historical context of the development of CBT and LICBT.
- To be aware of systems of stepped and matched care that support the practice of LICBT.
- To have knowledge of the other aspects of service delivery (for example, service promotion and self-referral), which are required to maximise the impact of the approach.
- To understand the economic argument which justified the English LICBT (IAPT) scheme, and to be aware of the effectiveness of LICBT.

Introduction

The 'core mission' of this book is to teach the reader how to perform low intensity cognitive-behavioural therapy (LICBT). This is a new form of CBT that is used to treat mild to moderate, common mental health problems over a shorter length of contact, through the use of therapy vehicles (such as supported self-help). However, before I turn to this important and fascinating topic, by way of an introduction I look at the varied contexts in which the approach has grown. These contexts have both enabled the development of the approach and are required to support its practice. These might be broadly described as *historical* (LICBT's origins), *service-related* (the arrangement of healthcare services which support LICBT), and *political* (the economic and political arguments that have driven the development of LICBT). To overview these, this chapter examines the principles of CBT and LICBT, then two of the psychotherapeutic approaches that have been instrumental in the development of CBT, the stepped care model of service delivery and latterly the English Improving Access to Psychological Therapies (IAPT) scheme.

Cognitive-behavioural therapy

The CBT approach assumes that emotions, behaviours and physical symptoms (which are core components of common psychological disorders) are influenced by thoughts, beliefs and images that exist in individuals' minds. These mental processes are termed 'cognitions'.

A classic example of this process in action is illustrated by the following situation: imagine that you are walking along a street and you notice that an acquaintance is approaching, walking towards you but on the other side of the street. You try to catch their attention but, rather than wave back, this person carries on walking without acknowledging you with their head remaining bowed down. Let us suppose the thought then goes through your mind: 'What have I done to upset them, why doesn't this person like me?' These cognitions might naturally cause you to become worried about your relationship with that person and more generally about how others perceive you. You might later also experience some physical symptoms that commonly accompany worry such as difficulty sleeping and restlessness while the matter plays on your mind. Now, let us imagine an alternative cognitive response to the situation. In this instance you think instead: 'They seem preoccupied, I wonder what is concerning them?' This line of thought is likely to have impacted less upon your mood because it is enquiring about their situation rather than reflecting negatively upon your own. As such, it will probably lead to a different course of action, perhaps contacting the acquaintance to check if they are in any difficulty.

The CBT approach provides a framework for understanding how individuals' interpretations of events may lead to the development and maintenance of psychological disorders (such as depression and anxiety). CBT treatment then involves the use of techniques to change dysfunctional patterns of cognition and behaviour that are central to such psychological difficulties. This approach emerged in the 1950s and 1960s, both arising out of 'behavioural approaches' that were popular at the time and as a reaction to 'psychoanalytic psychotherapy'. Before investigating CBT further, I first explore these therapeutic approaches to help us to understand its roots.

Psychoanalytic psychotherapy

Psychoanalytic psychotherapy has been in existence for over a century and, over this time, it has developed into numerous models of the mind and human nature. Therefore, you should bear in mind that below is a brief, basic summary of one (the Freudian) model that is informed by Atkinson, Atkinson, Smith, Bem and Hilgard (1990) and also Smith (1995). The psychoanalytic approach assumes that various tensions or conflicts exist within an individual's psychological 'make-up' or personality. These conflicts arise as a result of competing demands made by three different components that exist in the person's mind. These are termed: *id, ego* and *super-ego*. The id develops earliest in life and consists of our basic impulses, motivations and drives (for example, the need to eat and to gain sensual pleasure). Later, as infants learn that these impulses cannot always be satisfied immediately, they develop another element or aspect to their personality: the ego. This is essentially the manager of the id. It juggles the competing demands of the id, the real world and also the super-ego. The super-ego consists of the values and morals of society that are taught to the child by their parents and other adults. This is the part of the mind that rewards the individual for being good and punishes them for being bad.

Sigmund Freud (1856–1939) was the principal originator of this approach (in the late nineteenth century). He proposed that some difficulties emerged from tensions or conflicts between these elements. He also pictured the mind as having a similarity to an iceberg. Most of the iceberg is not visible because it is below the water's surface. Similarly, much of the activity of the human mind occurs below the surface of our consciousness, therefore occurring on an unconscious level. When there is a severe conflict, the ego can protect the individual by pushing it into the unconscious. So, for instance, an anxiety disorder might be fuelled by the presence of unconscious, unacceptable or dangerous impulses that are kept in check (or repressed) because they might impact upon a person's self-esteem or relationships. However, this is not a permanent solution and this unconscious material exerts pressure. At times this finds expression through irrational behaviour, dreams and possibly psychological difficulties if the ego is unable to sufficiently manage the situation.

Psychoanalysts seek to help their clients by bringing their conflicts into their awareness, ideally transforming symptoms into insights. They attempt to uncover the unconscious conflicts through use of techniques that facilitate their expression. These include:

- free association – unconscious conflicts can be revealed by the client saying what comes into their mind without any conscious editing;
- dream analysis – dreams are considered to contain unconscious desires in a disguised form;

- analysis of 'transference' responses – the client's unconscious feelings towards the thera-pist mirror childhood responses to parents that can explain the origins of conflicts; and
- interpretation – the client is helped to develop insight by the analyst feeding back or interpreting the understanding that they have learned about the client's resistance and motivations.

The process of psychoanalysis is lengthy and intense. It traditionally involves therapy sessions for several times per week, for at least a year and often longer. Its protagonists believe that, as unconscious material is brought to light and understood, symptoms are dissipated.

In understanding the historical development of CBT I draw upon Morrey (1995) as well as France and Robson (1997). CBT pioneers such as Albert Ellis (1913–2007) and Aaron Beck (1921–) were originally psychoanalytic psychotherapists who, in the 1950s and 1960s, came to understand that there were radically different ways to make sense of clients' psychological difficulties. Another key individual is the clinical psychologist George Kelly (1905–1967). He also developed an approach in 1955 that emphasised certain principles that were common to CBT. I focus below on Beck's model because it has been the most intensively researched and is the most popular form of CBT practised in the UK (Morrey, 1995). Indeed, Beck's approach has become synonymous with the term CBT, although it needs to be noted that there have been other contemporary CBT approaches that remain popular (for instance, Rational–Emotive Therapy). There have also been important developments in the field of CBT in recent years (such as Mindfulness-based CBT).

Beck originally sought to experimentally investigate the psychoanalytic proposition that depression was fuelled by repressed hostility. He did this by surveying the dream content of depressed individuals. His results contradicted this hypothesis and he found that their dreams were characterised by pessimism rather than anger. Likewise, within his therapy sessions, when clients were asked to free associate, the content of this process was not always of relevance to what was hypothesised to be the roots of their difficulties. Rather, their thoughts revolved around more immediate reactions to their situation, such as worrying about how Beck would judge a comment that they had made. Upon further investigation, he found that many depressed clients reported these types of thoughts and that they seemed to occur as much in their everyday lives as in the therapy session. He labelled these as 'automatic thoughts' because they occurred rapidly and fleetingly without conscious prompting. While some of the thoughts were plausible, many seemed irrational or without basis, yet at the moment they occurred they were accepted unquestioningly by the client. They were often negative in nature and hence became known as *negative automatic thoughts*. Beck came to see these patterns of thinking as a distorted lens through which clients saw both themselves and their surroundings. He helped his clients to explore a method of correcting these patterns by challenging these thoughts with questions such as: 'What is the evidence for … [their interpretation of an issue or situation]?' and 'Is there an alternative explanation?'

He found that, as clients used this technique to develop an alternative perspective, their difficulties rapidly improved – these observations forming the early building blocks of CBT (Beck, 1976).

Exercise 1.1   The origins and basics of CBT

Learn about the fundamentals of CBT by watching these internet clips:

- Beck describes the origins of CBT – www.youtube.com/watch?v=g879IJmAQCM& feature=related
- Beck's psychologist daughter (Judith) talks about the basics of CBT – www.youtube. com/watch?v=45U1F7cDH5k
- David Clark (an eminent UK clinical psychologist) explains the principles of CBT in a way that a client can understand – www.youtube.com/watch?v=JSO6iAFekPw
- A client describes her experience of receiving CBT – www.youtube.com/ watch?v=GVX4iVXtT-o&feature=relmfu

---

Behaviour therapy

Behaviour therapy refers to a number of different therapeutic approaches based on the principles of learning, which were established in the early to mid-twentieth century. Learning theory pioneers such as Ivan Pavlov (1849–1936) and Burrhus Skinner (1904–1990) found that animals and humans alike learn in two primary ways. Together, these form the building blocks of learning (Atkinson et al., 1990). The first of these is termed *classical conditioning* and refers to learning that one event will follow another. For example, a baby learns that milk will follow from the sight of a breast. In his classic experiment, Pavlov retrained a dog's salivation response. Naturally, when a dog sees food (the food in this context is termed an 'unconditioned stimulus'), it salivates (an 'unconditioned response' to this stimulus because it is a natural one). However, let us suppose a bell (a 'neutral stimulus') is also rung each time that the food is presented. Over time, the dog will associate the bell with the food and then salivate to the sound of the bell alone (this then becomes a 'conditioned response' to the 'conditioned stimulus' – the bell).

The second form of learning is termed *operant conditioning* and refers to learning that a behaviour will be followed by a consequence. For example, a child learns that hitting a sibling will result in disapproval from a parent. Skinner found that, if an animal is given a reward (such as food), after performing a behaviour (like pressing a lever), the frequency of that behaviour increases dramatically. In this way, rewards (or 'reinforcements') increase the rate of behaviour occurrence. There are two types of reinforcement:

positive and negative. Positive reinforcement occurs when a behaviour increases or is strengthened following the provision of a satisfying stimulus. So, a person might work harder or take on more duties if they are paid more. Negative reinforcement occurs when a behaviour increases or is strengthened as the result of taking away an unpleasant stimulus. In this way, a person might learn to improve poor work performance in order to avoid disapproval from their manager or take aspirin to remove a headache. Punishment differs from reinforcement in that it consists of providing an unpleasant stimulus after a behaviour (for example, slapping a child for throwing some food). This will tend to suppress the behaviour. However, as punishment fails to convey an appropriate alternative behaviour, its effects can be unpredictable. In addition, it can instil fear and aggression, and so for these reasons it is seen as a less effective form of learning. Later, psychologists also identified learning that occurs through observing others (Bandura, 1973).

Aspects of the development and maintenance of clinical difficulties can be understood in terms of learning theory. For example, a phobia might be developed through classical conditioning. This was demonstrated by John Watson (1878–1958) when he introduced a nine-month-old baby (Little Albert) to a number of objects (including a rat). Initially, Albert did not exhibit fear in response to these. However, as Albert was subsequently introduced to these objects a loud, frightening sound was made. Consequently, Albert made a link between the conditioned stimulus (the rat) and the conditioned response (fear), illustrating a mechanism for the development of a phobia. Clients sometimes report similar origins to their own phobias. A phobia of public transport might develop after experiencing an extremely humiliating experience on a bus such as involuntary defecation. Fear may then be maintained by operant conditioning as the avoidance of aversive states is reinforced through avoidance of the feared stimulus (Mowrer, 1947). This can be illustrated with the example given above where, by avoiding public transport, the person does not experience the high anxiety associated with this situation. This encourages them to continue to avoid public transport in the future.

Exercise 1.2   The application of learning theory

A mother is travelling on a bus with her four-year-old son. The son has a temper tantrum because he is bored and wants to go home to play with his toys. The mother, feeling embarrassed, removes her son from the bus, abandons her trip and takes him home. Which behaviour is being reinforced? What form of reinforcement is being used?

When the mother and child get home, the child quietly plays with his toys. At this point the mother shouts at her son for embarrassing her earlier. Despite the mother's intentions, which behaviour is actually being punished at that point?

Is the mother's behaviour helping the child? If not, give some thought to what responses would be more helpful for him.

Behaviour therapy uses the principles of learning theory in order to help people to overcome their psychological problems. For instance, the treatment of phobias involves a process of de-conditioning. This approach was termed 'systematic desensitisation' (Wolpe, 1969) and has similarities to 'graded exposure'. This approach involves substituting a response to a feared stimulus that is incompatible with anxiety, in this case relaxation. The client is taught skills that allows them to relax, prior to them being introduced to the anxiety-provoking stimulus. The client's task is then to relax while being exposed to the stimuli, thus breaking the relationship between the object/situation and fear. Exposure is graded in that the process starts with a stimulus that provokes a lesser degree of anxiety such as a picture of a cartoon rat rather than a live one. Then, after anxiety lessens through repeated exposure to this stimulus, increasingly challenging ones are then confronted (see Chapter 10 for details of graded exposure).

Cognitive therapy practitioners originally emphasised the use of cognitive techniques to alleviate distress, but then later integrated behavioural perspectives to form CBT. For example, Clark's (1986) approach to the treatment of panic disorder uses both cognitive techniques (identifying the thoughts that drive anxiety, then challenging these thoughts and substituting them with more functional alternatives) and behavioural ones (using behavioural experiments to disconfirm panic-related thoughts and exposure to confront avoided stimuli; see Chapter 10 for details regarding the theory and implementation of these techniques). However, it should be noted that similar developments also developed from another source in that behaviour therapists such as Martin Seligman (1942–) began to incorporate cognitive mechanisms into their approach in the mid-1970s (France & Robson, 1997).

Key features of CBT

Having examined the fundamental roots of CBT, I now turn our attention to the key features of the approach. A number of texts have overviewed CBT features (for instance, Blenkiron, 2010; France & Robson, 1997; Westbrook, Kennerley, & Kirk, 2011) and I draw on these below.

Firstly, whereas psychoanalytic psychotherapy takes the view that difficulties often have their roots in past conflicts and unconscious processes, CBT's focus is more upon what is happening for the client in the present. In particular, it is concerned about the relationship between their symptoms together with the triggers, modifiers and cycles that maintain them. This is not to say that CBT ignores the influence of past experience; rather the focus of treatment tends to be on how problems are being maintained in the present.

Secondly, the CBT approach assumes that the different kinds of symptoms interact with each other. These occur over the domains of cognition, behaviour, emotion and physical/autonomic. In the example I provided earlier in the chapter (walking along the street), cognition ('I wonder what is concerning them?') is seen to impact upon the emotion (anxiety), which then affects behaviour (telephoning the friend). However, other psychological 'chain reactions' are possible. For instance, physical symptoms, such as an increased heart rate, may lead to the thought 'I'm having a heart attack', which may influence the person's behaviour: they may call emergency services or withdraw from the situation. The CBT approach investigates and defines the relationships between these phenomena through use of a formulation. This is a kind of map of these relationships (see Chapter 3). CBT helps clients to work on their problems and goals by allowing them to break these patterns and substitute them with more helpful alternatives.

Thirdly, CBT is defined by an ethos of 'operationalism' and scientific study. This means that the CBT approach is defined (or operationalised) relatively precisely to allow practitioners to be trained to adhere to structured (or manualised) approaches to deliver the therapy (the LICBT interview protocols are outlined in Chapter 5). An example of a CBT manual for the treatment of chronic fatigue syndrome is available at: www.pacetrial.org/docs/cbt-therapist-manual.pdf; another for the treatment of depression in adolescents is available at: https://trialweb.dcri.duke.edu/tads/tad/manuals/TADS_CBT.pdf. Other manuals are published in book form, for example Beck, Rush, Shaw and Emery (1979). These typically outline key topics such as the length and phases of treatment, the structure of the sessions, how to understand the disorder in question and explain the relevant concepts to clients, as well as how to implement the CBT treatment techniques. CBT is also based upon and modified according to the results of scientific investigation, rather than being slavishly derived from theory. In this way, research is used to identify which methods of treatment are the most effective. This ethos is also fundamental to clinical practice, where both practitioner and client must be willing to test out and experiment with ideas. The term *collaborative empiricism* is used to describe this process.

Fourthly, CBT is an approach that is characterised by high levels of collaboration between the practitioner and the client. It requires both parties to work together, with initially the practitioner sharing the principles of CBT with the client, and the client sharing the details of their difficulties with the practitioner. Practitioner and client then work together to allow the client to achieve their goals, the client taking increasing responsibility for change as the therapy progresses. The practitioner aims to generally avoid instructing the client. Rather, the aim is to allow them to discover the relationship between their symptoms and the solutions to their difficulties through guided discovery. This is achieved through behavioural experiments and Socratic questioning. Socrates (470–399 BC) was a Greek philosopher from ancient history who resisted instructing or arguing, alternatively asking questions as if he were a naïve enquirer. Through his careful questioning, eventually his students and philosophical opponents would be obliged to recognise the weakness of their arguments. Socrates saw his role as helping individuals to 'give birth' to understanding as a midwife helps in the delivery of a child. CBT practitioners have adopted some of the principles of this approach: 'Through sensitive questioning, clients are encouraged to use what they know, to discover alternative views and solutions for themselves, rather than the therapist suggesting them' (Westbrook et al., 2011: 138).

Finally, the CBT approach is structured. For example, it is 'time-limited'. This means that clients are offered a set number of sessions, the number of which will depend upon the difficulties that they experience. Other forms of structure include the setting of an agenda with the client at the beginning of each session. This details the topics that the practitioner and client will cover within the session. Clients are also given homework tasks to complete between sessions that can form a vital part of the change process. In the assessment stage, homework might involve completing diaries that help the practitioner and client to understand the problem better. In the treatment stage, homework consists of tasks that aim to highlight and change unhelpful patterns (see Chapters 8 and 10). An important aim of this structured approach is to maximise learning through the use of recording and measuring. In this way, the client is enabled to become more aware of their pattern of symptoms and the factors that affect these. This can also help to provide evidence of progress that can be used to boost motivation in future tasks. Similarly, the therapy is evaluated by repeating standardised measures with clients at regular intervals (see Chapter 3). This allows the practitioner and client to determine the effectiveness of the treatment. It gives practitioners the chance to reflect, both individually and through supervision, upon the influences on clients' progress. It also enables CBT services to demonstrate their effectiveness to managers and service commissioners.

Key features of LICBT

Low intensity CBT has emerged over the last decade to become a pivotal component of English mental healthcare services. This followed the implementation of the government's Improving Access to Psychological Therapies scheme (see below). However, developments in the approach are also occurring in Australia, Sweden, Canada, The Netherlands and the USA (Bennett-Levy et al., 2010b). The terminology of high intensity CBT (HICBT) and LICBT is linked to the stepped care model of service delivery (see below). LICBT has evolved from the traditional or high intensity model of CBT therapy outlined above, which is described in many key texts (for instance, Beck et al., 1979). It shares HICBT's principles in that it is present-focused, views difficulties in terms of interacting clusters of symptoms, based on a scientific approach, and also both collaborative and structured. However, it is distinct in terms of its use of differing forms of therapy delivery. As such, the following additional principles both apply to and define the approach.

A first tenet of LICBT is one of efficiency. LICBT is a high volume approach that enables a practitioner to expertly help many more clients than can be reached with a high intensity format. This is achieved through the brevity of the therapy duration (typically six to eight weekly appointments) and the length of each session (about 30 minutes), or through delivering an intervention to many clients simultaneously (via large group formats; see White, 2010).

A second principle is associated with the use of specific vehicles to facilitate the delivery of CBT. These vehicles are instrumental in allowing the practitioner to administer an intervention at an accelerated pace. These typically include self-help materials, but also large format groups and computerised CBT. Naturally, to be in keeping with the scientific approach, these materials should be based on established CBT techniques and ideally have a strong evidence base (although this is not always possible owing to the current early stage in the evolution of the approach; see Chapter 2).

A final LICBT principle is one of early access to services. For clients to make best use of this form of CBT and to maximise service effectiveness, individuals need to be able to access services early on in the development of their mental health difficulties. At this stage, a relatively small amount of therapeutic input may significantly shift the trajectory of the client's problems. As time goes by, problems may become entrenched and chronic in nature. Negative cycles involved in the development and maintenance of difficulties then become embedded within a person's lifestyle, which can, in time, reduce the client's ability to respond to a low intensity approach. As such, integral to the LICBT approach are mechanisms that increase early access to services such as self-referral systems and the promotion of services within communities. Additionally, for those with more chronic or severe difficulties, there is a need for HICBT and LICBT services to be closely coordinated. It is this service delivery context that I consider next.

LICBT and service delivery – stepped care

I have introduced both HICBT and LICBT, and now take a step further back from the client to consider the broader perspective of how services should be structured to allow these forms of CBT to be delivered. This is done via the *stepped care* approach.

LICBT is an effective approach for most mild to moderate presentations of common mental health problems. However, like any psychotherapeutic approach, it is not a universal panacea. Because of this, it is important that LICBT practitioners are situated within a broader mental healthcare network to allow non-responding clients to be directed to other treatments. The recommended method of coordinating these services is a stepped care system (National Institute for Health and Clinical Excellence, NICE, 2009a). Within stepped care, clients usually move through treatments that are based on different 'steps' (or intervention levels) until their needs are met. These interventions increase in intensity (and often cost) over progression through these steps. The system is designed to be self-correcting in that the client's reaction to treatment is monitored and individuals are 'stepped up' to the next step if they do not respond to the treatment situated in their current step. Thus, some individuals will only experience one step, whereas others may experience different components of the service that are based on other steps.

Let us consider a simple example of a stepped care system for acute migraine headaches. Lipton et al. (2000) detail a two-layer, stepped care model for pharmacological treatment. The first step involves the use of asprin (800–1,000 mg) plus metoclopramide (20 mg). Those patients who did not have a beneficial response to this treatment are then to be offered a step two treatment of zolmitriptan (2.5 mg), which is more expensive and which has a risk of more significant adverse effects. In this way, clients are initially offered a less expensive treatment, before being offered a more targeted one which, for many individuals, will be unnecessary. A variant of the stepped care model that is also described in Lipton et al. (2000), is 'matched' or 'stratified' care. Here, rather than work up the steps until treatment is successful, attempts are made to match individuals at the outset to the step that is best suited to their needs. This will be based mainly upon the individual's particular problem presentation (in this instance the severity of their headaches).

Exercise 1.3   The experience of stepped care

Either on your own or in a small group, pick an activity that is commonly learned or developed through self-help (such as car maintenance or cookery). If possible, individuals in a group should pick different activities. Do not pick psychology or therapy-related ones! Now consider whether you would: (a) prefer to use, (b) use at a push or (c) never use self-help as a vehicle to learn this? If the latter, why not? If you are in a group, through discussion begin to understand differences between individuals' preferences (for example, is this due to a lack of confidence, differences in learning style or prior experience?). Attempt to pinpoint and categorise factors that feed into this variability within the group. If you are doing the exercise individually, consider this through self-reflection.

Now consider a stepped care model for help with learning this activity. This consists of: step one where learning is entirely self-administered (self-taught through use of book, audio or video instruction); if this is ineffective, step two is learning through minimal professional contact (self-taught but expert support is available to monitor and assist); if this is also ineffective, finally step three consists of intensive, expert tutoring. What would be the effects of this stepped care approach upon your own experience? What might the positive effects be? What are any potential negative effects? What factors lie behind these?

CBT has been considered to be an ideal candidate for stepped care for two reasons (Bower & Gilbody, 2005). Firstly, the infrastructure exists for it to be delivered at differing 'intensities'. Secondly, it has been highlighted as one of the psychotherapies of choice for a number of common mental health disorders (NICE, 2005, 2007, 2009b).

To illustrate, a stepped care treatment model for depression (which includes only the CBT approaches) is listed in Table 1.1 (based on NICE, 2009b). Here, the initial step is likely to occur in the community at the practice of the client's primary care physician (PCP), but also possibly in other general healthcare settings. At step one, PCPs are alert to possible illness in their patients, for example, offering screening for high-risk groups such as those who have experienced depression previously or who are suffering with significant physical health problems. Where mild to moderate depression is identified, LICBT can be initially offered (step two) to help with the client's difficulties, medication being offered only to those who do not then respond to LICBT (thus there is a form of micro-stepped care that operates within step two).

Table 1.1   Recommended stepped care system for CBT approaches for the treatment of depression (based on NICE, 2009b)

Step	Location	Service	Intervention	Responsive conditions	Possible outcomes
Step 1	Primary care physician's clinic	Primary care physician or nurse	Recognition, assessment, CBT-based psycho-education, monitoring	Mild, self-limiting	Client recovers or is stepped up
Step 2	Primary care mental health team	LICBT practitioner	LICBT (including guided self-help and CCBT)	Mild to moderate	Client responds or is stepped up
Step 3	Primary care mental health team	HICBT practitioner	HICBT	Moderate to severe	Client responds or is stepped up
Step 4	Mental health specialists including community mental health teams and crisis assessment teams (CATs)	Multi-disciplinary	Treatment usually incorporates CBT	Treatment-resistant, recurrent, atypical or psychotic depression and those at significant risk	Client responds or is stepped up
Step 5	Inpatient care, CATs			Risk to life, severe self-neglect	

Step three consists of treatments to help those with moderate to severe depression, as well as those who have not responded to step two. These individuals will usually be offered anti-depressant medications prior to, or in conjunction with, a psychological approach. This will be HICBT. More complex forms of depression such as treatment-resistant, recurrent, atypical and psychotic depression will need to be treated by specialists. In the UK these are usually based in community teams at step four. Finally, step five is for those who require inpatient care, for instance owing to the severity of their disorder, suicide risk or concerns with self-care and neglect. This recommended stepped care system is, strictly speaking, a mixed stepped and stratified model in that clients may enter step three directly depending on both their preference and how they have responded to treatments previously, and also step four if they are assessed as requiring specialist input. This overcomes a criticism that, for some clients, a stepped care system might contribute to feelings of hopelessness where the system necessitates that they endure treatment failures prior to them eventually getting their needs met.

The National Institute of Health and Clinical Excellence (NICE, 2009a) recommends that common mental health problems are treated within a stepped care process. This model incorporates guidance for a number of disorders and focuses on steps one to three where care is offered in the community by mental health professionals. Readers are referred to this reference, but the interventions and services associated with these steps are broadly the same as indicated in Table 1.1. However, how the model is implemented in practice will depend on service- (local networks) and client-related factors (such as client preference and motivation).

As important asides, it should be noted that LICBT practitioners cannot function without adequate supervision (and this is covered in Chapter 13) and so the provision of this supervision needs to be in place. Likewise, planning associated with information technology support needs to be undertaken prior to the setting up of new services.

Exercise 1.4 Getting to know stepped care

The stepped care systems outlined by NICE (see www.nice.org.uk) are based on the best evidence available at the time that they were written. Review the stepped care systems that they propose for depression (NICE, 2009b), anxiety (NICE, 2007) and obsessive–compulsive disorder (NICE, 2005). See how they relate to the general model for common adult mental health problems proposed by NICE (2009a).

Improving access to psychological therapies

A number of factors persuaded the UK Government to invest in a massive spend-to-save model that principally consisted of new, nationwide, CBT, stepped care services in England. LICBT has now become firmly established in English healthcare following the introduction of a new profession of low intensity workers (later called psychological well-being practitioners) who were employed to deliver this approach. These professionals are the main providers of psychological therapies for step two of the stepped care model. The scheme was called *Improving Access to Psychological Therapies* and started with an evaluation of two pilot sites (2006). Following this, 11 pathfinder sites were funded before the process of rolling services out across the nation started in 2008.

The precipitant to this scheme was a powerful argument outlined by a group of economists, health service managers and mental health professionals (Layard et al., 2006). This was constructed from several points:

- Mental illness represents an enormous cost to the nation with some 40 per cent of all disability resulting from mental illness and one in six individuals in society experiencing anxiety or depression.
- There is a large human cost to those suffering with these forms of difficulty and, at that point in time, only two per cent of National Health Service (NHS) expenditure was directed towards treatments for anxiety and depression.
- The financial cost to the government in terms of loss of work output was estimated at £12 billion (this figure was later revised to £17 billion).
- However, with the introduction of the proposed IAPT scheme, the projected cost to treat these individuals was estimated to be as little as £0.6 billion.

This was based on a forecast of IAPT delivering a 50 per cent success rate, together with a reduced chance of relapse (in comparison to pharmacological treatment). In this way, it was expected that the IAPT scheme would more than pay for itself, even without taking into account the knock-on benefits of both reduced medication and other healthcare costs.

It was planned that IAPT services should be delivered via the stepped care model proposed by NICE, IAPT practitioners being initially trained in HICBT or LICBT (although other evidence-based therapies were later included). The original estimate was that about 10,000 new therapists would be trained within a seven-year scheme. This estimate was later reduced to 'at least 3,600' (Clark, Layard, Smithies, Richards, Suckling, & Wright, 2009b: 1). The expectation was that these individuals would work together in teams. These would include other individuals such as senior therapists who would be available to provide supervision and other professionals (such as employment advisors) who could help individuals with important practical matters such as clients' return to work. Clients would also be able to self-refer themselves into services that would be delivered close to their homes in community venues. The outcomes of services would be monitored (which is in keeping with the scientific perspective of the CBT approach, see above) to demonstrate the effectiveness of the scheme.

At the time of proposal, the scheme provoked debate within the clinical psychology profession. Critics raised some issues that were based primarily upon misconceptions (Clark et al., 2009a). Despite this, one of these issues is worth noting. In many instances, psychological distress is caused and maintained by social and economic factors that CBT alone cannot address. For example, it is well established that levels of deprivation influence mental and physical health. A male working in an unskilled manual job is likely to live almost eight years less than one working as a professional. Similarly, those unemployed or insecurely employed are over twice as likely to experience poor mental health (Wilkinson & Marmot, 2003). Likewise, those with an absence of social support are more likely to experience psychological difficulties (for example, Brown & Harris, 1978).

While CBT cannot be an answer to all of these problems, within IAPT there is some attempt to address individuals' social and economic needs through the inclusion of employment advisors in the matrix of services. Additionally, a vital part of the well-being practitioners' role within the scheme is liaison with, and signposting to, agencies delivering occupational and other forms of support (such as debt management). This entails the use of some generic liaison skills and decision-making options which will be locally determined (see Chapter 12).

Exercise 1.5   Developing a community resource portfolio

The community resource portfolio (CRP) is an invaluable tool that allows the practitioner to help clients to access relevant community resources to meet their needs. These meet their social, community, education, vocational and some clinical needs. It is usually an electronic resource that can be kept on laptops or memory sticks alongside an electronic collection of CBT-based self-help materials. This facilitates the transportation of the CRP between community venues. Relevant segments of it are printed off for clients or emailed to them as appropriate. This exercise involves constructing a CRP for yourself or your service.

This portfolio will contain the relevant sections:

- Employment – different forms of vocation training from employment and voluntary services; opportunities for voluntary experience; and agencies that will facilitate and support individuals in ongoing training, and in maintaining their voluntary or paid employment.
- Welfare benefits – information about the level of benefits that clients can receive when they are not working; information about 'therapeutic work' that individuals can undertake while remaining on welfare benefits; as well as resources and supports that will facilitate individuals in claiming and knowing their entitlement.

(Continued)

(Continued)

- Clinical – relevant clinical services and supports for individuals, including both statutory and non-statutory resources.
- Educational – leisure and formal courses available at local schools, colleges and community venues.
- Social – hobby, club and leisure activities; other means of socially enriching lifestyle (for example, friendship and dating resources).
- Other – helpful resources such as the Citizen's Advice Bureau, who straddle several of these categories.

There are various sources of information for your CRP. These include: the internet, contacts listed in self-help books, existing resource directories that are published by other services, and feedback from colleagues as well as clients. It may also be useful to contact other organisations for further information and, if possible, to visit them.

The IAPT scheme received government support and Clark et al. (2009b) report on the performance of the two IAPT pilot sites. One of these (Doncaster) is of particular interest as it had a marked emphasis on low intensity work (particularly guided self-help). Clients were offered therapeutic contact on average 21 days following referral and they received an average of 4.9 sessions. Only 3.8 per cent of clients seen at step two were subsequently stepped up to step three. Of the clients who received treatment, 56 per cent had recovered at the time that they were discharged from the service. Fifty per cent of all treated clients maintained recovery at 10 months follow-up. The expected number of clients had returned to work and, as predicted by the model, higher recovery rates were observed in those who had experienced difficulties for six months or less. In this way, the pilot site evaluation report found LICBT to be a highly effective approach. Consequently, the IAPT scheme was rolled out across England and there are plans to set up similar services in the rest of the UK.

Summary

- LICBT is defined by a number of key principles. It is a high volume approach that uses therapy 'vehicles' to deliver treatment and it assumes that domains of symptoms interact with each other. Additionally, it is a more present-focused, scientific/operationalised, approach that involves high levels of collaboration between practitioner and client.

- A national service evaluation has demonstrated that it is an effective approach for the treatment of many mild to moderate, common mental health problems (Clark et al., 2009b).
- The approach is also seen to be cost-effective. According to economic modelling, access to treatment is much less expensive than the impact of not offering an intervention in terms of the costs of loss of work output (Layard et al., 2006).
- A 'stepped care' matrix of appropriate services needs to be in place to support LICBT. This includes HICBT practitioners as well as operational links with other services (such as crisis services). Other workers who can provide support in regard to economic and social issues (for example, employment advisors) also need to be included in this system.
- Finally, efforts also need to be made to promote services within communities and to other health professionals, as new services will require changes in referral behaviour and the approach is facilitated by early access to services.

Further reading and activities

At the end of each chapter we provide some options for you to learn more about the topic:

- Find out about the English government's IAPT scheme by exploring www.iapt.nhs. uk/. The background to the initiative is detailed at: http://cep.lse.ac.uk/textonly/ research/mentalhealth/DEPRESSION_REPORT_LAYARD2.pdf
- Discover how an example of a computerised client management system can be used to support LICBT services by exploring www.iaptus.co.uk/ or www.pc-mis. co.uk/
- Learn more about the impact that work and the environment has upon mental health by looking at Wilkinson and Marmot's (2003) paper, which is available from: www.euro.who.int/__data/assets/pdf_file/0005/98438/e81384.pdf

2

The Role of the LICBT Practitioner

Mark Papworth

Learning objectives

- To be aware of the factors that influence client suitability for psychological treatment.
- To know the background and evidence base associated with the effectiveness for guided self-help, computerised CBT and psycho-educational groups.
- To know the advantages and disadvantages of these methods of therapy delivery.
- To understand the fundamental, broad principles of using these vehicles as a means to deliver LICBT.
- To understand the principles of ethical practice.
- To be aware of situations which are likely to raise ethical issues and be able to use these principles as a problem-solving guide.

Introduction

The role of the LICBT practitioner can be seen to encompass a number of elements. These include the structure of the clinical interviews, the appropriate interventions available at step two of the stepped care model, the therapeutic relationship that the practitioner develops with the client, and the resources or vehicles that they use to facilitate recovery. LICBT is dependent upon these vehicles, which are guided self-help (GSH), computerised cognitive-behavioural therapy (CCBT) and the psycho-educational group (PEG).

In this chapter I consider the background and evidence base associated with these vehicles and also some key principles associated with their practical use. The structure of the clinical interview and more detailed descriptions of LICBT interventions are discussed later in this book. More latterly, I consider one aspect of the therapeutic relationship: the ethical principles that underlie it. Chapter 4 focuses upon the therapeutic relationship more generally.

While Clark et al. (2009a) found LICBT to be an effective approach (see Chapter 1), comparing the evidence base across these vehicles for delivering LICBT will inform and update the expertise of the practitioner, and also provide a knowledge of the evidence that lies behind the general, published guidance (for example, NICE, 2009a). Inevitably, the main area of attention will be GSH, as this has been the main focus for LICBT to date. However, before considering the LICBT role and GSH in some detail, I briefly discuss the topic of client suitability for CBT.

Client suitability

Not all individuals engage with or respond well to psychotherapeutic approaches. Traditionally, those that fall into the stereotype of YAVIS (young, attractive, verbal, intelligent and successful) have been considered to be better responders (Schofield, 1964). In terms of CBT, Blenkiron (1999; after Segal, Swallow, Bizzini, & Rouget, 1996) notes that several factors are suggestive of a better outcome. Firstly, the individual should be capable of pinpointing the problems and issues that are impacting upon their life, and have sufficient levels of motivation to enable them to complete therapeutic tasks away from contact with the practitioner. They should be able to access their own cognitions and emotions, and their life should be stable enough for the practitioner and client to focus upon one main problem for the duration of treatment. The individual should also have sufficient tolerance to manage the degree of distress that is often involved in overcoming their difficulties, for example when engaging in graded exposure.

Helpfully, Blenkiron (1999) notes that there are practical indicators that signal whether or not these factors are present. While one of these alone would not be sufficient to inform decision-making, a constellation of factors together with a lack of clinical response may alert the practitioner that contact is less likely to be successful and that an alternative approach might be preferable (such as medication rather than stepping the client up to HICBT). This is, additionally, important because the process of treatment failure can be detrimental to a client's condition (for instance, by increasing the levels of their hopelessness; Gloaguen, Cottraux, & Cucherat, 1998).

These practical indicators include clients possessing a more rigid, biological understanding of their difficulties (for example, seeing their problem as due to a 'chemical imbalance') or expecting the practitioner to 'fix' their difficulties rather than actively engaging in the process themselves. A client who is unable to identify the cognitions that were experienced within a recent, upsetting situation or who is unable to recognise or reflect upon shifts in mood within the appointment is also less likely to be able to utilise the approach. Poor rapport during the interview, as well as a tendency to idealise or blame previous practitioners is also a negative indicator. Clients who have a chronic rather than an acute difficulty, or where the nature of the problem is vague or unfocused, might also have a reduced likelihood of a positive outcome. In contrast, it is a positive indicator if they respond well to the initial presentation of the CBT model and also if they are able to benefit from a trial intervention; Blenkiron (1999) gives an example of getting the client to hyperventilate in order to reproduce some of the physical symptoms associated with anxiety.

There is little if any research to suggest that clients' personal or psychological characteristics will influence whether they benefit most from GSH, CCBT or PEG. Decisions about allocation should therefore be negotiated with the client. This will be influenced by the client's preferences and their practical circumstances, as well as the intervention options that are available locally.

Guided self-help

Self-help texts have been in existence since the birth of civilisation and written language. Tews (1970) notes that the great libraries of three millennia ago bore the inscription: 'Medicine (or remedy) for the soul'. The ancient Greeks and Romans wrote plays and texts to help others be more content with their lives (for example, Cicero, Lucretius and Seneca), and the psychologist Albert Ellis highlighted the psychological change elements within religious texts such as the Bible and the Koran (cited in Barrera, Rosen, & Glasgow, 1981). The French writer, priest and physician, François Rabelais (1494–1553) prescribed literature for his patients as part of their treatment (Schneck, 1944), and during the eighteenth century, several progressive mental asylums systematised this approach by housing libraries containing texts that were available to patients for use under therapeutic guidance (Weimerskirsh, 1965).

The use of books for self-help has occurred in mental health for well over half a century. Initially, this was based on the assumption that the reading of carefully chosen imaginative fiction can provoke similar therapeutic processes to face-to-face contact. As such, it was used as an adjunct to psychoanalytic psychotherapy. The assumption was that the reader consciously or unconsciously relates to the protagonist within the story and, in doing so, can model their own thoughts, feelings and actions upon their mental image of this person (a process termed 'identification'). Over the course of the story, emotions can be purged and conflicts expressed, potentially triggering insight in the reader (Lenkowsky & Lenkowsky, 1978). Since the 1960s, with the advent of CBT, a different type of self-help book has emerged that is written in a new style, where the reader is encouraged to interact with the materials. These might broadly be described as therapy treatment manuals that are written to be implemented by the reader. CBT self-help treatment manuals are the books used by the LICBT practitioner to help the client to overcome their difficulties.

It is important to emphasise that, for the appropriate client group, GSH is not a 'second best' option in comparison to HICBT. In fact, it has a number of advantages (Papworth, 2006). Firstly, while the practitioner must be discerning in choosing GSH materials from the hundreds of texts that are available (see below), as some texts are written by experts in their field, an informed choice of materials by the practitioner means that clients will receive the best guidance available for help with their difficulties. Additionally, this will be a standardised package of treatment that should be in keeping with best practice recommendations made by authorities such as, in the UK, NICE. Secondly, clients can refer to the materials at their own convenience, looking back over them as often as they wish and working through them at their own pace. As such, they are highly flexible and very convenient, allowing clients to work on their difficulties in a manner that is in keeping with their lifestyle. Thirdly, if the client is supported through contact with the practitioner via the telephone, this can result in personal cost savings for clients through reduced transport and childcare costs, and will therefore not exacerbate matters where economic hardship is an issue. This flexibility also facilitates access to psychological therapies for those where geographical distance proves to be an obstacle and who have limited choices in terms of public transport (such as those without a car who live in rural communities). Fourthly, supported self-help is an inherently empowering approach because it more explicitly entails individuals using their own psychological resources to bring about change. In this way, progress can be more unambiguously attributed to the client's efforts over contact. Indeed, if difficulties recur in the future, the client can also refer back to the materials. In this way, the approach is empowering in terms of reducing reliance upon services. Next, as self-help can be accessed remotely (for example, by post or the internet) and supported at a distance via the telephone, it minimises any potential negative impact of stigmatisation (feeling socially disgraced) that some clients perceive in the process of help-seeking for psychological difficulties. This also has the advantage of reducing obstacles for clients who may find it difficult to attend clinics because of their difficulties (for example, where they experience anxiety associated with leaving the house). Finally, they offer considerable cost-savings to services as a consequence of the reduced practitioner contact arising from the approach.

There are various possible levels of support for clients who wish to make use of self-help materials. Glasgow and Rosen (1978) established categories for these: (a) entirely self-administered; (b) minimal contact, for example, weekly brief telephone, mail or personal contact; and (c) practitioner-administered, which usually involves regular, professional contact associated with clarifying or elaborating on the materials. The

LICBT practitioner role is in keeping with the last of these options, which is associated with better *outcomes* and a *reduced level of risk*. These two issues are elaborated further below.

Outcomes

There is a long history of research looking at the effectiveness of GSH. To overview this research concisely, I summarise the more recently published reviews. Lewis et al. (2003) looked at the impact of self-help materials on a variety of mental health problems. Although these authors highlighted major weaknesses in many of the studies' designs, within these limitations they broadly found that the use of self-help materials produced statistically significant improvements (the results are considered not to be the result of chance) for generalised anxiety disorder (GAD), panic disorder and depression. There was too little high-quality research in regard to obsessive–compulsive disorder (OCD) for any conclusions to be drawn about effectiveness with this condition. Likewise, Mataix-Cols and Marks (2006) focused on OCD in their review and found no robust studies in the area. As such, they concluded that there was only limited evidence for effectiveness of self-help with OCD.

In a review focusing on self-help and depression, Gellatly, Bower, Hennessy, Richards, Gilbody and Lovell (2007) used a statistical technique ('meta-regression') to scrutinise 34 studies with a view to determining the factors that impact upon the outcome of treatment. Overall, they found a large effect size for GSH (which included some CCBT) in the treatment of depression (statistically, an effect size is a measure of the strength of a relationship). They found that outcomes were more successful when participants were recruited from non-clinical populations, provided with guided rather than self-administered self-help and given CBT-based materials. When individuals are not recruited from clinical populations, this is usually done via adverts in the media. These individuals are likely to respond more positively as they are likely to be more highly motivated having referred themselves for help, rather than having been referred by a health professional.

The review by Cuijpers, Donker, Van Straten, Li and Andersson (2010), which included 21 studies (17 using media recruitment), considered whether GSH (and to a lesser extend CCBT) was as effective as face-to-face psychotherapy in the treatment of anxiety disorders and depression. The study found no significant difference between the two forms of intervention, although the drop-out rate was slightly higher for the GSH interventions (although this was not a statistically significant difference).

Coull and Morris (2011) looked at GSH treatment for anxiety disorders and depression. They combined the results of 11 studies (using a statistical technique called 'meta-analysis') and found that GSH offered benefits to participants. However, as indicated by

Gellatly et al. (2007), there was a large effect size for those recruited via the media while a smaller effect size was observed for studies involving participants recruited in clinical settings. However, three of the six more clinically representative studies included participants with severe levels of symptoms (which are less amenable to GSH interventions). Additionally, the training and supervision of the practitioners involved in the studies was poorly reported. As such, the authors concluded that the effectiveness of GSH (particularly at a follow-up period) has yet to be determined. However, they state that it is likely that certain types of GSH will be effective for some disorders when delivered by appropriately trained and supervised professionals.

Thirty-one studies were included in Lewis, Pearce and Bisson's (2012) meta-analytic review of randomised controlled trials (RCT; see Table 2.1 for a definition) that considered the impact of GSH on anxiety disorders (although CCBT was also included in the analysis). They found significant evidence of effectiveness for its use with GAD, panic disorder and social phobia, with no difference between GSH and an equivalent face-to-face intervention in OCD and panic disorder. No evidence was found for its effectiveness with post-traumatic stress disorder (little research had occurred with this condition). The overall analysis demonstrated a large effect size in support of the approach.

In summary, it appears from these reviews that, for depression, panic disorder and GAD, the evidence supports the clinical effectiveness of GSH, but more high-quality research is required to increase the level of certainty in this regard. Among the studies, there are indications that CBT-based materials are the most effective resources for this purpose and that outcomes are improved with practitioner support – both of which are in keeping with the LICBT approach. Finally, outcomes are better for those who are recruited via the media which, once again, is in keeping with the service promotion and self-referral aspects of the LICBT model.

Risks associated with the use of self-help materials

The practitioner-administered approach reduces the risk to the client associated with the use of self-help materials (and CCBT, see below). This is not just because it allows an ongoing process of risk monitoring to occur (see Chapter 6). Rather, practitioner contact allows the therapeutic work to avoid the possible pit-falls of self-administered self-help (Barrera et al., 1981). One of these pit-falls is that it relies upon individuals diagnosing their own difficulties prior to them choosing a text for help with this. This is a far from straightforward task for an untrained individual, some symptoms (such as dizziness) being common to a variety of clinical difficulties. Incorrect conclusions arising from self-assessment might result in individuals labelling themselves as ill when they are not. Alternatively, it might result in misdiagnosis and attempts to adopt incorrect treatment strategies for either misdiagnosed difficulties (such as attempting to use CBT to treat dizziness caused by anaemia) or difficulties that have not as yet been found to be amenable to self-help. As a result, these efforts may delay the person in seeking appropriate professional help. Grant, Townend, Mills and Cockx (2008) list a number of physical health difficulties that can be confused with anxiety and depression.

Exercise 2.1   Physical problems that mimic anxiety and depression

Use a medical encyclopaedia to research the following conditions: hyperthyroidism, hypothyroidism, hyperventilation, hypoglycaemia and caffeinism.

What are the symptoms of these conditions? Which psychological difficulty do they mimic? How can you differentiate between the physical cause and the psychological difficulty? What is the impact of this in terms of your initial assessment? What is the impact of this in terms of the LICBT practitioner working with the primary care physician?

Another potential problem which is linked to using self-help resources without guidance is the danger of choosing poor-quality or ineffective materials. Pharmacological interventions for mental health are carefully controlled by being required to go through research trials before being given to the public. Additionally, there are processes for prescribers to report dangerous adverse effects as a result of their use (a 'yellow card' reporting system in the UK), which can result in the withdrawal of medication from use. In contrast, the arena of self-help is unregulated. Books have carried exaggerated and unsubstantiated promises on their covers. Such misrepresentation leaves the consumer less able to make the correct decision about which materials are likely to be the most effective to meet their needs. Additionally, some poorer or older materials offer advice that is counter to best practice. Finally, people may be less likely to see the self-help programme through to its final stages when they are without support. Unfortunately, ending treatment early could exacerbate difficulties, for example through increasing levels of hopelessness in someone experiencing depression. Practitioner support makes early termination less likely and, should a client fail to respond, they can explore alternative options with the client.

Principles of good practice

I describe the interview structure for LICBT in Chapter 5. However, lying behind this contact are two principles that are important to maintaining good practice (aside from the principles of ethical practice, see later). These are based partly on those proposed by Pardeck (1998) and Turpin (2010). The first principle is associated with continuing professional development (CPD). LICBT is an evolving, evidence-based approach. For the practitioner, this necessitates attendance at post-qualification training events and keeping abreast with the LICBT literature (both research evidence and materials). Additionally, LICBT practitioners need to be professionally accredited. The process of maintaining this accreditation will involve sustaining levels of CPD.

Exercise 2.2   Keeping up to date

In the UK here are some of the journals which publish information about LICBT:

- *Behavioural and Cognitive Psychotherapy*: http://journals.cambridge.org/action/displayJournal?jid=BCP
- *CBT Today*: www.babcp.com/Membership/CBT-Today.aspx
- *Clinical Psychology Forum*: http://dcp.bps.org.uk/dcp/dcp-publications/clinical-psychology-forum/clinical-psychology-forum_home.cfm
- *Journal of Mental Health*: http://informahealthcare.com/journal/jmh
- *The Psychologist*: www.thepsychologist.org.uk/

Within some of these, post-qualification courses are also advertised. Discover by using the internet which journals might be appropriate and available that will allow you to keep abreast of LICBT developments. Think about the journals that are the most suitable for your service and see whether it is possible to obtain regular access to them. Consider how keeping up to date with new developments in LICBT can be made a regular and entertaining habit. This might be through a reading group or a monthly meeting where individuals take turns to more formally present relevant articles.

A second principle is to remain up to date in terms of maintaining a critical awareness of the existing self-help materials. This involves more than having a broad knowledge of which materials are available. Rather, it involves knowing key differences between the materials (such as the published reading age required to fully access them, see www.cimt.plymouth.ac.uk/resources/topical/reading/reading.htm), as well as their strengths and weaknesses. This is important because it enables the practitioner to choose the most appropriate materials for each client, matching the materials to their characteristics and needs. An intimate knowledge of the materials also allows the practitioner to match the terminology and illustrative examples that they use in their sessions with those used by the materials' authors.

To help evaluate the available materials, there are a number of helpful criteria or 'tests' that can serve as a guide. I have already noted that many of the most effective materials for common mental health problems are based upon the CBT model (Gellatly et al., 2007; Turpin, 2010). Therefore, when scrutinising the materials, a first test for the LICBT practitioner is to examine carefully the material's content; how well does it present the reader with the CBT treatment approach, including the use of homework tasks? Secondly, there is evidence that clients appreciate materials that include stories of other clients' journey to recovery. This might include reports of how they have made progress as well as the struggles that they have experienced along the way. These stories normalise clients' difficulties and help them to relate to the materials. Therefore, a second test involves determining if the materials contain clients' stories (Turpin, 2010). A third test is associated with the client's individual needs. Do the materials meet any special requirements that they might have? For instance, the format and illustrative examples in a book written for teenagers are likely to differ from those designed with older people in mind. Some clients have a greater reading ability than others. Do the materials match the client in terms of ease of reading? Some clients may require large print or translated materials. Are these versions available?

Exercise 2.3   Translated materials

Explore the materials that are available from the internet which are appropriate for ethnic minority groups, for example:

- www.workingforwellness.org.uk/resources/general-information/translated-materials/
- www.getselfhelp.co.uk/links6.htm
- www.migranthealthse.co.uk/mental-health/accessing-services/language-and-communication/translated-materials
- www.dhi.health.nsw.gov.au/Resources/Search/default.aspx

Surprisingly, not all popular materials have been scientifically evaluated. So, a final test is associated with estimating the evidence that a particular self-help book is both effective and relevant. In terms of effectiveness: do the book's authors refer to any studies that they have undertaken to evaluate the materials? Can you find any studies that evaluate the materials on the internet (often the materials' authors have a personal website that lists their research publications). The relevance of the study might be investigated through considering factors such as its size (the number of clients included), how similar the clients are to the ones referred to your service (whether they have a similar diagnosis and severity of symptoms – usually average inventory scores are reported within studies), whether the materials were practitioner-supported, and the strength of the design of the study. Table 2.1 details a hierarchy that will help to determine the strength of a study's design.

Table 2.1 A measure of the strength of a study's design (based on NICE, 2007)

Design strength	Type of study	Description of study
Highest	Randomised controlled trial (RCT) or meta-analysis of randomised controlled trial	RCTs use a comparison group. Clients are randomly allocated to the treatment group or the comparison group where, in the latter, they usually receive practitioner support but in implementing an established (such as equivalent face to face CBT) or a relatively benign intervention (for instance, relaxation training). The effect of the novel treatment can then be compared with the established intervention or no intervention. A meta-analysis is a means of statistically combining studies.
	Controlled study without randomisation or quasi-experimental study	In controlled studies without randomisation, a comparison group is used but participants are not randomly allocated to the groups (perhaps with clients choosing their treatment). This design is weaker because there may be differences between clients that inform their choice and these may affect the outcome (for example, clients in one group might be more highly motivated or have a greater symptom severity). Quasi-experimental designs are other study designs where not all elements are controlled for. For example, only one group is used in the study where symptoms are measured immediately prior to the intervention, post-intervention and at six month follow-up. This design does not control for 'maturation' (difficulties improving as part of their natural course).
Lowest	Non-experimental descriptive studies	These studies do not use an experimental design. An example is a case report.

Exercise 2.4 Developing a critical awareness of materials

Gather the materials together that you personally have or your service uses. On your own or ideally with your peers, scrutinise these resources. Each pick one set of materials and explore the answers to the following questions in regard to them (adapted from Turpin, 2010):

- Do the materials offer the client an appropriate CBT treatment for their difficulties (do they include methods of exploring and monitoring symptoms to allow self-discovery, up to date and relevant techniques and homework assignments)?

(Continued)

(Continued)

- Are the materials available in different formats (translated or large print versions, and versions with differing reading ages)?
- What is the range of clients that will find the materials acceptable or unacceptable (the level of education required to understand them, their cultural acceptability and the relevance of the examples used)?
- Do the materials contain client case studies?
- What is the strength of the evidence base for the materials (for example, the size, number and quality of any evaluation studies)?

If you work in a service, present your answers to these questions to your peers by way of a presentation, a summary e-document and/or a laminated information sheet that might be stored with printed versions of the materials.

Computerised cognitive–behavioural therapy

With advances in technology, naturally GSH evolved to be delivered in new media. From the 1970s, this evolved through the use of audiotape, broadcast television, videotape and automated telephonic services. Then, with the advent of the relatively inexpensive personal computer, and as computers and internet connection became fast enough to run video, sophisticated programs or packages emerged that deliver CCBT to clients who experience some mild to moderate difficulties. As with GSH, CBT lends itself to computer-based delivery owing to its structured and operationalised nature. Examples of these programs are: Beating the Blues (www.beatingtheblues.co.uk), Living Life to the Full (www.livinglifetothefull.com), FearFighter (www.ccbt.co.uk) and MoodGYM (www.moodgym.anu.edu.au).

CCBT programs typically feature a range of interactive media (such as videos and online diaries) and offer six to eight interactive sessions that are normally undertaken weekly. As with the other vehicles, homework is set to be completed between sessions. The packages often provide a therapist narrator, client case examples and feedback regarding clinical progress. Worksheets can be printed from the programs to be used to help with homework. An initial assessment will need to take place with the LICBT practitioner in order to explore and confirm suitability for CCBT (NICE, 2006). This will involve making judgements regarding whether the client is sufficiently computer literate, has access to a computer and internet connection, and regularly uses a computer. Clients can then either access the program on their own computer or attend a community venue where a CCBT service has been constructed. As with GSH, there tend to be better outcomes when CCBT is supported by practitioner contact (NICE, 2006).

Computerised CBT shares many of the benefits of GSH. Recommended programs are written by expert practitioners and so clients can consistently receive high-quality help. If the client possesses a computer and an internet connection, they can fit their therapy around their personal commitments. Practitioner support can be offered via the telephone and so the intervention can be accessed remotely. Once again, as the approach involves an increased reliance on clients' personal resources, it is a relatively empowering approach. Finally, cost-savings arise from the relatively reduced level of practitioner contact in comparison to HICBT.

For those who are suited to the CCBT approach, computer programs offer unique benefits associated with an increased level of interactivity (for instance, via automated graphs that illustrate progress) and they can provide a greater variety of styles of information provision, which can facilitate client learning (such as text, audio, video and animation). Disadvantages associated with the approach include a requirement for clients to reach a minimum level of computer literacy in order to be able to comfortably access the materials and a lack of foreign language versions of programs. For services that have to buy computers and licences for the software (some programs are available online for free), there can be significant costs. Also, if the programs are being delivered by clinicians without specialist IT training, there may be a need for technical support. Owing to the personal nature the content, some patients will be reluctant to access the materials in situations where members of the public can overlook the screen content (for example, if using computers in public libraries).

When considering whether CCBT is a suitable option, the practitioner should bear in mind that depressed clients often have difficulties in terms of motivation and concentration, which may impede their ability to engage with CCBT and GSH. Similarly, owing to the increased reliance upon personal resources involved in these approaches, in the event of limited progress, clients may attribute this to their own shortcomings, which can increase hopelessness and risk. These issues underline the importance of ongoing practitioner contact and support. With regular support and monitoring, risk can be managed and trouble-shooting can occur. For instance, if a client becomes overwhelmed, the practitioner can break down a task into smaller steps for them. Similarly, CBT interventions for anxiety disorders usually involve live exposure tasks that involve managing some level of distress. Unless these tasks are supported by a practitioner, they can result in clients dropping out of treatment (Barrera et al., 1981).

Outcomes

To consider outcomes, I look at several reviews that have focused on CCBT. A useful starting point is the update by NICE (2006) of their 2002 guidance. This was, in turn, informed by a review by Kaltenthaler et al. (2006). These latter authors evaluated the use of CCBT with common mental health problems. They considered six studies that evaluated software programs used in the treatment of depression. From this sample, only one study identified a program that was ineffective. Similarly, 10 studies were included that evaluated its use with panic disorder and phobias, all finding CCBT to be effective to varying degrees. Four studies within the review considered its use with OCD and these offered mixed support. Bearing in mind these findings together with the costs involved in the various treatment options for these conditions, as well as the evidence presented by various organisations and experts, NICE (2006) recommended the use of Beating the Blues for mild to moderate depression and FearFighter for the management of panic disorder or phobias.

Griffith, Farrer and Christensen (2010) reviewed the effectiveness of internet-based CBT interventions for the treatment of anxiety and depression. Looking at 26 trials they found that 23 of these demonstrated evidence of effectiveness in comparison to a control group. Eight of these focused on depression and 16 on an anxiety disorder, with two further studies focusing on both anxiety and depression. There appears to have been a wide variety in the recruitment methods, the practitioner time involved in supporting the interventions and the severity of symptoms. Six of the studies focusing on depression yielded significant, positive results and all of the anxiety studies yielded positive results on at least one of the measures used. These authors conclude that internet-based packages can be as effective as face-to-face and pharmacological approaches for these conditions. Griffith et al. (2010) note that one study compared a self-administered with a therapist-supported approach. They found superior outcomes with the latter but concluded that an optimal amount of input had yet to be established.

Newman, Szkodny, Llera and Przeworski (2011) attempted to address this question by undertaking a systematic review that aimed to establish the optimal amount of therapeutic contact for use with CCBT. For mixed anxiety disorders and panic disorder, the authors found that most findings from controlled studies suggested that a degree of contact with a practitioner was optimal (more than 1.5 hours over the course of treatment), with potentially less being necessary for the treatment of some simple phobias. Likewise, practitioner contact was a critical change mechanism in the CCBT treatment for OCD.

Finally, Foroushani, Schneider and Assareh (2011) investigated the effectiveness of CCBT in treating depression through use of a 'meta-review'. This is an approach that draws together the findings of previous reviews in a systematic fashion. They found 10 relevant reviews and concluded that MoodGYM, Beating the Blues and Colour Your Life improve the symptoms of depression, with CCBT being broadly as effective as therapist-led CBT. The evidence does not suggest that any of one of these packages significantly out-performs the other two.

In summary, the reviews I have sampled appear to consistently conclude that CCBT is likely to be of benefit for depression and anxiety problems (but less so with OCD), although each includes the caveat that more research is necessary in the area. Additionally, in keeping with the LICBT role, evidence tends to suggest that this should be practitioner-supported in order to maximise effectiveness.

The advantages of CCBT in terms of risk management and the principles of good practice are similar to those of GSH (see above). However, it should be noted that CCBT programs can regularly assess mood and risk, alerting a health professional directly or telling the client that they need to contact a health professional should the need arise.

Exercise 2.5   Developing a critical awareness of materials (part 2)

Consider the CCBT materials that your service uses or is considering using in the future. With your peers, once again work through the questions listed in Exercise 2.4 and present your findings to your service. If you do not work in a service, carry out the exercise by applying the criteria to the programs that are available freely on the internet.

Psycho-educational groups

CBT was originally developed as a therapy for individuals, with the subsequent development of a group format occurring in the late 1970s (Beck et al., 1979). There are differing ways of delivering therapy in groups. These include group therapy and PEGs. I will discuss these in turn.

The treatment of clients' mental health difficulties through the use of group therapy emerged during World War Two. At this point, staff shortages necessitated the development of the approach (Free, 2007). In group therapy (including group CBT), one primary area of focus is the interactions between the group members. This can be used within the therapy process to help clients to overcome their problems (Bieling, McCabe, & Antony, 2006). Yalom (1995) described nine factors that influence change within group therapy. These are:

- the installation of hope – an emphasis upon potential positive outcomes;
- universality – the discovery that others experience similar difficulties to their own;
- imparting information – providing information and advice;
- altruism – the opportunity for clients to benefit from helping each other;

- the corrective capitulation of the primary family group and interpersonal learning – helping individuals to identify and change dysfunctional relationship patterns that developed in childhood;
- the development of socialising techniques – the learning of social skills through techniques such as 'role play';
- imitative behaviour – learning through observing others;
- group cohesion – the development of trust and support which enables individuals to discuss their difficulties; and
- catharsis – a process of sharing and unburdening.

Typically, the group therapy format includes seven to 12 clients (with an expectation that one or two will drop out) and two practitioners. The length of each session is usually 90 minutes to two hours, with longer meetings including a break (Bieling et al., 2006; Yalom, 1995). Group therapy which is based upon a CBT approach is commonly up to 20 sessions in length (for example, group treatment for bipolar and eating disorders; Bieling et al., 2006). Because of the nature of this format, group therapists require experience which enables them to interpret and work with the interactions occurring in the group, deal with the issues that are likely to arise over the course of therapy and pay careful attention in a one-to-one screening process to the mix of individuals who are invited to attend. The latter is partly to avoid the possibility of one client's difficulties adversely impacting upon others.

Like group therapy, PEGs also have a long provenance having been used since the early twentieth century to teach patients to manage their physical health difficulties. The approach has been used to help clients with mental health difficulties since the 1930s (Free, 2007). In contrast to group therapy, this format relies heavily on the use of educational methods such as lectures and homework tasks to impart the knowledge and skills associated overcoming mental health difficulties. As with GSH and CCBT, the structured/operationalised nature of CBT, together with its focus on present experience, means that it lends itself extremely well to this format.

PEGs may be much larger in size, particularly if lecture hall-type venues are available to the group leaders (they are usually run by two practitioners). This is the approach that is the focus for the LICBT practitioner. Programmes are typically six to eight sessions, similarly each being about two hours in length (including a break; White, 2010). In comparison to the group therapy approach, there is a differing emphasis upon change factors, with group interactions having a more minor part to play in the change process (see Table 2.2). The 'installation of hope' and 'imparting information' factors remain highly relevant. Clients are usually given information associated with the strong evidence behind the CBT approach early in contact to increase their level of engagement and motivation. Likewise, there is an increased emphasis within the lecture format on providing clients with the necessary rationale behind the development, maintenance and treatment of their difficulties. Another of Yalom's change factors that is important within PEGs is 'universality'. Attending a venue for an initial meeting and finding 50 other individuals attending with similar difficulties is a powerful 'normalising' experience. They are confronted with a fact that, rather than being unique, their difficulties are relatively commonplace. This can also be helped by the inclusion of video clips of ex-clients giving an account of their recovery stories within the lecture presentations. Clients will be experimenting with new ways of coping outside of the sessions as outlined in the lectures and homework tasks. However, as they will not be imitating the strategies demonstrated by other clients attending the PEGs, they are accessing a different variety of sources for 'imitative behaviour'.

Yalom's other group therapeutic factors are of less relevance in PEGs. Within the lecture format, interaction between clients is minimised and so there are limited or no opportunities for altruistic activities where group members support each other, share their own experiences and help each other to understand their difficulties. Owing to the large numbers of individuals attending, group cohesion is likely to be weak. For example, members are less likely to exchange contact details and meet of their own accord outside of the PEG setting. Likewise, individuals do not have an opportunity to disclose much personal information (an aspect of catharsis). Finally, owing to CBT's focus upon the present, there will not be a focus on individuals' developmental experiences within the PEG – an aspect of the process of 'corrective recapitulation'.

Table 2.2　A comparison between group therapy and psycho-educational groups according to Yalom's (1995) therapeutic factors

Therapeutic factor	Group therapy	Psycho-educational group
Instillation of hope	Relevant	Relevant
Universality	Relevant	Highly relevant
Imparting information	Relevant	Highly relevant
Altruism	Relevant	Less relevant
Corrective capitulation of the primary family group and interpersonal learning	Relevant	Less relevant
Development of socialisation techniques	Relevant	Highly relevant but occurs outside of group
Imitative behaviour	Relevant	Relevant
Group cohesion	Relevant	Less relevant
Catharsis	Relevant	Less relevant

While the evidence base for PEGs is less established in comparison to GSH and CCBT, the format has been used extensively by LICBT services. This is because it offers considerable advantages in terms of capacity. White (2010) describes PEGs that are designed to treat those experiencing anxiety and stress, but also (if present) an additional secondary depression. These are reported to accommodate up to 160 participants. One possible disadvantage is that, inevitably, the PEG necessitates a greater distance between the practitioner and client in terms of the therapeutic relationship, and therefore dilutes the practitioner's knowledge of the client's situation and progress. For instance, for larger classes it is impractical for all attendees to be screened by the practitioner. Clients are often simply invited to attend or might be prompted to see their PCP for referral. The latter introduces a basic check by a health professional which determines whether a class is likely to be appropriate for the individual. It requires that the PCP is fully briefed about the purpose of the PEG as well as its inclusion and exclusion criteria. Additionally, it is not possible for the PEG leaders to monitor participants and tailor individualised support for each attendee. Thus, clients who are not highly motivated or who are less able to rely on their own resources may find the group overly challenging and drop out. Services need to give consideration to how these individuals can be encouraged to re-attend at a later date, channelled to alternative LICBT vehicles or stepped up.

While the effectiveness of the PEG can be measured by providing individuals with self-administered assessments at each session (suitable assessments are listed in Chapter 3), a further disadvantage is that individualised risk assessment is more difficult. Additionally, clients (or possibly also their PCP) may not diagnose their difficulties accurately and so PEGs need to be designed to operate 'trans-diagnostically' to help with a broader range of presentations that the audience is likely to present with. This lack of individualised care may lessen effectiveness. Additionally, a requirement for larger venues means that some clients will need to travel a greater distance for their LICBT in comparison to the other modalities that can be accessed in their own home (although public transport to these venues is usually good). Finally, a limitation of PEGs is that they require a minimum level of literacy and usually services find it impractical to develop parallel foreign language PEGs for minority populations.

Outcomes

Given the long history of psycho-educational approaches, it is disappointing to note that research into the topic appears to remain at a relatively preliminary stage. There appears to be only one recent review that has attempted to evaluate the effectiveness of psycho-education in treating common mental health problems that were without physical health complications. Donker, Griffith, Cuijpers and

Christensen (2009) evaluated the effectiveness of psycho-education with anxiety and depression through use of a meta-analysis. Their review aimed to cover a range of psycho-educational approaches ranging from brief leaflets to PEGs. Studies were required to meet review inclusion criteria. Only those focusing on depression and 'psychological distress' were included in the final sample of studies for the review. All those that focused upon depression noted significant improvements. This suggests that providing clients with information about their condition can be an effective intervention. The authors note the importance of providing evidence-based content within these approaches. However, unfortunately they only included 'passive' information-giving approaches in their review. Thus, topics associated with active psychological treatments (such as components of CBT) were excluded. In this way, arguably the review has excluded the very studies that will have used the most powerful approaches. Additionally, another limitation is that, in their final sample, no studies were included that used PEGs as a vehicle for the intervention.

However, inevitably there is a delay between research studies being completed and them being included in a review. Also, whether or not research is undertaken can be determined by a variety of factors that are not necessarily linked to an approaches' effectiveness (for instance, how topical a focus is in terms of current government policy). To investigate the effectiveness of the approach further, I next look at some research associated with one specific PEG programme as a form of 'case study'.

Cuijpers, Muñoz, Clarke and Lewinsohn (2009) undertook a meta-analysis that combined the results of a number of high-quality studies that each evaluated the 'Coping with Depression' (CWD) programme (Lewinsohn, Antonuccio, Brechenridge, & Teri, 1984). This is one of the most widely available and longest standing interventions of its kind. It has been translated into several non-English versions and adapted for use with adolescents (see Cuijpers et al., 2009). The programme is based upon CBT and has been delivered via the PEG approach, but is also available as a self-help manual with both formats being included in the review. Studies were included where the programme was used as a preventive approach (to prevent depression occurring in those who were not having an episode at that point) and also as a treatment approach for those currently experiencing depression. Twenty-five studies met the review inclusion criteria, six of these being preventive in nature with the remainder being treatment-focused. Of these treatment studies, it is of interest that they had a relatively wide variety of target populations. Programmes in eight studies were aimed at adolescents, three were directed towards older people and five at ethnic minority groups. Attendees at the preventive groups were significantly (38 per cent) less likely to develop a depressive disorder. When the programme was delivered via self-help, the results were significantly better for those who had practitioner support – echoing the results described earlier for GSH in this chapter. A key finding was that, while the results were fairly modest, when an alternative psychotherapy was included as a comparison group, there were no

significant differences between the effects of CWD and those of the other psychotherapies. However, a separate analysis was not performed to investigate the effectiveness of
PEGs alone.

In order to address this question I summarise a high-quality, PEG-based study that
evaluated the effectiveness of an eight session, CWD-based programme for depressed
individuals living in Oslo, Norway. In this study by Dalgard (2006), attendees were
recruited through the media. The group size was relatively modest (eight to 10 attendees). In total, 155 individuals who went through the programme were included. The
authors found a significantly greater improvement in the treatment group in comparison to their control group and this was maintained at six-month follow-up. They concluded that the intervention effect was of the same magnitude as that found in studies
of other forms of therapeutic approach. Brown and Lewinsohn (1984) compared the
results of the CWD programme when delivered over a PEG, GSH and minimal contact
formats. They noted significant improvements over all conditions.

As such, it is possible to conclude from these findings that a CBT-based, PEG
approach shows promise, but as yet the status of the field is at a more preliminary
stage. Sampling of the research suggests that information-focused approaches can be of
benefit, potentially to the extent that they are equivalent in effectiveness to other established forms of psychotherapy. Additionally, these approaches appear to be appropriate
to be delivered early in the evolution of an individual's difficulties. Nevertheless, more
research needs to be completed before this can be established with certainty.

Principles of practice

White (2000) and Bieling et al. (2006) outline a number of principles of good practice for running PEGs (while the latter authors are focusing more on HICBT group
therapy). I distil some key principles and list them below. These are associated with
promotional activities, the content of promotional material, and also the structure and
delivery of the presentations.

An initial principle is associated with the promotion of the PEG. I have already
determined that services should facilitate early access to LICBT in order for clients
to gain the most from the approach (see Chapter 1). Services that host PEGs need to
allocate sufficient time to promote them to the local communities. This will usually
involve advertising the classes within healthcare settings, but also in other contexts
such as the local press, supermarkets, libraries and churches, using a variety of media
(for example, posters, leaflets and DVDs).

To reduce stigma and increase attendance at the initial class, the terminology
within the promotional literature needs to be pitched in terms of health rather than
illness. This might include the sessions being described as classes rather than groups

(prospective attendees might be reassured by details of the seating arrangements and the structure of the sessions). The focus should be described as 'stress control' or such like, rather than containing more medical terms such as 'treatment' or 'disorders'. Details of the PEG should be described to the client in the promotional literature and in the closing stages of the initial assessment (if this has occurred). This may help in addressing any negative assumptions that they hold that may deter attendance (for example, 'I will need to stand up and talk to strangers about my problems' or 'some people attending will be unpredictable because they are mentally ill'). Individuals should not be coerced into attending but rather feel that they are attending upon the practitioner's recommendation under their own volition. Clients should be provided with a manual or handouts that contain the contents of the PEG, as well as details of homework tasks together with the relevant materials to be completed.

There are a number of good practice principles associated with a good presentation style. These are documented more fully elsewhere and these texts contain detailed exercises that are designed to improve presentation skills (example sources are given in Exercise 2.6). Typically, exercises are associated with the development of voice skills, non-verbal communication and managing performance anxiety as well as the use of visual aids and handouts. Below I outline some key principles associated with a general approach as well as the structure and the style of the presentations.

Firstly, in regard to the general approach, as with the use of GSH, PEG leaders should be highly familiar with both the presentation topics and the materials. The use of client vignettes and analogies (as well as the presentation of the theory behind the approaches) facilitates learning by helping an audience with differing learning style preferences to access the material. Likewise, audience interest can be maintained through the use of a variety of teaching methods (such as the use of video as well as live verbal presentations), and also by adding images, film and animation to PowerPoint slides.

In terms of the structure, presenters should be aware of the dangers of 'overhead overkill' or 'visual aid fatigue'. The use of too many slides or 'visuals' is likely to create audience fatigue. It is important to ensure that the font of the slides is clearly legible from the back of the room. It is also better to make brief points rather than use full sentences on the screen and punctuation within slides should be minimised. Likewise, visual materials such as photographs and video should be of high quality. Within the presentation, enough time should be allowed for the audience to digest each slide before moving onto the next one and diagrams need to be fully explained rather than simply displayed. At least some classes need to be held in the evenings or weekends to allow those in employment to attend. Sessions should end punctually as attendees may have arranged to be collected by taxi or have buses to catch.

Finally, in regard to style, presenters should speak clearly and at a reasonable pace. Therefore, consider whether voice amplification may be required for larger venues. Beware of the habitual use of 'filler' words such as 'sort of' or 'you know', or other repetitive presentation habits. These can be distracting to audience members. Leaders should also ensure that they face and make eye contact with the audience while talking rather than read from the projection screen (using notes as prompts if these are needed). The inclusion of large chunks of text in slides for the audience to read should be avoided. Likewise, simply regurgitating the content of slides is not engaging; rather, presenters should talk around the points being presented.

Exercise 2.6   Developing presentation skills

In Exercise 2.2, I recommended that practitioners present journal articles and summarise workshops that they have attended for the benefit of their peers. Ask your colleagues for feedback after these presentations. Video record yourself while giving the presentation and evaluate your own performance against the following domains:

- Knowledge and skills – did you present information in a way that all of your colleagues could understand? Were you able to answer all of their questions adequately? Did you use a variety of teaching methods?
- Structure – were the slides presented in a logical order, was the talk delivered to time? Did the presentation have a natural beginning or introduction, middle and end? Did you include early on in the presentation a slide covering what you were going to present in the session? Did you close with a summary or a list of key points?
- Delivery and materials – did you use the right amount of slides (not more than approximately a slide per minute)? Were the slides clear in terms of content and font? Were the slides and the presentation visually stimulating? Did you manage to avoid using habitual, repetitive habits? Did you avoid appearing outwardly anxious? Was the volume and pacing of your speech appropriate? Were you facing the audience for most of the presentation and making eye contact with them?

If there are issues here, why not focus on one of these as a means to improve your performance and volunteer to do the presentation again to a different service (or video yourself doing it again without an audience). Try to obtain feedback and repeat this process as required. There are a number of resources available to help you learn about presentation skills. Many university courses require students to present and so they have some useful information (see http://lorien.ncl.ac.uk/ming/dept/tips/present/present.htm). Likewise, there are books published on the topic, for example McCarthy and Hatcher (2002) and Van Emden and Becker (2004).

Finally, research the presentation design considerations that need to be incorporated to facilitate access for those with special needs (for example, individuals with dyslexia tend to prefer white script on a dark blue background).

> ### Exercise 2.7   Developing a critical awareness of materials (part 3)
>
> Consider the PEG materials that your service uses now or is considering using in the future. With your peers, once again work through the questions listed in Exercise 2.4 and present your findings to your service.

Ethical practice

The final aspect of the role I would like to cover in this chapter is that of ethical practice. It is vital that all health professionals work ethically. Ethics are fundamental principles of morally correct behaviour that inform the nature of many aspects of contact with clients. This is particularly important with clients who are experiencing mental health problems because these difficulties can heighten individuals' vulnerabilities. These are summarised for professionals in their codes of conduct. These principles discourage professionally undesirable behaviour, and form the basis of judgements associated with disciplinary or legal action against the practitioner by allowing others to scrutinise their work. Codes of conduct cannot cover every eventuality. Rather they are a general decision-making tool that allows the practitioner to determine for themselves the right course of action. Additionally, individual organisations may have policies that are relevant to ethical issues. Naturally, these issues are also properly discussed within supervision and reported to managers.

By way of an introduction, the common principles of ethical practice in healthcare are overviewed before the principles that are more closely linked to the practice of psychotherapy. I then look at issues that are of particular relevance to ethics, before finally presenting some ethical dilemmas (within an exercise) that are associated with clinical practice.

Common principles of ethical practice in healthcare

Each of us behaves according to a personal moral code that we have developed for ourselves. This 'internal compass' helps us to determine right from wrong. Should we give money to charity? Should we buy organic food? Is an extra-marital affair acceptable? People differ in their morality and this will also probably change as individuals mature. In professional practice, it is unacceptable to leave moral or ethical practice to personal choice. Rather, to protect members of the public and also, to a lesser extent, the reputation of the professional group, professions publish codes of conduct that attempt to define appropriate limits to behaviour and guide decision-making.

Codes of conduct incorporate four general ethical principles that have been offered for the implementation of healthcare (Beauchamp & Childress, 1994). The first of these is a *respect for autonomy* of the client. This principle warns against failing to involve the client in decisions about their care. The next principle is *non-maleficence*. This means that above all, the clinician should not harm the client. While some aspects of LICBT treatment might be difficult and challenging for clients, these techniques have been found to be effective and therefore are ultimately beneficial rather than harmful. In this way, their use is ethically justified. This principle warns against poor practice, which might, for example, involve departing from established LICBT principles. This could entail using techniques that are outside of the LICBT practitioner role, training or job description. Alternatively, it can also involve 'medium intensity drift', where the practitioner's practice might shift over time into attempting to use LICBT with step three difficulties or to use HICBT models or interventions inappropriately within a step two context. The third principle of *justice* is associated with fairness. One application of this principle is the availability of services for all. Arguably, with its focus upon the engagement of individuals from diverse groups and a focus upon open access (self-referral and remote forms of intervention), the LICBT approach is a particularly just one. The final, more general principle of ethical healthcare is one of *beneficence*. This obliges the practitioner to act in a way that helps people, although not at the expense of others (including the practitioner themselves).

At times, these principles can contradict each other. For instance a suicidal client may require, against their wishes, a referral to a crisis team. In this situation, there is a tension between the principles of 'respect for autonomy' and 'non-maleficence'. This forms the basis of an ethical dilemma (although the appropriate action here is clear, see Chapter 6).

Ethical principles of psychotherapy

Practitioner codes of practice differ in style and content, but typically incorporate the principles described above. However, they also explicitly include a need to respect colleagues, be competent (for instance, by maintaining CPD or not practising if significantly affected by health/personal circumstances) and maintain integrity at all times (a characteristic that is associated with consistent adherence to moral principles). They also describe appropriate behaviour for other scenarios: *dual relationships* refers to the possibility of establishing a relationship with a client (or ex-client) in another capacity. In its most extreme form, this might involve forming a sexual relationship with a client (a situation that can result in the practitioner being 'struck off' from professional registration).

Codes commonly also describe appropriate approaches to taking care of *information about clients*. This encompasses standards associated with good note-taking, as well as judgements about confidentiality and the situations in which information might be shared. This topic is also relevant to the secure storage of information within services. *Misrepresentation* by practitioners is also an important issue. An example of this is that of a worker, either directly or through implication, misrepresenting their professional role or qualifications (for instance, failing to correct a client if they inappropriately call the practitioner 'doctor' or a student failing to make the client aware that they are a trainee practitioner). Also discussed within codes are the appropriate responses to *risk* (either to the client or the practitioner), as well as the acceptance and incorporation of the *client's diversity* within contact (see Chapter 11). *Financial matters* and conflicts of interest are usually included as well. These are commonly associated with seeking or receiving inappropriate financial gain from contact with clients, for instance the receipt of expensive gifts.

A final area of ethical conduct is associated more directly with how clinical services are delivered. Issues here include the delivery of assessments and interventions in a manner that is in the best interests of the client. In this way, asking questions within an assessment to satisfy personal curiosity alone is completely inappropriate. Only effective interventions should be used and they should be delivered in a manner that allows them to be evaluated. Interventions should be terminated rapidly if they are found to be ineffective, with clients being referred speedily on to others if required.

Exercise 2.8   Working with ethical dilemmas

Here are some ethical dilemmas to test your 'moral compass'. Variations of all of these have occurred in my career. Think through, in turn, how you would respond to these situations. As a guide, you can consult these codes of conduct: British Association for Behavioural and Cognitive Psychotherapies; British Association for Counselling and Psychotherapy; and the British Psychological Society. If you are working in a service, discuss your decisions with your supervisor and seek out any relevant organisational policies that your employer might have.

- Personal relationships – (a) an acquaintance from many years ago is referred to your service; (b) after beginning therapy with a client, their partner attends, who you find is an acquaintance from many years ago; and (3) the first time you meet a client you realise that he or she works at your favourite local café, where you usually have lunch.

(Continued)

(Continued)

- Dual relationships – (a) you are single and, after a chance meeting, a discharged client who you are attracted to asks you to join them for a drink after work; (b) a client who you discharged a year ago approaches you and makes conversation while you are waiting for a friend in a bar; and (c) an ex-client joins your service in some capacity.
- Financial matters – (a) a client presents you with a bottle of wine for a Christmas present or at the end of contact; (b) they offer you an opportunity, through their contacts, for a very good discount on a holiday; (c) they ask you to circulate to your colleagues an advertisement for their ailing business; and (d) by way of thanks, a client gives you a gift of jewellery or a new briefcase.
- Confidentiality – (a) a client requests to see copies of your case notes; (b) they ask you not to write down sensitive information about their history or condition; (c) they ask you to omit certain information from your letter back to the referrer; (d) your client is aged 18 and his mother rings up while extremely distressed with concerns about the client, wishing to discuss his progress; and (e) a client admits to some form of benefit fraud or illicit drug use.

Summary

- Not all individuals engage with or respond well to psychological therapy. Generally, those who are more likely to respond are motivated to work on their difficulties and are able to tolerate the distress involved in confronting some aspects of their difficulties. They are also able to pinpoint their own problems and issues, have a degree of stability in their life to allow them to focus on the therapy, and have sufficient self-awareness to be able to access their relevant cognitions and emotions.
- The main focus of this chapter has been introducing the vehicles of LICBT: guided self-help, computerised CBT and psycho-educational groups. One key advantage of these is their relative low cost in comparison to HICBT. Additionally, GSH and CCBT share major benefits associated with convenience and flexibility for the service user.
- Research examining the effectiveness of these vehicles remains in a relatively early stage, particularly regarding PEGs. However, within the limitations of the research, these findings indicate that they are effective for depression and some anxiety disorders.
- The level of practitioner contact that is involved in GSH and CCBT vehicles minimises the risk of adverse effects, reduces the likelihood of client drop-out and also maximises the effectiveness of the approach.

- Finally, principles of ethical practice are the bedrock upon which other skills and competencies are built. Ethically informed problem solving will be necessitated by a variety of clinical situations. This should draw upon the core principles of ethical conduct: respect for autonomy, non-malificence, justice and beneficence.

Further reading

- Bennett-Levy et al. (2010b) details the full variety of different LICBT activities and approaches.
- Turpin (2010) is available from: www.iapt.nhs.uk/silo/files/good-practice-guidance-on-the-use-of-selfhelp-materials-within-iapt-services.pdf. It offers further, useful advice in choosing self-help materials and promoting services within communities.
- White (2000) describes a PEG approach in detail.
- Details of the Coping with Depression course is available at: www.ori.org/Research/scientists/scientistPublications/Lewinsohn/CWDC.pdf

3

Understanding the Client's Problem

Brad Martin

Learning objectives

- Understand the different ways that problems can be understood and how these may fit into a stepped care model.
- Recognise the different influences on our understandings of problems.
- Consider the range of outcome measures available, including psychometrics and know how these can be an important part of assessment and treatment.
- Review collaborative formulation and problem statements as client-centred ways of understanding problems.

Introduction

Making LICBT work is all about ensuring that people get the right treatment for their problems at the right time. To accomplish this, we need a clear and specific understanding of the problems being experienced. In LICBT, more than with higher intensity treatments, it is important to make this understanding as accurate as possible because, once the treatment is underway, there is less opportunity for the practitioner to review this phase of the process. Also, this is important because low intensity materials are often focused on particular problems, so working on the wrong thing might mean that the real problem is ignored.

As we have seen in the Introduction (Chapter 1), a person's progression through the various care services can be thought of as passing through different steps, with two-thirds of people likely to need a low intensity treatment (NICE, 2011a). Each step brings some form of assessment, and offers its own perspective or understanding of the problem. This chapter will consider five increasingly specific ways of understanding a problem, namely:

1   using common language;
2   diagnosis;
3   psychometrics/outcome measures;
4   a formulation based approach; and
5   problem statements.

Each way of understanding the problem offers a unique perspective (see Figure 3.1). Because there is no single 'right' way of understanding a person's difficulties, it is often worth considering more than one perspective, and triangulating your understanding.

The job of the practitioner and client is to distil the most relevant information and emphasise the key information in a way that helps to make sense of the client's experience. The information that is relevant for one person may be very different from the specific information that is relevant for another person. Thus, a centrally

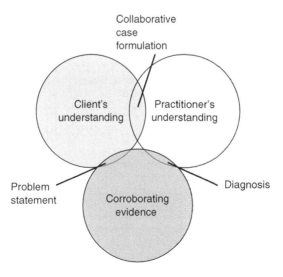

Figure 3.1   A balanced picture of the client's difficulties

important part of the understanding is that it is collaboratively developed with both the practitioner and client, with both deciding which elements are important and which must be included in the process. As has been said many times before, the client really is the expert in regard to their experience. Likewise, the practitioner is the expert in the mental health side of the puzzle. By bringing these together, we can get a very individualised picture of the person, their difficulties, and how the different pieces fit together into a story that allows us to describe, understand and predict the problem.

As a person moves from the initial tiers of a stepped care model through to higher tiers, the focus of our understanding may take different forms and the language we use to describe the problem may change (see Figure 3.2). There is a risk that, with very complex problems, in particular where the client's functioning is greatly impaired, the explanation may be hard to understand. This is one rationale for LICBT being most suited to mild to moderate common mental health problems. When trying to understand a problem, low intensity working balances problem complexity with an understanding of the problem that makes sense to most people.

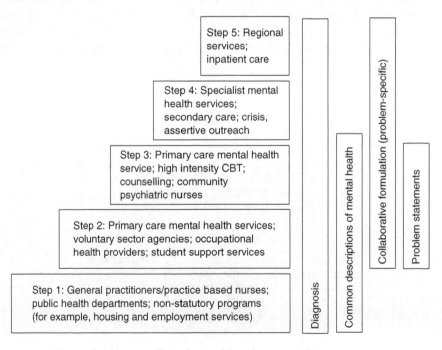

Figure 3.2 Ways of understanding the problem in stepped care

Using common language: the client's understanding

Collaborative working is at the heart of LICBT. In practice, this can mean different things, depending on the task at hand. In agenda setting it might involve considering what each person (including the practitioner and the client) wants to focus on; with goal setting it may include prioritising treatment components according to what is most valued and what the evidence says is most important. Within the context of understanding a problem, it is important to get the person's *own* grasp of their situation and use that to inform your *shared* understanding.

Most people try to make sense of their experiences. When they encounter something unusual they gather information about it, consider their existing knowledge, make new observations and reflect on their direct experiences. In putting this information together they are able to form an opinion about what is happening for them. Depending on what information they draw on, their opinion might be pulled in one direction or the other and so should always be considered as part of the story, but not necessarily the whole story. By starting with the client's perspective, noting their language and ideas, then looking to build on this rather than challenge it, we begin the process of understanding the problem from a common ground.

Exercise 3.1   Considering the client's subjective viewpoint

When Mary had her handbag stolen while walking home one evening, she was understandably upset. Her first reaction was to stay home and she even described feeling afraid when people came to the house. Over time, and after talking to friends, she developed her understanding of why the theft occurred. She believed that it was all her fault. Mary reported that she should have known better than to walk in that neighbourhood alone at night because a lot of crimes happened at this time. Despite the fact that she blamed herself for what happened, this explanation of why it happened gave her a sense that she could control the danger by making better choices. Now Mary is leaving the house but only during certain daytime hours and only when she is with friends. Unfortunately, it also left her very angry with herself for previously going out during the evening in what she thought was a foolish decision.

- Is Mary right about herself being to blame?
- If this explanation is helping her get out of the house and back into a more active lifestyle, is her understanding adaptive or maladaptive?
- How might you respond to this if Mary presented at your clinic?

Table 3.1 considers some of the things that the client can uniquely contribute to the shared understanding.

Table 3.1   Some of what the client brings

Beliefs about	What the problem is
	Where the problem comes from
	What the problem means
	Seeking help
Decisions about	What their goals for treatment are
	What they are willing to contribute to therapy
Evidence for	Their subjective experience
	The results of treatment
	Their motivation

There are, however, some problems that we might find ourselves getting into if we rely too heavily on a person's subjective opinion. For example, we know that current mental health state (for example, a lowered mood) can distort their perception of the situation. This is known as a *mood-congruent bias*. A number of authors have considered the effect that this bias can have on our thinking (see Watkins, Mathews, Williamson, & Fuller, 1992 for a nice example). There seem to be three main ways that this happens.

1 The first is that your current state can lead you to pay *extra attention* to things that support the way you are already feeling (for example, only noticing bad things when you are feeling low).
2 The second is through the *enhancement* of certain information (and the marginalising of other information), with higher emotion making certain beliefs more vivid.
3 Finally, there is a *recall* bias, with memories that match the current situation being more accessible than non-matching information.

Exercise 3.2   Distortion in thinking

By overly relying on only one perspective of the problem, there is a chance that the shared understanding gets 'contaminated' by the characteristics of the problem being looked at. Problems with anxiety may seem exceedingly dangerous or threatening;

problems with depression may seem hopeless. The clinician's expert knowledge and willingness to introduce questions can provide a valued alternative perspective.

Can you think of a time when something bad happened to you? Maybe achieving a low grade for an assignment, or getting a speeding ticket?

What kind of mood did this put you in? What sort of thoughts came to mind?

If you are like many people, the bad news might have had quite a wide impact on how you were feeling and the sort of things you were thinking about. You may have felt low, frustrated or fed-up. You may have thought: 'I have all the bad luck' or 'bad things always happen to me' or perhaps the last time something like that happened came to mind. That may seem obvious, but imagine what effect this might have on someone who suffers from chronic depression or anxiety. How could their condition distort their understanding of the problem?

Over-reliance on a person's own understanding of their difficulties has another possible problem, namely that the person's understanding might be based on inaccurate information or beliefs. Within individuals, families, communities or age cohorts there are beliefs, understandings and interpretations that may bias understanding and cause incorrect conclusions to be made. This even happens among qualified mental health professionals (Rippere, 1977). When the basis for the incorrect understanding is shared by others (as in the case of a communal belief), there may be little opportunity to naturally collect new information or challenge this way of thinking.

Exercise 3.3   The influence of thoughts, beliefs and context

Read Elena's story below:

Elena is a 68-year-old pensioner. She has been staying home a lot during the colder winter months and not seeing many of her friends. For the last few weeks she has noticed herself feeling quite low and is often tearful. She is asked about her mood during a routine visit to her GP, but attributes how she has been feeling to 'just the winter blues and feeling my age'. Elena goes on to say 'besides, I don't want to be a bother to anyone, I'm sure you have better things to do than listen to me complain'.

Can you think of any factors that might cause Elena to have the understanding of her difficulties that she does? What information or questions can you think of that might help us to develop a clearer picture of her problems?

What we see, as demonstrated in the points above, is that the client can be a source of rich information, which may be impossible to generate in any other way. There are, however, many ways that our own thoughts, opinions, beliefs and attitudes can be misinformed or biased. Working collaboratively does not mean that every source of information is weighted equally, but rather that all relevant sources of information are considered and valued for what they can contribute to the shared understanding of the situation. As such, we want to make sure that we are drawing from more than just a subjective position.

Diagnosis

A diagnosis is a way of describing a problem that is defined by a specific set of criteria according to standardised categories of information (the most familiar example of this is the *Diagnostic and Statistical Manual of Mental Disorders* from the APA, 2000). One of the premises that such a system is based on is that the conditions being evaluated can be understood and described according to set qualities, and that these have consistent features that are shared by all of the people with the condition. In psychiatric diagnoses, like with physical conditions, the labels used tend to refer to constellations of problem characteristics, rather than a single symptom in isolation.

This way of understanding problems has sometimes been likened to a recipe, bringing together a range of ingredients, in set quantities and in a particular order, which results in a final product. The combination of these elements is often recognised by a common name (a 'cake', perhaps), has consistent features (like sweet, light or textured) and may have a range of subtypes (for example, carrot cake or black forest cake). We all recognise that not every food item that uses eggs and flour is a cake (such as pasta) and that sometimes things with very different characteristics may belong to the same main category. Likewise, different mental health problems may share common features but can be distinguished from each other by critical differences.

Many scientific disciplines use diagnostic categories, although typically this is done when things can be directly observed. Diabetes, for example, is a category of metabolic disease that is defined by the failure of the pancreas to produce enough insulin to process the sugar in a person's diet. It can be evaluated indirectly by watching for the symptoms that untreated diabetes causes (such as frequent urination and unusual thirst) or it can be measured directly, in the case of diabetes by testing the blood for sugar levels. Because many different conditions could cause the outward signs of diabetes (for example, both diabetes and a urinary tract infection can cause frequent urination), the diagnosis would only ever be confirmed through a direct test.

Testing for a condition that cannot always be directly seen or measured, like many psychiatric problems, is not easy. As such, our ability to diagnose these conditions is limited to how closely we define and identify the criteria that we include in the condition, and the quality of the data that we have to base our decisions on. As Summerfield (2001) helpfully reminds us, diagnostic categories are established and agreed by experts, rather than being fixed and inherent, so we should think of them as ways of understanding, rather than true facts.

In the UK there are no universally agreed standards for who can offer a formal mental health diagnosis. Traditionally it was only certain professional groups that could do so, including medical doctors (such as psychiatrists) and clinical psychologists, although this is no longer the case in practice. It is not necessary to formally diagnose someone in order to use our understanding of the categories to help us understand and treat common mental health problems.

One of the functions that diagnostic categories can offer is to guide treatment decisions. Much of the evidence for treating mental health problems is based on evaluating a particular treatment (such as cognitive therapy) for a set diagnostic category (for example, a specific phobia). By matching a person's presenting problems with a diagnostic category, a practitioner can consider treatment options that are known to offer the best outcomes for those particular difficulties.

Of course, the fact that a particular treatment has (or has not) worked for someone else with a similar problem in the past does not mean that it will work for someone else now. Generalising from the literature to a specific person depends on many variables including client characteristics (including person-specific variables such as the level of motivation), whether the treatments are administered correctly and whether the conditions necessary for the problem to resolve are all present (for example, whether there are over-riding pressures such as escalating debt which need to be prioritised). These are just three qualities that must ideally match. The better the fit between the current circumstances and the one a treatment has been tested on, the more likely it is that we will get a similar result, but there are never any guarantees.

Exercise 3.4   Exploring diagnoses

LICBT is recommended for mild to moderate common mental health problems including depression, panic, phobias and generalised anxiety disorder. Pick one of these conditions that you believe that you have some prior knowledge of and make a list of all of the symptoms that you are aware of. Once this is done, use either the DSM-IV (APA, 2000) or the ICD-10 (WHO, 2008a) to list all of the formal symptoms for the condition you selected. (This is a useful site if you do not have access to these texts: http://behavenet.com/apa-diagnostic-classification-dsm-iv-tr.) Finally, look on a popular

(Continued)

(Continued)

website for signs of the same condition. What differences do you notice? Which factors do you think offer the greatest clarity? Which factors most differentiate the condition from other similar conditions?

Despite the challenges of generalising from what worked for one person, by drawing on the whole of the outcome literature, we can make reasonable predictions about what has the greatest chance of helping. Considering the tens of thousands of outcome trials published, we are fortunate that there are already reviewers that have filtered through the literature and made some recommendations about what is likely to offer the best treatment. Some sources, such as Roth and Fonagy (2005) or the Cochrane Reviews offer sophisticated reviews and overall guidance based on a systematic analysis of the best available literature.

Diagnostic decisions are based on information collected either by asking questions in a discussion with the client (or others who know about the client), as in the case of a routine clinical interview, or through a more standardised process like with the Structured Clinical Interview for DSM (First, Spitzer, Gibbon, & Williams, 2002). As information is collected, the practitioner is required to fit the available information about the client into pre-existing categories. Through this process, the presence or absence of clinical characteristics can either disconfirm a particular diagnosis or make others more likely.

By asking the right series of questions, tailored to the information from the client, and by listening carefully to the answers, the practitioner can start to narrow down their beliefs about the most likely category of problem the person is presenting with.

Completing a diagnostic interview correctly requires a lot of knowledge about the categories of mental ill health, what key characteristics might distinguish one disorder from others, otherwise known as *differential diagnosis*, and the shortest line of questions to get from not knowing to knowing. Many different authors have attempted to standardise the decisions involved in this process, using things like decision trees and standard questions. In practice, most practitioners learn this skill through a lot of clinical work and close supervision from more experienced practitioners. The core skills, however, most of us learned in primary school playing games like 'I Spy with My Little Eye' or 'Animal, Plant, Mineral'. In these games, we have a shared understanding of the categories and possible options; we ask increasingly specific questions to rule out some options and refine our understanding of the most likely category.

Outcome measures and psychometrics

Low intensity psychological interventions have grown out of two compatible needs. The first is to deliver high quality interventions that work and the second is to do this as efficiently as possible. Many services are pressured to deliver as much clinical treatment as possible, and manage both outcome and waiting lists (Rizq, 2012). With such pressure, why would we choose to invest in measuring the results of what we are doing? After all, the treatments being delivered have been designed by experts so they are already proven to work, right?

Low intensity interventions are routinely based on strategies that have been proven effective. Despite this, each clinical application is different. In measuring and monitoring outcomes, we have a chance to evaluate the treatment being offered with reasonably sensitive, accurate and valid measures – ideally guiding us to improve as we go (Barkham et al., 1998). The perceived benefits of measuring outcomes vary according to the groups using them, ranging from the individual (clients), through practitioners and services and up to a national scale. I describe these in turn.

Firstly, the most immediate benefit to collecting and monitoring outcome data can be for the service user. Clients often report benefits of monitoring. Standardised instruments validate personal experience, in part by demonstrating that their problems are common enough to be collated into an already made instrument (Proudfoot & Nicholas, 2010). Importantly, it also provides a valuable window into how problems are responding to treatment, to highlight accomplishments and as a reminder of progress. Finally, keeping an eye on well-being is a very good way of monitoring risk that should be used in conjunction with standard risk management practices (see Chapter 6 on Risk Assessment).

There are several ways that practitioners can directly benefit from routine monitoring of outcome data. Right from the first point of contact, outcome data (in the form of initial screening questionnaires) can be used to: help guide assessment (Wright, Williams, & Garland, 2002), inform treatment decisions (Thomas, Bruton, Moffatt, & Cleland, 2011), gauge the severity of the problems (Warner, Reigada, Fisher, Saborsky, & Benkov, 2009) and provide a level of specificity that non-standardised means (including clinical interviews) do not match. Of course there is also the possibility that outcome measures, as another form of information, can help to triangulate the information provided and could offer a different perspective to that provided by other sources. Lastly, bringing outcome data to supervision is promoted in the 'Good practice guidance on the use of self-help materials within IAPT services' (IAPT, 2010). The recommendation is that understandings informed by outcome data can help with decisions regarding the suitability of the treatment, the client's readiness for discharge and more generally the efficacy of the service being delivered. If all those reasons were not enough, Miller, Hubble and Duncan (2008) report that the process of following up on clinical work and reflecting on the results is the single defining characteristic of the best performing therapists, as it affords them the sort of information that is helpful in refining what they do with service users.

In regard to services, despite the time challenges that data collection, management and interpretation make, there are several good reasons why it is worthwhile. Even though most low intensity interventions are largely manualised, there is still a large amount of variability in how the treatments can be delivered. Routine monitoring allows for local decisions about best practice, enabling managers to identify and promote the methods that work best (Perry et al., 2011). It also affords services an opportunity to identify outstanding gaps in provision and areas for service development (McCormack & Farrell, 2009), and to identify residual difficulties for individual service users throughout the course of their involvement with the service (see the sections in Chapters 8 and 10 on relapse prevention and management). In services that are made up of practitioners from different professional backgrounds, routine use of standardised measurement instruments can also provide a common language to help describe and understand problems and service pathways, and to evaluate the various treatments provided using common standards.

Finally, on a national scale, outcome data can be collated and used to evaluate treatment/programme efficacy (such as the Doncaster and Newham IAPT pilot sites that led to the national commissioning of new services), identify examples of best practice (such as those in Gyani, Shafran, Layard, & Clark, 2011) and identify outstanding gaps in service provision. While much of this happens at a level beyond that which most people are able to observe, the process itself is entirely driven by the data that is developed by practitioners and service users. The better the quality of the data being fed into the system, the better the quality of the conclusions they are able to draw. At a local level the goals and guidelines agreed at a national level translate directly to the objectives that local health commissioning bodies or health management organisations use to guide where they spend their money.

What sort of variables might be important to measure?

Each service will have its own standards for what needs to be monitored and evaluated. There will often be a minimum that may be based on service preferences, commissioned targets or national guidance, and this may be enhanced according to the needs of the practitioner or the service user. For services involved in the IAPT programme there is the minimum data set (MDS), which includes free to use measures that collect data ranging from demographic information to routine psychometric data (including the Patient Health Questionnaire, PHQ-9, the Generalised Anxiety Disorder screening tool, GAD-7, the Work and Social Adjustment Scale, WSAS and the IAPT Phobia Scale, each of which are discussed below). When there is a minimum standard, it usually includes common psychological factors, such as mood, anxiety and well-being. If we think about the reason that people come into mental health services, however, those variables might not be the only ones that matter.

Other variables that are worth considering include:

- health;
- employment;
- insight;
- work or education;
- lifestyle;
- activity;
- relapse;
- personal skills (such as coping).

Types of outcome measures

Depending on the difficulties that are being targeted, the ability of the service user to offer information and the needs of the service, there are many different ways in which we can collect data. Each of these presents its own challenges, benefits and qualities. For some people, we may use multiple measurement forms.

One easy source of data that we can use to consider to measure change is *naturalistic data*. This sort of data is always being generated and is easily accessible. If a person is fearful of driving, for example, perhaps old mileage forms from their work could be used to monitor changes in distances travelled. For someone who is spending too much money, bank statements provide a helpful way to monitor spending.

We will look at generating problem statements (Richards & Whyte, 2009) later in this chapter, but in brief, they comprise a short description of the problem and are generated by the client at the beginning of treatment. This 'snapshot' of the problem provides a concise baseline measure of the difficulties. By comparing the mid or end of treatment situation with the original problem statement, we can monitor and evaluate change. A simple way to do this is to ask how much the person agrees with the original statement. If the statement is less accurate or true than it was when treatment began, change is likely to have occurred.

Box 3.1   Trainee practitioner's experience

I first took the patient to supervision, as a new patient, after completing an assessment in session one. The questionnaires were useful in contributing to the formulation – the client presenting with symptoms associated with social phobia but with the generic features of common anxiety that you would expect in most people. No

(Continued)

(Continued)

low mood or depression was identified. It was agreed in supervision that I would work with their common anxiety symptoms with a view to 'stepping up', if appropriate, at the end of treatment. This treatment plan was discussed and agreed with the patient.

During treatment the questionnaire scores (in particular the anxiety-focused one) reduced at each session. I took the patient to supervision again for a four-week review. The mood questionnaire had remained at 0 throughout the sessions and the anxiety one had gone from 13 (moderate severity) to 3 (below clinical caseness). However, the quality of life and phobia scale remained high with little change and no change in employment status. We agreed in supervision that the scores on the anxiety scale demonstrated that the treatment had been effective in reducing the anxiety.

However, the quality of life scale indicated that the symptoms of social phobia may still be impacting on the patient's level of functioning. In this case, the outcomes made for a difficult decision regarding 'stepping up' upon completion of low intensity treatment. It was agreed in supervision that this would be considered with other members of the management team. The outcome was to offer bibliotherapy for social phobia which was considered to be a suitable option after considering the patient's previous successful engagement with self-help materials, with the option of re-referring back into the service for step 3 (high intensity CBT) if needed.

Psychometric tests

Here we will look at measurement and outcomes, and consider how measuring a person's difficulties can help us to understand them more clearly. Any instrument that can quantify (assign a number value to) a psychological quality or characteristic of a person is a psychometric test or instrument.

The word psychometric comes from two separate words: *psycho*, which is derived from the Greek *psyche*, which in this context means mind, spirit or soul; and *metric*, which means to measure. In other words, psychometric tests are designed to measure some quality (or qualities) of a person's inner self. The range of available psychometric tests is immense, from instruments designed to assess common mental health problems like anxiety disorders and depression, to tests that can help people to identify professional options for a career path that best suits their personality, or peer into their unconscious and pull out 'hidden mysteries'. As you might expect, some psychometrics are more successful than others at accomplishing their goals.

In the UK there has been a huge uptake of standardised measures in recent years. It is now common for a referral from a primary care physician to come to a mental health service with scores from a test of anxicty and depression that can then offer the service some quantified sense of the difficulties that the individual may be encountering. The most common of these in current use in the UK are the PHQ-9 (Spitzer, Kroenke, & Williams, 1999) and the GAD-7 (Spitzer, Kroenke, Williams, & Löwe, 2006).

IAPT outcome measures

With the development and expansion of the IAPT initiative, we have seen the routine use of outcome measures and data collection on an unprecedented scale (Clark et al., 2009b). The IAPT programme requires services to collect and report on a set of specific measures, including demographic information and psychometric variables at set points in the service users' progress through treatment. While some of these relate to information that is useful at a service level or above (for example, the average age of people accessing the service), some are directly relevant to the clinical assessment and intervention.

Of the measures that are most directly of clinical interest, there are four core measures, including:

- *Patient Health Questionnaire* (Spitzer et al., 1999). The PHQ-9 is a nine-item, self-report questionnaire designed to identify symptoms of lowered mood and depression. Each item is scored 0–3 with high numbers indicating more frequent symptoms. The PHQ-9 is a very simple form of psychometric test that offers a total score that is calculated by counting the symptoms (Tavabie, 2007), where each of the diagnostic criteria for depression is weighted equally. The authors suggest using cumulative scores of 5, 10, 15 and 20 as cut-off points to indicate mild, moderate, moderately severe and severe levels of low mood, respectively (Kroenke, Spitzer, & Williams, 2001). While this is easy to use and fairly intuitive, this system of grading the severity of depression is no more valid than a cake recipe that instructs you to add equal parts of flour, eggs, vanilla extract and sugar. Anecdotally, and in at least one significant study (Kendrick et al., 2009), it seems to indicate worse mood disruption than is apparent from clinical interview or by most other ways of assessing low mood. Overall it is as good a brief measure as is available for use free of charge (Coyne, Thombs, & Mitchell, 2009; Gilbody, Richards, Brealey, & Hewitt, 2007).
- *Generalised Anxiety Disorder Scale* (Spitzer et al., 2006). The GAD-7 was developed by the same team who developed the PHQ-9. It uses the same system of adding up the symptoms to estimate severity and utilises the same categories of severity. While it was originally developed as a measure of GAD, the properties of the instrument suggest that a high score is equally likely to indicate GAD, social phobia, post-traumatic stress disorder (PTSD) or panic (Kroenke, Spitzer, Williams, Monahan, & Löwe, 2007). As such, it may be better at measuring global anxiety symptoms than specifying any unique condition (Löwe, Decker, Müller, Brähler, Schellberg, Herzog, & Herzberg, 2008).

- *Work and Social Adjustment Scale* (Mundt, Marks, Shear, & Griest, 2002). The WSAS is a five-item, self-report inventory that measures work, social and leisure functioning, in addition to relationships and home management. Each item is rated on a scale of 0–8 (0 = not at all, 8 = very severely). A score below 10 indicates that there is no significant impairment in this area; between 10 and 20 indicates impaired functioning; above 20 indicates moderately severely impaired functioning. Mataix-Cols, Cowley, Hankins, Schneider, Bachofen, Kenwright and Marks (2005: 223), when evaluating the ability of the WSAS to measure adjustment in people with phobias, reported that it is 'a valid, reliable, and change-sensitive measure of work/social and other adjustment'.
- *IAPT Phobia Scale* (IAPT, 2008). This is a three-item measure that has been specifically developed for use in IAPT programs. While it does not claim to be the most technically accurate measure of phobias, it combines a brief gauge of user-defined phobias (assessing social, panic and specific phobias), with good face validity (a way of describing whether something makes sense to your average person). While there have not been any evaluations of this instrument, its use in the scientific literature (as in Cavanagh, Seccombe, Lidbetter, & Bunnell, 2011) suggests good uptake.

For less common problems a set of free-to-use psychometric tests are recommended. These include:

- Social Phobia Inventory (Connor, Davidson, Churchill, Sherwood, Weisler, & Foa, 2000);
- Obsessive Compulsive Inventory (Foa, Kozak, Salkovskis, Coles, & Amir, 1998);
- Impact of Event Scale – revised (Creamer, Bell, & Failla, 2003);
- Health Anxiety Inventory (Salkovskis, Rimes, Warwick, & Clark, 2002);
- Fear Questionnaire (Cox, Parker, & Swinson, 1996);
- Penn State Worry Questionnaire (Meyer, Miller, Metzger, & Borkovec, 1990).

For samples of these free resources in a range of online and printable formats, search with any popular internet search engine. An excellent online resource for all of the standard instruments is: www.goodmedicine.org.uk/goodknowledge/increasing-access-psychological-therapies-iapt-outcomes-toolkit

While these free resources provide a generally good level of measurement, and are certainly better than not measuring and monitoring outcomes, practitioners are advised to be familiar with the qualities and characteristics of the questionnaires and take care in interpreting the results. Some good questions to ask when relying on any instrument include:

- Has the instrument been tested and confirmed to work in the way it is designed, and is the normative data (the information that tells you how the instrument performs with different groups of people) available?
- Is the instrument designed for the population that you are using it on? (for example, was it designed for working age adults or children?)

- Are there factors that could distort the results? Some factors (such as a low reading ability) may make self-report measures unable to offer a good assessment of the problem, while some conditions (including poor physical health or recent serious stressors) may lead to inflated scores on some measures (Johnson, Pollard, & Hennessey, 2000).

No questionnaire (especially brief, self-report questionnaires) can provide a robust and clinically complete picture of a problem in isolation, so they should never be used without clinical judgement (Coyne et al., 2009) and never to diagnose a condition. Used sensitively, though, they can enhance our understanding (see Figure 3.1), offer a great way to monitor change and a quantitative sense of the severity of a problem (relative to the service users' understanding of the questions) and act as a good screening instrument to highlight features of the problem that might otherwise get missed, ignored or forgotten.

Psychometric data can be used in a number of ways, from basic to increasingly sophisticated:

1 At the crudest level, the information from the psychometric test can be used to simply order which problem is the worst, so that it can be treated first. There is some advantage of this sort of strategy, as opposed to a fixed point of entry into a treatment programme (including services where every person starts in a psycho-education-based stress class).
2 At the next level up, psychometric data can be used to inform clinical assessment interviews by identifying specific areas to discuss. It is not uncommon for people to fail to mention certain information, either because they do not realise it is relevant or because they are embarrassed to discuss it. Questionnaires that consider all different aspects of a condition remind both the service user and the practitioner that the information is relevant and appropriate to discuss. This may be particularly helpful during the assessment phase of your work together.
3 Finally, psychometrics can be used to inform ideas about diagnosis, gauge the severity of a problem and evaluate changes in the intensity over time.

Exercise 3.5   Other influences on psychometric assessments

In Primary Care settings, the most commonly occurring mental health difficulties relate to anxiety and low mood (McManus, Meltzer, Brugha, Bebbington, & Jenkins, 2007) with about 10 per cent of people affected (Cape, Whittington, Buszewicz, Wallace, & Underwood, 2010). Both of these broad categories of mental ill health have many psychometric instruments designed to assess the presence or absence of the condition. For the most part they are usually self-report questionnaires that ask the person to rate the frequency or intensity of the symptoms being investigated.

(Continued)

(Continued)

While we treat these carefully designed instruments as if they are a valid gauge of the respondent's well-being, let us consider two scenarios and the impact that a person's current state might have on their response patterns:

- James is talking to you on the telephone during his lunch break. Earlier that day he attended a meeting with his managers where they reported that the business was having financial troubles and would be cutting back on employees. Since then he has not been able to think about anything but the idea of being unemployed.
- Ryan has been referred into your service for agoraphobia, which causes him to avoid ever leaving his house. His anxiety is only really active when he goes out, which he has not done for weeks. His family is hugely supportive and make sure that he has everything that he needs in the house, as well as providing company for him.

For James and Ryan, consider what their answers might be for the following questions: 'In the last two weeks, how often had you felt nervous, anxious or on edge?' (adapted from the GAD-7); 'In the last two weeks, how often have you worried too much about different things?' (adapted from the GAD-7). Answering from their current contexts, how might you expect James and Ryan to answer these questions? Would this give an accurate representation of the intensity of their anxiety?

While psychometric tests can offer a rich source of information and are easy to administer, they are not without their limits. Self-report questionnaires are infamously sensitive to influences from factors other than what they are meant to measure, and are unable to take contextual factors into consideration. For example, people may want to appear less well or unwell than they really are; they may respond in the way that they think the practitioner wants them to respond; or they may use the opportunity to communicate about factors outside the focus of the questionnaire. We would be foolish to not capture the information that they can offer, but it would be equally unfortunate to use the data incorrectly or value it over its actual significance.

Some problems with outcome measures

In low intensity work, the trick to getting the greatest value for your service users is knowing where to invest effort and how much to invest. Outcome measures provide us with a quick means of assessing the state of a person and they (in particular the standardised ones) do this very efficiently. Unfortunately, routine use of these instruments can cause practitioners to over-rely on them – trusting the results of the measures and not following through to develop a fuller understanding of the problem.

When our understanding of the problem is excessively influenced by the results of the measures, it can lead us into the wrong treatment decisions, make us think that a treatment is working when it is not or is not working when it is. Comorbidity is common in mental health problems, even in the mild to moderate range. It is more normal for a person to have features consistent with both depression and anxiety than either of these conditions alone (Kaufman & Charney, 2000).

Despite this, there are very different pathways that can result in these combined presentations and equally different 'best choices' for treating them, according to which condition came first, which is most severe, which is prioritised by the service user or which would be the most likely to result in treatment gains (Balta & Paparrigopoulos, 2010). The NICE guidance for comorbid anxiety and depression suggests treating the most severe first (NICE, 2011b) or the primary problem (NICE, 2009b). If either the depression or anxiety is severe, the problem is not suitable for LICBT.

Exercise 3.6   The danger of relying solely on questionnaires

Consider this case vignette: Dwight has a big problem with anxiety – so much so that he has increasingly withdrawn from his normal life. When he goes out or even thinks about doing things, he becomes so anxious that he gets nauseous. His range of activities has become increasingly small, and now there is little that he enjoys. The benefit of this avoidance strategy is that he is now better able to manage some of his chaotic anxiety symptoms; the downside is that his mood has crashed and he is very cross with himself.

When Dwight came to the service he was asked to complete some standard questionnaires. Among them was a set of questions that asked about his experience of anxiety over the last two weeks. Because Dwight was so avoidant and spent most of his time away from the things that cause him anxiety, he had not actually had cause to experience much of his problem recently. As such, his anxiety did not show up on the questionnaires as a concern. In contrast, he scored very high on the depression measure, in particular, the questions about feeling hopeless, down and having little interest.

1   What might the questionnaires lead us to conclude about Dwight's situation? What impact might that have on his treatment, and ultimately on whether his condition improved? How could we build in safeguards to our practices to prevent such easy misunderstandings?
2   If Dwight's problem was thought to be low mood and his treatment included increasing his activity levels, what would you expect would happen to his anxiety scores?

(Continued)

(Continued)

As we have seen above, there are many ways of looking at a problem. This includes using outcome measures, but also your clinical impression, the service user's understanding, and the shared formulation (see Figure 3.1). The more complete the information that you use to understand the problem is, the more likely it is that your understanding will point you towards that best treatment options.

Formulation

The term *formulation* is one that is frequently used in the therapeutic literature (it is also sometimes called *conceptualisation*). Grant et al. (2008) provide a helpful breakdown of the functions and roles of a formulation. They include being able to:

- help the client link thoughts emotions, behaviours, and the environment;
- help both the client and the therapist recognise the maintaining cycles (vicious circles);
- help to set the therapeutic priorities;
- provide a clear rationale for the treatment plan;
- offer the client a sense of hope and optimism;
- enhance motivation for the client;
- help to understand how the problem started.

The formulation is used to describe a personalised description of a situation. Some formulations can include diagnostic information, but generally they include a lot more personally specific information. Formulations offer a psychologically informed idea about the relationship that certain factors within the problem might have to each other. It is, in short, a simplified model of the very complicated people that we all can be.

Formulations vary between problem categories, so a formulation for a phobia and a formulation for depression may appear quite different. Each person brings a unique (and uniquely complicated) blend of variables that have combined in a (you guessed it) unique way, resulting in their experiences. No formulation could be expected to comprehensively capture every bit of information, although in CBT formulations there will usually be some forms of thoughts, emotions and behaviours included, at a minimum.

Collaborative case formulation is as much a process as it is an outcome. To collect a valid picture of a person's difficulty, each participant is required to contribute information on experiences, understandings and knowledge. Obviously these are not all equally distributed between the service user and the practitioner. For the formulation to be collaborative, each person's contributions must be used for what they can best offer. Despite the fact that there is no single system that offers the best formulation, one way of formulating the problem frequently used in LICBT is the 'hot-cross bun', so named for the shape it takes when drawn out (see Figure 3.3).

The 'hot cross bun' representation of the interactions between the situation, thoughts, feelings, physical and behaviours was introduced by Padesky and Mooney (1990). This way of representing a problem has been used in popular and widely read low intensity materials (such as Padesky & Greenberger, 1995; and Williams & Garland, 2002), amongst many others. The ubiquitous use of these five factors highlights both the functionality of the hot cross bun-based formulation and its adaptability. It can be used to provide an accessible and informative 'picture' of the problem.

Starting with only the most basic information (the area covered by the medium grey outline, see Figure 3.3), and adding information as it is available, provides a fuller and more complete understanding of the problem (such as with the 'trigger' information included in the area covered by the light grey outline). The 'hot cross bun' name is taken from the graphical form that the formulation takes when it is completed. It is very well suited to capturing specific situations and describing the direct inter-relatedness of the variables.

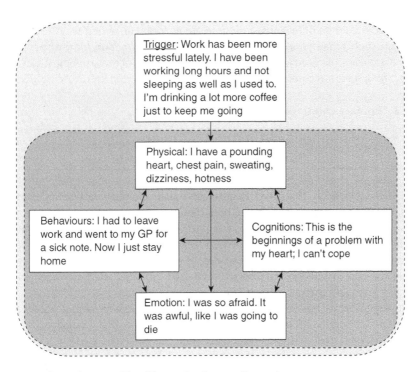

Figure 3.3   Case vignette 'Tom' from the Appendix

Variations of hot cross bun formulations include several categories of information including:

- *Situation or trigger* – often clinical problems occur within certain specific environments or contexts that have a direct bearing on the form of the problem. Under 'normal' circumstances most people are able to manage the demands of their environments. When circumstances become more demanding or less predictable, or appear less safe, this disruption of the status quo threatens to undermine all of the strategies and systems that the person has painstakingly put in place. This risks exposing them to their feared dangers, or the world to their hidden badness. Understandably, this can be very unsettling.
- *Cognitions* – what thoughts, beliefs, assumptions and mental images does the person have that are active with the problem(s) reported? It is worth noting here that these may not always be immediately identifiable by the person. In some cases these may be experienced automatically and as such an integrated part of an experience that they are not immediately recognised. In such an instance, careful questioning may help the client to recognise key thoughts. It can also be helpful to ask the person to run through the experience as though it were happening in that moment. This can help to trigger memories of exactly what they were thinking at the time of the experience.
- *Emotions* – when the problem is present or active, what feelings are encountered? People can consider a range of feelings, and there are no 'right' or 'wrong' ways to feel about a given situation. While it may be possible to solicit this information with an open question, some people are less used to talking about their feelings. For these people it may be helpful to offer a set list of common emotions (see Table 3.2).

Table 3.2   Primary emotions (Plutchik, 1994)

Joy	Acceptance	Fear	Surprise
Sadness	Disgust	Anger	Anticipation

- *Physiological/physical* – this category attempts to capture the way a person's autonomic reactions (factors including increased breathing, sweating and heart rate) contribute to the situation. In some problems, this is a particularly important variable, as the physical information is central to the person's understanding of their experience, especially in anxiety (see Chapter 9). Physical factors can be important when they are elevated (as is usually the case in anxiety), but also when they are inhibited (such as when feeling very tired or having low energy, as tends to occur in depression).
- *Behaviours* – what we do in a situation is an important variable, which this quadrant attempts to capture. The specific information here may relate to a cause of the situation, or a reaction to it. Behavioural factors are unique among the four categories included in this model in that they are directly under the control of the person's will. While it may be impossible to stop an intrusive thought, or prevent an emotional or physiological reaction, behaviours can (sometimes still with great effort) be controlled and regulated with greater success.

Problem statements

One of the things that you might have noticed so far about different ways of understanding the problem is that they can be quite tricky to understand themselves. Even the most straightforward system of just asking the person to tell you in their own words can be a challenge, and even then there is no telling what sort of information you will get or how useful it will be. Because of this, while each of the ways of understanding the problem already discussed offers its own perspective on the person's situation, none of them easily stands alone as an ideal candidate in low intensity settings, where the client is expected largely to be able to self-direct their treatment (albeit with support).

Within LICBT, there is an expectation that the service user will be able to play a lead role in both the prioritising of the problem(s) and the selection and administration of the treatment(s). One approach that has been promoted within LICBT is the *problem statement* (Richards & Whyte, 2009). A problem statement is a concise summary (usually only a few sentences) of where a problem comes from (the trigger), the symptoms being experienced by the client (including the cognitions, physical and behaviour), and some sense of the impact upon the client's life.

Problem statements are developed together with the client, towards the end of the first session, once a shared understanding of the difficulties has already been considered and discussed. This collaborative process does not require that either the client or the practitioner necessarily be the one to actually put the specific words or problems into a statement. Instead, as a collaborative process, the problem statement should be each person contributing what they can to the process. Ultimately though, it is the client's statement, so they have final say about what is included in the statement, what is prioritised, and the goals that are defined. Where possible, the practitioner should use the person's own words, giving them an opportunity to correct any misunderstandings.

While a problem statement is initially developed together to help prioritise the various difficulties and steer the decision-making process, as treatment progresses it can also be very effectively used to monitor change. As discussed above, if the problem statement is a summary of the problem at the point of the person beginning treatment, how much the same problem statement is still true later on can help to gauge the success of treatment.

A word of caution to keep in mind when drawing together a problem statement: when you bring together all the bad things that are going on for a person into a single declaration, there is a lot of unwelcome experience crammed into a small space. For some people it may be the first time that they have spoken about their difficulties. A little empathy from the practitioner can go a long way to moderate this and to normalise the impact that hearing the problem out loud can cause (see Chapter 4 for more guidance on this).

Exercise 3.7   Constructing the problem statement

Here are some sample problem statements:

- Ever since my friend moved away I have felt low and sad. I never go out any more and I hardly ever see my friends. My energy is so low that I can't concentrate and I find it difficult to focus. This has got in the way of my work and I am worried that I might be fired if my boss notices.
- As long as I can remember I have never been able to relax at bedtime. When I go to bed I spend hours just thinking about anything and everything and my mind races. This has caused me to be really tired all the time and I've started being irritable with my friends and family.

Using the case material for Tom in the Appendix, can you hypothesise what his problem statement might be?

Whatever system of understanding the problem that you are using, it is important to recognise that no single model ever captures the breadth of a whole situation and none has a monopoly on providing a way of understanding people. However you base your understanding, there is always something to be gained by considering another way of understanding a problem. By bringing together different types of information, we are more likely to avoid the biases and shortcomings that any given system has, and to acquire a more accurate, valid understanding of the situation. Hence, the LICBT assessment protocol brings together both the clinical interview and the use of psychometric measures (see Chapter 5).

Exercise 3.8   Bringing together diagnosis and formulation

One of the problems that using a diagnostic model poses to practitioners is that many mental health problems do not fit neatly into prescribed categories, even in low intensity working. Likewise, a purely formulation-based approach risks developing something so non-specific that you are unable to match the problem to an evidence base. In real life, people have broad, multi-dimensional experiences, where emotion, thoughts, activity and environment all interact and blur together, overlapping with the person's history and current situation. If diagnoses offer a shortcut to identifying conditions that helps us predict the progress of a problem and plan treatment according to the best available evidence, and formulation offers a personalised understanding of the problem, but is less able to draw from the wealth of specific knowledge that the literature can offer, what balance can be struck here?

Consider a situation where there could be both a diagnosis and a formulation.

How might these two ways of understanding a problem work together? Can you use both with the client? What role does the client's understanding have alongside these two more formal systems?

Conclusion

Although every person is different, many of our experiences and reactions are similar. By understanding our problems using common categories, we can use standardised assessments and treatments to offer high quality treatment to many people quickly and efficiently. There are many ways to understand a problem, and sometimes the best strategy is to combine several different approaches, including psychometrics, formulations, diagnostic categories and problem statements, as well as the person's own understanding of the problem. In Chapter 5, a structured way of undertaking this is presented. Then, through a clear understanding of the problem, we can make informed decisions about treatments choices and the same understandings can guide how we monitor and evaluate change.

Summary

- There are many options for understanding problems, ranging from very simple explanations in a client's own language to complicated psychological models or psychiatric diagnoses. Each system offers unique strengths and limits.
- Routine outcome measures (including psychometric instruments) can help us to assess and monitor specific aspects of a problem.
- In LICBT both collaborative formulation and problem statements offer specific, client-centred ways of describing problems and their maintenance, and proposing treatments that might help.
- By using more than one source of information, we can reduce the probability of bias distorting our understandings of the problems and improve our chances of offering meaningful interventions.

Further reading and activities

While the understanding of problems that we generate with clients in LICBT needs to fit with our standardised ways of working, there may be times (for example, as part of a reflective practice exercise or in supervision) where it may be helpful to consider additional details. One option that can be used to enhance our understanding of problems is the '5 Ps', which is based on a briefer 4 Ps version by Weerasekera (1996). It offers a simple descriptive model of formulation that is designed to promote a broad-based understanding of the current situation that goes beyond understanding the problem and includes information about the context to help us understand why this, why now and what can we do about it. The 'P's to consider include: *predisposing*, *precipitating*, *presenting*, *perpetuating* and *protective*. Cottam (2012) has also suggested that an additional 'P', namely *plan* should routinely be considered when understanding problems with this system.

To work effectively with LICBT you need to be clear that the client and the client's problems are suitable. When conventional, standardised ways of understanding the problem fail to capture the complexity of the situation, it may be an indicator that LICBT is not suitable. For those interested in learning about understanding more complex problems, I would strongly encourage you to review Kuyken, Padesky and Dudley's (2009) book on collaborative case conceptualisation.

The Therapeutic Relationship

Big deal or no deal?

Anna Chaddock

Learning objectives

- To gain an understanding of the nature of the therapeutic relationship in CBT and more specifically within LICBT.
- To gain a deeper understanding of what it means to be 'empathic' in the context of LICBT.
- To give examples of and to provide opportunities to practise some of the interpersonal skills that are important in engaging clients.
- To promote observation and reflection on your current practice and interpersonal skills.

Introduction

Warmth, empathy, listening skills, reflection, summarising, questioning skills and collaboration have been identified as essential qualities and methods for establishing and maintaining the therapeutic alliance (IAPT, 2010). However, these attributes and skills are not independent of one another, but form part of a process of relating effectively with other people. The result of this 'interpersonal process' is the formation and development of a relationship. In CBT, we define a relationship as 'therapeutic' when it is a collaborative one, and one that allows the client to embark upon the process of change. However, whereas the therapeutic relationship in traditional therapy may be described as dyadic (between two people: the client and therapist), in low intensity interventions the relationship is triadic, consisting of interactions between client, practitioner and intervention materials. This clearly has implications for the nature of the therapeutic relationship in LICBT.

You could take the view that, since a low intensity delivery model by definition relies on 'limited practitioner contact time' (Bennett-Levy & Farrand, 2010), interpersonal factors such as the development of a therapeutic relationship are less important. I would argue the opposite. It is precisely because you will have limited contact with the client that interpersonal factors are so important. As a LICBT practitioner you have less time to elicit the information needed to understand the client's difficulty, to develop rapport and facilitate their initial engagement with the intervention materials, and to overcome any difficulties that arise. The challenges of the therapeutic relationship may be different with time- and contact-limited interventions, but they are certainly not less (Farrand & Williams, 2010). The fact of the matter is that, regardless of your level of practice (low, high or stratospheric), the nature of the relationship you form with a client is the foundation on which all assessment, understanding, intervention and outcome is built. Dissatisfaction with the therapeutic relationship is reported to be the most common reason given by clients for disengagement or 'drop-out' and for not complying with treatment (Reis & Brown, 1999). There is also some evidence to suggest a stronger association between the therapeutic relationship and outcome in CBT than in other therapies (Bohart, Elliott, Greenberg, & Watson, 2002; Stiles, Agnew-Davis, Hardy, Barkham, & Shapiro, 1998). I believe that the therapeutic relationship is a big deal and I hope that, by the end of this chapter, you will too.

My objectives are therefore two-fold. I want to equip you with the theoretical knowledge you will need to understand the nature of the therapeutic relationship both in CBT in general and in its specific application within LICBT interventions. This will form the first half of the chapter. The second part of the chapter will be more practical, explaining and giving you chance to practise the interpersonal skills required to engage your clients. Engagement is the term often used to describe the nature of a client's commitment and involvement with the intervention. While there may be many peripheral signs of engagement (for example, attending sessions and completing homework tasks), an engaged client is essentially one who is actively involved in their own learning and in effecting change.

The nature of the therapeutic relationship in CBT

The therapeutic relationship is often referred to as a 'non-specific' factor in therapy (for example, Richards, 2010c). Non-specific factors are those that are common to many different forms and models of therapy, and you will also hear them referred to as 'common factors'. For example, warmth, genuineness and empathy are often identified as common factors (more on these three later). Specific factors refer to technical features that are unique to a particular therapy (Katzow & Safran, 2007). For example, the structure of sessions and the development of a problem statement would be defined as some of the therapy-specific factors in LICBT. However, Castonguay and colleagues (Castonguay, 1993, 2000; Castonguay & Holtforth, 2005) have argued that, in fact, many variables that are considered 'common' may actually have quite therapy-specific applications or be used in ways that are idiosyncratic to a particular type of therapy. So when we refer to the therapeutic relationship in any type or form of therapy, it is important to be specific about what we mean.

'Collaborative empiricism' is the term used to define the therapeutic relationship in CBT (Beck et al., 1979). The 'collaborative' part refers to the fact that, unlike many other therapies, the practitioner and client in CBT are active and equal team members who are working together towards change (Beck, 1995; Blackburn & Twaddle, 1996). In standard CBT, the therapist brings their knowledge and experience in treating a range of different problems using CBT, and the client contributes their knowledge and experience of themselves. The relationship becomes therapeutic when both sources of knowledge and experience are brought together, and when both participants are working together and participating in the process. Gilbert and Leahy (2007) liken this to a dance between two partners. Ideally both move together, in time with the music. This is essentially what we aim for: the therapist and client 'stepping' together, with steps matched and in time, the movement of one supporting and allowing the movement of the other.

This is a defining feature of CBT. It is what makes the relationship in CBT unique and specific. In no other therapeutic approach would you find the therapist and client working together in that way. This kind of collaboration allows a therapist and client to develop a shared understanding of their difficulties, and to make discoveries together to effect change in cognition and behaviour. This is where the 'empiricism' part of the definition comes in. The therapist and client work together like 'personal scientists' (Beck et al., 1979). They test out theories, try new and different ways of doing things and then evaluate the outcomes of these experiments. You can see that, in describing the nature of the therapeutic relationship in CBT, we are also describing the very nature of CBT.

> ## Exercise 4.1   Reflecting on personal experience of collaboration
>
> Think about a time when you have worked well with someone on a project or towards reaching a decision.
>
> - What sorts of things made it easy or difficult to work with the other person?
> - What did you and the other person do to facilitate joint working or collaboration?
> - How did it feel when you were collaborating?
> - What are the implications of your learning so far for your clinical practice, and specifically for your role in facilitating a collaborative relationship with your clients?

The role of the therapeutic relationship in CBT

In some forms of therapy, the therapeutic relationship is considered to be the main factor in bringing about change in the client's difficulties. In CBT, Beck and colleagues (1979) describe the role of the therapeutic relationship as the *context* within which therapy happens. We need to be careful here that we do not misinterpret the use of the word 'context'. Here, context is not synonymous with *background*. While many misinterpret or misquote the original text, there is no 'merely' or 'only' as a preface to describing the therapeutic relationship as a context for further intervention. The therapeutic relationship is therefore not *merely* the context. For example, we would not say that the death of a loved one is *merely* the context for their grief. Loss and grief are interrelated; you would not usually see one without the other. In the same way it can be argued that the relationship and technical parts of the therapy are inextricably linked within CBT. Therefore, while the therapeutic relationship may not be considered *sufficient* in and of itself to effect change, it is certainly a *necessary* part of the change process (Beck et al., 1979). For example, we could say that water is necessary in order for a plant to grow. However, water is not the only thing a plant needs (it also needs light, oxygen and nutrients). Without water the plant is unlikely to do well, but similarly, with only water it is unlikely to flourish. The water is necessary, but it is not sufficient in and of itself.

The nature of the therapeutic relationship in LICBT

So far we have identified that a defining feature of CBT is a therapeutic relationship characterised by collaborative empiricism. However, your role as a LICBT practitioner differs considerably from that of the more traditional 'CBT therapist'. In this section we will be identifying some of the implications of these differences for the therapeutic relationship in LICBT.

In LICBT, client–practitioner contact time is reduced by providing group based deliveries and shorter sessions that are limited in number (Bennett-Levy, Richards, & Farrand, 2010a). The focus is on engaging clients with interventions materials and in supporting them as they work through them. We could therefore summarise that, in LICBT, the therapeutic relationship between practitioner and client is characterised by *collaborative engagement* rather than collaborative empiricism, since much of the testing of thoughts and experimenting (for example, with behaviours) would be initiated within the CBT materials.

> The CBT now largely resides *within the materials,* rather than within the therapist. It used to be said that the therapist brings to the table their expertise in CBT, while the patient brings their expertise about themselves. Now the materials bring their expertise about CBT, and the LI practitioner brings their experience in providing valuable guidance and support. (Bennett-Levy et al., 2010: 13)

This has a number of implications for our understanding of the therapeutic relationship in LICBT. Firstly, in contrast to a traditional client–therapist relationship, which may be described as dyadic (between two people), the therapeutic relationship in LICBT is triadic, since it consists of three participants: the client, practitioner and the materials. If we extend Gilbert and Leahy's (2007) dancing analogy, the contrast would be similar to coaching a dance partnership, rather than being one of the dancers. To coach or choreograph a dance you need to have knowledge and skills in dancing in order to do a good job, but you utilise your skills in a different way to bring out the best in the dancers you are coaching. In the same way, good interpersonal skills are essential to relating well to your client, but also in order to help your client relate well and get the most out of the CBT materials. A good dance instructor knows the steps required by both participants and can give instruction, advice and encouragement to make sure the dance partners are 'stepping in time' and working together in the best way possible. In the same way, a good LICBT practitioner has knowledge of the client and their difficulties, as well as knowledge and experience of CBT materials, and can therefore give instruction, tips, advice, encouragement and support in order to help their client work with the materials in a way that maximises their potential to benefit from them.

Engagement and support can be arranged through almost any form of communication you could imagine, including face to face, by telephone, email, the internet, traditional mailed letters, groups and courses. This also has implications for the skills and practitioner behaviours involved in promoting collaborative engagement. For example, in traditional face-to-face sessions we would expect non-verbal communication to play a big role in communicating warmth, genuineness and empathy (for example, through eye contact, facial expression, tone of voice and posture). However, many of these non-verbal cues are not available to us when interacting with our clients via telephone or email. It is, unfortunately, beyond the scope of this chapter to address these issues adequately. Good practice guidelines for engaging clients by telephone or via email are available and Chapter 5 also describes some of the practical issues associated with telephonic working.

It seems fair to say that in LICBT, the practitioner and intervention materials share the role of therapist. So whereas Beitman, Goldfried and Norcross (1989) describe the therapeutic relationship as the personal qualities of the client, the practitioner and the interaction between them, in LICBT this becomes the personal qualities of the client, the practitioner, the intervention materials and the interaction between them. This means that, when we are engaging our clients with intervention materials, we need to consider their interpersonal qualities as well as our own. The suggestion that there may be relational aspects to self-help materials is a controversial one, although there is increasing evidence of this within the self-help literature (Richardson & Richards, 2006; Richardson, Richards, & Barkham, 2010). However, anyone who has ever been absorbed in a good book can tell you it is possible to relate to and feel related to written materials. Often what moves us most are the parts that in some way relate to some part of ourselves, our feelings as a parent, the loss of a loved one, a betrayal or the breakdown of a relationship. We feel in some way that the author or character understands something about ourselves, that there is a connection. In the same way it can be incredibly powerful for a client to read a passage which they feel describes what they are experiencing, or when a suggested activity moves them or affects change. Good quality materials will therefore be able to communicate to the client that the authors understand what it is like for them in the midst of their distress. Richards and Farrand (2010) advocate an empathic approach to selecting self-help materials for a client by putting yourself in the client's shoes and asking whether they would feel engaged by the way the material communicates with them. This implies that effective promotion of CBT materials requires the practitioner to have a detailed knowledge and understanding of them. There is some evidence to suggest that practitioners who practise CBT techniques and materials on themselves can develop a deeper level of understanding of CBT and experience a greater sense of empathy for their clients (Bennett-Levy, Lee, Travers, Pohlman, & Hamernik, 2003; Farrand, Perry, & Linsley, 2010; Thwaites, Bennett-Levy, Davis, & Chaddock, in press).

In summary, together we have identified that the therapeutic relationship is characterised by collaborative engagement, and that the relationship has three participants (the client, the practitioner and the CBT materials). We have acknowledged that good interpersonal skills in relating to others are essential in promoting a client's engagement in LICBT and specifically in promoting the client's engagement with the CBT materials. In addition, there may be specific considerations or adaptations of good relating style required for engaging a client by telephone or through the written word. Finally, we have highlighted the need to consider the interpersonal qualities of CBT materials when selecting appropriate materials for a client to engage with.

The practitioner's role in promoting a collaborative relationship

Fundamental to the CBT view of the therapeutic relationship is the idea of teamwork, requiring the client and therapist to be 'in tune' with each other and to work together towards shared goals. A collaborative relationship is established when the client perceives the therapist as someone who is tuned in to their feelings and attitudes, understanding and accepting, and when the therapist feels concern and care for the client and senses that they are operating on the same wavelength. This clearly requires the therapist to use all of their perceptive skills in listening, perspective taking and communication. These skills and attributes are commonly summarised within the literature under the headings of warmth, genuineness and empathy.

The CBT literature defines a therapist's warmth as 'a type of softness and gentleness that *conveys caring concern*' (Gilbert, 2007), and genuineness as an honest response to the client without pretence, overstatement or acting (Beck et al., 1979). Empathy is much more difficult to define. It relates to our perception of the client's experience (Burns & Auerbach, 1996; McLeod, Deane, & Hogbin, 2002; Overholser & Silverman, 1998), and our sensitivity and attitude towards understanding how they feel and think (Bennett-Levy et al. 2003; Hoffart, Versland, & Sexton, 2002). It means taking the perspective of the client and a having a felt sense of what it is like to be in their shoes (Bennett-Levy et al., 2003; Burns & Auerbach, 1996; Deffenbacher, 1999; Sloan, 1999). It also encompasses our skills in communicating all of this to our client, so that they know that we have been trying to understand, and how close we are to understanding their experience.

Here, the focus will be on empathy over warmth and genuineness for a number of reasons. First, because when you compare the three concepts, empathy seems to have the most to offer in terms of facilitating collaboration and that 'team work' attitude. This is important because, as we have already identified, you will have limited time to focus explicitly on relational factors owing to the limited time you have within your contact with clients, and therefore keeping one concept in mind is likely to be more realistic than keeping three. Moreover, while it is possible to be warm and respond genuinely to a client in the absence of empathy (without taking the element of perspective-taking), you cannot truly respond empathically without also demonstrating warmth and genuineness. A cold and insincere response is unlikely to fit the criteria for empathy.

To help us understand empathy further, we are going to use the analogy of one of those old-fashioned, analogue radios, the ones with a dial that you have to manually turn in order to tune in to a particular frequency to pick up a particular station. If you are not tuned in properly to the right frequency, the sound is distorted and disguised by white noise and you may also be picking up frequencies from other stations. In the same way, 'tuning in' to your client's mood or emotional state, which is sometimes referred to as *attuning*, is something that you actively have to do by paying attention to all the signs and signals your client is 'transmitting'. Tuning in or *attunement* is an important component of therapeutic empathy, which is defined by Thwaites and Bennett-Levy (2007) as a *perceptual skill*. Think of it this way: if you are not on the same wavelength as your client, you are going to be limited in the extent to which you are able to engage them collaboratively.

The main clues to understanding things from the client's perspective come from the things our clients say or write to us. However, further clues can be picked up from their choice of words, the *way* they say things (for example, word emphasis, tone, pitch or rate of speech), their eye contact, facial expression, posture, whether they are washed, shaven, how they smell, even a client's breathing can communicate something of their experience. These are all clues from the client to help us tune in to what our client is feeling and thinking. Therefore, your perceptual skills in picking up on these cues are also part of the range of skills that enable you to be empathic. In telephone work or in communication via email, the range of cues may be limited, and in these cases you may need to be even more explicit in asking your client and clarifying with your client what it is that they are feeling and thinking.

Exercise 4.2   Practising perceptual skills

You will need some ear plugs or head phones and someone to act as 'communicator'. This could be a colleague, supervisor, willing family member or friend. You could even use some recorded dialogue from a TV programme, anything in which someone is talking about an experience they have had.

The role of the 'communicator' is to briefly describe an experience or event for a couple of minutes. This could be in role as a depressed or anxious person talking about their difficulties, talking about a real-life problem difficulty or really anything the person is comfortable to talk about (for example, how their day has been, what they did at the weekend, the last film they saw or something that has moved them).

I would advise the communicator not to pick something distressing or difficult to talk about (no more than a 4/10 on a subjective units of distress scale). The purpose is to practise actively attending to and perceiving communications from the other person. As they are describing, you (the 'perceiver') gather as much information as you can from their communication. Do this in three stages under three conditions:

1 With ear plugs in or headphones on so that you cannot hear the person.
2 With a blindfold on, or sitting with your back turned to the communicator so you cannot hear them.
3 With eyes and ears unimpeded so that you can hear and see them.

If you are using a scene from a TV programme or film, you could watch with the sound off, seated looking away from the screen, etc.

Exercise 4.3 Reflecting on practice (perceptual skills)

In relation to the previous exercise consider the following:
  For each condition:

- What were you observing/perceiving? What information have you gathered about the communicator's experience?
- What was it like trying to understand the communicator's experiences based on the information available to you?
- Do you have any initial hypotheses about this person's thinking, emotional experience or behaviour based on what you have seen and/or heard?
- Did you experience any internal response to their communications?

Overall:

- What are you learning about picking up on communications from others based on your experience within this exercise?
- What are the implications of this learning for your clinical practice?
- Are there any specific implications for working with someone over the telephone or through an interpreter?

Like any skill, it takes practice to develop a level of artistry in perceptual skills. Almost any social situation can be utilised to practise these skills because it is largely a case of looking, listening and paying closer attention to what is being communicated by other people's words, way of speaking and body language. Even the queue at the supermarket can become an opportunity to practise noticing what people might be thinking, feeling and doing.

Exercise 4.4   Practising communication skills

Think about how you demonstrate that you are listening and paying attention to the other person communications. Repeat the exercise with the 'communicator' from Exercise 4.2. This time ask your communicator to talk to you about any topic or issue (for example, their last holiday, a recent film or interest) under the following conditions:

1   While they are wearing the blindfold, or with their chair turned so that they cannot see you.
2   With ear plugs in so that they cannot hear you.
3   Without ear plugs or blindfold so that they can hear and see you.

Your job is to respond as you usually would to what they are saying. After each condition, ask the communicator to feed back to you how effective you were at demonstrating you were listening and paying attention to them, and also *what you did* that showed them that you were. For some extra practice you could reverse roles to get an experience from the communicator's or client's point of view.

Exercise 4.5   Reflecting on practice of communication skills

Think about your experience of the previous exercise.

• Was there anything that surprised you?
• What was difficult and what came more easily?
• What are you learning about communicating to others based on your experience within this exercise?
• What are the implications of this learning for your clinical practice?
• Are there any specific implications for working with someone over the telephone or through an interpreter?

Going back to our radio analogy for understanding empathy, once you pick up on the client's 'frequency' the next step is to interpret what you have seen, heard and smelled so that you can 'fine tune' and clarify what it is that you are picking up. Summaries, reflections and clarifications can all be described as empathic communications since they can all be used to get closer to the client's experience and emotional state as well as to let the client know that you are making an effort to understand (see Table 4.1). These techniques, as well as providing the opportunity to communicate

Table 4.1 'Fine tuning' behaviours

Client communication:
'I didn't do very well with it this week. After last session I really felt motivated to start doing some of the things we talked about, but when it came to, it was much harder than I thought. I didn't do too bad on the days when I was able to get up straight away like we said, and I even managed to get to see my friend in hospital on Tuesday I think it was. I think she really appreciated me going. But some days are harder than others, you know what I mean?'

Practitioner behaviour	Description	Examples
Summarising	A brief statement pulling together or 'chunking' what the client has said	'It sounds like you don't think you did very well this week, but you managed to do some things, even though it was more difficult than you'd first thought'
		'OK, so you've not achieved all you'd hoped, but you did manage to see your friend, which sounds like it was important to both you and to her'
Reflecting	Playing the client's words or experience back to them in the same way that a mirror reflects back the image in front of it. Reflecting often also refers to acknowledging that you have picked up on a client's mood or emotion	'So some days are harder than others'
		'So you don't think you did very well this week'
		'So you've been giving yourself a bit of a hard time this week about how much you've achieved'
		'You seem disappointed'
Clarifying	Asking a question to check that your understanding is correct. Clarifications can follow either a summary or reflection	'Am I right in thinking that you are a bit disappointed with yourself this week, that you've not managed to do more?'
		'So it sounds like you've been giving yourself a bit of a hard time this week. Is that right?'

empathy, can also in turn make a session more accessible to a client by giving it more structure and in drawing out the most important points for the client to be recognising. Summarising is probably the most useful in terms of helping to keep a contact focused and 'on message'.

Different people express their emotions in different ways. Some people are more able than others to share their distress openly with you or may even be actively trying to disguise their distress. Interpreting the meaning of non-verbal communications is not always easy, especially when you consider the impact of context. For example, avoidance of eye contact in a session with you may indicate that the person is bored, disengaged, irritated, shy or has feelings of shame and embarrassment depending on the context in which it is observed. Silences may signify that the client is thinking, that they are angry, that they do not know what to say or that they do not understand. This is really about piecing together what you already know with what you are observing and the context in which you are observing it and then checking out your understandings with the client.

Exercise 4.6   Interpreting behaviour

Imagine you are with a client. Consider the following non-verbal communications and think about what meaning they might have. Generate as many possibilities as you can.

1   Sitting slumped forwards in the chair.
2   Speaking very slowly.
3   Breathing fast and audibly.
4   Speaking very quietly.
5   Very active, making gestures and shifting about in the chair.
6   Smiling as they are telling you things, making jokes and laughing.

Now compare notes with a colleague or supervisor.

Exercise 4.7   Reflecting on interpreting behaviour

• Was there anything your colleague or supervisor thought of that you did not?
• If there were differences, does this represent a gap in your experience, knowledge or attitude towards any particular communications or presentations?
• What are the learning points for you from this exercise?
• What do you need to follow up in order to improve your practice?

I have not given you any 'answers' or a list of possible interpretations of the clients' behaviours because trying to make sense of what a client is communicating to you is not really about being right or being wrong. I would argue that much more important to your client is that they can tell you are making an effort to understand. Thwaites and Bennett-Levy (2007) identify empathic communication as another important component of therapeutic empathy. Taking a broad view, this means any active communication back to the client that you are making efforts to 'tune in' and to understand. Experience tells us that our client's do not necessarily come into therapy expecting us to be able to understand what is going on for them. In fact, clients often come with the expectation or experience that other people do not understand or struggle to understand their problems. The fact that you are showing them that you are making the effort to try to understand can be an important factor in facilitating collaboration because it shows that you are on their side and trying to work with them.

However, assuming that you have an accurate understanding can be counterproductive to collaboration. Notice that, in Table 4.1, the therapist has fed back their understanding in tentative, rather than absolute, terms. Tentative expressions of understanding, such as 'So what I hear you saying is ...; You seem to be telling me ...; Am I right in thinking that ...', can help lessen the impact of a therapist's misunderstandings because they are communicating that you are checking out with the client that your understanding matches theirs (Beck, 1995) and, as such, are less likely to be perceived as you telling the client what they are thinking and feeling.

When we think about working collaboratively with someone, 'being on the same wavelength' is certainly going to help. So far we have considered things from the point of view of the therapist and their efforts to tune in to the client. However, it is also important to consider how we support clients to get on our wavelength and attune to us. Feedback is one of the most important ways of ensuring this. This means first getting the client to feed back to you where they are in terms of their understanding of a task or concept or how well they think things are going. Table 4.2 gives some examples of times when it might be useful to elicit some feedback from a client.

It can be difficult to feed back to a client that they have not understood something correctly or when they have got off-track in some way. At these times, taking the client's perspective and asking yourself how you might like this put to you can help keep your feedback in that empathic, collaboration-building zone. Giving positive feedback to your client is also important and something that is often forgotten. Positive feedback

Table 4.2   Eliciting feedback

Feedback scenario	Example
Understanding their five areas assessment	'This seems quite important what we're doing here so I'd like to just pause for a second and make sure we're both on the same page with this. What sense are you making of what we've done so far?'
The accuracy of the problem statement	'If this is the statement we are going to be working from, it seems pretty important that we're satisfied with it. So how well do you feel it sums up the problem?'
In general how well the sessions are going	'OK so we've met a few times now and I'm interested from your point of view how you think it's going so far'

might come in the form of praise or affirmations (for example, 'You've really impressed me with the way you've approached this') and encouraging statements (for example, 'This stuff isn't easy, but you're on track with it and doing really well. Let's see what more we can achieve this week'). The important thing is that your praise and encouragement are given in response to something, otherwise it may seem insincere and even patronising.

Exercise 4.8   Practising joined up empathy skills

This time ask your communicator to talk to you about any topic or issue (for example, their last holiday, a recent film or interest, etc.). You can do this face to face, facing away from one another or even, for a little added realism, over the telephone. Putting into practice all that you have learned so far about empathic attunement and communication, respond to what the person is communicating to you. Make sure you ask your communicator for feedback on how you did.

Now go back over this section of the chapter and identify (perhaps with help from the communicator) the practitioner behaviours you were demonstrating.

Exercise 4.9   Reflecting on practice of empathy skills

Thinking about your experience:

- Was there anything that surprised you?
- What was difficult and what came more easily?
- Was there any behaviour or set of behaviours that you missed out?
- What are you learning about relating well to others based on your experience within this exercise?
- Are there any specific implications for working with someone over the telephone?

Thinking about empathy in general:

- What is your understanding of 'empathy' so far? What are its key features and what does 'being empathic' entail?
- How do you know when you have been or are being empathic?
- How do you think a client might experience empathy?
- What are the implications of this learning for your clinical practice?

Exercise 4.10   Reflecting on your response to the chapter

Thinking about the chapter as a whole:

- What has stuck out for you, surprised you, inspired you, confused you?
- What has provoked your thinking?
- Did you learn or realise anything about your client's experience of LICBT?
- Is there anything in the chapter that you feel you need to follow up with a tutor, supervisor or through further reading?
- How could some of what we have talked about today be applied to your practice?
- Is there anything that you might want to change about your current practice? If so, what, and how might you go about doing it?
- For you, what is the most important thing to 'take away' about the therapeutic relationship?

Conclusion

The aim of this chapter was at least to add to your knowledge and understanding of these issues, and to give you some insights into what constitutes effective and empathic practice. The intention has also been to make the chapter as accessible as possible and to support, encourage and motivate you to engage in developing your knowledge and practice further, in the same way that you would hope your clients are supported, encouraged and motivated by your work with them.

Summary

- A collaborative therapeutic relationship is a defining feature of CBT at whatever level you are practising.
- Some of the greatest strengths of LICBT are time efficiency, flexibility in mode of delivery, and an emphasis on empowering clients to help themselves. These are the very features that pose particular challenges to a traditional view of developing a therapeutic relationship.
- Empathy is a powerful tool in engaging clients. It is a process that encompasses perception of the client's experience, a felt sense or understanding of their experience, and your communicated response. It is not an add-on to the rest of your LICBT practice; it is more a way of being with a client and of engaging them with the key tasks of LICBT.

Further reading and activities

- Thwaites and Bennett-Levy (2007) is the 'must read' paper on empathy in CBT.
- For further information on selecting self help materials, see Richards and Farrand (2010) and www.iapt.nhs.uk/silo/files/good-practice-guidance-on-the-use-of-self-help-materials-within-iapt-services.pdf
- Bennett-Levy, Thwaites, Chaddock and Davis (2009) explore the importance of reflection in the development of CBT skills, including interpersonal skills. Most of Bennett-Levy's publications can be accessed via the University of Sydney University website: http://sydney.edu.au/medicine/people/academics/profiles/jbennettlevy.php
- Josefowitz and Myran (2005) present an interesting perspective on how some key elements of CBT may be intrinsically relationship-promoting.
- Lovell (2010) identifies in more detail how best to engage clients by telephone.

As identified in the chapter, videotaping and reviewing your practice and interpersonal skills can be extremely helpful. However, we often have the tendency to be our own worst critic, so it is advisable to review this with a supervisor or trusted colleague so that you can get that second, balancing opinion. It can also be helpful to observe or review other people's practice. You may wish to ask whether you can sit in on a session with your supervisor or an experienced colleague (or review a video of their practice). Think about what worked well, what did not work so well, whether there was anything that was particularly effective and reflect on how you might like to adjust your practice. Remember that some supervisors and colleagues may not feel comfortable with you doing this and some services may not have the facilities for recording sessions with clients.

You could also monitor your own skills over time. Self-monitoring focuses you on specific aspects of skill or practice, and enables you to start to think about ways you could improve on your practice. Select one or two skills (for example, summarising or encouraging) and then over a period of time (for example, over the course of a week, over a number of sessions, or over a course of sessions with one client) take notice of what you do and how you do it in relation to that particular skill. Some of the reflective questions we have been using together in the chapter so far might be helpful in structuring your reflections on your skills and in thinking about how or what you might need to do to change or further develop your skills. Abstract: Enhancing Self-Practice/Self-Reflection (SP/SR) approach to cognitive behaviour training through the use of reflective blogs.

Self-Practice/Self-Reflection (SP/SR) is increasingly beginning to feature as a central component of CBT training programmes (Bennett-Levy et al., 2001). Programmes including a reflective element, however, are not unproblematic and it has been documented that simply setting time aside for reflection does not necessarily result in trainees using such time to reflect. Such limitations may be overcome by including a requirement to post reflections on reflective blogs.

5

The LICBT Interview Structure

Mark Papworth

Learning objectives

- To understand the rationale for the structure of the LICBT assessment and treatment interviews.
- To be able to use the interviews to understand the difficulties that the client is experiencing and to address their difficulties.
- To be able to make adjustments to the interviews to allow them to be delivered over the telephone.

Introduction

The interview structure is the framework through which the practitioner delivers their help. It supports the LICBT approach (like a skeleton supports the muscles) and allows the practitioner to cover the content required to help the client within the allocated time. This is typically six to eight, weekly, 30 minute sessions. As such, it is crucial that the practitioner learns the interview structure in order to allow this to occur. If trainee practitioners are not well versed in this, they find it difficult to deliver the session within the time frame and may commit fundamental clinical mistakes. These include: missing out important sections of the interview, creating barriers to engagement by placing sensitive sections of the interview (such as risk assessment) too early in the structure or de-motivating the client by asking them to do homework without giving them a rationale for the intervention.

Below I introduce the interview structure of the LICBT approach (assessment interview and treatment interview). I will illustrate how this is used in practice by reproducing an interview with Judy. This client was referred because of difficulties that had occurred at work (see more detail in the Appendix).

The assessment interview

The assessment interview serves several important functions (Grant et al., 2008). Firstly, it has an educational role for the client in terms of providing information about LICBT and the nature of their problems. As the practitioner asks questions and helps the client to discover connections between symptoms and triggers, the client is able to construct an informed picture of their difficulties in tandem with the practitioner. Towards the end of the interview, a problem statement is produced with the client. This provides a shared understanding of the presenting difficulties and serves to guide both the client and practitioner to the therapeutic work that lies ahead. In this way, the assessment instils a sense of hope in the client, letting them know that their problem is fathomable, not unique to themselves and also treatable. This, in turn, motivates the client and strengthens the therapeutic relationship.

The initial assessment might well be the first personal contact the client has with the LICBT service (if they did not receive a prior 'triage' consultation). As such, in this first meeting the practitioner is the 'face' of the service. The client is likely to feel particularly vulnerable, anxious and uncertain about attending. Thus, the practitioner should make full use of their interpersonal therapeutic skills (see Chapter 4). Indeed, upon first greeting the client in the waiting room, they should take care to do so in a warm and appropriately welcoming fashion. Additionally, it is helpful if their appearance is in keeping with what is generally considered to be appropriate for a health professional. If the client needs to be led some distance from the waiting area to the therapy room, neutral, casual conversation may help to put them at their ease, for example: 'Did you manage to find the clinic okay?' Likewise, a similarly neutral question can also help to place the client more at ease when they first sit down in the clinic room:

Practitioner: How did you feel about coming along here today?
Client: OK, but I am feeling a bit nervous – I wasn't sure what to expect.
Practitioner: I guess that is to be expected in this situation. People usually settle as they start talking, I wonder whether we can try that and see how we go?

The formal structure of the assessment and treatment interview is set out Table 5.1. I will review this structure in more detail for the assessment interview, illustrating it with excerpts from an interview with Judy. This structure is given as an example and is taken primarily from the English IAPT scheme (Richards & Whyte, 2009), also drawing upon Grant et al. (2008) and Westbrook et al. (2011). It is designed as a guide, but in practice, deviation from this is inevitable and it is best used flexibly in a patient-centred manner. However, there is a logical order to the structure and so I recommend that, particularly in training, this broad order of events is followed where possible. An example record sheet for the interview is provided in Figure 5.1, although some services may be using fully computerised record systems (see www.iaptus.co.uk/; www.coreims.co.uk/About_CORE_IMS.html and www. pc-mis.co.uk/).

Table 5.1   Structures of the assessment and treatment LICBT interview

	Assessment interview	Treatment interview
1. Introductions (5 minutes approximately)	Practitioner and client names; practitioner explains their role and the structure of the session, also explaining the limits of confidentiality and the role of note taking	Recap of information covered in the Introduction at assessment (other than confidentiality and note taking)
2. Information gathering (reviewing, 10 minutes approximately)	Gather information about the problem; complete the risk assessment and review the outcome measures; explore why they are presenting for help at this point; review of onset, modifying and maintaining factors; note the client's expectations and goals; review past episodes and treatment as well as alcohol, drug and caffeine use; review medication use and attitudes towards this; finish by considering other issues such as diversity-, debt- or work-related ones	Review of problem statement and monitor change in this; review of risk assessment and outcome measures; review of medication and previous session's homework
3. Information-giving and shared decision-making (looking ahead, 10 minutes approximately)	Produce the problem statement and check this with client; present information about appropriate treatment options and determine the preferred option with the client; summarise the session	Discussion of next intervention options; introduce the next focus for LICBT; develop an action plan to be completed over the next week; summarise the session
4. Ending (5 minutes approximately)	Next steps agreed, including next appointment and referral to any other agencies (for instance, employment advisor)	Next steps agreed, including next appointment, how to maintain activities arising from previous homework tasks and additional approaches/input where indicated

Client name *Judy Jenkins*   Client DoB *1-3-66*

Practitioner name Ⓨ/ N   Client name Ⓨ/ N   Preferred name Ⓨ/ N
Practitioner role Ⓨ/ N   Agenda Ⓨ/ N   Timescale Ⓨ/ N
Confidentiality Ⓨ/ N   Note taking Ⓨ/ N

Presenting problem (4Ws: what, where, when with whom)

What: Depression, low mood.
Where: Ongoing low mood, unable to socialise currently, has difficulties leaving house.
When: Occurs throughout day, worsens if out, particularly in social situations.
Whom: Is more dependent upon partner and relatives at the moment, is able to do more
       with husband John present.

(Five areas: emotion, physical, cognition, behaviour, triggers)

Emotional: Low mood, tearfulness, guilt.
Physical: Tiredness, fatigue, loss of concentration, difficulty sleeping.
Cognitive: Worry, 'I am a failure', 'I am holding John back' and 'I am imposing on others'.
Behavioural: Inactivity, avoidance, at home most of the day.
Triggers: Ruminates about work which worsens mood; low mood is worsened by contact
              from work; feels worse in the mornings.

[Risk (see proforma for this section: Figure 6.1)]

Impact of problem:

Is on sickness absence from work; is unable to undertake household chores – is relying
on family to help with this. Has affected lifestyle – the couple are socialising less together and with others (husband has increased work commitments). The relationship is
supportive.

Outcome measures:

PHQ-9: 16   GAD-7: 10   WSAS: 29

Onset, modifying and maintenance factors:

Onset: Work-related issues, promotion (four months ago) and subsequent diffi-
              culty in coping; occurred approximately one month ago.
Maintenance: Avoidance behaviour (socialising, activities in the community); general
              reduction in activity.
Modifying: Improvement when husband is able to give her attention; practical support
              from others results in worsening of mood (thoughts of failure).

Client expectations and goals:

Wants most to improve ('get back to old self') and also return to prior levels of activity
(coping with housework). Goal to return to work but is uncertain whether she can cope with
prior role.

Medication and client expectations:

Fluoxetine, 20 mg/day

Other relevant (for example, employment, family situation):

Currently is away from work. Work are keen for her to return. Client currently cannot face discussions with her employer. No financial stresses.

Problem statement:

About four months ago, I got a promotion at work. I found it difficult to cope and I made mistakes. I feel down and guilty, I am tired and have difficulty sleeping. I think I am failing and that I am letting people down. I am now not socialising and I am unable to keep up with the housework.

Agreed action:

Client agreed to 6–8 sessions of GSH; I gave client the depression recovery manual and asked her to read the clients' recovery stories. I asked her to consider whether a referral to this team's Employment Advisor might be helpful, with a view to the advisor facilitating an initial discussion with the employer. Further appointment arranged in one week.

Figure 5.1   Example of completed assessment interview recording sheet

Introductions

It is likely that the practitioner will have already briefly introduced themselves when collecting the client from the waiting area. However, to avoid any confusion, it is best to start the interview with confirmation of the clinician's name, the client's name (and what they would preferred to be called: Mr Smith or John) and the client's date of birth (so the clinician can confirm they have retrieved the correct files). This is particularly important in telephone LICBT where the practitioner will not be clear regarding who has answered the phone and also because in some families it is not unusual for members to share a Christian name. Additionally, if there is a national or regional electronic patient record system, it is likely that others with the same name will be included.

Next, the practitioner should state their professional role (for example, low intensity CBT practitioner, CBT coach or psychological well-being practitioner) and their remit. This might involve explaining that the practitioner works with mild to moderate psychological problems and uses evidence-based approaches, primarily through the use of guided reading or computer-based packages. The practitioner should then provide an agenda for the session (checking that the client is happy with this) and let them know how much time the session will take.

It is vital to discuss confidentiality before the client starts to recount their problem. Clients sometimes attend with an assumption that what that they say within the therapy room cannot be revealed to anyone else under any circumstances. On the contrary, session content is routinely shared with the practitioner's supervisor, correspondence is usually sent as a minimum to the client's primary care physician and confidentiality may need to be breached if the client indicates that anyone is at risk (see Chapter 6). It is important that the client is aware of the limits of confidentiality to enable them to make an informed decision regarding whether or not to continue with the session. Finally, the clinician will usually let the client know that they will be taking notes as part of their role. This will be to aid memory, to enable the supervisory process and as a record in case any other practitioners need to have contact with the client (for instance, if the client is to be stepped up).

This introductory segment is brief and is primarily concerned with setting the scene for LICBT through giving the client information about the clinician and the session plan. Nevertheless, it is undertaken in an interactive way, with the practitioner intermittently checking out whether the client has understood the information or needs anything clarifying.

Information gathering

After this scene-setting section, the practitioner moves on to enquiring about the difficulties for which the client has been referred. This section is a collaborative process of discovering and mapping the various elements that constitute the individual's distress. Often the client will have mentally rehearsed this section of the interview prior to attending. So for some clients, this section is focused on guiding and steering the client in the telling of their story.

To ensure that the various essential dimensions of the problem are covered, it is useful to consider the '4Ws' and the 'five areas'. These are overlapping frameworks that act as a guide for assessment. They have their origins in the 1960s (for instance, Lang, 1968) and variants have been the basis for formulations within many self-help books (Greenberger & Padesky, 1995; Williams, 2003). The '4Ws' consist of the following areas: *what* the problem is (for example, 'Can you tell me what the problem is that has led to you coming here to see me today?'); *where* the problem occurs ('In what situations do you get these symptoms?'); with *whom* the problem gets better or worse ('If you are with anyone, does that change how you respond in that situation?'); and *when* the problem happens ('Is there any time of the day when your symptoms become better or worse?'). The skilful clinician will explore these areas (and those described below) sensitively using a funnelling framework (see Exercise 5.1), rather than using these (and other examples) as stock questions to ask in each assessment. For educational purposes I have broken down the interviews into discrete sections. However, for the experienced LICBT practitioner, the interview will flow seamlessly from one section into another. The use of summaries is helpful as a tool to bridge sections and steer the interview: 'From what you have said, it seems that [summary]. Can I just pick up on what you were saying about [new topic contained in the summary]. Can you tell me a little more about this?'

The 'five areas' are the elements of the 'hot cross bun' model (described in Chapter 3). These prompt the practitioner to obtain information about the interacting dimensions of client symptomatology. The first of these is the *emotional* dimension. Usually, it is this dimension that prompted the client in their help-seeking and so they will usually report on this spontaneously when asked about their problem: 'I feel depressed most of the time'. Thoughts and emotions are frequently confused by clients and they can be helpfully labelled in this section of the interview for the client. Some individuals (such as older people) are more likely to report the *physical* dimension of their difficulties ('I feel tired all the time and I have lost all my spark'). In such circumstances, questioning about emotions may be required, for instance: 'Have you noticed any difference in your mood since you started experiencing these changes?' Examples of physical symptoms include sweating, increased heart rate and shaking in anxiety, as well as loss of energy, sex drive and appetite in depression (see Chapters 7 and 9). An example of a question that encourages clients to elaborate on their physical symptoms is: 'Is there anything else that changes in your body while this is happening?'

The third dimension consists of thoughts or *cognitions*. It is important initially not to use jargon such as 'cognitions' with clients, although as contact progresses it is useful to match the terminology used in the session with that contained in the self-help materials. Cognitions are the words or images that pass through the client's mind while the difficulties are occurring. This dimension is sometimes more difficult for individuals to access. The client might be helped to recall cognitions by being asked to describe in fine detail the most recent time when they experienced significant symptoms. This can be followed up with a question such as: 'What was running through your mind at the time?'

The *behavioural* dimension encompasses the activity or actions that have changed for the client. These might include new behaviours such as checking (for example, to see where the public toilets or other areas of 'safety' are), the avoidance of specific situations, the adoption of safety behaviours or a more general reduced level of activity (see Chapter 9). Examples of questions that probe these changes are: 'Is there anything that you have been doing less since you developed this problem?' and 'Is there anything that you do to help yourself cope in that situation?'

The final and fifth area to explore before moving on from this section is the day-to-day *triggers* to episodes of distress. These are factors that make distress more likely to occur and can often be classified for the client according to a common theme. For instance, for a client whose anxiety is triggered by busy supermarkets, the cinema and crowded public transport, the theme may be busy public spaces where escape is more difficult. Identifying the theme allows both client and practitioner to predict and explore the range of situations that might be problematic for the client. This will be helpful in the treatment phase of LICBT.

By this stage in the interview, the practitioner will have mapped out a broad picture of the client's immediate problem. It is now usually useful to present the client with a summary of the practitioner's understanding of this before moving on. This affirms that the practitioner has captured the detail and scope of the problem, and thus will avoid the need for later 'back-tracking'. It is also facilitative for the client in terms of making sense of the relationship between the different aspects of their difficulties. This might be in the form of a few sentences or delivered by talking through and completing with the client a diagram reproduced from a self-help book (in particular, one that they might be likely to use if they choose the option of guided self-help to help them with their difficulties; see Williams, 2003: 1a6). This process is illustrated below in an excerpt of the initial interview with Judy:

Interview with Judy: excerpt of the initial assessment interview, the 4Ws and the five areas

Practitioner:	… I appreciate that is a lot to get through there and a lot to take in [the information given in the Introductions section], but I am wondering whether we can take about five or ten minutes to try and get an idea of what is going on for you. I think Dr Jones mentioned that you felt your mood had dipped considerably.
Client:	Yes.
Practitioner:	I am wondering if you could give me a bit of an idea of what is going on for you?
Client:	Well, I have not been at work for a little while now. I think it has been about a month and I am not my old self. I am tired.
Practitioner:	Yes.
Client:	Sometimes I feel tearful even.
Practitioner:	Right.
Client:	And I mean, it feels like I am a bit of a shell of who I used to be.
Practitioner:	OK.
Client:	And I just really feel fed up about things.
Practitioner:	It's coming across as if things are quite difficult for you at the moment. You've noticed how you are not how you used to be, quite

tired and tearful a lot of the time. Are there any other changes in your body that you have noticed?

Client: Yes, I can't really concentrate on things anymore. I struggle to take anything in.

Practitioner: Anything else?

Client: I am finding it more difficult to sleep than I used to. I think my worrying is keeping me awake?

Practitioner: OK, so you have talked about some symptoms you are getting in your body: you're more tired, you're finding it difficult to concentrate on things and you are not sleeping as well as you used to?

Client: Yes.

Practitioner: And you say you have been off work for a month?

Client: Yes.

Practitioner: And I suppose if you look back at what has been going on for you around about a month ago, before that has there been anything that has been particularly stressful?

Client: Well, I think things have built up a bit at work. I work in a large garage. I always thought I was very good at my job. People used to say that. But then I had an opportunity and I have been helping out the manager, acting up [a promotion for a trial period].

Practitioner: So you have been acting up?

Client: Yes, and there were a couple of things that have gone wrong and I have just lost all my confidence.

Practitioner: Yes.

Client: I mixed up one of the staff rotas. I am still on the desk sometimes and the phone, and I got a couple of customer appointments mixed up. The manager had me in and we had a conversation about it: whether I was the right person for that role. I just got myself into a real 'tiz' about things and I just found it was very difficult to keep going. I just felt I was under scrutiny so that's what led to me coming away from work. Also, there is a bit more pressure at home and my husband John (again it's another good thing happening), he's got a new role and he is doing more training now rather than being directly involved in sales. But that involves him travelling around more and preparing things in the evening.

Practitioner: Yes.

Client: And I just felt, you know, we were having no time together.

Practitioner: So it sounds like there's been a lot of change going on, for not only for yourself but John as well?

Client: Yes.

Practitioner:	And initially you were saying that things seemed quite positive with the extra responsibility at work. But it sounds like there has been a period of change and things haven't gone as well. There has been a mix up with this rota?
Client:	Yes.
Practitioner:	And I suppose for any of us going into a new role we are unlikely to get it right first time. We're bound to make a few mistakes.
Client:	Yes, that is what John says but …
Practitioner:	But it sound like being called into the manager's office, that sounds … I think I would find that quite intimidating for that to happen.
Client:	Yes.
Practitioner:	And you are saying that a month ago, you thought you couldn't face going into work?
Client:	That's right.
Practitioner:	And again with John there, he's had a few changes, again these are positive. But it sounds as if there's not as much support at home and there is change there with him travelling more.
Client:	Yes.
Practitioner:	And you're saying that he has to do work in the evenings as well.
Client:	Yes, so that is more pressure. But I feel really guilty because he's really enjoying the new role, so I don't want to put the brakes on him.
Practitioner:	So, you're saying work has been an issue to the point that you've had to go off, and also in terms of home life John is under a lot more pressure. Are there any other aspects to the problem? For instance, in your activities at home or your social life, how are these at the moment?
Client:	Well, it's not that good you know. That's another thing that I feel quite bad about. We've got two children: Jack is six and Julia is seven. My mum is coming over and helping out, and John's mum is coming over and helping out. I am not able to keep on top of the washing anymore and sometimes I am just too tired to get going in the morning. It's just very difficult at the moment. I feel like I'm failing at home as well.
Practitioner:	So those kind of day-to-day activities at home, the cooking, the cleaning and washing; you feel that that takes a huge effort.
Client:	Yes.
Practitioner:	Because you are feeling so tired you are struggling at home. You said that your mum and your mother-in-law are helping out.
Client:	That's right.

Practitioner:	But you are feeling quite guilty there. You said that you are having thoughts that you are failing and you seem to think you are imposing on others which is making you feel guilty?
Client:	Yes.
Practitioner:	Is there anything else on your mind when you are feeling low?
Client:	At the moment I just feel so useless; I can't do anything.
Practitioner:	So, that's something else that runs through your mind: you think you are useless?
Client:	Yes.
Practitioner:	So it seems to have hit you on all sides there. Work has been a huge issue for you and it also seems to have affected your home life.
Client:	Yes.
Practitioner:	And in terms of going out with friends, or with you and John going out, has there been much change there that you have noticed?
Client:	Well, we are not doing very much any more. I mean John with his work, and I don't feel I would be very good company if I went out. It's a big step for me to go out the house at the moment, let alone go to the pub or meet friends for a meal or something.
Practitioner:	So that is something you are avoiding at the moment?
Client:	Yes.
Practitioner:	Is there anything else that you are not doing that you were a few months ago?
Client:	I think socialising is the main one; we used to go out a lot more.
Practitioner:	It seems to be impacting for you on all areas at the moment. It seems to have had a big effect on your lifestyle. You don't seem to think you would feel comfortable socialising anymore? Is that it, or do you feel that you have lost your confidence in other ways?
Client:	I think it's about feeling I don't have much to talk about anymore other than what I am failing at.

Exercise 5.1   Identifying therapeutic processes

There are a number of key interpersonal strategies. Some of these are described in detail in Chapter 4. These include:

- Empathic statements (demonstrating verbally that you understand others' situations and feelings).

(Continued)

(Continued)

- Paraphrasing (restating the meaning of what has been said but through the use of different words).
- Reflecting (echoing back the last part of what has been said to you).
- Summarising (restating in a briefer manner a number of issues/problem elements that have been reported).
- Funnelling or the use of 'open-to-closed cones' (a process of moving from open through to closed questions while exploring an interview topic). In this way an initial open question exploring a topic might be: 'Can you tell me about the problems that you are experiencing?' The conversation will then cycle through more specific open questions such as: 'Could you tell me what was running through your mind at the time?' and 'Were you experiencing anything different in your body?' The final stage in the process is to pin down the detail through more closed questions (prior to then usually summarising): 'Do you notice these changes whenever you enter a crowded situation?'

Go through Judy's transcript above and identify these therapeutic processes.

Additionally, determine whether all aspects of the 4Ws and the five areas were adequately covered? If not, can you say which aspects were and which were not?

It is likely that, at this point in the interview, the practitioner is in a position to consider a provisional diagnosis for the difficulties that the client is experiencing. The formation of a diagnostic hypothesis is crucial in that it helps to determine which materials might be of benefit to the client and where they should be placed to best have their needs met within the stepped care system (see Chapter 1). Should the client attend with a difficulty that is inappropriate for LICBT, options for services should be discussed with the client in the shared decision-making section towards the end of the interview. An abbreviated guide to diagnostic categories is given in Table 5.2. More detailed information about anxiety and depression presentations is provided in Chapters 7 and 9.

The next element of the initial interview is the risk assessment. This is covered in detail in Chapter 6 and so is not discussed here. Following this, the interview moves on to explore the *impact* of the problem upon the client. Typically, problems interfere with the client's lifestyle, particularly if they have been present for some time. This might be in the form of interference with their ability to keep performing at work, manage their household responsibilities, engage in social activities, maintain their hobbies and sustain their relationships with others. Questions that enquire about the impact of difficulties include: 'Could you let me know how this problem is affecting your daily life?' and 'If I watched a video of your weekly routine that was taken before these problems developed and compared it with one taken recently, what differences would I notice?' The next section of the interview involves a review of the outcome measures. This is explored in Chapter 3 and so, once again, it is not discussed here.

Table 5.2   Some selected diagnostic features of disorders and recommended services

Group of disorders	Disorder	Selected features of disorder[a]	Appropriate step (see Chapter 1)[b]
Anxiety	Agoraphobia with panic	Worries about panic attacks and their implications; anxiety about being in places where escape is difficult or help is unavailable	Mild to moderate, step two; mild to severe, step three
	Generalised anxiety disorder	Excessive anxiety and worry that is difficult to control	Mild to moderate, step two; mild to severe, step three
	Obsessive compulsive disorder	Obsessions (cognitions or impulses that are experienced as intrusive) and/or compulsions (repetitive behaviours such as hand-washing that are a response to the obsession or performed according to rigid rules)	Mild to moderate, step two; mild to severe, step three
	Post-traumatic stress disorder	Previous exposure to a traumatic event; recurrent recollection/re-experiencing of the event	Step three
	Social phobia	Marked and persistent fear of social performance situations that are predicted to be humiliating or embarrassing	Step three
	Specific phobia	Marked and persistent fear caused by a specific or object or situation (for instance, animals)	Not specifically covered by NICE/IAPT, but as agoraphobia: mild to moderate, step two; mild to severe, step three
Eating disorders	Anorexia nervosa	Refusal to maintain body weight; fear of weight gain and disturbance in how weight/shape is experienced	Initially, step four outpatient care
	Bulimia nervosa	Recurrent episodes of binge eating and inappropriate behaviour to prevent weight gain (such as self-induced vomiting)	Mild to moderate, step two; mild to severe, step three (not part of UK IAPT scheme)
Mood disorders	Major depressive disorder	Depressed mood and loss of interest (with other depressive symptoms) over a two-week period	Mild to moderate, step two; non-response to step two and moderate to severe, step three; severe and complex, risk to life or severe self-neglect, step four

(Continued)

Table 5.2 *(Continued)*

Group of disorders	Disorder	Selected features of disorder[a]	Appropriate step (see Chapter 1)[b]
	Bipolar disorder	At least one major depressive and one manic episode (a period of persistently elevated mood lasting at least one week)	Step four, multi-professional care
	Dysthymic disorder	Depressed mood for most of day more days than not for at least two years (not enough symptoms to meet the criteria for major depression)	Step one or step two
Personality disorders		Enduring, pervasive pattern of experience and behaviour that deviates markedly from norms	Borderline personality disorder, step four, multi-professional care; anti-social personality disorder, usually step four, interagency work
Schizophrenia		Delusions (beliefs held despite overwhelming evidence to the contrary) or hallucinations (vivid perceptions with no basis in reality)	Step four, multi-professional care

[a] For full descriptions see DSM IV-TR; [b] based on NICE/IAPT guidance

The interview then moves on to investigate the circumstances surrounding the development of the problem, as well as maintenance factors and fluctuations in symptoms. Sometimes the client can remember a *triggering event* or set of circumstances that led to problem development. Alternatively, they may recall a broader pattern of issues or stresses that were present around the time of onset. Examples of questions that enquire about problem onset are 'Can you think of the first time you experienced these problems?', 'What was happening at that time in your life?' and 'Were there any stresses that you were experiencing at the time?'

Maintaining factors serve to keep the problem going for the client. These (together with modifying factors) may have already been mentioned by the client within the '4W/five areas' section of the interview. However, this might not necessarily be the case and this is an appropriate point to check whether these have been comprehensively covered. Examples of maintaining factors include those associated with safety behaviours, escape/avoidance, activity reduction or scanning/hyper-vigilance (see Chapters 7 and 9 for more detail regarding these). An example of questioning regarding maintenance factors is 'Sometimes people with your difficulties carry things with them or do things to help themselves to cope. Can you think of anything which works like that for you?'

Modifying factors alter how challenging the problem or situation is for the client. These are linked to variables that are situational or geographical (how busy a shop is or how far it is from the client's home for a client who experiences agoraphobia), social (whether they are accompanied or not), physiological (a client's menstrual cycle) and mood-related (boredom). A question enquiring about modifiers is 'Can you think of anything which makes the problem/situation better or worse?'

We are now approaching the end of the information-gathering section of the interview. However, there are still a few areas to cover. The first of these involves enquiring about *why the client is presenting* at this point in time. This might, for instance, be due to the recent development of difficulties or to symptoms beginning to have a greater impact upon lifestyle. For example, a relationship might be under stress or the client could be finding it difficult to remain at work. This may influence the client's *expectations* about treatment and the *goals* that they wish to work towards within their LICBT. Both client and practitioner need to reach a shared understanding regarding what they are both working towards in terms of therapeutic outcomes. Goals are also beneficial in that they focus the client on future possibilities rather than the difficulties that exist for them in the present. They also provide a further opportunity to evaluate progress within the contact (together with the use of the outcome measures and checking back against the problem statement). This point in the interview is also an opportunity to modify unrealistic goals and expectations (such as to never be sad or anxious) and, where required, to frame them in a more helpful manner. A further part of this process is to enable the practitioner to explore whether other services may be required to accompany the LICBT (for instance, an Employment Advisor to help with a return to work). These can be presented to the client as options later in the interview.

Goals should be framed as something positive that the client is moving towards, rather than something negative that they are moving away from. Clients may have mentioned their goals earlier in the interview, for example, 'I wish I could get back to work again'. If so, this is an opportunity to check whether all of them have been captured. If not, certain questions can help focus the client on their goals: 'If you didn't have these problems, what would you be doing that you are not doing currently?'; 'If all of your problems were to magically disappear what would be different and how would your life appear to others?' Additionally, it is helpful if goals are detailed and specific. So if a client stated that they 'just wanted to feel normal again', the practitioner might ask 'If you were normal again, how would life be different for you? What would you be doing that you are not doing now?'

Next, the practitioner enquires about any *past episodes* of psychological difficulties that the client has experienced (particularly those that have any similarities to the current episode) and the treatments that they have received. Clinical responses to previous treatments are of importance because they indicate what might be helpful and unhelpful in regard to the current difficulties (for instance, 'How did you respond to the medication?'). This is also an opportunity to explore the client's attitudes towards different treatments ('How would you feel about taking medication again?') and whether this has influenced their understanding of their condition ('My mood responded last time to tablets which corrected a chemical imbalance in my brain'). This information may potentially act as a cue to obtain reports from other agencies, consider integrating certain strategies that were found previously to be helpful and orientate the client towards a CBT approach before beginning LICBT proper.

Additionally, in this section the practitioner explores with the client whether they are taking any *substances* that may interact with their difficulties in some way. As a minimum, it is useful to enquire about their intake of alcohol, caffeine and non-prescription/recreational drugs. Excessive use of either alcohol or non-prescription/recreational drugs might indicate an addiction or a dysfunctional coping strategy. The added complications of trying to break these powerful habits are likely to mean that the client is less appropriate for LICBT within a primary care setting (although alcohol-related problems have responded well to self-help administered within a specialist setting; Apodaca & Miller, 2003). Excess caffeine can result in symptoms such as irritability, headaches, tachycardia (increased heart rate), palpitations and insomnia. These can be confused with anxiety symptoms and practitioners may help clients to reduce caffeine intake as part of their treatment. Similarly, excessive alcohol intake can result in fatigue and sleep disruption, and often has a link with depressive symptoms.

Collaborative care is a model that aims to integrate specialist mental healthcare with primary care (Mullican, 2011), psychosocial issues being relevant to some 70 per cent of primary care consultations (Fries, Koop, & Beadle, 1993). With this in mind, the IAPT scheme has included a review of current medication with a particular focus on the client's attitude and adherence, the LICBT practitioner having an explicit role in working with the primary care physician in this regard. This may not necessarily be a component of LICBT in general, but within IAPT, the step two worker role incorporates this collaborative care/case management component (Katon et al., 1999; Richards & Suckling, 2009). Details of this aspect of the role are beyond the scope of this book, but information regarding it can be found in Myles and Rushford (2007), and Healy (2009) is a useful introductory text about medication (see also www.nhs.uk/Conditions/Pages/bodymap.aspx?r=1&rtitle=Health+Encyclopaedia).

Finally at this point, any other relevant information might be obtained that is pertinent to the client's problem. Depending on their circumstances, this might include details about their employment situation, levels of debt and any issues associated with their welfare benefits (such as an impending review interview). For most clients, it is not usually necessary to enquire about their family background and their developmental history because this is of limited relevance to LICBT intervention options. For clients who have diverse backgrounds, any relevant information that might be required to enable the practitioner to tailor contact to meet the client's particular needs can be obtained. Hays (2001) provides examples of useful, facilitative questions, for example, in regard to disability:, 'Do you have experience with disability?' and 'Are there ways in which your disability is part of the difficulties you have attended here to address?'

Information-giving and shared decision-making

In this section of the interview, the focus shifts towards summarising the information from these earlier sections and then considering the intervention options for the client. In first element of this section, the practitioner collaboratively devises the problem statement with the client. The accuracy of this is then checked with the client. As the problem statement is discussed in detail in Chapter 3, I do not elaborate on it here.

The treatment options will depend upon the interventions that have been established as being effective for the client's condition and also the services that are available locally. Typically, the LICBT practitioner will provide a number of options to the client with further information about what each will entail, highlighting the pros, cons and practicalities of each. For instance, it might be that computerised CBT is a more flexible approach in that the client is able to work on this at home over evenings and weekends, and they could start it almost immediately. However, depending upon the pattern of local services, CCBT clients may get less personal support from the practitioner in comparison to those undertaking guided self-help. After hearing about these options, a client may have an immediate preference or, if they are uncertain, they might wish to take away some information leaflets and discuss their decision with the practitioner during a booked phone call or a further face-to-face contact. Additionally, the client may have goals or issues that require input from other agencies (such as an employment advisor, debt management advisor or the Citizen's Advice Bureau). These options, together with the practicalities associated with the client accessing them, can also be discussed at this stage.

The final element of this section of the interview involves the practitioner summarising the content of the session for the client. There is a balance to be struck here between a long summary that contains too much information for the client to comprehend, and a summary that is so short that it consists merely of set headings with little if any client-related content.

Ending

We are now at the end of the assessment interview. What remains is for the practitioner to confirm the steps agreed within the session, together with who is responsible for what (for example, will the client refer themselves to the debt advisory service or is it the practitioner who is going to make the referral on their behalf). Assuming that a further meeting is to take place, the arrangements for this are then made. Final enquiries should be about whether the client has any outstanding questions and also a request for feedback can be made regarding how the client found the session (see also the Patient Experience Questionnaires at: www.iapt.nhs.uk/services/measuring-outcomes, and the Client Satisfaction Questionnaire, Wilkin, Hallam, & Doggett, 1992: 249–50). The client's feedback can be noted and, where possible, used to inform the subsequent sessions.

Exercise 5.2   Practising the initial interview

Form into a group of three with some colleagues. The exercise involves rotating through the roles of practitioner, client and observer. Here, within a role play exercise, you will practise the initial interview. Base the client on one of the assessment case studies from the materials in the Appendix or a case of your own that you know well. If the practitioner gets stuck or misses out part of the interview, the observer can prompt them and the role play can then continue. Refer back to the chapter and the materials as needed. Aim to have covered all the relevant sections before you stop. After the role play ends, all those involved can consider:

- What went well?
- What went less well?
- Which aspects might benefit from further practice?

Pay particular attention to the skills described in Exercise 5.1 and your non-verbal style/interactions (such as eye contact, facial expression and posture). Then, rotate the roles and repeat the exercise.

   IAPT video excerpts that are in keeping with this interview format can be found at: www.iapt.nhs.uk/workforce/low-intensity/reach-out--students-menu/

Trouble-shooting

Carlat (2005) gives useful advice in regard to countering difficulties that can arise in the initial interview. A summary is provided below of ways of managing such difficulties. Some clients may find the practitioner's questioning to be threatening when discussing their problems. This can result in them withholding important information. Levels of threat can be reduced by 'normalising' within questioning. This involves implying that the client's response to a situation is an understandable or predictable one, for instance: 'Sometimes, when people experience these kinds of difficulties they drink more alcohol. Have you been affected in this way?' Clients may simply find it difficult to recall specific facets of their difficulties (for instance, their cognitions). As noted earlier, in these instances recall can be improved by asking the client to consider in detail a recent situation where difficulties have been encountered. For clients who are more reluctant in their communication, the increased use of open questions as well as the use of reinforcing, continuation techniques ('that's very interesting, can you tell me more', the practitioner nodding and maintaining good eye contact) can encourage them to disclose. Other clients may be overly talkative. For these individuals, an increased use of closed-ended questions and gentle interruption ('I'm sorry to interrupt you again but we have about ten minutes left and still need to talk about how your difficulties are impacting upon your situation') should help the practitioner to keep the interview on track. Finally, some clients can understandably become tearful when describing their difficulties. At such points, as well as offering an empathic response, providing tissues together with the waste-paper bin for the spent tissues implicitly gives the client permission to express their feelings. Additionally, such distress can be tactfully used to helpfully explore the client's presentation, for example, 'Can you tell me what we were talking about which triggered your sadness?', 'What went through your mind at that point?' or 'What was running through your mind while you were upset?'

The treatment interview

You will see from Table 5.1 that the treatment interview structure has many similarities to the assessment interview. Additionally, as some of the techniques and processes associated with LICBT intervention have been described previously in this chapter and elsewhere in this volume, this interview is described in less fine-grained detail. The function of the treatment interviews, which follow the initial assessment, is principally to maintain the client's movement through cycles of learning and change (although it might also involve other goals such as medication management and signposting onto other services). This learning involves the application of LICBT to enable clients to overcome their difficulties. It can helpfully be considered to consist of a number of stages that the client moves through (Kolb, 1984; see http://serc.carleton.edu/introgeo/enviroprojects/what.html or www.faculty.londondeanery.ac.uk/e-learning/facilitating-learning-in-the-workplace/theoretical-perspectives-on-workplace-based-learning/). The client may enter at any point in the cycle. For instance, they could progress through the following stages: (a) abstract conceptualisation (understanding the concept associated with a topic – say, behavioural activation); (b) active experimentation (making changes in keeping with this understanding – the use of diaries and planners to consider changes in activity); (c) concrete experience (being aware of what has occurred – an increase in positive activity); and (d) reflective observation (understanding the meaning of the experience, what was beneficial and how – the engagement in certain activities results in an improvement in mood). The cycle is then repeated but is associated with new learning about the same topic or a new topic altogether.

The treatment interview is now described, but I will refer back to the description of the sections previously mentioned in the initial assessment where there is overlap or duplication. I also highlight how aspects of the interview relate to this learning cycle to illustrate this process of psychological development.

Introductions

In this section, the practitioner welcomes the client back, restates their own name and confirms the client's, and reminds them of the practitioner's role. This reviewing process is particularly important when conducting LICBT by telephone, so both the client and the practitioner can be absolutely sure of the identity of the person they are talking to before disclosing any personal information. The introduction section also provides the client with a reminder of the possible and agreed scope of contact, as well as what issues the practitioner can and cannot help them with. Once again, an agenda is set and a time-scale for the interview offered.

Information gathering

This section of the interview commences with reviewing the problem statement that was constructed with the client in the initial assessment. In the second session (before any formal intervention has been administered), this has a function of checking that, after a period of reflection, the client feels that no important aspects of their clinical presentation have been omitted. However, for subsequent sessions, the clinician uses the problem statement to monitor change in the client's condition by referring back to its content. Where positive change has occurred, this can be used to motivate the client by reinforcing progress. In the later sessions, it is also useful to review progress against the goals set in the initial session.

Next, the risk assessment is reviewed to determine whether there has been any change in this aspect of the client's condition (see Chapter 6). Then, the weekly outcome measures are examined (see Chapter 3). Additionally, if collaborative care is part of the practitioner's role, it is appropriate for medication to be reviewed at this point. Last but not least, this section of the interview concludes by reviewing how the client has found any tasks that were set in the previous meeting. This might include reading self-help chapters, completing diary sheets, performing activities that may have arisen from the self-help information as well as contacting other agencies.

As the practitioner reviews these tasks, they might also check that the changes and routines established in the earlier sessions have been maintained and that no obstacles have arisen in regard to these. The practitioner reviews the previous week's homework by enquiring what the client has done and how they have found it. Together, client and practitioner can consider what the client has learned from the tasks, whether any difficulties have arisen and what influenced these. The practitioner should also try to facilitate the consolidation of understanding and respond to any queries that the client might have. In this way, the practitioner is focusing on 'concrete experience', 'reflective observation' and 'abstract conceptualisation' elements of the learning cycle.

It is important that the client has gained the appropriate insight from these homework tasks before the practitioner moves the session on and considers further work for the forthcoming week which may, at least in part, be based upon this learning. For example, a client may have been asked within their reading to complete a three-column thought record task to identify the cognitions that underlie their difficulties (see Chapter 7). In this instance, the purpose of the task is to enable the client to become aware that there are common situations where they experience distress, and that when problematic emotions or physical sensations occur they are usually preceded by particular cognitions that fuel these symptoms. The practitioner enquires about this through the use of the funnelling format, before summarising and moving the questioning onto a new topic. An example of this line of questioning would be 'How did the diary task go last week?' If the relevant understanding is not expressed, then 'What did you get from the exercise?' If the level of understanding remains uncertain, 'Did you notice a pattern to the situations where you became down?' If more questioning is necessary, 'Most of your dips in mood seem to be preceded by communication with your partner when you perceive him to be criticising you. Could that be relevant?' Depending on whether or not this learning has occurred, the practitioner may either negotiate homework with the client that is linked to a new chapter or consider modifying the original tasks and continuing to focus on the previous chapter.

The practitioner should attempt to generally adopt an accepting, warm, curious and praising approach when reviewing the homework. In this way, LICBT is like other psychotherapeutic approaches where an interpersonal style that displays the common therapeutic factors (such as empathy, warmth and genuineness) is the bedrock upon which the approach is established. This will encourage disclosure and investment from clients. For instance, some individuals may be initially embarrassed about either the standard of their written work or their more limited understanding of psychological theory/techniques. A positive approach from the practitioner will build confidence and momentum, whereas a critical or aloof one is likely to reduce the chances of the client completing their homework and attending for the next session.

Trouble-shooting

Where difficulties have arisen, the practitioner needs to move into a trouble-shooting mode to find possible solutions. If the client has been unable to complete the home-work, this should be gently explored with them. Typical difficulties may include too much homework being set, homework which does not match the client's problem, the client having difficulty in understanding the reading, the task set being too difficult (perhaps because it provoked too much anxiety) or (in the case of depression) it requiring too much effort. Gently exploring these issues in a non-judgemental fashion with the client is very important as it will help to identify any obstacles to treatment. At times, it may be helpful to go back over content covered in the previous session as a check of the client's understanding. It can also be helpful to break tasks down into smaller goals so that the client feels less overwhelmed. Another possible difficulty is that the client may have other distracting issues going on in their life that interfere with their ability to focus on the treatment for their identified problem. In these circumstances, it may be important to discuss whether the sessions would be best postponed.

Unless solutions or compromises can be agreed upon, there is a risk that the client will lose faith in their ability to benefit from the approach. Ideally, problems with the homework can be addressed in the session with the client. However, at times the practitioner will not have the answer to a question or the resources for a solution to hand. In this situation, if possible, the practitioner should try to park the issue ('I don't have the answer to that right now, but I will find out for next week') while they do some research or seek guidance.

Information-giving and shared decision-making

Once the practitioner is satisfied that the client has understood the previous homework tasks and has been able to put these into practice, they can turn their attention towards thinking about the next week's focus. This will be informed by the client's provisional diagnosis, problem statement and goals, the resources that the practitioner is working through with the client, how the client has reacted to the resources to date and the client's preferences. Different individuals also have different styles or preferences in the way that they learn (Kolb, 1984). Some clients may be relatively independent and able to work through the resources almost unaided. However, many will benefit from introduction and discussion of the materials prior to them leaving the session. In this way, the practitioner is easing them into a new cycle of learning, usually by working through the abstract conceptualisation and active experimentation phases of the cycle.

The LICBT practitioner should aim to be expert in explaining the tasks and concepts contained in the materials in a manner that responds to different individuals' learning preferences. So, for instance, some individuals may find it easier to understand the *theory* behind a concept and will therefore find it better to enter the learning cycle at the abstract conceptualisation stage. The theory behind an approach might be introduced in a number of ways:

- working with diagrams that are contained in the materials (for example, in behavioural activation, a low mood and inactivity cycle; Blenkiron, 2010: 90);
- use of theoretical examples ('I wonder how you would feel if you were in a prison cell for a week? What would influence this?'); or
- use of a verbal anecdote or visual image that encapsulates an idea.

An example of the latter is that, if we do not put effort into long-distance relationships by making phone calls and writing letters, then we do not usually get much communication back (positive reinforcement), rather only bills and telesales calls. This, in turn, lowers our mood and so we are even less inclined to write letters to friends.

Others might find concepts more difficult to grasp theoretically and might be aided through reflective observation regarding their own previous experience (for instance, being helped to notice that attending at the clinic on that day resulted in some change in their mood). Alternatively, some clients may be more comfortable with active experimentation in terms of change, feeling more comfortable in seeing what emerges from their efforts. In this way, LICBT practitioners must be willing to introduce topics in a variety of ways that allow the client to enter a new cycle at various possible points.

Once the client has entered this cycle, they can then be set homework to consolidate this through set reading and exercises that will have been introduced in the session, as negotiated with the client and according to their ability. I have adapted Blenkiron's (2010) 10 Rs into principles of good practice for the purposes of the treatment interview:

- *respond* to the difficulties the client presents;
- *relate* these difficulties to the materials;
- make sure that the materials you provide for the client are the most *relevant* available for them;
- be *realistic* in regard to the homework negotiated with the client;
- *review* the homework with the client;
- *reinforce* the client's efforts and progress;
- help the client to *record* progress through use of diaries and measures;
- *rehearse* tasks with clients;
- *revisit* previous homework tasks in subsequent sessions; and
- help clients to *reintegrate* and consolidate positive coping strategies back into their lives.

Ending

As with the assessment interview, the practitioner closes the session with a summary of the contact, also re-confirming the next steps. These might include completing the reading/exercises as noted above, other actions such as maintaining previous homework initiatives, initiating or maintaining contact with other agencies, and arranging the next meeting with the LICBT practitioner.

Exercise 5.3   Practising the treatment interview

Go back into your group of three. Once again, you will rotate roles: practitioner, client and observer. Perform a role play exercise that covers the treatment interview using the case example given in the Appendix (Julian). Again, if the practitioner gets stuck, the observer should prompt the practitioner, the role play then continuing until the end of the interview. Refer back to the chapter and materials as needed. Once again, reflect upon the performance (as in Exercise 5.2) before rotating roles and repeating the exercise.

Remember that IAPT video excerpts in keeping with this interview format can be found at: www.iapt.nhs.uk/workforce/low-intensity/reach-out--students-menu/

Adapting the approach for work over the telephone

There is limited research evidence associated with use of the telephone as a modality to deliver GSH, but it is seen to be a promising approach that is viewed as preferable by many clients (Bee et al., 2008). Indeed, telephone consultation has both advantages and disadvantages in comparison to face-to-face contact. The advantages include an ability to increase access for those who find it difficult to attend at a health or community venue (for example, because of agoraphobia, depression or a physical disability). Additionally, it is much more time-efficient for the practitioner than home visits. It also reduces the costs involved in attending sessions for clients (such as for childcare, parking and transport costs). It is less stigmatising for clients than attending at a local clinic where others might see them being called from the waiting room by a mental health professional. As the practitioner is not seeing the client at a local clinic that is scheduled within a weekly time slot in the practitioner's diary, often greater flexibility is available to the client in terms of the timing of the contact. This would ideally include evenings and weekends for the convenience of those who are in day-time employment. The disadvantages are associated with the lack of visual contact with the client and also a lack of awareness associated with what is occurring in the client's environment at the point when they receive the telephone call.

Working over the telephone, therefore, needs to compensate for the practitioner and client's 'blindness'. While the interview structure remains the same, the client needs to be asked in the introductory section whether they are able to talk to the practitioner at that particular time (for instance, they may have unexpected company), and if not, when would be a good time for the practitioner to call back. The practitioner also needs to check whether the client has all the materials to hand (such as pen, paper, outcome measures and self-help resources), some of which will need to have been sent through to them previously. In the closing stages of the interview, a date needs to be set if the client is to send through to the practitioner a copy of their completed written tasks, to allow the practitioner to review them prior to the next telephone consultation (or an alternative format for review agreed). Lovell (2010) also recommends making information about the practitioner available to the client, prior to the initial interview. This might include a photograph and some detail about their professional experience, or access to an internet video clip of the practitioner talking about such topics. This helps the client to form a picture of the practitioner in their 'mind's eye' which, in turn, facilitates the development of the therapeutic relationship. Alternatively, Richards and White (2009) recommend that an initial face-to-face interview is scheduled where a working relationship can be established and the practicalities of the telephone contact discussed.

Lovell (2010) also recommends alerting the client to the fact that long pauses may occur in the conversation while the practitioner is completing notes or attending to the live supervision that is available via some telephony systems. Additionally, if the client needs to end a call prematurely, for instance if someone has unexpectedly entered the house, a code word can be decided upon that indicates to the practitioner that the call needs to end abruptly. Practitioner and client need to agree what should occur if someone other than the client answers the phone, and whether it is acceptable to leave a message on an answering machine if the client is out at the scheduled time of contact. The absence of visual contact might mean that the clinician tends to rely more heavily on either the materials or anecdotes to explain concepts, rather than the completing of personalised diagrams for the client. However, Lovell describes how clients can be helped to draw and understand cycle-based diagrams by asking them to draw a clock face and then to add labels to be placed at points that coincide with the different numbers on the face.

Exercise 5.4   Telephone contact role play

Repeat Exercises 5.2 and 5.3 over an internal telephone line with a colleague. Alternatively, try doing the interview with the practitioner sitting back-to-back with the client (to limit the availability of visual cues). Practise making the adjustments outlined in the last section. Explore how this experience felt different. How did the adjustments work within the situation? Once again, reflect upon the performance (as in Exercise 5.2), rotate roles and repeat the exercise.

Summary

- There are two interview formats that are fundamental to the LICBT approach: assessment and treatment.
- Both of these include introductory stages, information-gathering and information-giving sections, as well as ending stages.
- The outcomes of the initial interview include the production of the problem statement for the client, specifying goals and expectations and the identification of a provisional diagnosis. The latter is instrumental in determining whether the client is appropriate for LICBT and, if so, which resources might be appropriate to meet their needs.
- A learning cycle has been used to frame the function of the treatment interview, this structure enabling the client to engage in a continuous cycle of learning to help them utilise LICBT to counter their difficulties.
- There are a number of adaptations that are required to allow the interviews to be performed over the telephone.

Further reading and activities

Recommended further reading is:

- Grant et al. (2008) and Westbrook et al. (2011) are primarily concerned with HICBT, but aspects of these texts cover relevant models (five areas) and also provide examples of useful assessment strategies/questions.
- Healy (2009) is an introductory text to medication.

Continue to practise these interviews through role play exercises. The observer can use the assessment rating scales provided by Richards and Whyte (2009) to assess the practitioner's performance. Use video to record the exercises and rate your own performance. Ask your supervisor to rate your performance by using the scales; ask for feedback and repeat, repeat, repeat! You are in a learning cycle as well. The more experience and feedback you are able to obtain, the quicker your skills will develop.

The Assessment and Management of Risk

Mark Papworth

Learning objectives
• To understand the rationale for risk assessment and management.
• To know the risk factors which need to be covered in suicide risk assessment.
• To understand how these factors are used to inform suicide risk.
• To be able to assess risk through the use of hierarchical questioning.
• To understand the principles associated with managing risk.
• To be aware of risk factors associated with violence to others and indicators of self-neglect.
• To be aware of tools that can facilitate the assessment of risk.

Introduction

Practitioners will inevitably have contact with individuals who are at risk. Suicide is one of the most difficult therapeutic issues that are faced by mental health workers. Overall, the annual number of suicides is decreasing in England, having been one of the targets for mental health services for over 10 years (Department of Health, 1999). However, it is estimated that in England someone takes their own life every two hours

(Department of Health, 2002). Given that fewer than one per cent of individuals with affective disorders commit suicide (Bryan & Rudd, 2006), the great challenge for the LICBT practitioner with their large caseload is predicting the risk of occurrence of such an infrequent but extremely serious event.

This chapter introduces the reader to a risk assessment approach. It draws upon relevant principles, evidence and guidance from the UK's Department of Health (Department of Health, 2007) and the American Psychological Association (APA, 2003), but also adapts and draws heavily on Bryan and Rudd's (2006) decision-making model, which is in keeping with the LICBT role. Additionally, within the English Improving Access to Psychological Therapies scheme, the main focus for risk assessment is suicide risk and so this is reflected within the focus of framework presented below (although risk to other people and self-neglect are also considered to a lesser extent). The chapter then examines the principles of risk management and then, more latterly, it discusses some other forms of risk that might be encountered within LICBT practice. Finally, practitioners should be aware of and ensure that their practice is in keeping with their own organisation's policy for the management of risk. This would normally dictate that practitioners remain up to date with their statutory and mandatory training, which usually encompasses the protection of vulnerable adults and children.

Background – setting the scene

The goal of risk assessment is to identify and balance the factors that the client possesses that influence their risk of suicide. While the LICBT role does not encompass the treatment of suicidality, suicide-related factors will at times occur within mild to moderate presentations of anxiety and depression. It is vital to be able to assess risk because this is one of the factors (together with patient's choice, their diagnosis, severity of difficulties and other characteristics) that determine where the client is placed within the stepped-care system. This should be carefully monitored and this task is integral to therapeutic contact: 'The worker will … strive to ensure that any assessments/interventions will be in the best interests of the service user, minimising any possible harm and maximising benefits over both the short and long term while at the same time balancing these against any possible harmful effects to others (British Association of Behavioural and Cognitive Psychotherapy, n.d.: 1). Some 45 per cent of individuals present the preceding month within primary care before their suicide (Luoma, Martin, & Pearson, 2002). Even more worryingly, some 20 per cent attend the previous day (Pirkis & Burgess, 1998). Thus, practitioners should be constantly vigilant in monitoring risk. Unfortunately, there is no rating scale or clinical decision-making process that is completely reliable in the prediction of suicide (Department of Health, 2007). However, there are a number of relevant factors and principles that inform best practice decision-making.

The aim of suicide risk assessment is not to eliminate risk altogether. This is ultimately impossible. It could also be counter-productive, given the potential for rupturing the therapeutic alliance by breaking confidentiality or involving clients with crisis services unnecessarily. In this way, over-reactivity in terms of risk assessment can result in barriers to clients in receiving appropriate help and might inhibit their help-seeking behaviour in the future. However, under-reactivity will result in inappropriate care for the client, leaving them in a situation of risk, and may result in professional liability issues for the practitioner who could be deemed as failing in their duty of care.

Within the IAPT LICBT framework, risk assessment occurs in the initial assessment session as part of the information-gathering section of the interview (see Chapter 5). This initial risk assessment is then revisited on each subsequent meeting to check that it remains accurate. This is important because risk is based upon both *static* factors (for example, previous historical events) as well as *dynamic* ones (such as relationship stability). The latter may change on a weekly basis (see below). If the client's circumstances change (perhaps a worsening in their levels of mood, hopelessness or ideation) or their level of disclosure increases so as to indicate increased risk, the risk assessment should then be reviewed in detail. Best practice in regard to risk assessment conforms to relevant guidelines, is based upon the information available (empirical evidence and client reports), is thoroughly documented, and the relevant people associated with client responsibility and care are informed (Department of Health, 2007).

A theme that is revisited within this chapter is a need for a shared language through which to communicate concepts about this crucial topic with other professionals, for example within supervision. I discuss categories for levels of risk later in the chapter, but there are also standard terms for describing the risk-related phenomena with which the client may present. These range from suicidal ideation through to a suicidal attempt that resulted in injuries (O'Carroll, Berman, Maris, & Moscicki, 1996, as cited in Bryan & Rudd, 2006). The range of these presentations is summarised in Table 6.1.

Table 6.1   The range of suicide risk-related behaviour

Suicide attempt with injuries	A non-fatal outcome, the evidence suggesting that the client intended to kill themselves, the attempt resulting in injuries
Suicide attempt without injuries	A non-fatal outcome, the evidence suggesting that the client intended to kill themselves but no injuries occurred
Instrumental suicide-related behaviour	Behaviour that could potentially have resulted in self-injury, the evidence suggesting that the person did not intend to kill themselves but rather intended to achieve another goal (for instance, to seek help, to punish others or to receive attention)
Suicide threat	An action which stops short of self-harm that suggests to others that suicidal behaviour may occur in the future
Suicidal ideation	Self-reported thoughts of engaging in suicide-related behaviour

There are several approaches to risk assessment (Department of Health, 2007). *Unstructured clinical judgement* refers to a process in which risk assessment information is gathered unsystematically as part of a broader clinical assessment. The disadvantage of this approach is that important risk-related factors can be omitted, particularly as some suicidal clients can present as calm and composed, attending with a seemingly minor problem. Additionally, clients who are not suicidal during initial sessions may, during the course of therapy, become suicidal. An *actuarial approach* focuses on static risk factors, which are entered into a formula that estimates risk over a time period. This approach is more usually used to calculate risks in groups of individuals and is less appropriate for use with individual service users. Finally, *structured clinical judgement* involves the practitioner making a decision based upon the best research evidence and the clinical contact with the client as well as the client's own view of their situation. I advocate this latter approach. Bryan and Rudd's (2006) framework offers a means of framing decision-making that is particularly useful for practitioners, and also provides a shared language for categorising risk that is useful in the process of case management supervision.

Many self-rating scales that measure either depression or general psychological dysfunction contain at least one item that asks the client about suicidal thoughts. I recommend that this information be discussed independently of the risk assessment segment of the interview. In other words the risk-related inventory question should not be used as a 'lead-in' to the risk assessment interview segment. This is because clients may disclose differing amounts within a self-rating scale and the face-to-face interview. Keeping these two sources of information separate allows the clinician to compare these sources as a 'double-check'. A risk response that is indicated on a self-report inventory in a later section of the interview can then cause the practitioner to re-visit the earlier risk assessment section of the interview: 'We thought that your thinking about suicide had not changed since our last meeting. However, I can see that your response has changed on this item of the scale. I wonder what was going through your mind when you circled this response?'

The relevant factors for suicide risk

Below I now explore the suicide risk-related factors upon which decision-making is based. I then look at how to balance these factors to make decisions associated with client care. Finally, I look at how to structure the interview to best obtain this information. The relationship between these factors is a complex, but generally additive one. Aside from the 'protective characteristics', the more of these factors that are present for the client, the greater the risk. The factors are predisposition to suicide, symptomatic presentation, precipitants or stressors, presence of hopelessness, nature of suicidal thinking, previous suicidal behaviour, impulsivity and self-control, and protective characteristics (Bryan & Rudd, 2006). I describe these in turn, also drawing upon APA (2003) as a source for the probability statistics reported below:

Predisposition to suicide

A susceptibility or predisposition to suicide can be determined by a number of individual characteristics. These will usually be identified from the other parts of the information-gathering section of the assessment interview, a service triage assessment (which, if part of the care pathway, will have preceded LICBT contact) and the referrer's letter. These characteristics include a previous history of psychological problems (for instance, those experiencing clinical depression have a 20-fold greater rate of suicide), discharge from inpatient treatment over the previous year (particularly male), same-sex sexual orientation, chronic physical illnesses (such as HIV or pain syndromes), male gender (the rate of suicide is approximately four times greater for men with a further increase for those aged over 65), single status (the suicide rate being twice that for those who are married), and a history of childhood abuse (the rate increases approximately 10-fold) or domestic violence.

Symptomatic presentation

The presence of a psychological disorder is probably the most significant risk factor for suicide, with more than 90 per cent of individuals who commit suicide having a diagnosable psychological condition. Information regarding this factor will be obtained from the earlier sections of the information-gathering section of the interview. Mood disorders, primarily in depressive phases, are the diagnoses most associated with suicide deaths. There is an estimated 12-fold increase in risk with dysthymia (a chronic, lower level form of depression; see Chapter 7) and this rises to a 20-fold increase in risk with major depression. However, anxiety conditions are also associated with a 6- to 10-fold increase in risk, although usually as part of a co-morbid pattern of symptoms. Eating disorders (particularly anorexia), borderline and anti-social personality disorders are also associated with increased risk, and alcoholism is estimated to increase risk by 6-fold.

Precipitants or stressors

Precipitants also are usually identified in the early sections of the information-gathering section of the interview. These typically include events or factors associated with loss, such as a relationship conflict, breakdown or bereavement (suicide rates are higher among the widowed than the married, especially with older men); also loss of health or job (risk is particularly elevated for those under 45 in the time following the job loss, there also potentially being knock-on effects of increased alcohol intake) or financial issues. If these factors have not been identified earlier in the initial assessment interview, examples of relevant questions to explore this factor include 'How have things been for you recently?', 'Can you tell me about anything in particular that has been stressful for you?' and 'What has triggered your contact with our service at this point in time?'

Presence of hopelessness

Hopelessness is linked to cognitions and beliefs that are associated with a negative expectation regarding oneself and the future. Usually occurring with depression, hopelessness is more closely related to suicide than any other depressive symptom. It has been determined to be a more powerful predictor of suicide than a global assessment of depressive symptoms. This needs to be explored in the risk assessment element of the information-gathering section of the initial interview. Examples of questions that explore levels of hopelessness include 'It is not uncommon when depressed to feel that things won't improve and won't get any better; do you ever feel this way?' and 'Does it seem as if things can never get better?' Bryan and Rudd (2006) state that the presence, severity and duration of hopelessness should all be investigated with the client. One means of measuring severity is to ask the client to rate how hopeless they feel on a scale of zero (not hopeless at all) to 10 (as hopeless as they could ever imagine).

The nature of suicidal thinking

This factor is at the heart of the client's suicidality and so should be carefully assessed in the risk assessment element of LICBT interview. Suicidal thinking precedes suicide but is also a common phenomenon, with over 13 per cent of individuals experiencing it at some point in their lives (APA, 2003). Thus, it is essential to consider other suicide-related factors in conjunction with it. Additionally, as suicide is more strongly associated with the worst previous episode of suicidal ideation (the process of having ideas about suicide) rather than the current one, it is important to explore past as well as present experience.

Bryan and Rudd (2006) state that frequency ('How often have the thoughts occurred?'), intensity ('On a scale of one to 10, how strong are these thoughts?') and duration of suicidal thoughts ('When did you start to have these thoughts?') should be explored. They also suggest that individuals may feel more comfortable discussing their past experience of suicidal thoughts and so the practitioner might, with some clients who find disclosure more difficult, start with past experiences before moving on to the current episode (see 'hierarchical questioning' below). It is useful to distinguish between suicidal ideation ('I feel like killing myself') and non-suicidal morbid ideation that includes thoughts about death without suicidal content ('I just can't go on'), the former having stronger links to suicide than the latter.

If the client has a suicide plan, this increases the level of risk. Generally speaking, risk increases if the plan is more detailed, lethal and feasible. With this factor, disclosure may be dependent upon cultural and/or religious beliefs, and so the practitioner will need to research and explore these for some members of minority groups (see Chapter 11). If we find that the client has a plan, questioning should pursue this by exploring whether the individual has taken any preparatory steps towards completing this (for instance, hoarding tablets or pinpointing a location to jump from). Appropriate questions include 'Have you thought about how you might want to kill yourself?', 'Have you considered when you might do this?', 'Do you have access to [the means]?', 'How close have you come to following this through?' and 'How likely do you think it is that you will carry this out?' When clients are at imminent risk of killing themselves, they may even make arrangements to sort out their affairs to minimise difficulties for their loved ones. Examples of questions to ascertain this include: 'Have you been putting your will in order?' or 'Have you recently given away any of your possessions?' It is recommended that the practitioner asks about the planned method of suicide at least twice ('Have you considered any other methods?') as clients sometimes do not report their most lethal or accessible method upon initial questioning.

The practitioner will also need to make informed judgements regarding the client's intent (their aims) which draw from differing sources. We have heard what the client has told us; this is their *subjective* intent (what they say to the practitioner). However, clients may not be aware of or may not always accurately report their 'internal world' to us. They may be unwilling to disclose their intent for fear that the practitioner will take steps to keep them from acting upon it, or they may overstate intent where their statements and behaviours associated with self-harm have an alternative purpose to suicide (for instance, to receive attention). In this way, we also need to consider the client's *objective intent*. This is based upon environmental and behavioural factors such as the presence of any past attempts, as well as both the lethality of these past circumstances and method chosen. Objective intent may or may not coincide with their subjective intent. Where there is a discrepancy between objective and subjective sources, the practitioner should explore this with the client to try and increase the overall accuracy of their estimation of intent, for example, 'You've said that you do not have thoughts of suicide, but when your relationship previously broke down you took a serious overdose. Do you remember having any thoughts of suicide or making any plans back then?'

Previous suicidal behaviour

A history of previous suicide attempts is one of the most significant risk factors for a future attempt. Up to 80 per cent of completed suicides were preceded by a previous attempt, and the presence of a previous attempt represents a 38-fold increase in suicide risk for the client. As such, the practitioner should explore the timing and detail of these within a risk assessment. This will usually include the precipitants, alcohol/substance use at the time and the potential lethality of the attempt. Questions that probe this factor include 'Have you attempted to kill yourself or hurt yourself in the past?', 'What was happening at this time?', 'Why did you choose that method?', 'Did you inform anyone of what you were planning to do?', 'Did you believe someone would find you or were you found accidentally?', 'Did you seek help afterwards yourself or did someone get help for you?' and 'Are there other times in the past when you've tried to harm or kill yourself?'

Impulsivity and self-control

Impulsivity and the linked characteristics of hostility and aggression increase suicide risk. Impulsivity is a personality trait characterised by an individual tending to initiate actions without adequate forethought regarding the possible consequences. Because many suicide attempts are a reaction to a precipitant or stressor, levels of impulsivity may have a greater predictive value than the presence of a suicide plan. As impulsivity is considered to be a stable personality trait, those with high levels of impulsivity and who have previously made a suicide attempt should be considered to have a long-standing risk for the future.

Alcohol and drugs can increase impulsivity. Up to one-third of all suicides have alcohol as a contributory factor, with as many as 50 per cent of individuals who have committed suicide having been found to be intoxicated at the time of their death. The suicide mortality rate for alcoholics is six times greater than for the general population; relationship issues are both a possible consequence of alcoholism and a precipitant to attempts. Approximately 50–75 per cent of alcoholics who commit suicide have also suffered with major depression. Abuse of other substances is also associated with suicide, a history of attempts being common amongst individuals experiencing substance use disorders. Questions that will elicit information associated with this factor include 'Do you ever have times when you feel out of control?', 'What happens when you feel like this?', 'Has this ever led you to doing things you have later regretted?' and 'Have you ever got into trouble as a result of this?' Linked to this, it may be important to ask about use of alcohol or illicit drugs: 'Do you drink alcohol or use recreational drugs?', if so 'How often do you do this and how much do you use?'

Protective characteristics

The presence of protective characteristics makes suicide less likely to occur and so these should be explored in the risk assessment section of the interview. There are a variety of protective characteristics that individuals can possess. One example of such a characteristic includes having good coping skills, for example being able to work through problems rather than avoid them. Additionally, those with strong religious beliefs tend to have a reduced risk, many faiths providing purpose and support as well as seeing suicide as morally wrong or sinful. Levels of social support can act as a protective factor. Support networks can be informal (family or friends) or be developed by contact with self-help organisations. However, as I have already noted, relationship discord can increase suicide risk and so it is important to assess the status as well as the presence of such networks. Family and children are often cited by clients as being a barrier to suicide, the presence and number of children at home decreasing risk, particularly for women. Examples of questions that inquire about protective characteristics include 'Do you have family and friends around you who you can talk to and depend upon?', 'Are there other people in your life who would be unable to go on without you?' and 'When you are thinking about suicide, what helps you feel more hopeful about life?'

Making decisions based on the suicide risk assessment

We now know the factors that are relevant to determining the level of suicide risk. How do we use this information in a structured way to decide whether the client is safe? If they are not, what we should do about it? Helpfully, Bryan and Rudd (2006) have developed a decision-making guide and an adapted version of this is reproduced in Table 6.2. In the first column are the eight (numbered) factors listed above. The indicated responses for the differing levels of risk are provided at the bottom of the table. The estimation of risk level is based upon the best possible matching of the client's pattern of risk factors to the description of risk level given in rows two to five of the table. A *non-existent* risk category is used where there is no ideation or other identifiable risk factors. For this category, no changes in the treatment plan are required. The *mild* risk level is used where dysphoria is rated as mild, there is limited activity in terms of suicidal thinking, good levels of self-control and protective characteristics are present, and few other risk factors are identified. This level of risk will trigger a more attentive evaluation of risk at each session.

Moderate levels of risk should always be discussed within case management supervision, usually to consider where to refer the client when stepping them up within the healthcare system. The decision regarding when to step up and to whom, will, to some extent, be dependent on the role and provision of other services available within the local stepped care system (and so will vary according to local resources). Moderate risk levels are indicated by more significant dysphoric symptoms and frequent levels of ideation with accompanying plans. The client may have good levels of self-control and protective characteristics, but other risk factors are also present. In terms of the client's needs, Bryan and Rudd state that the client is likely to need increased clinical involvement and open access to specialist crisis services (for example, via a telephone emergency number). Active involvement of the family should be considered as well as an increase in the frequency of therapeutic appointments, together with the use of

Table 6.2   Client presentation and indicated responses

	Risk level			
	Non-existent	**Mild**	**Moderate**	**Severe**
1. Predisposition to suicide		Few risk factors	Some risk factors present	Multiple risk factors
2. Symptomatic presentation		Mild dysphoria	Limited dysphoria	Severe dysphoria
3. Precipitant		As 1	As 1	As 1
4. Hopelessness		As 1	As 1	As 1
5. Suicidal thinking	No identifiable ideation	Ideation of limited frequency, intensity and duration; no identified plans; no intent	Frequent ideation of limited intensity and duration; some specific plans; no intent	Frequent, intense and enduring ideation; specific plans; no subjective intent but some objective signs
6. Previous suicidal behaviour		As 1	As 1	As 1
7. Impulsivity		Good self-control	Good self-control	Impaired self-control
8. Protective characteristics		Identifiable protective characteristics	Identifiable protective characteristics	Few if any protective factors
Indicated response (see text for more detail)	No changes to treatment plan, routine monitoring	Careful monitoring	Consider step-up, need for increased involvement, support and careful monitoring	Need to step-up immediately and involve specialist services

Source: Bryan and Rudd, 2006: 198 © 2006 John Wiley and Sons; adapted and reproduced with permission.

telephone contact for monitoring purposes. The primary care physician would usually be contacted to consider a medication review, and the mental health practitioner who receives the stepped-up referral would construct and rehearse a crisis response plan with the client. This would set out specific instructions for the client to follow if they were to encounter a period of crisis (see Bryan, Corso, Neal-Walden, & Rudd, 2009). The management plan would include self-management strategies, methods of marshalling protective features of the client's life such as social support, and the involvement of relevant external organisations (including an out-of-hours contact).

A *severe* risk level requires rapid contact with crisis/specialist services. This category is used where severe levels of depressive symptoms are present, with frequent and enduring ideation and specific plans. The individual will also have impaired self-control, few protective features and multiple other risk factors. Bryan and Rudd also use an *extreme* category of risk. However, this category is not listed because it has the same indicated response as the severe category and so has limited additional practical utility. However, in instances where a client contacts a service in desperation or when monitoring the client by telephone, a clinician may need to alert emergency services where the risk is immediate and extreme, for example after taking a potentially fatal overdose.

Exercise 6.1   Setting the foundations for risk management

Now discuss this model with your supervisor and/or manager. Does it apply to your practice? If not, what are the areas where there is deviation (perhaps because of differences in your role or in the provision of local services)? If required, adapt the model to apply to your service. If you are a trainee practitioner, what are the differing levels of risk that you are expected to 'carry' both as a trainee and then upon qualification?

Check whether your service has supervisory support systems that can be called upon over the working week at short notice (on-call supervisors and holiday cover/rota for supervisors and managers). If so, how do you access them (for example, if you are working away from base at a community venue)?

Look at your job description (both now and periodically re-read it) to check that you are operating within your job role. Operating outside of your role puts both client and practitioner at risk.

Exercise 6.2   The categorisation of risk

Consider the following case example (which is also summarised using an example proforma in Figure 6.1).

Jane is 35 years old and attends for her LICBT appointment complaining that 'she just can't go on'. Upon further questioning she describes having had such thoughts frequently for several weeks. However, she states that she would not kill herself. She has three children aged 8, 10 and 14 years, and has been living with her mother for the past 12 years. She recently lost her job as a cleaner because of redundancies at her firm. She has been treated for depression twice previously over the past 10 years and did take an overdose of her tablets when she last experienced similar problems. Her symptoms include low mood and tearfulness and she scores 21 on the PHQ9. She states that she currently feels very hopeless most of the time. She feels intermittently suicidal and has saved a lethal quantity of her medication in case she 'can't cope any more'. There is no family history of suicide or abuse. She does not use alcohol or recreational drugs, but does describe herself as being erratic and impulsive at times. She has never been married, but does have a current boyfriend, although this relationship is at times unsupportive.

What category of risk would you use to describe this client? Which of the indicated responses (if any) do you consider are necessary?

Client name: Jane Smith   Date of Birth: 8-3-77   Client number: 808445
Session number: 2   Date: 3-2-12

Predisposition to suicide History of two previous depressive episodes.	
Symptomatic presentation Low mood, tearfulness, PHQ9 = 21.	
Precipitants or stressors Job loss after redundancies at work, some relationship issues.	
Presence of hopelessness Very hopeless for much of the time (more than half the days), 5/10 for severity.	
Nature of suicidal thinking Frequent thoughts of 'just can't go on' for several weeks, many times daily, 5/10 for strength. No subjective intent. Specific plan, potentially lethal and initial steps made.	
Previous suicidal behaviour Previous overdose of tablets provoked by relationship breakdown. Reported to be potentially lethal although cannot recall number or type of tablets. Partner found her and called emergency services.	
Impulsivity and self-control No excessive alcohol or substance abuse, 'erratic and impulsive', relationship issues.	
Protective characteristics Three children (8, 10, 14), in a stable relationship, and contact with mother.	

Level of risk	Indicated response
[Reader to consider]	[Reader to consider]
Risk to others or self-neglect	*Indicated response*
Some impulsivity (see above), no significant impact on children; no signs of self-neglect.	[Reader to consider]

Figure 6.1   Possible format for recording a risk assessment (paper or electronic)

The structure of the interview

Having described the risk factors that need to be assessed and how to make decisions based on this information, I now focus on how to obtain this information within the LICBT interview structure. Risk should be explored at the initial assessment, with information being appropriately incorporated from other sources such as the referrer. A section of the interview is entirely devoted to assessing risk, although the practitioner needs to be attentive to any indications of risk throughout the assessment process. Of course, this section of the clinical interview is no different from the others in that it requires high levels of skill to engage the client to enable an accurate risk assessment to take place. For some clients, this section of the interview explores particularly personal thoughts that they may not have disclosed to others. For these individuals, intense feelings associated with guilt, shame or sadness might arise from the discussion, as well as anxiety associated with their concerns about the practitioner's possible reaction. It is important for the practitioner to remain non-judgemental and contain any personal feelings of anxiety and also boredom or fatigue. Instead they should, rather, attempt to work through the elements of the risk assessment in a calm, empathic and caring fashion. Thus, practitioner responses such as exclaiming 'I don't know what to do!', expressions of horror, steering the client away from risk-related topics or glancing at their watch all convey the message to the client that their statements are not being attended to. This, in turn, might be experienced as rejection or failure, which might further heighten risk or lead the client to disengage with services.

To facilitate disclosure, risk assessment follows an initial, broader exploration of the client's problem to enable a therapeutic relationship to be established prior to discussion about suicide risk. It also precedes the discussion in the interview around the completed outcome measures to allow the clinician to compare the information between two sources (face-to-face and self-report feedback), as noted above. In situations of significant risk, the remaining other sections of the interview may need to be postponed or abandoned to allow risk to be fully explored and an action plan developed that is based upon the guidance for indicated responses (as provided in Table 6.2).

Bryan and Rudd (2006) recommend that the risk assessment follows a format that they term to be a *hierarchical* questioning style. This refers to a gradual increase in the intensity and sensitivity of the questioning as the discussion continues. This method is likely to increase client engagement and disclosure within the process. In this way, rather than beginning the risk assessment with a core question such as: 'Have you been feeling suicidal?', less sensitive questions precede this topic and normalise the client's experience, thus encouraging the client to more readily report any symptoms if present.

A typical risk assessment structure is presented in Figure 6.2. Here, example questions are listed to demonstrate the hierarchical interviewing process and where the risk assessment information is drawn from within the initial interview format. Details about symptomatology, precipitants and the client's predisposition are likely to have been at least partially covered in the information-gathering section of the interview

A. Example questions to illustrate possible interview order for information obtained in the preliminary 'information-gathering' section:

1. Can you tell me what led to you coming along to see me today? (predisposition/symptoms/precipitant, open question)

2. Tell me more about what you experience when you 'feel down'? (symptoms; specific open question)

3. When was the last time that you felt tearful? (symptoms; closed question)

4. What was running through your mind while you were tearful? (symptoms; closed question)

5. [So, from what you have told me … (summary)]

6. How have things been going for you recently? (precipitants; open question)

7. Etc.

B. Example questions to illustrate possible interview order for information obtained in the 'risk assessment' section:

8. You mentioned earlier that you were 'feeling down'. It is not uncommon when people feel like this for them to feel that things won't improve and won't get any better. Do you ever feel this way? (hopelessness; normalising, hierarchal question picking up from 1)

9. People feeling depressed and hopeless sometimes think about death and dying? Have you ever thought about killing yourself? (suicidal thinking; normalising, hierarchical question)

10. Have you thought in this way in the past? (suicidal thinking; increasing disclosure by starting with past events)

11. Have you previously attempted suicide or tried to harm yourself in some way? (previous suicidal behaviour, hierarchical question)

12. Could you tell me more about this [how many times, triggers, intent, plan, lethality, event details]? (previous suicidal behaviour, hierarchical question)

13. Have you recently made any plans to act on this? (suicidal thinking; hierarchical question)

14. Sometimes people who have previously made attempts see themselves as being more impulsive. Would that description apply to you? (impulsivity; normalising, hierarchical question)

15. However, you are seeking help for your problems. That suggests to me that you have some reasons for living. Can you think of what they might be? (protective factors; hierarchical question)

16. [It seems from what you have said that … (summary)]

C. Example questions to illustrate possible interview order for information obtained in the 'routine outcome measures' section:

17. Looking at this question [Q2, PHQ9], you have indicated that you feel down, depressed or hopeless for more than half of the days. Could you tell me more about what you were thinking about when you picked this response? (double-check of items 2 and 9)

18. This question [Q9, PHQ9] suggests that you have had thoughts of hurting yourself or death for most of the days since I saw you last. What came to mind when you were thinking through what box to tick here? (double-check of items 9 and 12)

Figure 6.2   Example questions to illustrate the possible chronological, hierarchical risk assessment structure within the initial assessment

(see Section A, Figure 6.2). Levels of hopelessness, the nature of suicidal thinking, past suicidal behaviour, levels of impulsivity and the presence of protective characteristics will be covered hierarchically in the risk assessment section (Section B). Finally, the risk information is triangulated with the self-report measures which are discussed in the routine outcome measures section (Section C).

Examples of risk assessment

In this section I look at some examples of risk assessment in practice by presenting excerpts of two LICBT risk assessments. Initially, I look at our assessment of Judy (who we first met in Chapter 5), which indicates a mild level of suicide risk. I then look at the risk assessment of Kate, where a severe level of risk is indicated. Within the first excerpt I provide an abbreviated running commentary to illustrate both the functions of the questioning and the intentions of the practitioner.

Interview with Judy: excerpt of the initial assessment interview, risk assessment (commentary in brackets)

Practitioner: You've told me that you've been down after experiencing these difficulties at work, and they have affected your ability to cope at home? Also, changes in John's work seem to have had an impact here as well. You said that you had been feeling low, sometimes thinking that you were failing quite a bit. Sometimes, when people get depressed and low, they become a bit hopeless about things. I'm just wondering whether that is something that has happened with yourself? (enquiring about hopelessness; normalising)

Client: Well I suppose so. I am worried about my job, I know in some ways I am lucky with my family; but sometimes, yes it does feel quite hopeless. I don't really know where to go from here.

Practitioner: OK, and sometimes when people feel hopeless, if they think that they can't go on, they might think 'do I want to be here?' and they have thoughts of self-harm, that sort of thing. Can I ask whether you have had any of those sorts of thoughts? (enquiring about suicidal ideation; normalising)

Client: I suppose I would be lying if I said no. It crossed my mind that it could be easier just to not wake up tomorrow morning, not have to deal with how that day is going to be. But I don't think I actually would.

Practitioner:	So you've had some of those thoughts; thoughts of suicide, but you don't think you would act on them. Is that what you are saying? (enquiring about plans; hierarchical questioning)
Client:	I don't think I could. I think I'm probably too much of a coward. I don't really think I could do that to my family. I know people still care about me, just sometimes it feels that all is lost.
Practitioner:	OK. So it sounds as if you haven't thought it through in any more detail than just having these thoughts that go through your mind? You haven't made plans or anything like that? (paraphrasing)
Client:	No.
Practitioner:	OK, I'm pleased to hear that. Can I just ask: your doctor said something about you having some counselling before? (enquiring about past events)
Client:	Yes, before I met John I had quite a bad break up and I remember that that was a low period then. There used to be a counsellor who they had at the doctor's practice and I think I saw them for ... I think it was six sessions.
Practitioner:	How long ago was that?
Client:	It must be around 10 years ago now.
Practitioner:	Can I check whether you had any of these kinds of thoughts at that time? (enquiring about suicidal thinking linked to past events)
Client:	Again, I suppose I thought things are so difficult and it feels like such an effort to carry on, but I don't remember thinking that much about these things at the time.
Practitioner:	So, it seems that you may have had the odd thought, but you didn't plan or act on it back then? (enquiring about plans linked to past events)
Client:	No.
Practitioner:	And are there any other times in your life when you have felt this bad and had these kinds of thoughts?
Client:	Not as bad as this, no.
Practitioner:	OK. Can I just also check the sort of person you are because sometimes people are more impulsive than other people, and sometimes people act more spontaneously? What sort of a person would you say that you are? (enquiring about impulsivity)
Client:	I wouldn't say I am massively spontaneous. I mean, no not really. If I have one too many drinks I might make a decision I wouldn't have done otherwise, but I don't think that is any different from anyone else.
Practitioner:	And you also mentioned something about not harming yourself because of family members. Can you tell me a little bit about

	what's stopping you acting on these thoughts? (enquiring about protective factors)
Client:	I guess I know that I have people who really care about me, and I have a great family and I know they are trying their best to support me. I couldn't hurt them.
Practitioner:	So it seems from what you're saying then that you have been depressed, and… [summary given of the stresses/precipitants]. You have been having the odd thought about hopelessness, and not wanting to go on and do suicide; but you haven't got any plans and haven't thought those thoughts through in any more detail. You have folk around you who are supporting you now. Is that a fair summary?
Client:	Yes.
Practitioner:	OK, that's fine.

Interview with Kate: excerpt of the initial assessment interview, risk assessment

Practitioner:	OK Kate, You've told me that you have unfortunately lost your job and also have recently broken up with your partner, and that just sounds really difficult. Sometimes when people experience these things and they are feeling so bad, they sometimes have thoughts about not being able to go on. I am just wondering whether that is something that has ever gone through your mind?
Client:	Well, what is the point? I have got nothing any more.
Practitioner:	Tell me a little bit more? You say you have got nothing, is that the thought that goes through your mind?
Client:	That's the truth isn't it? I have got no job, and with the state of things at the moment, who on earth is going to employ me. There is just no hope of that. I haven't got a relationship any more and how or where will I ever get to meet anyone else? That's it, that's never going to be again is it? Just what have I got? I am going to lose my house. I am loathsome to be around. My friends and family are not going to put up with me much longer are they? There is just nothing.
Practitioner:	I can see that things are feeling really hopeless for you at the moment. You don't seem to see anything ahead for yourself is that right?
Client:	Not at the moment. I don't think there is!

Practitioner:	That sounds like a really painful place to be. And sometimes when people are in a lot of pain like that, they can feel like ending their life. I am just wondering whether that has ever been something that has gone through your mind?
Client:	Every day.
Practitioner:	And so you think about suicide, have you thought about this in any more detail than that?
Client:	I have done a little bit of research I suppose. I have got quite a few tablets in the house and, you know, I know I can get more. I think that with a bottle of wine … and everything will be a lot simpler wouldn't it?
Practitioner:	So you have stockpiled your tablets by the sound of it, is that right?
Client:	Well, I have got about six packets now.
Practitioner:	How long have you been saving those up for?
Client:	I suppose the last week. Any time I am in town really.
Practitioner:	So, things have changed for you over the last week?
Client:	I guess. Nothing is getting any better and there's just no way forward. Yes.
Practitioner:	And so these thoughts about ending it, taking these tablets; you say you are getting those very frequently. Is that something that is on your mind a lot of the time or is that something that comes into your mind just at certain points?
Client:	No, it is on my mind a lot of the time. It's kind of getting the courage.
Practitioner:	So, you are building up to this by the sound of it?
Client:	Yes, I suppose. But I'm such a weak person. I am probably too weak even to do that. I am just pathetic.
Practitioner:	You spoke about a bottle of wine. Do you drink very often?
Client:	It dulls the pain a bit, doesn't it? But money is getting a little tight as well now. Yet another way of coping that I am not going to have shortly!
Practitioner:	So things are getting worse and you can't see a way out really? You are having these thoughts of suicide and you have stockpiled some tablets; and you're thinking you might do it at some point when you have some wine; and the money is running out. So in your mind, do you have a time-frame for this? I'm just wondering how far the planning has gone?
Client:	Well, I'm thinking maybe if I get another few packets, maybe three packets – I'm popping into town after this. I've got another appointment with the doctor tomorrow. So I thought I could go to the pharmacy while I am there. Maybe within the next few days if I can.

Practitioner:	So that sounds like you're feeling really desperate. You said you had a difficulty in the past where a relationship broke up and there were some problems. Have you tried anything like this previously?
Client:	Yes, another failure though! I think I got through about 15 pills or something, and about half my bottle of wine and then my mum came round. She took me to hospital. I can't even do that right!
Practitioner:	Did you know your mum was going to come over or was that unexpected?
Client:	No, I didn't know. She did pop round quite frequently. She knew I was really upset but we hadn't planned it.
Practitioner:	OK, is that the only time or have you taken other overdoses before?
Client:	Not overdoses. I mean, there was a time when I was a teenager when I used to cut my arms, and my legs and things. I don't think that was ever with the intention of ending my life.
Practitioner:	From what you say then, things sound really bad for you at the moment. You seem quite desperate about things: building up these tablets and thinking that you might kill yourself in the near future. I am wondering whether you have had any other thoughts or any other plans about how you would kill yourself?
Client:	Well there is a section of the railway track that is really easy to get to, and that I have sussed out. I suppose sometimes I think that that would be a lot easier. There would be no-one coming in or anything like that. It would be quicker; I suppose that I don't think you would need as much courage. It wouldn't take as long.
Practitioner:	So, that sounds like a well thought through plan as well? You have said about the tablets and it's going to take you a little while to build up those tablets. You are going to see the doctor about getting another prescription; and tell me about the railway track. Is that something you had thought to do instead of the tablets or if the tablets didn't work? How does that figure into things?
Client:	I guess it is just an option and I go down to that section of the railway track every day now, and I just sit there and 'mulch'. I guess I find some comfort in it.
Practitioner:	OK, so you go down there. You are obviously still with us; you haven't jumped in front of the train so far. What is keeping you from doing that?
Client:	I don't really know. I guess the courage thing and I'm slightly concerned about the driver. Kind of how they would feel; I wouldn't want them to think it was their fault. I am sure that they wouldn't.

Practitioner:	I am just trying to gauge how you are at the moment and whether you … You said something about seeing the GP tomorrow and I am wondering whether you're planning on doing that still, or whether you could go off today and jump in front of a train?
Client:	I haven't been there yet today. So I will go there this afternoon. I don't know.
Practitioner:	So, in terms of going there; presumably you get comfort from it, but there is a bit of you that thinks 'I might jump in front of a train', from what you're saying. Is that right?
Client:	Yes, I suppose the comfort comes from knowing that there would be a way out.
Practitioner:	So, thinking about it today on a scale of zero to 10, with 10 being 'I'm definitely going to jump in front of that train' and zero being 'I'm just going down there because it helps me to think or feel better', where are you at on that scale?
Client:	At this point seven maybe.
Practitioner:	Seven. OK, so that is veering much more towards wanting to kill yourself isn't it? I have heard what you have said and I have to say I am a bit concerned about you; about your safety. Often what happens is that when people are depressed they become suicidal, and that is part of the crisis and the depression that they are experiencing. I wonder if you can look back to that time 10 years ago when you took that overdose. Did life improve at some point after that?
Client:	Yes, I guess so.
Practitioner:	Life is tough at the moment, but it got a bit better after that. That is often the case, people improve. So, some people make attempts and then regret it, no matter how determined they feel at that point. For that reason, what I would like to do is … I have some colleagues who work in a team who deal with people when they are in a state of crisis and try and support them through it. To some extent it's up to you how much you work with them, but at this point I would like to let them know about your situation and what you are going through. I'm just wondering how do you feel about that?
Client:	Well, I thought these sessions were confidential?
Practitioner:	Well they are, but remember how we had a discussion at the start: how if anybody is at risk …; and you have told me that you are at risk, haven't you? My duty above everything else is to protect you. Part of that involves, if I can't do it on my own, bringing in other people who can help you and give you the support that you need.

Is that something you really would not like or is that something you've got mixed feelings about? Where are you at about this at the moment?

Client: I guess they can try, but I don't see what they can do. I don't see what anybody else can do.

Practitioner: Yes, but I just wonder whether it's worth considering whether that might be part of the condition you're experiencing at the moment. This is something, as I say … You had something a little while ago and came through it. So if you are feeling fairly comfortable with it … It's not easy 'cause you were expecting to come along to see me and all of a sudden, I am suggesting that somebody else might be involved. I'm just wondering whether I can ask you to have a seat in the waiting room again and I'll give them a ring and talk about your case, and see what they say. How about that? Then I can come and fetch you and we can have another chat again about what they think is the best course of action for you. We can then take it from there. Does that sound all right?

Client: Yes.

Practitioner: OK.

Exercise 6.3   Making sense of the interview with Kate

I have indicated the purpose of the questioning within the abbreviated commentary in the interview with Judy. See if you can identify where the practitioner discusses the different risk factors within Kate's transcript. Have any of these been omitted?

Exercise 6.4   Putting it into practice

If you are in a service or training in an educational setting, form a group of three with some colleagues. You will rotate through the roles of practitioner, client and observer. Use a case from the Appendix (or a case of your own) and role play the information-gathering section of the initial assessment (which includes risk assessment) – aim to complete this within 20 minutes. Imagine you are role playing a client who has a moderate or severe level of suicide risk. You will need to adapt the case to be in keeping with this risk level. Use the hierarchical model as a guide and the example questions from Figure 6.2 if you get stuck.

The clinical skills associated with the management of risk

Having described the decision-making process, I will now consider some clinical approaches that are helpful in moderating suicide risk. These are loosely structured around some of the APA's (2003) suggested components: the therapeutic relationship and attending to the client's safety, facilitating contact and support from others, 'tipping the balance' away from suicide, reducing the impact of stressors, developing a therapeutic plan and maximising adherence to treatment. The LICBT practitioner will refer the client to specialist services if a severe level of risk is noted. However, some immediate moderation of risk at this step may be possible and would be desirable because there will inevitably be a delay in the client receiving specialist support (although it is important that attempts are not made to treat or 'contain' severe levels of risk within LICBT). Some principles and brief interventions are overviewed, although few of these will be able to be integrated in the remaining time of the LICBT interview following the establishment of such risk. Attending to the client's safety (and therefore continuing to helpfully engage with them in the session) is of primary importance. The other components are best implemented in a patient-centred way, according to client need and the intervention opportunities presented within the session.

Maintenance of the therapeutic relationship

Firstly, the client is likely to have invested a degree of hope in the LICBT contact prior to attending, particularly if they have made the effort to physically attend at a local clinic (rather than opt into a telephone assessment). It is important that the practitioner does not undermine this, despite potentially having to break confidentiality in order to move the client onto another service and also end the LICBT contact because of the client's level of risk. Many clients do not object to this if they are given an appropriate rationale. It is vital that these actions are done with sensitivity (using fully the interpersonal skills described in Chapter 4) because the withdrawal of care can be a trigger for suicide.

The breaking of confidentiality will be eased by sensitively reminding the client that this situation had been discussed at the beginning of the first meeting, and that the practitioner's paramount concern is the client's safety. Thus, they have a duty to involve others (this conversation occurred in interview with Kate above). In this way, despite this action being sometimes against the client's wishes, the practitioner is able to convey that it arises from a position of care and concern. The involvement of crisis services can be facilitated by referring to them as 'colleagues' who work with the practitioner in the locality, but who are specialists in helping people who may be in a crisis such as the client's. In this way, despite the contact with the practitioner being withdrawn, the client is made aware that ultimately this will lead to a greater chance of their needs being met. It is recommended that services are closely dove-tailed together so that the client leaves the session with the knowledge that they remain involved with services. This can be done by telephoning the crisis services while the client is still present in the clinic, and then 'feeding back' to them the arrangements that have been made prior to them leaving. Additionally, the practitioner can arrange with the client to contact them briefly by telephone after they were due to meet the crisis service, to check that the meeting has taken place and that they are now engaged in this service (taking appropriate action if this has not occurred).

Attending to the client's safety

The practitioner must additionally attend to the client's safety by removing their means of harm wherever possible. This might involve, for example, obtaining a commitment from a client who has been stockpiling medication to return the unused tablets to the pharmacist for safe disposal or involving a partner in doing so. Also, this would involve informing the client's primary care physician of the situation so that they might potentially prescribe in smaller quantities, switch to a less toxic alternative and closely monitor medication adherence. Family members can also be involved to maintain vigilance in the situation. Bryan (2007) reports a US case study where the practitioner contacted a client's wife (with the client's permission) and asked her to change the combination of the gun safe and keep the new combination from the client. This demonstrates how the directness of the practitioner's actions can be dependent on the immediacy and lethality of the method.

Facilitating support

The practitioner might make efforts to mobilise social support for the client. This is beneficial in terms of increasing the level of monitoring of the client's situation. Suicidal individuals also often feel increasingly isolated and disconnected from others, believing that others would be better off without them (Joiner, 2005). The re-establishment of a support network disconfirms beliefs that others do not care for them. These efforts also demonstrate that the practitioner takes the client's views seriously and has their interests in mind. As such, contacting others can form part of an action plan (see below) or, with the client's permission, the practitioner can contact the client's closest supports to facilitate this. This might be particularly useful until specialist services become involved.

Tipping the balance

When clients report feeling suicidal, they are usually more accurately feeling ambivalent, torn between wanting to die and wanting to live. As such, the goal for the practitioner is to attempt to tip this balance towards the client choosing life (Beck et al., 1979). There are several strategies that are helpful in achieving this aim. The first of these is the engagement in an abbreviated form of problem-solving process (this is described in full within Chapter 8). Suicidal patients usually have real and significant issues in their lives, but often their problem-solving processes have broken down to a point where suicide appears to be an optimal option (Martell, Addis, & Jacobson, 2001). Helping the client to consider other angles to a problem can create the possibility of an unforeseen solution. This can instil hope and introduce viable alternatives to suicide into the person's mind. For example, Beck et al. (1979) describe a case where a man with a family lost his job. He experienced cognitions such as 'I am worthless' and 'my family would be better off if I were dead'. They describe the practitioner reframing the problem in terms of looking at how to find alternative employment (a referral to an employment advisor would be helpful here) and also obtaining sufficient financial resources to support the family until he is re-employed (contact with a welfare rights agency would allow him to see what welfare support he is entitled to). In this way, the practitioner repackages a seemingly impossible situation as a soluble one.

Beck et al. (1979) also suggest attempting to introduce 'cognitive dissonance' into the client's thinking with a view to tipping this balance. Cognitive dissonance occurs when an individual simultaneously holds contradictory views. In such situations, they have a natural tendency towards altering their cognition towards greater consistency. The technique involves the practitioner highlighting inconsistencies, either within the client's patterns of cognition or between their experience and their cognition, with a view to provoking a therapeutic shift. Beck et al. (1979) describe an instance where a woman attended for therapy following the break-up of her relationship with her second husband. When the practitioner enquired why she was harbouring thoughts of suicide she said that 'I can't live without Peter' and 'I just can't get along without a man'. The practitioner enquired whether this had always been the case. With an expression of enlightenment the client stated: 'Actually the best time in my life was when I was completely alone … [the client then elaborated upon this]'. This new item of evidence contradicted her cognitions and resulted in the beginning of a shift in her thinking. Similarly, in the interview with Judy above, the practitioner highlights through questioning that the client previously felt suicidal and recovered from this. This past experience was dissonant to her present view that nothing can improve in her future and change is not possible.

Additionally, both Beck et al. (1979) and Martell, Addis and Jacobson (2001) describe a two-part technique that is also designed to tip the balance. To engage the client in this approach, they must be willing to re-examine their situation objectively with the practitioner. The first part of the task involves listing the client's reasons for living. If the client has difficulty in considering this currently, they can be prompted to recall the reasons from a prior, happier period in their life (for example, to hold my grandson or to see a sunset). Then the practitioner considers with the client which of these past reasons remain applicable to the present. Frequently, the suicidal client displays distortions in both their cognition and recall, and is either ignoring or discounting these reasons in regard to their present situation. This part of the exercise allows the practitioner to form a counter-balance to the client's reasons for dying. This should be undertaken in a neutral, explorative manner because the exercise can be counter-productive if the client perceives that the practitioner is attempting to 'bully' them into a certain way of thinking. The second part of the exercise is less likely to be possible in the remaining time available to the LICBT practitioner. I nevertheless note it for completeness. The advantages and disadvantages of dying are then explored. It is important that the practitioner takes the client's reasons for dying seriously and avoids attempts of humour or flippancy during this exercise. After the exercise, the client frequently sees their situation more objectively and the reasons for dying seem less compelling than previously.

Removal of stressors

A further possible strand to an intervention is the reduction of any immediate stressors that the client is facing. This might involve discussing with the client the various options that might be a means to this end (such as attending debt advice services). Alternatively, this might involve directly intervening on the client's behalf, for instance writing a letter of support for re-housing to a local council for a client who is experiencing harassment from neighbours. In this instance, it is unlikely that the LICBT practitioner would be able to carry out these actions because of the need to rapidly step the client up, but they could highlight these to the client as options that are available to the specialist services they will be seeing in the near future.

Development of a plan

It is good practice to develop a plan with the client for them to take away, perhaps on a card that they can keep in a wallet or purse. This will usually detail the actions that they should put into place should they feel desperate. Such a plan might involve contacting close family or friends, the crisis team, voluntary 24-hour support services (such as the Samaritans in the UK) or the emergency services if the risk is immediate. It might also list activities (such as going for a walk) or memories/images that might be helpful (for example, of the client in a safe, comforting place). These action plans are considered to be more helpful than no-harm contracts, which involve the client agreeing not to attempt suicide over the course of contact. There is little if any evidence of benefit in regard to the latter (Bryan & Rudd, 2006) and it is clearly more helpful to consider positive ways of moving forward rather than simply asking that clients not engage in negative behaviour (Brown, Have, Henriques, Xie, Hollander, & Beck, 2005).

Maximising adherence

A final recommendation is to encourage the client to adhere to any treatment. Rather than asking clients to sign a no-harm contract, this involves guiding them through a discussion that highlights that depression can be viewed as a condition which commonly has suicidal thinking as a symptom (as demonstrated by the suicide-related items on depression inventories). Further, depression is treatable and, as individuals recover, so suicidal ideation reduces. In this way, the client can be encouraged to come to a reasonable position of aiming to see how they respond to a period of treatment before considering to act on their suicidal thoughts.

The assessment of selected other forms of risk

In this section I briefly consider some other forms of risk, namely, risk of violence to others, risk of harm to children because of psychological problems and risk associated with self-neglect.

It would be inappropriate for LICBT practitioners to treat individuals who pose a significant danger to others. As such, effective referral management systems should screen such cases out of service pathways prior to them being seen. However, such systems are not infallible and sometimes referrers may not be fully aware of individuals' situations at the point in time that a referral is made. Additionally, some appropriate referrals might be made for individuals who have committed violent acts in the past, but who have had no recent history involving aggression. Because the practitioner needs to protect themselves in their role and has a duty to also protect others from harm, it is important that they are aware of the risk factors for violence so that they know when to alert authorities or warn others. This should be discussed firstly with a supervisor, providing that a delay does not place an individual at risk. These risk factors are summarised below (Kropp & Hart, 1997; Webster, Douglas, Eaves, & Hart, 1997).

In terms of historical or 'static' factors, previous acts of violence against others correlate with a risk of violence occurring in the future. This might include criminal acts against strangers or acquaintances, or the assault of family members. Likewise, the earlier that a pattern of violence began for the individual, the more likely it is that this will continue. Substance abuse is a linked factor in that, if present, this statistically increases the probability that individuals have acted violently in the past 10-fold. Witnessing violent acts in childhood or adolescence is one of the more robust factors in terms of predicting spousal assault. Prior psychotic or mood disorders are considered to increase the risk of violence, but a stronger predictor (in terms of mental health difficulties) is psychopathy. This is a form of personality disorder where individuals lack a sense of moral responsibility. The stability of the person's relationships, both personal- and work-related, has also been found to be relevant. The less stable these relationships have been, the greater the risk of violence. However, this factor does not have as strong a predictive value as the presence of previous violence in the person's history.

Other clinical factors that correlate with violent behaviour include having a lack of insight (difficulty understanding why they react in a certain way), having misperceptions of others' behaviours or intentions (for instance, taking things personally when they were not intended as such), and minimising previous violent acts. However, an angry disposition (or a tendency towards angry states) is a stronger predictor, and any homicidal ideation or intent is also of relevance. There is a connection between psychotic states and violence, and just as impulsivity is relevant to suicide risk, it is also of relevance in regard to risk of violence to others. A number of factors associated with a possible lack of stability in the individual's future are likely to increase frustration and therefore risk associated with them. These include their plans lacking feasibility, exposure to daily hassles such as difficulties in housing and finances, and lack of social support.

An additional area to consider is a potential risk to children caused by a mental health difficulty, which may be present when the client is a parent. Professional regulations and organisational policies stipulate the importance of reporting physical, emotional and sexual abuse of children, and so this is not discussed here. Rather, all health professionals should receive mandatory training on this topic from their employer organisation and be guided by their professional bodies. However, in some circumstances, mental health difficulties can place children under subtler forms of risk in terms of limitations upon the emotional and physical care that a child receives. Examples of this might include a client with obsessive–compulsive disorder involving a young child in helping them with their compulsive routines, an individual with agoraphobia restricting their child from going out to play as they feel safer having them nearby, and a child doing housework and cooking meals to support a lone parent with depression. In this way, whenever a client presents with a clinical condition that is significantly restrictive in terms of their lifestyle, it is recommended that the practitioner asks whether there are children in the home, and determines their age(s) and the impact that the condition has upon them (clients may minimise this impact). Depending on the client's responses, advice may need to be sought from a child safe-guarding professional. These can be difficult judgements to make and practitioners should seek advice within their supervision where these issues arise.

Exercise 6.5   Protecting the children

Think about some of your own clients or discuss some of your supervisor's cases with them. If you are not working within a service, complete the exercise using the case examples provided in the Appendix. Whether or not these clients actually have children, think about the clients' difficulties and consider what impact that they might have on their care of children of differing ages. If the answer is little or none, ask yourself the question 'How severe would these problems need to become before it began to impact upon this child's care and development?' Next, explore with your supervisor the appropriate agency to call for advice or to more formally report that you have become aware of a child who is at risk.

A final area to consider is the risk of self-neglect. As home visits are usually not part of the LICBT practitioner's remit, they will be unlikely to be able to view the client's home environment. Consequently, they will be unable to determine whether the client's garden is well kept and free of rubbish, the house is maintained, and the interior of the house is similarly clean, tidy and hygienic. As such, judgements regarding self-neglect are limited by the information that the client gives the practitioner over contact (this might be explored in the initial interview when the client is asked about the impact of their difficulties) and how they present within the interview. So, for example, concerns might be raised if the client states that they are unable to shop or cook for themselves presently, have lost their appetite and appear underweight (which might be confirmed by determining their body mass index, see www.nhs.uk/Tools/Pages/Healthyweightcalculator.aspx). Other physical cues include uncombed, matted hair; long, dirty finger nails; poor skin condition or lesions; dirty or soiled clothing; and the client having an unhygienic smell. If these are present, concerns should be discussed with the practitioner's supervisor and then, depending on the outcome of this discussion, with a safe-guarding professional.

The role of rating scales

There are a number of tools that can assist the clinician in assessing risk. It is unlikely that it would be possible to integrate these routinely into the work of the LICBT practitioner without incurring considerable time costs. However, some tools may be useful following the identification of significant risk to inform the practitioner's judgement regarding its severity. However, it should be noted that, in isolation, these tools generally have a limited predictive ability in terms of identifying who will act on their intention/situation and who will not. A variety of tools are evaluated in detail in the Department of Health (2007) document. Therefore, a limited sample of the more widely used measures is described (Table 6.3) to give the reader an indication of the scope of the available tools.

Table 6.3   Sample of tools that may assist the practitioner in risk assessment

Title	Purpose	Type	Description	Website/contact
Beck Hopelessness Scale	Assessment of risk of self-harm/ suicide	Self-report tool	20 true/false items that assess the client's perspective regarding their future – hopelessness being an important risk factor	www.harcourt-uk.com/
Galatean Risk Screening Tool	Assessment of risk of violence to others, self-harm/suicide and self-neglect/ vulnerability	Structured screening tool	General screening questions covering the areas: suicide/ self-harm, damage to property, self-neglect and risk to dependents; sections lead to further questions where risk is indicated	www.egrist.org/
Historical Clinical Risk – 20	Assessment of risk of violence to others	Structured clinical judgement tool	20 items looking at historical, clinical and risk management items which are coded on a three-point scale	www.parinc.com
Suicidal Ideation Scale	To assess intention to die after a suicide attempt	Self-report or structured screening tool	21-item scale designed to look at intensity of ideation regarding an attempt which has occurred over the previous week	www.harcourt-uk.com/

Summary

- This chapter has focused primarily on suicide risk assessment. The goal of this form of risk assessment is to identify and balance the factors that the client possesses that influence their risk of suicide.
- Risk assessment should be repeated on each contact because risk is based upon both static factors and dynamic ones; dynamic factors potentially changing between contacts.
- There are eight factors that should be considered: predisposition to suicide, symptomatic presentation, precipitants, hopelessness, suicidal thinking, previous suicidal behaviour, impulsivity and protective characteristics. These can be used to make an informed decision about suicide risk using Bryan and Rudd's (2007) framework.
- These factors are best explored within the LICBT interview through use of a hierarchical questioning format.
- Once identified, there are a number of principles that can be used to manage risk. This can be done via consideration of the therapeutic relationship and the client's safety; by facilitating contact and support from others; through 'tipping the balance' away from suicide and reducing of impact of stressors; as well as by developing a therapeutic plan and maximising adherence to treatment.
- The practitioner should also assess the risk of violence to others, self-neglect and harm to children.
- There are a number of risk assessment tools that are available to assist the practitioner in these endeavours.

Further reading and activities

Bryan and Rudd (2006) outline the principles of suicide risk assessment. Beck et al. (1979) is a classic text that has a section on the means of managing suicide risk.

Find out about your local Crisis and Safeguarding Teams. Determine how to contact them, their inclusion and exclusion criteria, and what services they offer. If possible, try to arrange to meet with them to learn more about how they operate. Finally, obtain information regarding voluntary crisis support services that are accessible both locally and nationally. If possible, obtain cards or leaflets that list contacts for support services which can be given to some clients. Alternatively, design one of these for the service yourself.

7

Understanding Depression

Theresa Marrinan

Learning objectives

- To gain a clear understanding of what is meant by the term depression, including typical symptoms and formal diagnostic features.
- To have an awareness of common maintenance processes in depression.
- To be able to differentiate between different levels of severity in depression.
- To be able to distinguish depression from other disorders.
- To have knowledge of the key vulnerability factors for developing depression.
- To understand the importance of managing risk and relapse.

Introduction

The aim of this chapter is to give the reader a clear understanding of what is meant by the term depression (also referred to as clinical or major depression). There will be a consideration of the typical symptoms and formal diagnostic features, and an exploration of how the CBT model enables us to understand the processes by which depression may be maintained. As the role of the LICBT practitioner involves working with mild to moderate depression, the reader will be guided to means of distinguishing different levels of severity. In addition there will be a review of some of the complications that may arise in trying to make sense of symptoms, particularly where low mood may be indicative of a separate disorder, or where co-morbid anxiety symptoms cloud the picture. Finally, a brief overview will be provided of vulnerability factors and risk, and the importance of relapse prevention will be highlighted. The overriding objective of this chapter is to provide the LICBT practitioner with the knowledge to correctly identify those people who may be experiencing depression in the mild to moderate range, in order to ensure that the appropriate treatment may be administered. Some of the factors mentioned above, such as maintenance processes and relapse, will also be further elaborated in the following chapter, which describes the treatment of depression.

What is depression?

To help us explore this further, let us consider the following case.

Alison is a 39-year-old woman who has been referred for treatment. She describes herself as feeling weepy for most of the day, with little energy or drive to complete routine tasks such as looking after her children and her home. She works part time as a dental receptionist, but reports that she has to 'drag' herself to work. Once there, she feels restless and irritable, finding it difficult to concentrate or focus on her job, which in turn causes her to worry about making mistakes. Although she feels constantly tired, she has difficulty getting off to sleep at night. Her appetite has diminished and she has lost a stone in weight in the past month. The mornings are a huge struggle for her, and she has called in sick on three occasions over the past two weeks. She loves her husband and children, but feels 'trapped' in her life and finds it hard to see a future. This results in her feeling as though she is a 'bad mother and terrible wife'. She describes having felt like this for the past six weeks.

Alison is describing some of the typical symptoms we might expect to see in a person who is clinically depressed. Of course it is common for most people to feel fed up or dissatisfied with their life from time to time, so how do we determine whether Alison is just feeling a bit down or falls into the category of being clinically depressed? This is a question that will be addressed throughout the chapter. The UK's National Institute for Health and Clinical Excellence provides an excellent summary of the evidence base for treatments for depression (NICE, 2009b). Both this chapter and the next will draw heavily upon this guidance. Needless to say, it is crucial for those involved in the assessment and treatment of depression (or the supervision of such practitioners) to be familiar with such guidelines.

Exercise 7.1   What does it mean to be depressed?

To begin to understand what it means to be depressed it may be helpful to spend a few minutes on the following exercise. Think back to a time when you felt really down or fed up. Perhaps you had the sense that things were not going right in your life, maybe you had some disappointing news, or possibly a relationship ended. Consider the next four questions and take some time to write down some ideas.

- How did you feel (what was your mood), for instance, upset, angry, disappointed?
- What thoughts did you have, for example, did you blame yourself or others; or did it change the way you thought about yourself, your life or the future?
- How did you feel physically, for example, tired, energetic, restless, tense?
- What type of things did you do to cope, for instance, go to the gym, go shopping, keep busy, watch television, avoid friends, stay in bed?

Feeling low and fed up can be like a very mild version of depression, so how we feel, think and act at these times can be very similar to the responses of a person who is experiencing depression. When understanding depression within a CBT model we would tend to focus on the four key areas referred to in the above exercise, in other words: emotions, thoughts, physical reactions and behaviours. Each of the four areas will be described further below.

Emotions

Think back to Exercise 7.1 – were you able to identify the emotions you experienced? By emotions we are referring to mood states such as anger, sadness, guilt, shame, joy and fear, rather than thoughts such as 'I feel like a failure'; 'I'll never have another relationship'. A key symptom of depression is obviously low mood. Aaron Beck, a founding father of cognitive therapy (see Chapter 1), describes how the depressed person becomes almost incapable of experiencing a sense of pleasure or joy. They become a 'cerebral' person, able to see the point of a joke but unable to feel any amusement (Beck et al., 1979). Life in general becomes much more effortful as the activities a person previously enjoyed no longer provide pleasure. There may be a sense of purely going through the motions. Yet, while the person may seem incapable of experiencing positive feelings, negative emotions may be felt with a much greater level of intensity, which at times may seem unbearable. These negative feelings are not limited to sadness and despair but may also include guilt, irritability and anxiety.

Thoughts

Review your answers to Exercise 7.1 – what kinds of thoughts did you have when you felt low? Did you blame yourself? Did you view other people as having let you down? Did it make you question your understanding of the way the world works, for example whether the world is just or fair? When people feel depressed it can affect the way they view themselves, others and the world in general. They tend to focus heavily on the negative aspects of situations, often thinking the worst, which can exacerbate low mood. One reason this may occur is because emotional states are usually accompanied by thoughts that fit with the emotional state. For example, when we feel happy we tend to think more positively, whereas when we feel low we are more likely to experience negative thoughts. This is sometimes referred to as *mood-congruent thinking*. Another important aspect to consider is that thoughts are mostly automatic and unquestioned. In other words, we see our thoughts as a reflection of the truth (although later we may be able to apply a different perspective). Unfortunately, if a person is experiencing depression and consequently has enduring low mood, the negative thoughts are more likely to persist and they may find it extremely difficult to consider alternative ways of viewing their situation. This can have the effect of maintaining and deepening low mood. This is not to suggest that the depressed client's thoughts are invalid, simply that when low mood dominates the picture it can be extremely difficult to consider alternative or less negative explanations.

Through his work as both a psychiatrist and a researcher, Beck was able to study many depressed patients and as a result gained great insight into the kinds of thought patterns that can occur in depression (Beck et al., 1979). One common feature he observed was the phenomenon of *negative automatic thoughts* (NATs). These are thoughts that frequently pop into the person's mind regardless of the particular event or situation, such as 'it's all my fault', 'I've failed again' or 'I'll be alone forever'. Beck suggested that these might arise from more fundamental beliefs that the person holds about themselves and the world in general. As a result there is a tendency to view these as factual explanations, and accept them unquestioningly. Beck proposed that these negative thoughts cluster into three domains:

- *self*, for example, 'it's all my fault', 'I'm useless';
- *the world* – this may encompass current and past experiences, for example, 'people always let you down', 'life's unfair';
- *the future*, for instance, 'it's always going to be this bad', 'nothing will ever change', 'I'll be alone forever'.

This is known as the *negative cognitive triad*.

Beck further proposed that the depressed person may be subject to *faulty information processing*. This refers to a process where the individual is more likely to pay attention to those aspects of their experience that would seem to confirm or endorse negative thoughts, and ignore evidence that would be in contradiction of those same thoughts. For example, a person who views himself or herself as being a failure might feel devastated when they receive some constructive feedback, seeing it as evidence that they are useless, while on the other hand discounting any praise. They may recall previous instances where they experienced a sense of failure, such as not getting a job they interviewed for, while ignoring evidence that might suggest the opposite, for example previous successful job interviews. They might even actively search for evidence, perhaps from their memory or from events occurring in the present, that appears congruent with their negative belief. It is as if the person is experiencing the opposite of wearing 'rose tinted glasses'.

Beck suggested that this faulty information processing is the result of *systematic thinking errors*. In the self-help literature these are often referred to as *unhelpful thinking styles* (for example, Williams, 2009). One example of this is *selective attention*, where the person tends to overgeneralise from negative situations, discount any positives and exclusively blame themselves when things are going wrong (see Chapter 8 for further elaboration of these thinking styles).

A further difficulty for the depressed person is that they may interpret the very experience of being depressed negatively, for example believing they are a failure for not being able to overcome their low mood. Symptoms such as poor concentration may lead to the thought 'I'm stupid'; feeling exhausted may cause the person to conclude 'I'll never be able to get back to work', and so forth (Westbrook et al., 2007).

An overall consequence of these patterns of negative thinking is that assumptions are drawn about events in a way that tends to reinforce negative beliefs, so perpetuating low mood and leading to a sense of *hopelessness* – a very common feature of depression.

Physiological symptoms

It is important to recognise that there are extensive physiological symptoms associated with depression. Think back to the earlier exercise. Do you remember how you felt physically? When depressed it is usual to feel lethargic, listless and lacking in energy, even after extended periods of inactivity. Think back to a time when you slept in longer than usual, hoping for a rest, but woke up feeling more tired or sluggish. People with depression can feel like this for most of the time. Being in a constant state of tiredness leads them to believe that they need more rest in order to recover their energy levels. As a consequence, they tend to do less and sleep more, which unfortunately results in them feeling even more tired.

As well as feeling physically exhausted, the person may have great difficulty in focusing on mental tasks such as reading, because of difficulties in concentrating and paying attention. To others the person may appear 'slowed down', taking longer than usual to process information or respond to questions. This can present some important considerations for both the assessment and treatment of the client, as discussed in the following chapter on the treatment of depression.

Other physical symptoms may include agitation, tearfulness and a reduced interest in sex. Many people also report an increase in existing aches and pains, headaches and muscle tension. Indeed it is not uncommon for people with depression to present to their doctor with physical complaints, which may result in misdiagnosis if the depression is not recognised. Sleep problems are also commonplace. These can include difficulties in getting to sleep and staying asleep, and early morning wakening. Alternatively, the depressed person may sleep excessively or stay in bed most of the day. Appetite is usually affected. Some people find that they do not feel hungry and may lose weight as a result, while for others there can be a propensity to 'comfort eat', leading to weight gain.

Behaviours

Consider again your answers to Exercise 7.1. What kinds of things did you do when you felt fed up? Did you continue to go out, see your friends and stay active? What did you stop doing, or do less of? Typically, when people are depressed they become less active and withdraw from the outside world. Motivation reduces markedly and this, combined with lower energy levels and reduced concentration, means that the person struggles to carry out previously routine tasks. Consider a chore that you dislike doing and would avoid if at all possible, for example revising for an exam, ironing, filling out job applications or completing a tax return. For the person experiencing depression, they are likely to view most if not all activities in this way, even those that were previously enjoyable. Tasks that are necessary to perform in order to function effectively become very onerous. These can include paying bills, carrying out household responsibilities and going to work. A hitherto manageable load of ironing can feel like a 'mountain', unpaid bills may pile up, creating high levels of anxiety, and tasks such as shopping can feel completely overwhelming. The person often avoids social contact or hobbies because of the effort involved or as a result of predictions that they will not gain any enjoyment from these activities. There may also be a sense of shame about how others might view their condition. Consequently, the person becomes much less active and more socially isolated. The more they withdraw, the harder it can be to reinitiate social contact. However, despite lower levels of activity, they have less energy and feel more lethargic. In addition, by doing less they have more time to spend going over or *ruminating* about their difficulties.

At more severe levels of depression basic self-care can be affected, including getting up, dressing and washing. When depression becomes overwhelming, the person may experience a desire to give up on life completely. This can be a consequence of feeling utterly hopeless that anything will change and wishing to escape from a state that feels unbearable. Thus, suicidal ideation, self-harm and suicide attempts are common in depression. Careful risk assessment is therefore crucial (see section below on risk and Chapter 6).

Table 7.1 shows typical symptoms of depression. These are grouped into categories of affective (emotions/feelings), behavioural, physiological and cognitive symptoms.

Table 7.1   Typical symptoms of depression, grouped into affective, behavioural, physical and cognitive domains

Affective	Behavioural	Physical	Cognitive
Low mood	Social withdrawal	Lack of energy	Poor concentration
Feelings of guilt	Diminished activity	Reduced/increased sleep	Reduced attention
Anxiety	Rumination	Reduced/increased appetite	Negative thoughts about self, others and the future
Irritability	Comfort eating	Muscle tension	Pessimism
Sadness	Self-harm	Pains	Sense of worthlessness and helplessness
Despair	Suicide attempts	Agitation	Beliefs about deserving punishment
		Loss of libido	
		Tearfulness	

Exercise 7.2   Understanding symptoms

Consider the case of Alison presented earlier. Which symptoms does Alison display that indicate she may be suffering from depression? Try to group Alison's symptoms according to the categories of affective, behavioural, physical and cognitive.

Understanding maintenance processes in depression

You will now be familiar with the types of emotions, cognitions, physical symptoms and behaviours that are typically experienced in depression. In Chapter 3 there was a description of how, within the CBT model, these different areas are thought to link up and reinforce each other, thus maintaining the original problem. This is referred to as a *maintenance cycle*, or *formulation*. Typically in CBT formulations, five key areas or domains are considered (Greenberger & Padesky, 1995; Williams & Chellingsworth, 2010). In addition to the four areas already referred to above, the environment is also seen to play an important role. This includes any triggering of events or situations that elicit or perpetuate low mood (see Chapter 3). It can be helpful to identify the initial event that led to the person becoming depressed, such as the loss of employment or a relationship. In addition, it is important to identify typical situations in which the low mood occurs. One means of doing this is to ask the client to focus on a recent event or situation where they felt low, and look at their responses in each of the other domains. This can help to highlight characteristic responses, such as negative thinking or inactivity, that may be keeping the person stuck in the depressive cycle. An advantage of formulating a recent situation is that the client is likely to have good recall of the event, and so may be able to give more accurate descriptions of their responses.

This way of formulating is based on a *biopsychosocial* model as it takes into account, and incorporates, biological or physiological factors, psychological aspects such as the client's understanding or beliefs, and environmental factors. By considering possible links between the five areas we can begin to understand how the person's depressed mood may be triggered and sustained.

Depression can be understood in general as being maintained by a reduction in positive experiences, and an increase in negative experiences. Low mood is associated with negative thinking, and a drop in activity levels and social contact. As a consequence, the person has little opportunity for positive experiences such as enjoying time with friends, or gaining a sense of achievement from carrying out tasks. By not engaging in such activities the person's self worth suffers and they have more time to focus on their negative thoughts, which can then perpetuate low mood. Long periods of inactivity also increase feelings of lethargy, which can then feed into beliefs about not having enough energy to do anything or change their situation. Consequently, the person gets stuck in a negative cycle from which they feel it is impossible to escape. This can result in high levels of hopelessness and a belief that nothing will ever change.

To further understand how the five areas link to each other, it may be useful to study some of the possible maintenance processes for Alison. An example of a formulation, based on a recent event, is illustrated in Figure 7.1.

Alison's most recent low mood was triggered when she woke up thinking about not having attended her daughter's school assembly on the previous day. As a result she had the thought 'I'm a terrible mother'. This led to feelings of guilt, sadness and despair, which reduced her motivation to face the world. Consequently she stayed in bed, and

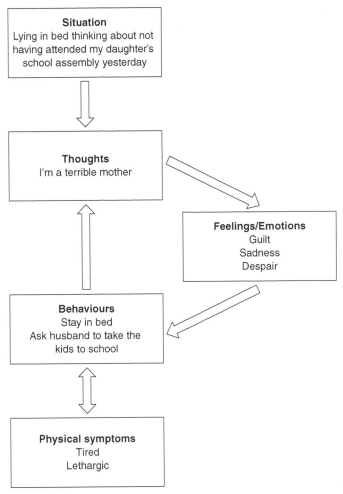

Figure 7.1   Example of a maintenance cycle for Alison (1)

asked her husband to take the children to school. This resulted in her feeling more tired, and staying in bed for longer, which reinforced her belief about being a bad mother. This increased her negative emotions, and so maintained her low mood.

Let us consider another example. Alison struggles to concentrate at work, which leads to thoughts that she will make a mistake. This causes her to feel anxious, and results in her checking information repeatedly. An upshot of this is that she finds it even more difficult to concentrate, thus reinforcing her negative thought that she will make a mistake, and keeps her trapped in a cycle of anxiety and low mood (see Figure 7.2).

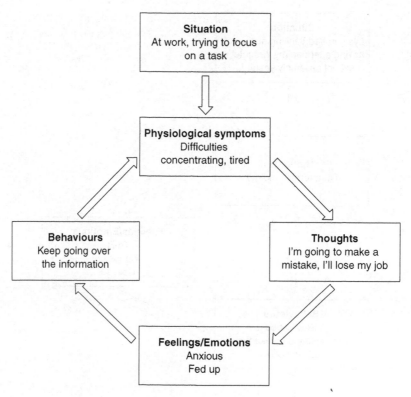

Figure 7.2   Example of a maintenance cycle for Alison (2)

The idea of maintenance cycles is key to the CBT model, and helps us to understand why low mood may persist long after the original triggering event has been forgotten. Mapping out these cycles is usually the starting point for treatment, as will be explored further in the following chapter.

Differentiating between normal low mood and major depression

As described earlier, the experience people have when they are depressed is fundamentally no different to how anyone might feel when they are down, fed up or demotivated. In this sense, depression can be seen as being somewhere on a continuum. At one end lies everyday, normal experience. At the other is severe depression where the person feels unable to function at all, and experiences urges to end their life. So, how can we differentiate between a person who is simply feeling fed up and someone who might be said to be suffering from clinical depression? Duration and severity are key factors to take into account here, and these will be considered further below.

Duration

Duration most obviously refers to the length of time that the person has experienced the depressive symptoms. Usually the symptoms need to have been present for at least two weeks for a formal diagnosis of depression to be made. In addition, it is important to consider the constancy or endurance of the symptoms, in particular low mood. To understand this, let us first explore what might be thought of as normal variations in mood states. As part of our everyday experience it is likely that we will all feel fed up or miserable from time to time. These feelings tend to lift naturally or something may happen to make us feel better. A person's mood tends to vary throughout the day, making it almost impossible to maintain one emotional state. Consider, for example, a positive emotion such as happiness. While it may be desirable to prolong this feeling for as long as possible, our moods shift over time and unfortunately the emotion will eventually fade. The flip side of the coin is that unpleasant emotions such as anxiety and anger also tend to ebb away, as they too cannot be sustained indefinitely. Furthermore, emotions are usually influenced by whatever else might be happening around you. So, for example, anger may diminish once an apology has been received, fear may dissipate once a threat is removed. This is the normal state of affairs. However, when people are depressed, the opposite is true. Low mood becomes a constant feature of the person's experience and they can seem immune to positive events. People describe waking up feeling depressed and remaining so throughout the day. If occasionally there is a brief improvement in mood in response to something positive happening, this does not last and the person's mood swiftly drops again. Thus, when assessing for depression it is important to consider both the persistence of the symptoms as well as their duration.

Severity

Another central indicator is the severity of the symptoms. This is usually determined by the extent to which the person's symptoms interfere with their ability to function at previously 'normal' levels. In more severe cases of depression a person may feel incapable of carrying out any of their usual activities, even the most basic, such as washing, dressing and eating. In milder cases, a person may appear on the surface to be functioning fairly normally and be able to go to work, despite having less motivation and finding it more difficult than usual to focus on tasks. Routine activities may be carried out but take more effort. Those that are less necessary, such as exercising and socialising, may be avoided. Obviously, judgements will vary over what is considered a normal level of activity. Thus, it is important to establish for each individual the extent to which his or her life has been affected. Useful questions might include 'What things have you stopped doing, or are you doing less of, since you began to experience low mood?' or 'Which activities have become more difficult to carry out?' This will help the practitioner to ascertain how much the person's functioning has been negatively affected and aid judgements regarding the level of severity.

Determining whether a person's experience of depression falls into the category of mild, moderate or severe is particularly important for LICBT practitioners. Treatment should be targeted at those people with mild to moderate depression, and those clients with more severe symptoms will need to be stepped up for a more intensive approach. In practice, the distinction is not always clear-cut and will be guided by the number, type and severity level of the symptoms. Knowledge of formal diagnostic criteria and the use of screening tools will also aid this process. These are discussed further below.

Formal diagnosis

The process of making a formal diagnosis of depression necessitates careful consultation of well-established, standardised classification systems, such as the *Diagnostic and Statistical Manual of Mental Disorders* (*DSM-IV-TR*) (APA, 2000). Whether or not practitioners have a formal role in making diagnoses, it helps to be aware of the agreed criteria in order to help guide treatment decisions (see Chapter 3). DSM-IV-TR lists a number of symptoms as needing to be present for a diagnosis of depression to be made. Briefly, these are: depressed mood; reduced interest or pleasure in most or all activities; significant weight loss or weight gain; insomnia or hypersomnia; agitation or slowing down; fatigue; feelings of worthlessness or excessive guilt; difficulties with concentration; and recurrent thoughts of death or suicidal ideation. At least five of these symptoms need to have been present for a minimum of two weeks, and one of these should be depressed mood or reduced interest/pleasure (APA, 2000).

One method for remembering the main diagnostic criteria is to use the mnemonic MISPLACED, which stands for:

- depressed **M**ood
- loss of **I**nterest/pleasure
- disturbed **S**leep
- un**P**lanned weight loss or weight gain
- **L**ack of self worth/guilt
- **A**gitation or retardation
- **C**oncentration difficulties
- loss of **E**nergy
- thoughts of **D**eath/suicidal ideation

Exercise 7.3   Using diagnostic criteria

Consider the case of Alison presented at the beginning of the chapter. In order to make a formal diagnosis, a full assessment would need to be carried out. However, we already have some indication of the symptoms Alison is experiencing. Which of these might fit with the formal criteria for a diagnosis of major depression? Consult the *DSM-IV-TR* and become familiar with the full range of criteria needed to make a diagnosis of major depressive episode.

Screening tools

Screening tools are a useful aid in the assessment process (see Chapter 3). Traditionally, measures such as the Beck Depression Inventory II (Beck, Steer, & Brown, 1996) and the Hamilton Rating Scale (Hamilton, 1960) have been used in the assessment of depression. However, within briefer treatments such as LICBT, it may be more efficient to use shorter instruments. These can be quicker and easier to administer, and lend themselves more readily to weekly reviews and telephone consultations. The Patient Health Questionnaire (PHQ-9) is one such instrument, and its brevity is thought to be a major advantage in enabling frequent and regular administration (Kroenke et al., 2001). It can be used both at the beginning of treatment in assessing the client's symptoms, and throughout, as a way of checking client progress.

Differential diagnosis

When making a diagnosis it is important to ensure that the symptoms present are not better explained by an alternative category of diagnosis. This is a process known as *differential diagnosis* and clear guidance around this is usually provided within diagnostic classification systems (for example, *DSM-IV-TR*; APA, 2000). Low mood may be symptomatic of a number of other conditions or disorders, thus it is important to rule these out. The main areas to consider are discussed below.

Medical conditions

Depressive type symptoms are often a feature of certain medical conditions such as diabetes, stroke, hyperthyroidism and cancer, thus it is important that where such conditions may be present, the symptoms are not better accounted for by these. Alternatively the experience of having a medical condition may lead to depressed mood, in which case this would generally result in a different diagnosis such as *mood disorder owing to a general medical condition* (APA, 2000). In older adults there may be particular difficulties in differentiating between depression and dementia, both of which frequently present in this age group (Maynard, 2003) and result in similar symptoms such as difficulties with memory and concentration (Wright & Persad, 2007). In addition, dementia and depression are often co-morbid. Where there are underlying medical conditions, accurate diagnosis is crucial as this has implications for providing appropriate treatment.

Substance misuse

Excessive use of alcohol or illicit drugs tends to have a significant impact on a person's mood and physiology. Dependency on such substances can result in similar symptoms to those experienced within depression. In these cases it is more appropriate to refer the person for treatment of substance misuse.

Other mood disorders

Perhaps a more difficult issue is distinguishing major depression from other types of mood and anxiety disorders. Table 7.2 outlines other mood disorders where low mood is a key symptom.

- Depression is considered *subthreshold* when a person is experiencing low mood or diminished interest, but their symptoms do not meet the full diagnostic criteria for major depression. *Dysthymia* also refers to a milder form of depression, but one that has endured for at least two years. The only distinction between subthreshold depression and dysthymia appears to be the length of duration of symptoms. Hence within NICE guidance, dysthymia is referred to as *persistent subthreshold depressive symptoms* (NICE, 2009b) and LICBT is recommended as a treatment. This reflects an increased recognition of the suffering caused by this condition, its relatively common occurrence and the risk that, if left untreated, its presence can increase vulnerability to developing major depression (NICE, 2009b).
- *Adjustment disorder with depressed mood* is diagnosed when the person experiences depressive symptoms as the result of a stressful life event occurring within the previous three months, but these are not sufficient to warrant a diagnosis of major depression (APA, 2000). This does not include bereavement, which is considered separately. LICBT is not usually suggested for this disorder, but if the symptoms last beyond six months it may be worth considering whether the person is developing major depression or another mental disorder.

Table 7.2   Differentiating depression from other mood disorders

Condition/disorder	Description
Subthreshold depression	Depression is considered subthreshold when a person is experiencing low mood or diminished interest, but their symptoms do not meet the full diagnostic criteria for major depression. It is thought to be more common in those with a history of major depression. While not classified as a disorder within current diagnostic systems, it may be a vulnerability factor for later development of depression.
Dysthymia	A milder form of depression, but much longer lasting. A diagnosis requires that sufferers experience mild symptoms of depression for most of the day, or on most days, over a period of two years. As there seems to be little evidence that dysthymia differs from subthreshold depression other than in duration, within NICE guidelines dysthymia is referred to as *persistent subthreshold depressive symptoms*. People experiencing dysthymia have been found to have a much higher chance of going on to experience major depression. It may therefore be important to offer some form of treatment as a preventative measure (NICE, 2009b).
Adjustment disorder with depression	This diagnosis may be given when a person has experienced a stressful life event that results in symptoms of depression, but these are not sufficient to meet criteria for major depression.
Bipolar disorder	This is characterised by periods of mania alternating with episodes of low mood. Manic episodes involve extremely high levels of energy and on occasion can lead to psychotic symptoms. A small proportion of those with major depression may go on to develop bipolar disorder. Low intensity interventions are not recommended for the treatment of this disorder (NICE, 2009b).

Anxiety and depression

Distinguishing depression and anxiety can be challenging as both regularly occur together (Brown, Campbell, Lehman, Grisham, & Mancill, 2001), and in practice the boundaries between them are often blurred (Blackburn & Davidson, 1996). When depression is accompanied by anxiety, determining which symptoms to treat is a key issue. To guide the practitioner, it is useful to consider the following questions.

- Is there an existing anxiety disorder, which preceded the depression?
  Where the person has an existing anxiety disorder, and comorbid major depression or depressive symptoms, it is important to consider treating the anxiety disorder first. There is evidence that some anxiety disorders, such as generalised anxiety disorder and social anxiety disorder, tend to precede the onset of major depression and appear to increase the person's susceptibility to developing depression (Belzer & Schneier, 2004). It is not difficult to understand why a person with an anxiety disorder may become depressed. The experience of being in a constant state of anxiety can be both

distressing and exhausting. In order to prevent high levels of anxiety, the person may avoid many situations. This can place great restrictions on their ability to function normally, for example not going out because of fears of having a panic attack, or shunning social situations to avoid the possibility of making a fool of oneself. The difficulties in overcoming anxiety can also lead to a sense of despondency or hopelessness, which can then result in low mood. Thus, the depressive symptoms may be secondary to the original anxiety disorder. In such cases, successful treatment of the anxiety is most likely to result in a reduction of the depressive symptoms.

- Are the anxiety symptoms part of the depressive disorder?
  It is very common for people with major depression to experience symptoms of anxiety without these symptoms being sufficient to warrant a diagnosis of anxiety disorder. Consider for example Alison, who was presented earlier. Alison experiences anxiety as the result of struggling to concentrate at work. In addition, she feels anxious about letting her children down, putting too much onto her husband and because she has difficulties in getting to sleep at night. In such cases the anxiety symptoms may be most usefully regarded of as part of the depressive disorder. Thus, treating the depression is most likely to result in a reduction of the anxiety symptoms.

- Is low mood affecting the person's capacity to engage in treatment?
  Because of the debilitating effects of depression, even where the person has an existing anxiety disorder, having low mood may interfere with their capacity to engage in treatment. They may experience a lack of motivation, poor concentration or high levels of hopelessness. Within the LICBT model the client is expected to play an active role in their treatment. Unless the depressive symptoms are treated first, it may be difficult to engage the client, and successfully treat the anxiety disorder. In addition there may be issues of risk, in which case the priority should be to improve the client's mood and reduce hopelessness. In these situations it is likely to be important, at least initially, to target the symptoms of depression.

Bereavement

Finally, it is important to consider bereavement. Grief is a normal reaction to loss, and the grief process should be allowed to naturally run its course. However, when the symptoms persist longer than would be expected, it may be important to consider whether the person has developed major depression. In practice it is difficult to determine the normal duration of grief, as this is likely to vary from person to person. Formal diagnostic criteria would suggest at the very minimum, no less than two months (APA, 2000). It can also be useful to consider whether the depressive symptoms are limited to triggers related to the bereavement, such as memories of the person they have lost or significant events such as anniversaries. If so, it may be more appropriate to allow the grief process to take its course or, if necessary, direct the person to bereavement counselling.

Having considered how to recognise major depression and differentiate this from normal low mood and other disorders or conditions, it is important to consider some of the other factors that LICBT practitioners need to be aware of in the assessment and consequent treatment of depression, in particular the importance of early detection of depression, consideration of who may be most vulnerable to developing depression, risk assessment and relapse.

The importance of early detection of depression

Depression has been found to be a very common disorder. Indeed, it has been labelled the 'common cold of psychiatry' because of its extensive occurrence (Seligman, 1973). Globally it is considered to be one of the leading causes of disability (WHO, 2008b). Worldwide estimates suggest that between 4 and 10 per cent of people will suffer an episode of major depression in their lifetime, and between 2.5 and 5 per cent will experience dysthymia (NICE, 2009b). In the UK it is estimated that anywhere between 2.4 and 11.4 per cent of the population are suffering from depression, or mixed anxiety and depression, at any one point in time (NICE, 2009b; Singleton, Bumpstead, O'Brien, Lee, & Meltzer, 2001). Yet despite its widespread occurrence, evidence suggests that people are often reluctant to admit to feeling depressed (Meltzer, Bebbington, Brugha, Farrell, Jenkins, & Lewis, 2000). Moreover, in primary care services, where most people with depression initially present and are then managed, it is often under-diagnosed (Goldberg & Huxley, 1992; Kessler, Lloyd, Lewis, & Gray, 1999).

Given their role in treating mild to moderate mental health problems, LICBT practitioners are in a prime position to detect the early signs of depression and offer a timely intervention. Prompt access to treatment is a core principle of LICBT, with the aim being to help the person to make changes in the initial stages before difficulties become more entrenched and harder to shift. This is particularly important because of the disabling nature of depression and the cumulative negative impact that it can have upon the individual when not treated early. A chronic course of depression can lead to multiple losses in areas such as employment and social support. This can result in dependency upon welfare benefits and increasing levels of isolation, which can further impact upon the individual's self-esteem, thus maintaining and possibly deepening the depression.

Who is most at risk of developing a depressive disorder?

When assessing for depression, there are a number of factors to be aware of that may increase a person's chances of developing depression. These tend to fall into four categories: recent stressful life events, demographic factors (in particular gender), difficult life history and personality influences (for example, Fava & Kendler, 2000). These are explored further below.

Recent life events

Significant life events such as divorce, job loss and health problems are common causes of stress and can trigger depressive episodes. However, it is clear that not everyone who experiences a stressful episode will go on to develop depression. As mentioned previously, many people may simply need time to adjust or to grieve a significant loss. It is likely that a combination of factors will determine who goes on to experience depression following such an event, and that vulnerability factors play a part in this.

Demographic

Studies consistently indicate that women are almost twice as likely as men to experience depression (Waraich, Goldner, Somers, & Hsu, 2004). Some researchers have highlighted factors such as relatively higher levels of poverty, inequality and discrimination to explain this (for example, Belle & Doucet, 2003). There is also some indication that women are more ready to seek help than men (Verhaak, 1995).

Amongst older people the increased incidence of factors such as physical ill health, disability and social isolation may increase their risk of experiencing depression. Indeed, it is thought to be the most common mental illness to occur in later life and yet often goes undetected and untreated (Anderson, 2001). This may be partly due to older people under-reporting symptoms such as dysphoria (Gallo, Anthony, & Bengt, 1994). There is also some suggestion that they may have less familiarity with the concept of psychotherapy (Knight & Poon, 2008) and a lack of knowledge about how to access services (Robb, Haley, Becker, Polivka, & Chwa, 2003; Segal, Coolidge, Mincic, & O'Riley, 2005).

Limited evidence exists to suggest that depression is more common amongst people from some minority ethnic backgrounds (for example, Bhui, Bhugra, Goldberg, Sauer, & Tylee, 2004), but findings vary. Culture is sometimes thought to play a part in how people present to mental health services. For example, it may be more acceptable to present physical, rather than psychological, symptoms to others (see Chapter 11 for further discussion). Research also indicates that depression may be under-diagnosed in those from a minority ethnic background, and they may be less likely to be offered a talking therapy (NICE, 2009b).

General socio-economic factors such as unemployment, poverty, belonging to a lower social class and lack of educational qualifications also appear to increase the risk of developing depression (NICE, 2009b).

Life history

Some research indicates that a link may exist between problems in childhood, such as physical or sexual abuse, or marital discord between parents, and the later development of depression (Fava & Kendler, 2000). In LICBT, these areas are generally not explored in any great detail. It is likely to be more appropriate to explore these factors where depression is more severe or entrenched, or low intensity treatment has not been successful. In these cases a more intensive treatment, undertaken on a higher step within the stepped care model, may be a more suitable approach.

Personality factors

Finally, it is thought that personality traits such as 'neuroticism' may be associated with higher levels of depression (Fava & Kendler, 2000). Hans Eysenck, a psychologist who wrote extensively in the field of personality, described the 'neurotic individual' as someone who is highly susceptible to negative emotional states, and experiences significant difficulties in dealing with stressful situations (Eysenck, 1947). Again this is an area that is likely to be beyond the remit of LICBT and may be more suitable for exploration within more intensive modes of therapy.

In summary, there are likely to be a combination of factors that make a person more susceptible to depression. Having a broad awareness of these can help the practitioner to pick up on relevant cues, although some of these may be more appropriately explored in high intensity treatment.

Risk

Risk is a particularly important area to explore for clients who present with depression. The high levels of misery and despair experienced in this disorder mean that suicidal ideation is commonplace, and suicide may be seen as a means to escape an intolerable situation (Beck et al., 1979). Those suffering with depression have been found to be at least four times more likely than the general population to commit suicide (NICE,

2009b). High levels of hopelessness in particular, appear to significantly increase the risk of suicidal behaviour (Beck, Kovacs, & Weissman, 1975; Beck, Steer, Kovacs, & Garrison, 1985).

Risk tends to increase with severity of symptoms, and where there are co-morbid mental or physical health problems (APA, 2003). However, those with mild depression or dysthymia are also vulnerable. Thus regular monitoring is crucial, and a risk management plan needs to be in place where risk is a significant issue (see Chapter 6). Practitioners also need to ensure that they pay adequate attention to risk issues where they have less direct contact with the client, for example where sessions are less frequent or conducted in different modalities, such as by telephone, in groups or using computerised CBT.

Regular case management supervision should be used to monitor any clients with issues of risk (see Chapter 13). When working at a low intensity level, it is usual to refer on those with moderate to high levels of risk. However, in doing so, it is important not to leave the person unsupported while they are waiting to be seen by another service. It is vital to provide interim support or ensure the person has ready access to other reliable sources of help.

Relapse

While depression is often characterised as a time-limited disorder with full recovery occurring after four to six months, for many people the symptoms can persist for much longer (NICE, 2009b). Studies show that at least half of those who have had an episode of depression will go on to have another, and those who relapse are even more vulnerable to further depressive episodes (Kupfer, 1991). Low intensity treatments should be targeted at those experiencing a first episode of mild to moderate depression. Those with more chronic depression will need to be stepped up to a more intensive therapy.

Given the high frequency of relapse in depression, it is essential to prepare clients for possible setbacks following recovery. In particular, clients are encouraged to consider strategies that they have found useful and can continue to apply to manage difficulties in the future. This is explored in more detail in the next chapter, which outlines LICBT treatments for depression.

Conclusion

The aim of this chapter was to provide a clear explanation of what is meant by the term depression. The reader should now be in a better position to conduct an effective assessment of those presenting with depressive symptoms, and to understand common processes in the maintenance of depression. This is an important starting point for determining which methods are likely to be effective in treatment.

Summary

- Depression is a common disorder.
- The particular area of focus for LICBT practitioners is in assessment and treatment of mild to moderate depression.
- Maintenance cycles are a helpful way of understanding why a person may get stuck in a depressive cycle.
- In the process of making a diagnosis it is important to ensure that symptoms are not better accounted for by an alternative diagnosis.
- When depression is accompanied by anxiety, the practitioner needs to make a careful assessment of which symptoms to treat first.
- Risk assessment and careful monitoring are vital as suicidal ideation is commonplace in depression.
- Studies show that relapse rates are high in depression, thus relapse prevention strategies need to be built into treatment.

Further reading and activities

Consider what you have learnt from this chapter. Which key points stood out for you? Make a list of significant issues that it will be helpful to remember when assessing clients with depression. If there are any areas of confusion, or if this chapter has raised particular questions for you, it may be helpful to discuss these further with a supervisor or tutor.

In order to build on what you have learnt so far, a number of texts are recommended for further reading. Williams and Chellingsworth (2010) provide a useful guide to formulation, while Part One of Williams's (2009) self-help guide illustrates how to orientate the client to understanding their own symptoms of depression. To get an insider's view of depression, it may be useful to read: *I had a black dog* (Johnstone, 2007). This provides a simple yet powerful insight into a former sufferer's experience of depression, and may be useful reading for clients. For further background on the CBT model Westbrook et al. (2011) is invaluable. Finally, it is recommended that you become familiar with the current NICE guidelines for depression.

8

Treatment of Depression

Theresa Marrinan

Learning objectives

- To acquire knowledge of the key treatment strategies for depression within the LICBT approach.
- To have an awareness of the evidence base for low intensity treatments of depression.
- To gain an understanding of how to implement treatment strategies and manage some of the difficulties that can arise in the process.
- To be able to use a relapse prevention approach to maintain improvements and manage possible setbacks.

Introduction

This chapter provides an outline of LICBT treatments for depression. It builds on Chapter 7, in which we looked at how to recognise depression and understand how maintenance processes can lead a person to become trapped in a depressive cycle. Readers will be guided to the main strategies used to treat depression within the LICBT approach, including a brief review of the evidence base. The case example of Alison, who was presented in Chapter 7, will be used again in this chapter as a means of illustrating how these strategies may be implemented. The chapter will finish by guiding the practitioner in how to set up a relapse prevention plan with clients to help maintain improvements and manage setbacks.

Overview of LICBT for depression

As the evidence base for CBT has grown, there has been a move towards developing briefer treatments for common mental health problems. As a result, treatment methods are becoming less complex, allowing many more practitioners to be trained in these approaches. This has been accompanied by the development of new methods of delivery, such as guided self-help and computerised packages. The result has been to pave the way for the wider dissemination of psychological therapies, so enabling effective treatments for depression to be made accessible to growing numbers of people. This is supported by large reviews of the research, which have shown that guided self-help, based on CBT principles, is effective in the treatment of mild to moderate depression (Anderson et al., 2005; Gellatly et al., 2007).

LICBT for depression is a brief treatment, typically delivered in six to eight sessions of 30 minutes duration, over the course of 10–12 weeks. It is targeted at people with mild to moderate levels of depression, using a guided self-help approach. Many self-help materials for depression exist. These include books (for example, Brosan & Hogan, 2007; Gilbert, 2009; Greenberger & Padesky, 1995; Williams, 2009), worksheets available from the internet (for example, Get Self Help, www.getselfhelp.co.uk, and the Centre for Clinical Interventions (CCI), www.cci.health.wa.gov.au), electronic packages, known as computerised CBT (for example, Beating the Blues, MoodGYM), and interactive internet interventions (for example, Living Life to the Full Interactive, www.llttfi.com).

In this chapter the reader will be signposted to a small sample of the many self-help materials currently available for the treatment of depression, in order to illustrate how these can be used in treatment. However, it is important that practitioners become proficient themselves at choosing appropriate materials (see Chapter 2 for further guidance).

An essential aspect of increasing access to treatment has been to provide clients with more choice over how treatment is delivered. Attending appointments in clinics can often be difficult for those experiencing depression because of the very symptoms that are part of the disorder, such as reduced motivation and low energy levels. Unfortunately, non-attendance often leads to assumptions about the client's supposed lack of incentive to change. Factors that can reduce attendance, such as the client's symptoms or fear of being stigmatised, are not always fully considered. Within the LICBT approach, there is an attempt to address this by providing treatments in different modalities, for example by telephone or email. This can be helpful for depressed clients in particular, who may find the effort involved in travelling to clinics prohibitive. The sections below outline the key tasks of assessment and principal treatment strategies employed within the LICBT approach for depression.

Assessment

The main focus of the assessment session will be to build up a clear picture of the problem, with an exploration of symptoms, triggers and possible maintaining factors. The assessment session also provides an opportunity to discuss the client's expectations, identify goals and treatment options, and make some shared decisions about how treatment will be delivered (see Chapter 5). Key aspects of the assessment session will be considered in further detail below.

Formulation

In the process of gathering information regarding the client's difficulties, a key function is to gain an initial understanding of the client's symptoms and how these are being maintained. This will involve an exploration of triggers, symptoms and the client's responses. In order to do this the practitioner should ask the client to identify a recent example of when they were experiencing low mood. Questions to elicit this might include the following:

- 'Can you think back to the last time you felt very low – what were you doing at that point?'
- 'What kinds of things were going through your mind?'
- 'What were you feeling?'
- 'What physical sensations were you experiencing?'
- 'Was there anything you were avoiding doing?'
- 'What did you do to make yourself feel better?'
- 'How did you feel after doing that?'

In gathering this information, the practitioner can build an initial formulation with the client, to help them begin to understand how their symptoms are being maintained or reinforced. Figure 8.1 illustrates a simple formulation constructed with Alison in her first session, to enable her to see possible links between symptoms. This process begins during the assessment phase and continues throughout treatment as further information emerges.

Chapter 7 shows some other examples of maintenance cycles that would have been developed with Alison during the course of treatment. Self-help materials (for example,

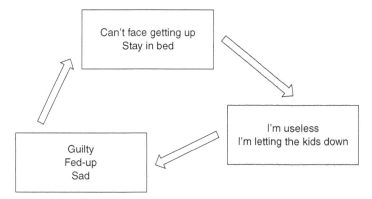

Figure 8.1   Simple maintenance cycle

Williams, 2009) often provide explanations of how these maintenance cycles occur, and a typical homework task from the assessment session or first treatment session will be to identify some more examples. This will help the clients to become familiar with their own patterns of response to low mood.

Exercise 8.1   Helping clients to formulate using self-help materials

Review some of the self-help materials available for depression, for example:

- Overcoming depression (Williams, 2009);
- CCI (Back from the Bluez workbook), available at: www.cci.health.wa.gov.au;
- Northumberland Tyne and Wear NHS Trust Self-help leaflets (*Depression and low mood*), available at: www.ntw.nhs.uk/pic/selfhelp

Choose one or two and consider how you might use them to help a client to understand their symptoms and map out a formulation.

Problem statement

Towards the end of the assessment session a problem statement should be generated, which captures the main elements of the person's difficulty. This will include triggers, symptoms and the impact of the problem (see Chapter 3). Below is an example problem statement for Alison:

> For the past six weeks I have been feeling down most days. I can't concentrate at work, and I'm too tired to look after the kids or spend time with my husband. I think I'm a terrible mum and wife and I'm scared that I'll never feel any better.

Some clients may be able to identify a clear event that triggered their depression, such as the break-up of a relationship or loss of employment. For others they may have experienced a gradual onset, with no obvious triggering event. In these circumstances, it may be helpful instead to include the duration of the problem.

Goal setting

A key task of the assessment process is to set some goals (see Chapter 5 for guidance around goal setting). Alison's overall goals for treatment have been provided as an example, see below:

- 'to improve my mood';
- 'to have more time for myself';
- 'to have a better relationship with my husband';
- 'to explore options for changing my job'.

During the treatment phase, general goals can be broken down further and specified more concretely. For example, a goal such as: 'to have a better relationship with my husband' might involve three components:

- 'to go out once a week with my husband';
- 'to share the household tasks more equally';
- 'to spend 30 minutes each day catching up with my husband, when the children have gone to bed'.

Orientation to treatment

The final task of the assessment session is to orientate the client toward the LICBT model, clarifying what treatment is likely to involve and discussing the active role that clients are expected to play. It may be useful to offer a sample of self-help materials (for example, Williams, 2009), or provide a short demonstration of computerised

CBT, to aid the client in making decisions about how treatment might be delivered (Martinez & Williams, 2010). Materials or links to websites that explain depression can be provided in the initial assessment and discussed further in the following session (for example, Brosan & Hogan, 2007; CCI – Back from the Bluez module; Williams, 2009). Clients can also be encouraged to consider practicalities such as setting up a file in which to keep materials, or arranging how telephone calls will be organised.

Treatment strategies

In this section there will be an outline of four low intensity treatments for mild to moderate depression, which are recommended by the National Institute for Health and Clinical Excellence (NICE, 2009b). These should be delivered using a guided self-help approach, and are listed below:

- behavioural activation;
- cognitive strategies;
- problem solving;
- sleep hygiene.

Deciding which of the strategies to implement will depend upon factors such as client choice, goals for treatment and decisions about which symptoms are to be targeted. There are various models for structuring treatment. Clients may be guided to systematically work through a given self-help package, or use components from different resources as part of an individualised package (see Williams & Morrison, 2010, for further discussion). The various treatment strategies and techniques will be discussed in detail below.

Behavioural activation

Typical symptoms of depression, such as poor motivation, lack of energy and feelings of hopelessness, usually result in withdrawal from social contact, or avoidance of tasks that are important for normal functioning. One negative consequence is that the person has less opportunity for pleasant or rewarding experiences. Referring back to Alison, for example, we can see that, when she feels low, she tends to stay in bed. Consider how this reduces opportunities to experience pleasant events, such as meeting up with friends or engaging in hobbies. People with depression also find it difficult to manage routine or necessary tasks such as going to work, shopping or paying bills, as these activities may be experienced as unrewarding or aversive. In Alison's case, she describes feeling constantly tired, with the result that she has to force herself to go into work. Once there, she experiences anxiety about getting things wrong as she struggles with her concentration. On her days off, following a restless night's sleep, she finds it difficult to summon the energy to get her children ready for school or carry out household tasks. In these circumstances it may seem easier to go back to bed. This may provide short-term relief, but as a result she may continue to feel tired or listless, and it is also likely to maintain or increase her sense of hopelessness. A further consequence of this avoidance is that secondary problems can be created as tasks build up, with the effect that life becomes even more overwhelming and difficult to manage.

Behavioural activation (BA) is a method of helping the person to become more active and tackle avoidance in a carefully structured way that is not overwhelming (Jacobson, Martell, & Dimidjian, 2001). This follows in the tradition of other behavioural methods such as *activity scheduling* – a means of planning and engaging in enjoyable or rewarding activities (Beck et al., 1979). There are six steps involved in setting up BA which are described in turn below.

1   Present a rationale

Suggesting to a client that they need to get more active, without providing a clear rationale, is likely to be ineffective and at worst may increase negative beliefs about failing. In any case, there is a good likelihood that someone in the person's support network has already made such a suggestion without this leading to significant change. Thus, it is important to acknowledge the client's difficulties and provide reassurance that reduced activity is a common feature of depression. Offering materials with case examples can be helpful to illustrate this (for example, Williams, 2009). However, the client also needs to understand how to break this cycle of inactivity. It is therefore essential to provide information that helps the client to understand that, contrary to what they may believe, the way to lift energy levels when they are depressed is to increase activity rather than rest. Referring back to the client's formulation can help to demonstrate how doing less tends to reinforce tiredness and can keep the focus on negative thinking. Explaining the model in this way provides an opportunity to engage the client more actively. The transcript below demonstrates how the practitioner introduced BA to Alison.

> *Practitioner:*   So Alison, it sounds as though it's very difficult to get going in the morning?
>
> *Client:*   I just can't seem to get myself out of bed … or do anything. I tell myself I should but I just can't seem to do it.

Practitioner:	It sounds like you want to but it's quite an effort? Can I ask what would you be doing if you did manage to get up?
Client:	Well … I'd have to get the children ready and then take them to school … then see all the other mothers …
Practitioner:	What would that be like?
Client:	It sounds really lazy but it's just so much effort – and then the thought of facing people … it's really hard.
Practitioner:	It sounds as though you think you should be able to do these things but the effort feels overwhelming. When you looked at the information I gave you about depression did you find any other examples where people find it difficult to get going when they're feeling low?
Client:	I think there was a man who had stopped working because he felt so bad?
Practitioner:	That's right, it's very common for people to struggle to get active when they feel very low – in fact it's one of the key aspects of depression. What do you make of that?
Client:	So it's not just me? But I don't want to be like this forever … I hate how it makes me feel.
Practitioner:	How does it make you feel?
Client:	Useless … like a neglectful mother, like my kids think I don't care about them.
Practitioner:	It sounds as though it's very difficult to get up in the morning and perhaps easier to stay in bed so that you don't have to do the things that take a lot of effort at the moment. But in the long run, it seems like it makes you feel just as bad to stay in bed?
Client:	I guess so.
Practitioner:	If you could get going again would that be something you would want to aim for?
Client:	I'd like to, but I have tried and it's so hard.
Practitioner:	I wonder if we need to break down the activities to make them more manageable. When you've been experiencing low mood for a while it can take an effort to get going again and we may need to think about building that up slowly. However, what we do know is that a person's mood tends to improve when they get more active and it can help them feel more in control of their life. What do you think?
Client:	Well … I would like to get out of this rut.
Practitioner:	Perhaps we could start by thinking about different types of activities that you used to do before you became depressed?

2 Identify some routine, necessary and pleasurable activities

Once the client has agreed to try the approach they can be guided to identify activities they used to do before becoming depressed. Three types of activities are targeted: *routine, necessary* and those carried out for *pleasure* (Richards, 2010a). These are described below.

- *Routine activities* are those we do on a daily or frequent basis, for example self-care and household tasks. Disruptions to such routines are thought to contribute to low mood (Jacobson et al., 2001).
- *Necessary activities* are those essential to effective functioning in life, for instance working, studying or paying bills. Carrying out such activities can also provide us with a sense of mastery or achievement, which is important for self-esteem. When such activities are avoided, problems may build up.
- *Pleasurable activities* are those that afford us enjoyment, for example hobbies, social events, relaxation and exercise. Avoidance of such activities reduces the potential to experience positive events and emotions.

Worksheets can be given out to guide clients with this, such as that provided in Figure 8.2, which includes Alison's list of activities.

List of activities		
List some of the activities you used to engage in regularly before you started experiencing low mood or alternatively some new ones that you would like to introduce into your life		
Routine For example: cleaning the house, shopping, cooking meals	**Pleasurable** For example: hobbies, social events, relaxation, exercise	**Necessary** For example: paying bills, maintaining the car
Have a shower Wash dishes Vacuum Ironing Go shopping Take the children to school Sort out packed lunches Cook a meal Do the washing Do the garden Go jogging	Go to the cinema with my husband Meet friend for a coffee Read a book Go to yoga class Go for a cycle ride with husband and children Go on holiday	Go to work Put the car in for a service Buy the children's sports kits Sort out payment for my daughter's dance class Look for a new job

Figure 8.2   List of routine, pleasurable and necessary activities

---

Exercise 8.2   Drawing up a list of activities

Make a list of activities that you have carried out over two or three days in the past week. Group these into routine, pleasurable and necessary. Did you have any difficulty in doing this? If so, what made this a challenging task?

Sometimes clients find it difficult to differentiate between routine and necessary activities (Richards, 2010a). This distinction is not crucial as long as there appears to be a balance across the three types. Where clients have had low mood for a long period of time, they may find it difficult to identify pleasurable activities. In these circumstances it may be necessary to help them to generate new ones. Self-help materials often provide examples of these (for example, CCI – Back from the Bluez workbook). Likewise, clients who have become depressed as the result of a medical condition may need to make lifestyle adjustments and consider new types of activities.

3   Devise a hierarchy of activities

The next step is to organise the listed activities into a hierarchy, from the least to the most difficult. The aim is to help the client take a graded approach to reintroducing activities, so preventing them from feeling overwhelmed by trying to do too much too soon. However, sometimes clients may also need to prioritise certain tasks that require immediate attention, such as paying bills. Figure 8.3 shows Alison's hierarchy.

Hierarchy of activities List your activities in order of difficulty. Include some pleasurable, routine and necessary tasks in each box	
Least difficult	Have a shower Wash dishes Go shopping Cook a meal Sort out packed lunches Do the washing Meet friend for a coffee Go to work

(Continued)

Figure 8.3   *(Continued)*

Medium difficulty	Ironing
	Do the garden
	Read a book
	Go to yoga class
	Put the car in for a service
	Buy the children's sports kits
	Sort out payment for daughter's dance class
Most difficult	Go jogging
	Take the children to school
	Vacuum
	Go to the cinema my with husband
	Go for a cycle ride with my husband and children
	Go on holiday
	Look for a new job

Figure 8.3   Hierarchy of activities

4   Plan some routine, necessary and pleasurable activities

After grouping the activities into a hierarchy, the client can use an *Activity Diary* to record those that they are planning to do during the week ahead. Most people benefit from engaging in a range of activities and their quality of life may suffer if this is restricted. Thus, clients should be encouraged to draw up a mixture of routine, necessary and pleasurable tasks. When planning activities, it is also important to try to make these manageable and realistic, breaking down larger tasks into smaller ones. The key is to set small discrete tasks which can be comfortably achieved. Figure 8.4 shows an example of Alison's activity diary with a plan of her activities for the week ahead.

5   Carry out the planned activities

The next step is to carry out the activities. It can be helpful for practitioners to warn clients that it may not be possible to achieve all of the planned activities and to build some flexibility into their homework. This can prevent the client from becoming discouraged if they are unable to stick rigidly to their plan.

Activity diary							
	Mon	**Tues**	**Wed**	**Thurs**	**Fri**	**Sat**	**Sun**
Morning	Have breakfast Wash dishes Shower	Have breakfast Wash dishes Shower	Work	Have breakfast Wash dishes Shower	Work		
Afternoon	Put some washing in	Spend 20 minutes weeding the garden	Work	Work	Go for a coffee with friend	Do shopping with husband	Go for Sunday lunch with family to mum's house
Evening	Cook a meal and eat with husband and children Watch TV	Cook a meal and eat with husband and children Watch TV			Cook a meal and eat with husband and children		

Figure 8.4   Activity diary

6   Review the outcome

Reviewing the diary with the client at the following appointment is essential. This serves to provide encouragement, facilitate learning and convey the message that the task is an important part of the treatment. It also allows the practitioner to check on the client's progress and help to problem solve any difficulties.

Use of self-help materials

Practitioners may wish to develop their own set of worksheets based on the protocol used in this chapter, or access existing resources. Self-help materials all vary slightly in their approach, each containing different amounts of detail, and some using a more problem-solving approach (for example, Williams, 2009). With experience, practitioners tend to discover which materials they prefer and those which suit different clients.

Common problems when implementing BA

There are a number of potential pit-falls when using this technique, which are discussed below.

- The client waits to feel less tired before carrying out the activities

Some clients may firmly hold onto the belief that they need to feel less tired or lethargic before they engage in BA (Jacobson et al., 2001). The practitioner should ensure they have explored this carefully with the client and clearly explained that in depression people usually feel more energetic once they start to engage in activities. Metaphors can be useful, for example the idea that getting active when depressed is similar to jump-starting a car with a flat battery (Stott, Mansell, Salkovskis, Lavender, & Cartwright-Hatton, 2010). If the client remains unsure, it may be useful to suggest taking a more experimental approach. One means of doing this is to encourage the client to try out a planned activity when feeling tired, and measure energy levels before and after.

- Goals are too ambitious

Another common problem involves having unrealistically high standards and setting overly ambitious goals (Westbrook et al., 2007). This can result in the client feeling overwhelmed and carrying out none of the planned activities. Setting vague goals also contributes to this, for example rather than 'do the housework' it is more useful to set a specific and manageable goal such as 'wash the dishes after breakfast' or 'spend 20 minutes ironing'. If necessary, these tasks can be broken down even further. The key here is just to get started. By encouraging the client to build up their activity levels gradually and set clear goals, there is a greater chance of success, which should result in increased motivation and optimism (see Box 8.1).

> ## Box 8.1 Difficulties in carrying out BA
>
> After some initial success at session two, Alison felt much more positive, and set some further goals of going jogging, doing the ironing and vacuuming, clearing the front garden and putting her car in for a service. However, at the third session she reported that she had not managed to do any of her planned activities. Her score on the PHQ-9 had increased and she reported that she was feeling hopeless about her depression ever lifting. Furthermore, she had almost cancelled the session because she did not want the LICBT practitioner to think she was not trying. The practitioner gently reassured Alison that reintroducing activities can be difficult initially, and asked how she

felt about the activities she had planned to do. Alison described feeling guilty about doing so little and realised she had been putting herself under pressure to 'get back to normal'. The practitioner explored whether it might be helpful to set more achievable goals in the short term. Alison agreed to this and they set a number of more specific goals for the week ahead. These were: to spend 20 minutes each morning carrying out one task in the house, such as vacuuming, or doing the laundry; to meet a friend for coffee once during the week; and to spend 30 minutes gardening. When she returned to the third session, Alison reported that she had completed her goals and was feeling more hopeful about the treatment. Her PHQ-9 score had also reduced and she felt able to increase her goals for the following week.

- Lack of pleasure

Some clients initially report experiencing a lack of pleasure when carrying out previously enjoyable activities, such as meeting a friend. Naturally this may lead the client to question the value of engaging in such activities. It can be helpful to warn clients that it sometimes takes a while to regain a sense of enjoyment, so persistence may be necessary (Westbrook et al., 2007). It is also important to establish that the client is choosing activities that have provided pleasure in the past, not simply those they believe *should* make them happy.

- Setting activities that are dependent on others or the weather

On occasion, activities are difficult to carry out because other factors get in the way. For instance, friends may be unavailable to meet up at specific times, or poor weather may make it difficult to do things outdoors. Where there is a likelihood of this occurring, it is useful to think ahead and plan some alternatives (Kinsella & Garland, 2008).

Evidence supporting the use of BA

Jacobson and colleagues developed BA as a stand-alone treatment after finding that clients who received pure BA had equivalent outcomes to those treated using full CBT, with improvements being maintained at six months (Jacobson et al., 1996). Systematic reviews of studies into activity scheduling and BA have since lent further support to this finding, suggesting that these methods can be as effective as standard CBT in treating depression, and superior to other types of treatment, such as supportive counselling and brief psychotherapy (Cuijpers, van Straten, & Warmerdam, 2007a; Ekers, Richards, & Gilbody, 2008). BA has also been shown to be effective when delivered as a brief treatment (Hopko et al., 2003). Reviewers have pointed to the possible advantages of offering BA over CBT, as it is a relatively straightforward intervention that does not require complex skills on either the part of the client or practitioner (Cuijpers et al., 2007a; Ekers et al., 2008). This suggests it may lend itself particularly well to low intensity interventions.

Cognitive strategies

Cognitive strategies are used in LICBT to help clients challenge negative thoughts and unhelpful patterns of thinking. Negative thinking is a key feature of depression. As described in Chapter 7, the CBT model of depression suggests that depressed people show cognitive biases or systematic errors in their thinking (Beck et al., 1979). These can be described as *unhelpful thinking styles*, which serve to maintain or worsen low mood. Table 8.1 shows types of cognitive biases, grouped into four main thinking styles (adapted from Westbrook et al., 2007). By identifying these styles of thinking, the client may be able to take a step back and begin to question some of their negative interpretations of events.

Table 8.1   Unhelpful thinking styles

Unhelpful thinking style	Examples
Self-reproach (a) Taking things personally (b) Self-criticism (c) Name calling	(a) My husband wouldn't be so tired if I was a better wife; my kids would do better at school if it weren't for me (b) I'm not a very good mother; I don't do my job well enough (c) I'm a loser, waste of space, neglectful mother
Intuitive thinking (a) Mind reading (b) Making negative predictions about the future (c) Basing reasoning on emotional responses	(a) Everyone knows I'm depressed; all the other mothers must feel sorry for my kids (b) Things will only get worse; I'll never feel any better (c) It must be my fault otherwise I wouldn't feel so guilty
Selective attention (a) Overgeneralising (b) Discounting any positives (c) Taking all the responsibility (d) Magnifying negative events	(a) I never spend time with the kids; my husband has to do everything (b) My manager only praised me because she feels sorry for me (c) It's my fault we haven't got enough money to take the kids on holiday; the house is a mess because of me (d) Forgetting to book in that appointment proves I'm bad at my job
Extreme thinking (a) 'All or nothing thinking' (b) Unrealistic standards (c) Catastrophising	(a) I *always* let people down; I *never* do anything right (b) Other people just get on with it despite their problems; no one else struggles with their lives (c) My husband's going to leave me; I'll lose my job

Some typical examples of Alison's thoughts are included for illustrative purposes. However, clients would not necessarily demonstrate all of these different styles of thinking. Self-help materials provide examples to help clients become familiar with their particular styles (for example, Brosan & Hogan, 2007; Williams, 2009; www. getselfhelp.co.uk).

As clients become aware of these unhelpful styles of thinking, they can also be guided to challenge specific negative thoughts as they arise. Thought records provide a useful means of doing this (Beck et al., 1979; Greenberger & Padesky, 1995). As mentioned in Chapter 7, negative thoughts are experienced in three domains: *self* (for example, 'I'm useless'), *the world* (for example, 'people always let you down') and *the future* (for example, 'I'll never feel any better'). This is termed the *negative cognitive triad* (Beck et al., 1979). These thoughts tend to form habitually and frequently in the person's mind and hence are labelled *negative automatic thoughts* (NATs). As a result, the person may accept them unquestioningly, seeing them as reflections of the truth rather than their own appraisals of events, which can make them very difficult to challenge. The use of thought diaries and thought challenging techniques helps the client, firstly, to become aware of these thoughts, and secondly, to evaluate their validity. Through this process, the client is guided to find other more balanced perspectives that may help them in breaking the vicious cycle maintaining their low mood. There are three steps involved in this process, which are outlined below.

1 Present a rationale

There are various means of introducing thought challenging techniques. One useful starting point can be the formulation or maintenance cycle, through which the client is guided to understand how their negative thoughts are maintaining their low mood. It can also be helpful to explain that thoughts tend to be subjective and rely on factors such as current mood, thus it is normal to think more negatively when one's mood is low. Self-help materials can provide explanations and exercises to illustrate this, and may be useful as preparation (for example, CCI – Back from the Bluez workbook). The transcript below illustrates the process of introducing the idea of thought challenging to Alison using Figure 7.1 (see Chapter 7).

Practitioner:	Looking at this cycle it appears that when you missed your daughter's assembly, it led you to think that you're a terrible mother?
Client:	Well I must be … all the other mothers were able to go.
Practitioner:	How did it make you feel when you had the thought that you're a 'terrible mother'?

Client:	Awful ... miserable. I just went back to bed and cried for hours.
Practitioner:	That sounds really distressing. How often do you have the thought that you're a 'terrible mother'?
Client:	All the time. I just wish I could get back to how I was.
Practitioner:	Did you always see yourself as a 'terrible mother'?
Client:	I'm not sure ... no I don't think I did ... not like this.
Practitioner:	So you've tended to see yourself in a more negative light since experiencing this depression?
Client:	I think so. I hate the way I feel at the moment.
Practitioner:	It sounds as though it makes you feel really miserable to view yourself in this way. Unfortunately, when you're feeling depressed it's quite normal to see yourself more negatively, but this can keep your low mood going for longer. We can see from this cycle that when you had the thought that you're a terrible mother, it seemed to make you feel a lot worse and led to you staying in bed for longer?
Client:	Yes, I felt so guilty that I just couldn't bring myself to do anything.
Practitioner:	That's understandable. You know sometimes it can be helpful to explore these kinds of thoughts further and consider how valid they are, since it may be your low mood that leads you to have this thought. What do you think?
Client:	It makes sense ... but I can't imagine thinking any differently.
Practitioner:	It's easy to see these thoughts as fact rather than a reflection of how we feel in a particular situation. However, there is a way to help you with this. Would you be willing to try this?
Client:	I can give it a go...
Practitioner:	OK, well I have a worksheet here which explains a technique for noticing and checking out these thoughts. Let's have a look at this together.

2   Identify 'hot thoughts'

The next step involves helping clients to notice their NATs by using a thought diary to record any situations where they have experienced negative emotions and accompanying negative thoughts. Emotions should be rated on a scale of 0 (no emotion) to 10 (the strongest emotion imaginable), after which the client notes down the thought associated with the most intense emotion. This is labelled the *hot thought* as it most closely corresponds with the strongest emotion felt in the situation (Greenberger & Padesky, 1995). Figure 8.5 shows an example of a thought diary completed by Alison.

Thought diary			
Date	**Situation**	**Emotion** Rate how strongly you felt the emotion (0–10)	**Negative thought** What was going through your mind? (Write down those thoughts which fit with the strongest emotion)
Wednesday 6th June	At work, made a mix up with one of the appointments	Anxious 6/10 Down 7/10[a]	I'm rubbish at my job
Thurs 7th June	Supposed to go shopping with husband – couldn't face it so he went alone	Miserable 8/10[a] Anxious 5/10	I'm a bad mother

Figure 8.5   Thought diary

[a] Strongest emotion.

When completing a thought diary for the first time it is important to ensure that the client understands the distinction between thoughts and emotions. The following explanation may help to clarify this.

- *Thoughts* are like a verbal commentary inside a person's head, and often consist of sentences such as 'I'm a failure', 'I'll never get better', 'I've let everyone down again'. They tend to reflect the person's perception of events or appraisals of themselves.
- *Feelings* refer to emotional states such as anger, sadness, fear and happiness. They usually consist of a one-word answer.

Self-help materials can also be useful in helping the client to understand this distinction (for example, CCI – Back from the Bluez workbook; Greenberger & Padesky, 1995).

Initially, identifying NATs is more of an exercise in *noticing* rather than *challenging* negative thoughts. Williams suggests that it may be helpful to label a negative thought as 'just one of those unhelpful thoughts' and simply register its existence (Williams, 2009). NATs may be viewed rather like a bully whose aim is to make the client feel bad. This may help the person to distance themselves from the NATs and see them as perceptions rather than facts. Furthermore, it can provide a rationale for distracting from the thought, for example by engaging in some potentially pleasant or absorbing activities, rather than getting caught in ruminating about the thought.

3 Evaluate and challenge the 'hot thoughts'

Once a client has become adept at identifying and monitoring the occurrence of NATs, the next stage involves learning how to evaluate and challenge them, with the aim of developing a more balanced perspective. This entails looking for evidence that either supports or contradicts the 'hot thought'. A worksheet may be used for this purpose. An example of one such worksheet, as completed by Alison, is shown in Figure 8.6.

There are a number of steps involved in completing the worksheet. The first involves deciding on a 'hot thought' to evaluate. Once chosen, this is recorded at the top of the worksheet. The person should then rate how strongly they believe the thought, from 0 (no belief) to 10 (complete belief). This can be helpful later to demonstrate any shifts that may occur as a result of completing the exercise.

Challenging Thoughts Worksheet	
Hot thought: I'm rubbish at my job How much do you believe the hot thought? 8/10	
Evidence for	**Evidence against**
I mixed up one of the appointments on Wednesday which led to a client missing their slot. Last week I forgot to remind one of the clients about their appointment this week. I struggled to organise the rota system and had to get some help from Jenny. My colleague said that I don't seem to be my usual cheery self at the moment.	I've never made a mix up with appointments before. I remembered to send out reminders to all of the other clients as I usually do. The other receptionist said she was surprised I'd made the mix up because I'm so conscientious. I was put in charge of reception last year because my manager said I was good at my job. A client sent a thank you card to the surgery last month and mentioned me by name as being kind to his daughter when she was frightened about the dental procedure.
How much do you believe the hot thought now? 5/10 Considering the evidence for and against the hot thought, is there another way to think about this? **Balanced thought:** Although I'm struggling to concentrate at work at the moment because of my depression, I generally do a good job.	

Figure 8.6   Challenging thoughts worksheet

Next the client is guided to provide some evidence that backs up their 'hot thought'. Usually clients can readily provide examples which support the thought; however, it is important that these are factual and specific, and not simply the result of unhelpful thinking styles. It can be useful to introduce a courtroom metaphor, where only concrete evidence can be accepted. For example, when asked to provide evidence for the thought: 'I'm rubbish at my job', Alison initially stated 'I'm always making mistakes'. With some gentle guidance from the practitioner to facilitate her in providing some specific examples, Alison realised she was only able to identify two instances where she had made an error.

Once the client has listed some evidence to support their 'hot thought', the next step is to look for any evidence that contradicts their thought. Not surprisingly, clients tend to struggle with this. It can therefore be helpful to use prompts designed to help them see things from another perspective. Self-help guides often provide these (for example, Greenberger & Padesky, 1995; Williams, 2009). See below for some examples of questions that can be useful:

- Have I had any experiences to show that this thought is not always true?
- What would a good friend/close work colleague say?
- What would I say to a friend who was in the same situation?
- Could I look at this from another perspective?
- When I am not feeling this way do I see things differently?
- In a year's time would I say the same thing?
- Am I jumping to conclusions?
- Am I setting the same standards for others as I set for myself?

When the client has completed both columns of the Challenging Thoughts Worksheet, they are asked to consider both sets of evidence. It can be helpful to return to the courtroom metaphor and ask the client to imagine how a judge would sum up the evidence for and against. By doing this Alison was able to generate the following thought: 'Although I'm struggling to concentrate at work at the moment because of my depression, I generally do a good job'. By taking this more balanced perspective, Alison felt less negative towards herself and reported an improvement in her mood as a result.

Use of self-help materials

The approach presented in this chapter is broadly based on the popular and influential self-help book: *Mind over mood* (Greenberger & Padesky, 1995). There are also other adaptations available (for example, www.cci.health.wa.gov.au; Williams, 2009). Working through the process of challenging thoughts can be time-consuming, so the practitioner's role would normally be limited to introducing the method and directing the client to appropriate self-help materials that can guide them through the various stages. Once familiar with the method, clients need to practise regularly, on a daily basis if possible, in order to become proficient at challenging negative thoughts.

Exercise 8.3   Challenging 'hot thoughts'

Think back to a recent situation where you noticed a negative shift in your mood. Using the thought diary provided in Figure 8.5, try to identify the 'hot thought' associated with this change in mood. Once you have done this, complete the challenging thoughts worksheet (Figure 8.6). Did your 'hot thought' change as a result? Were you able to come up with a more balanced thought? Did this have any impact on how you felt about the situation? What difficulties did you experience in completing this exercise?

Common problems when implementing cognitive strategies

There are a number of potential difficulties in using this technique. These are discussed below.

- Difficulties identifying NATs

As NATs are so frequent and habitual, they can be very difficult to spot. Encouraging the client to regularly practise spotting NATs through the use of thought diaries will help them to become more aware of their presence. A further complicating factor is that NATs can be difficult to distinguish from more deeply held beliefs. Within the traditional CBT model three separate levels of cognitions are described (Beck et al., 1979; Westbrook et al., 2007):

- o *Core beliefs* can be seen as the deepest level of cognitions and represent enduring attitudes about the self, others and the world in general (for example, 'I'm a failure', 'others will always reject me', 'the world's an unfair place'). These tend to develop as the result of early experiences and usually manifest as very general statements.
- o *Assumptions or rules for living* are the guiding principles a person lives by, which influence their interactions with the world (for example, 'if I work hard I'll succeed', 'I have to please others in order to be loved', 'being a good mum means always putting your children first'). These are shaped by the person's core beliefs and act as a kind of 'mental rule book' (Beck, 1976).
- o *NATs* are negative thoughts that habitually pop into the person's mind. They tend to arise from the person's core beliefs and rules for living, but are more specific as they reflect appraisals of the *immediate* situation (for example, 'no-one's rung me all week – they're all fed up of me', 'I did nothing all day – I'm so lazy', 'I couldn't get up today – I'm a bad mother').

By their very nature, rules for living and core beliefs are deeply entrenched and firmly held by individuals, which makes them very difficult to modify. There are effective strategies to do this; however, this work is complex and takes time. It is therefore more appropriately carried out using a high intensity CBT approach. Nonetheless, it is important for the LICBT practitioner to have an awareness of these different levels of cognitions in order to keep the client's focus on NATs, otherwise, the client may end up attempting to challenge deep-rooted beliefs. One means of doing this is to encourage the client to focus on thoughts that relate to the specific situation being appraised (Kinsella & Garland, 2008).

- Challenging NATs leads to limited change

There are occasions where clients experience little change in their belief ratings after challenging their thoughts. However, it is important to recognise that even small shifts can be helpful. It may also be useful to check that the client has selected a suitable 'hot thought' to work on. As mentioned in the previous section, attempting to challenge core beliefs is likely to result in little or no change. Difficulties can also arise when thoughts are expressed in the form of a question, for example: 'What if my kids think I'm a terrible mother?' or 'What if my husband decides to leave me?' Questions are difficult to challenge, so clients need to be guided to making clear statements. Questions may also represent worries about possible future events, which are inherently difficult to challenge without the aid of a crystal ball! Thus, clients should be guided to focus on their appraisals of what is happening currently, for instance: 'I'm letting my kids down' or 'my husband is getting fed up of me', as these types of thoughts are more accessible to being evaluated.

- The client's living circumstances are overwhelming

Many clients live in such difficult circumstances that low mood is an almost inevitable response (Brown & Harris, 1978; Hagan & Donnison, 1999). Living in an area of high crime, having insurmountable debts, being unemployed, or having an abusive or an otherwise dysfunctional relationship are all situations likely to result in low mood. In such circumstances, radical changes may need to occur in the person's environment. Problem solving and involving the wider system, for example employment advisors, debt counsellors, housing agencies or relationship counsellors, may need to be considered before cognitive strategies. Sometimes factors such as poverty and the resulting stress are inescapable. However, there are examples of psycho-education classes being used effectively within deprived communities, both to normalise how people are feeling and to provide strategies to cope with stress and depression (White, 2010).

Evidence supporting the use of cognitive strategies

Evidence from research trials suggests that guided self-help based on CBT principles is effective for mild to moderate depression (Anderson et al., 2005; Gellatly et al., 2007). It should be noted, however, that the self-help methods used in these studies generally use a combination of cognitive and behavioural techniques, without separating out cognitive techniques for specific consideration.

Problem solving

Effective functioning in life requires the skill of problem solving. Two key factors can interfere with this in depression. The first concerns depressive symptoms, such as reduced motivation, lack of energy, poor concentration, hopelessness, high levels of self-criticism and indecision. These symptoms can lead the person to feel more overwhelmed by difficulties and less optimistic about possible solutions. The second factor concerns the tendency to disengage from activities (as described earlier), which means that problems tend to accumulate, so consequently, solving them requires more effort. Problem solving approaches can be useful in helping the person to actively manage these difficulties, thus breaking the vicious cycle. This typically involves a number of steps (Myles & Rushford, 2007; Mynors-Wallis & Lau, 2010). These are detailed below.

1   Present a rationale

Having established early on in treatment the types of symptoms that the client is experiencing, it can be helpful to discuss how these can impede efforts to problem solve. It is also useful to explore the vicious cycle that occurs when the person feels too depressed to deal with difficulties and problems start to mount up. The practitioner should provide an overview of what problem solving involves, explaining that it requires an active approach by the client, with most of the work happening between sessions (Mynors-Wallis & Lau, 2010). Clients can also be directed to self-help materials, which explain the approach in some detail (for example, Brosan & Hogan, 2007; Williams, 2009).

2   Identify the problem

Once the client has agreed to engage in problem solving, the next stage is to define which problem to work on. Alison's problem list is presented below:

- I don't like my job.
- I feel fed up in my marriage.

- I never get any time for myself.
- I can't keep up with the housework and other tasks that need doing.

From the problem list the client chooses which one they wish to solve. The practitioner may need to provide some guidance here. For instance, it may be easiest to start with the least difficult problem. However, there may be problems that are more pressing and which, if they were resolved, would be more likely to lead to symptom relief.

3   Generate possible solutions

Once a clear problem has been identified the next step is to generate as many solutions as possible. Clients should be encouraged to include even those that are unlikely or extreme, for example 'win the lottery' as a solution to money worries. The aim of this is to help the client to think 'outside the box' and consider more creative solutions, in order to help them get unstuck from what may seem an insoluble problem. With help from the practitioner Alison was able to generate a number of possible solutions to her problem: '**I never get any time for myself**':

- Leave my husband and kids.
- Give up my job.
- Leave things how they are and stop expecting to have time for myself.
- Ask mum to have the kids more often.
- Ask my husband to spend more time with the kids.
- Spend some time doing nice things on my days off.

4   Choose a solution

Next, the client needs to decide on their preferred solution. A useful way to do this is to consider the pros and cons of each. Figure 8.7 provides an example of how Alison worked through this process.

5   Implement the solution

One aspect of feeling depressed is that the person may feel fairly despondent or pessimistic about their chances of successfully implementing the solution, or their low levels of motivation may act as a barrier. Thus it is important to set clear and manageable goals in this process. Alison's preferred solution was: '**to spend some time doing nice things on my days off**'. To help her do this, she planned an activity for each day: to have a coffee with her neighbour, to sit in the garden and read some magazines, and to visit a garden centre.

Problem: I never get any time for myself		
Solution	Advantages	Disadvantages
Leave my husband and kids	I'd have plenty of time for myself I'd be able to do whatever I want with my time	I'd miss them really badly I'd be lonely and more unhappy
Give up my job	I'd have more time for myself It would be a relief not to have to struggle with the work	We'd be much worse off financially We'd struggle to do nice things or have holidays
Leave things how they are	I'd stop expecting things to be better I might get used to the way things are	I think I might feel more depressed and hopeless
Ask mum to have the kids more often	I'd be able to relax knowing they were being well looked after I could do more things I want to do	I'd feel guilty – mum's not getting any younger and she gets tired easily now
Ask my husband to spend more time with the kids	I could go out on my own or spend time with friends My husband enjoys spending time with the kids	I'd feel guilty as he works long hours and comes home really tired He's already doing a lot to help out
Spend some time doing nice things on my days off	I could do things without my husband or the kids I wouldn't have to ask anyone else to help with the kids My mum and husband wouldn't have to do any more than they're already doing	I won't be able to keep up with the housework I'll feel guilty

Figure 8.7   Advantages and disadvantages of each solution

6   Review the outcome

Following implementation of the solution, the outcome should be reviewed to consider whether the problem-solving process has been successful. This can help to highlight both difficulties and achievements. A review can also help to consolidate learning and highlight any other issues that have been raised for the client. For example, Alison realised through this process that she was able to make time for herself, particularly on days when she was not working and her children were at school. However, previously, during these periods, she had not allowed herself to do anything enjoyable, as she felt guilty about not catching up with housework and other tasks. She also became aware that she found it difficult to share the responsibility for household tasks with her husband. As a result, Alison decided to discuss with her husband how they could allocate household responsibilities more equally.

Use of self-help materials

Within LICBT, problem solving may be used either as part of a package for managing depression (for example, Brosan & Hogan, 2007; Williams, 2009) or as a stand-alone treatment that can be delivered over four to six sessions (see Mynors-Wallis & Lau, 2010).

Exercise 8.4   Practising problem solving

Think of a problem that you have had recently and have not yet resolved, for example, difficulties with housemates, money worries or managing your time. Work through the problem-solving process. Was this helpful? Were you able to come up with a solution? What difficulties did you experience in working through the steps?

Common problems in using problem-solving approaches

There are a number of potential difficulties in using this technique. These are discussed below.

- Difficulty generating solutions
  The symptoms experienced in depression, such as poor concentration, reduced motivation and hopelessness, can make it difficult for depressed clients to be creative and generate solutions. Thus, the person may need more time and support with this. Practitioners can help by suggesting ideas. When undertaking the task for homework it may be beneficial for the client to enlist the assistance of a friend or partner.

- Lack of assertiveness
  Dealing with problems often necessitates the use of assertiveness skills, for example complaining about poor service, refusing to take on extra work and managing difficulties in personal relationships. Indeed, as we can see in Alison's example, solving her problem required a discussion with her husband about sharing the household tasks more equally. Where a client struggles with conflict, they may find it difficult to implement such solutions. In these cases, it may be useful to see negotiation of the conflict as a problem to be solved and help the client to work through this. Alternatively, clients may be directed towards psycho-education regarding assertiveness techniques (for example, Williams, 2009; www.cci.health.wa.gov.au).

- Rumination gets in the way of problem solving
  Some clients may spend a good deal of time ruminating about their problems in an attempt to understand themselves and their situation better. However, in practice, this generally results in reduced problem solving (Nolen-Hoeksema, 1991). In these circumstances, it is important to ensure that the client is taking an active approach and working through all stages of the problem-solving process.

Evidence supporting the use of problem solving

Large-scale reviews of studies into problem solving have found it to be an effective treatment for depression in both working age and older adults (Bell & D'Zurilla, 2008; Cuijpers, van Straten, & Warmerdam, 2007b). Studies also suggest that problem solving may be effective as a brief, stand-alone treatment, for people presenting with depression in primary care (Dowrick et al., 2000; Mynors-Wallis, Gath, Lloyd-Thomas, & Tomlinson, 1995).

Sleep hygiene

Sleep disturbance is a common symptom of depression. Indeed, convincing evidence exists to suggest that poor sleep may be a factor in the later development of depression (Ford & Kamerow, 1989; Riemann & Voderholzer, 2003). Studies indicate that as many as three-quarters of people presenting with depression also experience sleep problems (Staner, 2010). Difficulties include getting to sleep, staying asleep, early morning wakening and poor quality sleep. Excessive sleeping and napping through the day are also common. Many clients continue to experience insomnia even after recovering from depression, and this appears to increase their chances of relapse (Franzen & Buysse, 2008). Thus, improving sleep may be an important goal in the treatment of depression.

Having sufficient sleep is essential for effective functioning. As well as impacting on mood, lack of sleep can impair concentration, memory and cognitive abilities, lead to increased irritability, and lower our pain threshold. It is thought that people need on average between seven and nine hours of sleep a night, although some can survive on less and others require more. The number of hours of sleep needed tends to decline with age.

Sleep hygiene refers to the practice of developing healthy sleeping habits, which can be achieved by altering environmental factors and behaviours that contribute to sleep quality. Self-help materials are widely available to aid this process (for example, Espie, 2006; Maunder & Cameron, 2010; Moodjuice – self-help guide to sleep problems, available at www.moodjuice.scot.nhs.uk; Williams, 2009). The main areas to focus on are outlined below.

Establishing regular sleep and wake times

Disruptions to our internal body clock may occur when it is out of synchronisation with the natural environment, for example when travelling across time zones or because of irregular sleep patterns. Thus, a key strategy in sleep hygiene is to encourage clients to go to bed and get up at set times, and to avoid napping during the day. The establishment of a bedtime routine can also help signal to the body when it is time for sleep.

Avoiding stimulants, alcohol and excessive eating before going to sleep

Stimulants such as caffeine and nicotine tend to interfere with sleep, and some medicines may also keep the person awake if taken in the evening. Excessive alcohol intake and eating heavy meals late in the day can also result in more disturbed sleep and should be avoided.

Creating an environment conducive to sleep

The environment in which we sleep is also important to think about. It is helpful if the bedroom is comfortable, for example ensuring there is a good mattress, the room is uncluttered, not too hot or cold, and that it is reserved solely for sleep or sex. It is also important to control for noise levels and the amount of light coming into the bedroom.

Taking regular physical exercise

It is thought that regular physical activity can be beneficial in reducing insomnia and promoting good quality sleep (Driver & Taylor, 2000). However, intensive exercise for extended periods or in the evenings can be overly stimulating and detrimental to sleep. Thus, it may be more helpful to engage in fairly gentle exercise such as walking, cycling or swimming.

LICBT interventions for sleep hygiene can be delivered by providing psycho-educational materials alongside other treatment strategies as part of the treatment plan. Alternatively, sleep hygiene may need to be the main focus, at least initially, if sleep is particularly problematic or a priority goal for the client. Given how common sleep problems are in depression, services may consider running groups on sleep hygiene prior to, or alongside, individual treatment.

Relapse prevention

Having looked at treatment strategies in some detail, it is important to consider how the client can maintain improvements in their mood once treatment is complete.

Unfortunately, relapse is common in depression and may occur for at least half of the clients who present with this disorder (Kupfer, 1991). Hence, it is vital to discuss the possibility of relapse and help the client to plan how they might manage setbacks. Some clients may fear that *any* signs of low mood in the future will be an indication that they are becoming depressed again. Thus, as treatment moves toward completion, the client should be guided to think about how they will distinguish normal ups and downs in the future, and how they will know if they are experiencing a relapse. This can set the stage to establish a relapse prevention plan.

The model of LICBT lends itself well to relapse prevention. The client will be accustomed to taking a very active role in treatment. They will have collated and completed various materials, and be familiar with self-help resources. An explicit relapse prevention plan can be drawn up towards completion of treatment that consolidates this learning and details strategies for dealing with future setbacks. Templates are available in self-help books and on internet sites (for example, Williams, 2009). These will usually cover the areas described below.

What the client has learnt about depression

The first part of the relapse prevention plan involves a review of what the client has learnt about their depressive symptoms and how these may have been maintained, for example through inactivity, negative thinking styles or avoidance of problem solving. The client should identify which treatment strategies have been helpful in breaking this cycle, and which they might continue to use in the future.

Maintaining helpful ways of coping

Next, the client should be encouraged to think about how they will continue to implement treatment techniques that have proved beneficial. The use of a metaphor may be helpful here – such as the idea that in order to stay physically fit we need to eat well and stay active. Maintaining good mental health can be seen in much the same way, as an on-going process that requires continual practice of those strategies that have been effective in the person's recovery. For example, it may be beneficial to continue to practise challenging negative thoughts. Clients can be encouraged to keep spare copies of particular materials, such as behavioural activation diaries, thought diaries and sleep hygiene information.

What to do in the event of a setback

Planning for setbacks involves identifying signs and symptoms that may indicate if the person is becoming depressed again. These might include feeling overwhelmed by problems, high levels of self-criticism, becoming isolated or getting back into unhelpful sleeping patterns. Early recognition of these signs can act as a reminder to the client to implement strategies they have learnt in treatment in order to prevent a full relapse. It can also be useful to identify types of possible situations in the future that would be likely to make the person more vulnerable, for example stress at work, a relationship break-up, unemployment or illness (Williams, 2009). An emergency plan can be drawn up that includes particular treatment strategies to use, names of people they can approach in their support network and contact details for services.

The client should be encouraged to keep their relapse prevention plan in a safe place, where it can be easily accessed. A useful suggestion for clients is to plan in some time each month to review their progress, looking at what is going well and not so well (Williams, 2009). This can help them to stay vigilant for signs that things may be slipping back and promote an active approach to managing difficulties.

Conclusion

You should now have an awareness of the main LICBT approaches to working with depression and some knowledge of how to implement particular treatment strategies, including relapse prevention. The next step is to apply this to your practice. Hopefully this chapter has provided some helpful information regarding ways of managing some of the typical problems that can occur in the implementation of these techniques. However, there is no substitute for experience and it requires many hours of practice to apply these treatment strategies well. Supervision is a vital aspect of this process and will be discussed further in Chapter 13.

Summary

- The introduction of the LICBT approach in mental health services has increased access to treatments for depression, including more choice over how these are delivered.
- The main LICBT treatments for mild to moderate depression outlined in this chapter are behavioural activation, cognitive restructuring, problem solving and sleep hygiene. These should be delivered using a guided self-help approach.
- Relapse prevention is essential when treating clients with depression and a plan should be in place by the completion of treatment.

Further reading and activities

Consider what you have learnt from this chapter. Are there any particular points that stand out for you? If you are already working within a low intensity service, is there anything you would change about the way you are currently implementing treatment strategies for depression? Could you discuss this further in supervision? You have been guided towards some of the self-help resources that our services have found particularly helpful. You may find it useful to gather others that you can utilise with your clients (see also Chapter 2 for further guidance around choosing self-help materials). Begin to build up a file of relevant self-help materials that cover each of the treatment strategies outlined in this chapter.

A number of texts are also recommended for further reading. For extensive coverage of low intensity interventions see Bennett-Levy et al. (2010b). Williams (2009) is an excellent self-help resource for treatment of depression, and covers a range of treatment strategies. For further understanding of the CBT model read Westbrook et al. (2011).

Understanding Anxiety

Brad Martin

Learning objectives

- To recognise what anxiety is and where it comes from.
- To understand what causes anxiety to become a problem.
- To have knowledge of the types of anxiety that can be treated using the LICBT approach.
- To be aware of the key maintenance processes in anxiety.

Introduction

Human beings have evolved in environments that include danger and threat. Those who were best able to recognise and respond appropriately to the risk lived long enough to pass on their traits; the rest took their chances. As such, we all have a genetic heritage that is particularly good at tuning in to danger and responding in a way that is meant to keep us safe. Anxiety can focus our attention and can lead to adaptive changes in the brain and body. Anxiety only becomes a problem *when it is not helpful, lasts for longer than it should or is more intense than is proportionate to the situation.*

Although estimates vary considerably, between 13 and 28 per cent of people experience some form of clinical anxiety during their lives (Michael, Zetsche, & Margraf,

2007) and rates of comorbidity are high, with both comorbid depression and mixed anxiety disorders being common (Kessler et al., 1997). Ballenger et al. (2001) state that generalised anxiety disorder is the single most common cause of workplace disability. The World Health Organization estimate that the typical age of onset for anxiety disorders is 13–15 years old (WHO, 2000), meaning that anxiety disorders manifest earlier than any other major class of mental illness.

Exercise 9.1   Your experience of anxiety

Think about the last time you felt a high level of anxiety. Maybe it was before a job interview or when going into the dentist's office. What characteristics made the situation memorable? Was there something about the context that caused the anxiety (for example, was it novel or dangerous)? Do you remember any specific thoughts that you had at the time? What did the anxiety feel like in your body? Where did you feel it?

Other than the anxiety, could you identify any emotions? How would a typical person react to the level of anxiety you experienced? At what point would the reaction go beyond reasonable and be out of proportion? How do you gauge if your anxiety is proportionate and helpful, at the time of the experience?

Some of the more commonly reported features of anxiety include heightened *physical* states, such as breathing quickly or sweating a lot, or the opposite, including numbness, fainting and feeling like you are unable to move. There are often also *cognitive* symptoms including an over-estimation of the danger and/or an under-estimation of the ability to cope. Generally speaking, the symptoms are very unpleasant and people go to great lengths to avoid them. Some of the *behaviours* observed include avoidance and withdrawal (these can be very subtle and sometimes we are not even aware we are doing them). *Emotionally*, we can experience core (primary) emotions, including fear and anger, and more complex (secondary) emotions such as feeling overwhelmed, ashamed, humiliated and intimidated (Hackmann, Day, & Holmes, 2009). It is important to recognise that under normal conditions *these reactions and responses are entirely normal, appropriate and necessary for us to function safely*. We will explore each of these categories in greater detail.

What is anxiety?

Despite anxiety being a very common experience, it can be a very hard concept to define. In situations that are actually dangerous, anxiety is a completely normal and helpful reaction. It can help us respond in ways that minimise the potential for harm and increase the likelihood of us surviving the danger. Roth and Argyle describe anxiety in its clinical forms as 'an unpleasant emotional state experienced as fear or something close to it. It is unconnected with, or disproportionate to, environmental threats, and is associated with bodily discomforts' (Roth & Argyle, 1988: 33). This 'clinical anxiety' is the type that we will be focusing on here.

CBT is full of models to help explain the relationships between the different parts of the experience of anxiety. As you may have identified when you thought about your own anxiety experience, these models often include information on emotions, physical sensations, behaviours and cognitions. Perhaps the simplest example of the interactions of some of these symptoms is in David Clark's model of panic (Clark, 1986).

Emotional

Often our first indication that we are anxious comes from the *emotions* we feel rather than our thoughts. People may describe an experience of being uneasy, nervous or frightened, or a 'felt sense' of danger. Even without any other components, the emotional distress alone can be overwhelming and result in people wanting to avoid the feeling, its causes, or both. In the human brain, the parts that are most responsible for emotional responses are the amygdala, hippocampus and hypothalamus. These are part of a larger network in the body called the hypothalamic–pituitary–adrenal axis. When the emotional centres of the brain produce powerful emotions there is a release of several different stress hormones, including adrenaline, noradrenaline and cortisol. These hormones play a powerful role in how the body responds to the emotions.

Physical

The physical sensations that anxiety causes can be powerful and their effect on the person can lead to an enhanced sense of fear, danger or threat. While symptoms vary a lot between people, some of them may be familiar to you. Some common signs are listed in Box 9.1. The physical symptoms of anxiety show up in all of the anxiety disorders. Common interpretations of the physical symptoms include the belief that the person may be about to die, pass out, lose control, make a fool of themself or 'go crazy'.

Box 9.1   Physical signs of anxiety

- Fast or irregular heartbeats (palpitations)
- Sweating
- Face goes pale
- Dry mouth
- Muscle tension and pains
- Trembling
- Numbness or tingling in fingers, toes or lips
- Breathing fast
- Dizziness
- Faintness
- Indigestion
- Passing water frequently
- Nausea, stomach cramps
- Diarrhoea

Source: © 2011 Royal College of Psychiatry. Reproduced with permission.

Behaviours

The most common response to danger is to simply avoid or escape it! For example, most of us recognise that playing in traffic is unsafe, so we do not do it – this is common sense. By staying out of the street or crossing quickly we tend to avoid getting hit by cars. When these safety-oriented *behaviours* are proportionate to the actual danger they are healthy, appropriate and keep us safe. As Paul Salkovskis writes (see Further reading and activities): 'The avoidant behaviour of panic patients is normal and logical, in the sense that the fact that the reader of this article avoids drinking poison is normal and logical' (Salkovskis, 1991: 12). Avoidance or escape becomes a problem when it unnecessarily restricts our lifestyles, prevents us from functioning or distorts our ability to develop accurate appraisals of the danger present.

As we saw with the traffic example above, when anxiety appears in response to actual danger the responses can be very helpful (see Table 9.1 for further examples of symptoms of anxiety offering helpful reactions). Responses can help to limit exposure to the things that are dangerous or provide a means to manage a difficult situation (like lying down when you are breathless and think you are about to faint). Unfortunately, as we will see, sometimes the same sort of behaviours that keep us safe in dangerous situations can be unhelpful when used in less dangerous situations.

Table 9.1   Protective advantages of reactions to anxiety

What can happen	The benefit it may offer
Freezing (for example, when you cannot move while a big scary dog is barking and snapping his teeth at you)	If the thing that we fear is a possible predator, by staying very still we decrease either their ability to pick us out from our environment or the likelihood that they will see us as a threat. It can also help us to locate and identify potential threats. In the case of freezing when at a height, this protects us from moving around while on high ground and the risk of falling.
Fainting (for example, when exposed to blood or blood-injury)	Lying flat and still can reduce blood loss and allow time for clots to form. It can also cause an attacker to stop attacking.
Fidgeting (like when you are talking to someone that you are attracted to but are afraid might not fancy you)	Moving around, fooling around or fidgeting can help your body use up some of the stress hormones that are preparing you to react more dramatically. Presumably, it would be worse to run away or fight the person that you are attracted to, so fidgeting offers a more acceptable response.
Flight (for instance, running away when that same barking dog actually starts biting you)	Of course, if you can avoid being bitten by a dog by staying very still that is preferable, but if the dog starts biting, sitting still will result in injury. The best thing to do may be to get away from the source of danger.
Agoraphobia, or an avoidance of open public spaces	Back when our ancestors were living in natural settings, tall grasses, trees and other hiding places kept us safe. Big open spaces meant exposure to danger. This seems to be hard-wired into us, and some of us experience a sense of danger when out of familiar environments or around people we do not know.
Fighting (or just being aggressive)	Like any action movie character will tell you, sometimes the best way to keep yourself safe is to eliminate the threat at the source. By fighting, we can harm potential sources of threat and reduce their ability to hunt us.

Exercise 9.2   The role of safety behaviours

Can you think of a time when your anxiety prevented you from doing something that you wanted or needed to do? Alternatively, can you recall a time where you took extra care to prevent a bad outcome from occurring but your actions caused a problem (such as wearing a heavy jumper to stop people noticing you sweat, which actually made you so hot that you sweated even more)? What actions did you take to prevent the feared outcome? What were the unexpected effects of your action(s)? In hindsight, what other options may have been available?

The following situation encapsulates the phenomena:

A man is seen flicking his earlobes on the bus. The person beside him asks him what he is doing. 'It keeps the lions away' the man answers. 'But, there are no lions here' says the person. 'See … it works', says the man.

Actions that are intended to reduce threat or prevent a feared outcome are called *safety behaviours*. Salkovskis (1991: 10) discusses the need to recognise the difference between '*coping* behaviour and *avoidance* behaviour', even though both can look on the surface to be very similar. These can include actions to minimise exposure to predicted dangers (for example, by crossing the street to avoid a stranger), to neutralise consequences (such as quickly washing your hands after handling something 'contaminated') or to enhance your ability to manage a situation (including only doing things under certain conditions, like having water/medicine handy or only going out when accompanied by a friend/family). Simply put, a safety behaviour is anything that you do to keep yourself safe. Of course we all do things every day that are intended to keep us safe (like looking both ways before crossing the street), but with anxiety disorders, safety behaviours may be disproportionate to the situation or act to maintain the problem.

One problem is that people who rely on safety behaviours usually attribute the fact that their feared outcomes do not occur (or occur less intensely) to the use of the safety behaviour, rather than because their expectations were unrealistic. By relying on safety behaviours several undesired outcomes are achieved. When we use safety behaviours to enable us to engage with situations that we would normally avoid, we may believe that the only reason we avoided danger was due to *the safety behaviour*. For example, the person who always takes a friend with them to the supermarket never learns that they can cope by themselves.

Another problem is that, by restricting our contact with the feared situations, *we never learn corrective information* about the actual threat (or lack of threat) that may actually exist. For instance, a person who is afraid of dogs and avoids them may never encounter a friendly dog or learn that most dogs are not dangerous.

A further incidental result of the safety behaviour is that *we never develop a capacity* (or tolerance) for the things we are avoiding. Recall the first time you ever spoke in front of a group (or imagine what this would be like if you have never done it). If you are like many people, this would have been an anxiety-provoking experience. After some experience, a bit of encouragement and a few good outcomes your confidence may go up, your skills will almost certainly be greater and the intensity of the anxiety you experience may be less. Things that cause us anxiety can be a bit like eating olives – they may be unpleasant at first and, given the opportunity, you may choose to avoid them. However, with enough exposure you may grow to not only tolerate them but actually get a lot out of the experience.

Lastly, some of the things that people do that are intended to make someone safer can actually *make the feared situation more likely*. We can see examples of this in social anxiety, where the shy, retreating behaviour can attract undesired attention, or in panic, where a person fearing that they may pass out throws open a window and breathes quickly and deeply, causing hyperventilation.

Cognitive

Human beings are sense-making beasts. We are constantly examining our experiences and trying to understand them as best we can. Sometimes the basis for our understanding is well informed and accurate, but often we have to make use of less than complete information or adapt knowledge from other areas that may not be well suited to the current needs. The specific focus of the cognitions will vary according to the anxiety disorder (see Table 9.2), but the main features of the cognitions are fairly consistent. We will look at three forms of cognitive distortion where the thoughts that we have about a situation and our ability to be safe within it appear to be important in helping us to understand our anxiety. When the fear of the situation is too high and/or the expectations of safety are too low, problems occur. These three forms of distortion are next outlined and are:

1   over-estimating the likelihood of danger;
2   over-estimating the severity of the risk; and
3   under-estimating our ability to cope.

Probably the most typical types of anxiety-related cognitions are those related to *over-estimations of the likelihood of danger*. People with chronic anxiety tend to expect bad outcomes more often than they actually occur. Mathews and Mackintosh (2000) demonstrated that this pattern was linked to a bias in interpreting emotional information. As such, when someone *feels* like there is danger, they then *think* that there is danger.

Table 9.2   Focus of fears in anxiety disorders

Anxiety disorder	Fear of:	How the fear is expressed
GAD	The future	Worry
	Uncertainty	Over-thinking
	Anxiety itself	Problem avoidance
Specific phobia	Specific things, sometimes unique to the individual. Common examples include creepy crawly things (snakes and spiders), smelly and slimy things (for instance, rotten food), and heights or open spaces	Terror
		Panic when exposed to the feared thing
		Dizziness
		Sweating
		Nausea
		Avoidance

(Continued)

Table 9.2   *(Continued)*

Anxiety disorder	Fear of:	How the fear is expressed
Social anxiety	Situations that include being around other people, in particular people you do not know	Paying close attention to other people's behaviours
		Over-monitoring your own behaviour
		Believing that others are noticing you or judging you negatively
Panic	Physical symptoms of anxiety and the things that come with them (for example, fear of dying)	People are often avoidant of situations where they expect to encounter panic
	There is often a catastrophic nature to the interpretations of what is happening	Repeated health checks and attendance at hospital
OCD	Fear of responsibility for bad things happening, of contamination, of being a bad person	Monitoring/screening of behaviours and thoughts
		Checking, counting, ordering, hording, seeking reassurance

Exercise 9.3   Over-estimating danger

Think back to when you were younger and first watched a scary film. Many of us will have developed a genuine experience of fear. Immediately after watching the scary film, how reliable would your internal 'threat meter' have been? Imagine you were home alone and heard the house creaking. What ideas might you have had to explain the noises? Once some time had passed and you felt more settled, what changes would you expect with regards your ability to accurately predict danger?

When we are assessing this aspect of cognitions, it may be helpful to quantify the degree to which a person expects a bad outcome to occur to add specificity to the shared understanding of their anxiety. This can easily be done with scaling the risk (such as with a 0–100 point scale, where higher numbers mean that the event is increasingly likely to occur). The basis for these predictions can be tested out with cognitive restructuring and carefully designed behavioural experiments.

When you ask someone with chronic anxiety about their feared situation, they will often use terms like overwhelming, terrifying or intense. In this way they are *over-estimating the severity of the risk*. There is rarely a sense that the threat could be graded or less than a full dose – it is all or nothing. The prediction is not that it will be bad – it is that it will be disastrous.

Exercise 9.4   Exaggerating the risk

Imagine the following situation: you have just been in a car accident and have to be taken to the accident and emergency department at the hospital. Once you have generated a mental image of this scene, consider what injuries you might have sustained. Did you imagine that you were fine and maybe only had light scratches but were getting checked out just to be safe? A quick survey around my hospital generated responses such as 'I probably have a massive trauma including a lot of blood', 'multiple fractures' and 'I am in pain – I have physical injuries, shock, I'm crying, and I've wet myself'. These are all extreme injuries or worst case scenarios, and all from people without anxiety disorders.

It is not unusual for us to imagine unrealistically bad outcomes. In order to be prepared and consider the full range of our possible challenges, it is important that we consider the worst outcomes. For our reactions to be helpful, though, we would ideally consider the range of possible outcomes as well as mentally evaluate the likelihood of each scenario. The failure to evaluate the cognitions is the most important part in understanding anxious cognitions. If the person imagining the car accident scene above imagined that their legs were broken and this was so upsetting that they stopped driving in cars or leaving the house, this is problematic.

These first two types of cognition distortion are related to the presence of a danger. This final one, *our under-estimation of our ability to cope*, considers how well we could manage if a bad outcome occurred. Owing to a lack of positive experiences in dealing with anxiety and a lack of problem-solving skills, many people with chronic anxiety believe that they would not be able to manage if the feared outcome occurred. Even when there have been past experiences of managing successfully, high levels of anxiety can bias our memory and attention, and cause us to minimise or negate our resources.

The pressing demands of anxiety-producing situations, coupled with their novel nature, can sometimes leave us poorly prepared. People can underuse the skills and resources they have, or fail to creatively engage with new problem-solving solutions. The solution to both of these problems comes from Arthur Rubinstein who, when asked how to get to Carnegie Hall in New York replied 'practice, practice, practice'. For us to be able to use our skills when we need to, and for them to work well, we must get into the practice of using them. This means exposure to the conditions where the skills can be used and practice of the skills themselves.

For the purpose of this chapter, we will use the single term 'anxiety' to capture the whole range of conditions and symptoms described above. What it is important to remember when working with people who suffer from excessive anxiety is that it can have many faces and we often only find out about all of the characteristics of each person's anxiety when we ask about them explicitly. For more information on assessing anxiety and the outcome measures you might use, refer to Chapter 3.

Where does anxiety come from?

In their influential works on the evolutionary value of anxiety, McGuire, Marks, Nesse and Troisi (1992) and Marks and Nesse (1994) brought together a wide range of material related to the role of evolution in the development of different kinds of anxiety. In it they explain that anxieties, like other emotions (for example, love), developed alongside the environments within which they occur. Just as people feel love in response to romantic attachment, they may feel social anxiety in response to perceived disapproval from others. In this way, the emotions that we feel play an important role in helping us to respond appropriately to the range of situations that we find ourselves in. Anxiety states are uniquely capable of helping us to pull our attention away from less important things and onto the most immediate, dangerous ones.

Nobody would ever complain about running away from an attacking dog or avoiding areas of high crime at night, as both of these things would help keep us safe and are in proportion to the threat. Conversely, if we reacted to a fear of dogs by wearing body armour at all times, or insisted on travelling in an armoured tank around town, these actions might raise eyebrows. *Anxiety usually becomes a problem when it occurs in the absence of the thing it is meant to protect us from or is in excess of what is required to reasonably keep us safe in that situation.*

In modern times, it may not make a lot of sense for a person to experience such a high level of anxiety that they believe they are having a heart attack (this can be common with people experiencing panic) or to find themselves unable to leave the house (as in agoraphobia). So, why does it happen so regularly to so many people? It suffices to say that, when safety is involved, it is better to err on the side of caution and see danger where there is none, rather than miss actual danger when it is there.

For an example of this we need look no further than the wonderful horror films of the 1980s. The films usually open with a group of young people about to go camping near a lake. Unbeknownst to them, a violent killer has just escaped from a nearby prison and is looking for new victims. Usually, one of the campers hears a sound in the bushes and tries to raise the alarm. If the cautious person paid attention to their fear and escaped (as they never do in the film), they would avoid the killer. All of the others who assumed that it was only a squirrel would fall victim to the bad guy. Of course, in the film the escaped killer gets all of the campers, but in real life, the person who believed that there was danger in the bushes and escaped would out-survive those who were more casual with danger every time. In this way, *incorrectly identifying non-existent danger is a safer bet than ignoring actual danger.*

In a perfect world we would be able to accurately tell the difference between the noise of a squirrel in the bushes and an escaped murderer, but we often have to make choices with less than all of the facts and under pressure. When this happens, our natural tendency for risk-aversive decision-making (Holt & Laury, 2002) means that we are focused more on keeping safe and we can thus tend to overestimate risk.

What causes anxiety to become a problem?

As we have seen, the different elements experienced during anxiety (the cognitive, emotional, physical and behavioural) are entirely normal and even helpful in some situations. So when does it become a problem? Under typical conditions, when a person experiences the range of anxiety-related symptoms described above, they engage in a very important process of evaluating why they are anxious. Most people will spontaneously question their thoughts and check to see if they make sense and are realistic. They will then approach the fear (this can be literally approaching it physically or more generally by thinking about, talking about or otherwise experiencing the feared object). As they generate information about the situation, their fear, if it is unreasonable or excessive, will begin to ease (see Figure 9.1). As the fear eases, the person can engage with it more freely and this repeats until the person has developed more helpful ways of reacting to the feared object.

Anxiety becomes a problem when it appears at times when there is little or no actual threat; where the anxiety symptoms are disproportionate to the actual risk; where it prevents us from learning accurate and relevant information about situations; and where it causes us to engage in actions that make our situations worse (see Figure 9.2). In contrast to the adaptive approach to anxiety that most people (usually) take, unhelpful approaches to anxiety are often characterised by a lack of accurate information and a general pattern of avoidance. In describing the Glasgow Stress Control in 10 Words

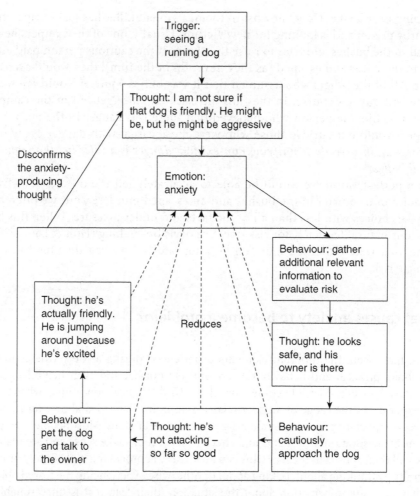

Figure 9.1   Example of an adaptive anxiety response

programme, Jim White described the first two principles as 'face your fears', and 'be more active' (White & Richards, n.d.).

Chronic anxiety may also be characterised by a self-fulfilling quality. As seen in the second dog scenario above, the person's anxiety caused them to run away from the dog, which in turn caused the dog to chase them. Ironically, the things that are intended to keep us safe can sometimes be those which put us at risk. By assuming that your initial reaction to a situation is accurate, by not finding out more reliable information and behaving as if something is dangerous, the likelihood of anxiety becoming a problem may be increased.

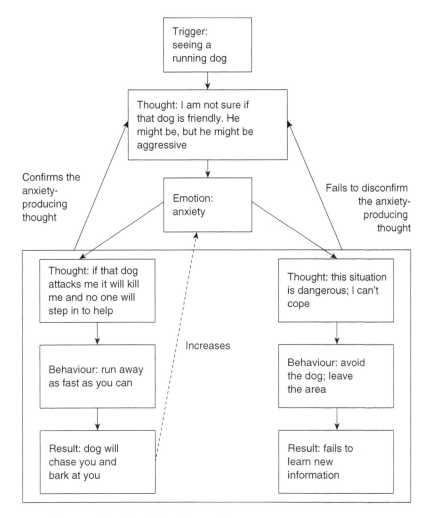

Figure 9.2   An example of maladaptive anxiety management

Categories of anxiety disorders

Because LICBT is one of the newest treatments, the established literature and evidence are limited and there are few robust studies evaluating the results. However, because LICBT is an adaptation of standard CBT, for which there is very good evidence, we can cautiously generalise some of the results. The greatest evidence for using LICBT with anxiety appears to be in treating *simple phobias, social phobia, panic, generalised anxiety disorder* and to a lesser extent *OCD*. There is a suggestion that LICBT may be an option for PTSD (McMullen, O'Callaghan, Richards, Eakin, & Rafferty, 2011), although at the time of going to press this is still some way from being firmly established. This is not to say that it is only helpful with these problems, just that the evidence may not yet be established beyond those yet, and the treatments may be beyond what is commonly available or offered. Because of the lack of evidence and suitable low intensity materials, we will not consider PTSD or health anxiety here. The treatment elements discussed below are all covered in Chapter 10.

Simple phobia

Simple phobias are intense fears to situations or objects that are excessive, or focused on objects that are not dangerous (see Figure 9.3). What separates phobias from normal fears is their intensity, which is hugely disproportionate to the actual danger that the object poses. Phobias can be focused on the same things that most people find uncomfortable (such as

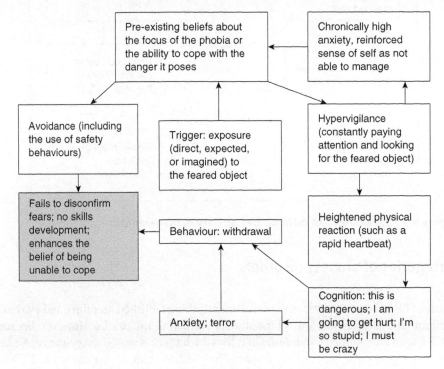

Figure 9.3 A cognitive model of simple phobia

creepy-crawly, slimy, stinky things), but with an intensity that prevents the person from functioning normally. Some of the more striking phobias are focused on things that most people are comfortable with, including fairly non-dangerous things like clowns (coulrophobia), being tickled by feathers (pteronophobia) or having contact with dolls (pediophobia). It is worth noting that these more remarkable phobias are highly uncommon compared with more typical fears, such as those of blood, dogs, heights and public speaking.

Panic

Panic disorder occurs when physical symptoms (such as shortness of breath or an unusual feeling in their body) cause a person to believe that the reaction itself is dangerous or that it is a warning sign of some worse physical reaction to come (see Figure 9.4). The person's reactions to the panic often make the situation worse (for example, breathing deeply, causing hyperventilation and a sense of dizziness). Panic can be experienced differently by different people so it is important to ask the person about their specific experiences. Some describe it as being like a heart attack, others like a stroke, or people may think that they are going crazy, choking or passing out. Because panic is based on both the physical arousal *and* the understanding that the person has of the physical experience, the treatment must address both of these aspects. There is, however, a decision that must be made about which path to follow (see Chapter 10).

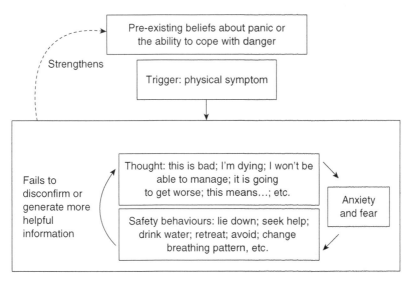

Figure 9.4   A cognitive model of panic

The central maintenance factor in panic disorder is that people think that the symptoms they are experiencing are dangerous when they are not. Thus, the treatment's focus can be either to reduce the symptoms or to reduce the interpretation and implications of the problem. From a purist CBT perspective we would normally think that it is better to challenge the belief that the problem has to be avoided or controlled, and work with the clients to develop better responses to the symptoms. Clients, however, may prefer to simply be given tools to better manage their body's reactions (such as with applied relaxation; Öst & Sterner, 1987). Indeed, better symptom management may provide a platform for working with people who are reluctant to engage with more conventional CBT. Clinicians and clients should be aware that some people with panic have an aversive response to relaxation (Cohen, Barlow, & Blanchard, 1985). As Lilienfeld (2007: 62) wrote 'it is likely that relaxation is useful for some anxiety-disordered patients but harmful for others'.

Social phobia

Social Phobia (also known as social anxiety) is an extreme fear of being negatively evaluated by others. People with social phobia may fear that they will act in a socially inappropriate way, leading to negative judgements by others, for example that they will be seen as stupid, ugly or incompetent (see Figure 9.5).

They may also believe that the consequences of the critical judgement are more severe than is likely. People often react to this intense fear with actions that are designed to prevent or soften the feared judgement. Unfortunately, avoidance or safety behaviours can actually increase the probability of a feared outcome occurring. An example of this is a person who is worried about mixing up their words, rushing what they are trying to say and ending up making a mistake.

Generalised anxiety disorder

Generalised anxiety disorder is a chronic state of worry that occurs frequently and intensively, or in situations where it is poorly suited to help the situation. Instead of worry being the source of the anxiety, in GAD worry is actually the strategy used to regulate the anxiety (see Figure 9.6). The near endless consideration of 'worst case scenarios' and 'what if scenarios' is used in a (usually futile) attempt to reduce the sense of uncertainty about what may happen. Kendal, Callery and Keeley (2011), in summarising the best practice guidelines for GAD, identified a broad role for LICBT, including education, active monitoring, entirely

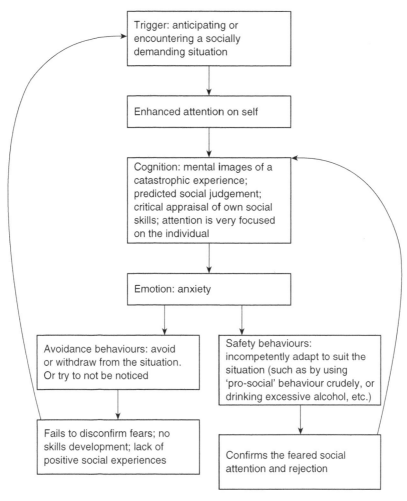

Figure 9.5   A cognitive model of social phobia

self-administered bibliotherapy (such as information leaflets available in doctors' surgeries), psycho-education classes, applied relaxation and guided self-help. Given the high reported rates of relapse in GAD (Allgulander, Florea, & Huusom, 2006), there may also be a low intensity role in managing medication compliance if medications are used. Wilkinson, Meares and Freeston (2011), in their excellent clinician's guide to treating GAD, provide a full chapter on low intensity options with GAD, and include recommendations for psycho-education, relaxation and problem solving.

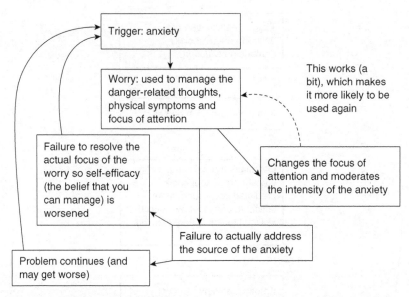

Figure 9.6   A cognitive model of GAD

Obsessive–compulsive disorder

Obsessive–compulsive disorder is a condition that occurs when a person experiences intense anxiety, often triggered by an intrusive thought where the anxiety is minimised, managed or neutralised by a compulsive behaviour. Taylor and Bryant (2007: 165) define an intrusive thought as 'a thought or image that you do not intend to think about, but pops into your head every now and then without you wanting it to', which is interpreted to be a threat or danger. The threat is so aversive that the person responds to it with a compulsion to manage or neutralise it.

Common types of intrusions relate to harm, contamination and breaches of moral codes (such as blasphemy). Typical compulsions include washing, ordering or hoarding. There is not always a clear logical link between the obsessions and compulsions (so someone who is anxious because they had a thought about hurting someone else may systematically arrange their clothing as a way of managing the anxiety). Because these compulsions are negatively reinforced through the instant cessation of the anxiety, the compulsion is repeated whenever the anxiety occurs (see Figure 9.7).

Compulsive behaviours can vary considerably between people, but also across time, with increasingly complex or pervasive compulsive responses developed to help manage anxiety. Compulsive behaviours include visible actions (such as washing your hands) and also covert behaviours (for example, praying or counting to a certain number).

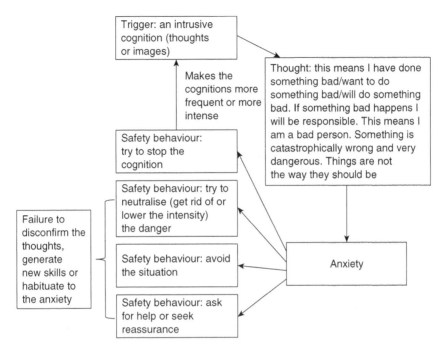

Figure 9.7   A cognitive model of OCD

Stress

One of the most common complaints in primary care health settings is stress (Dimsdale, 2008). Although stress is not technically a mental health diagnosis, it has been linked to mood and anxiety disorders (Lopez, Akil, & Watson, 1999). Technically *stress* is the term for the conditions that exert demands on a person and *strain* is the resulting effect on the person (Tausig & Fenwick, 2012), although for the purpose of this discussion we will use stress to describe both the situation and its consequences.

The word 'stress' comes from the Latin *stringere* meaning 'to draw tight', which is a pretty good description of what stress feels like. Common symptoms include emotional (feeling overwhelmed, exhausted or fed-up, having a negative attitude and lacking enthusiasm; Bassett & Lloyd, 2001), cognitive (reduced attention capacity and the consequent degradation of performance on cognitive tasks; Healy & Bourne, 2005) and physical symptoms (fatigue, headache, upset stomach, muscle tension, change in appetite, teeth grinding, change in sex drive and feeling dizzy; Dingfelder, 2008).

The sources of stress appear to depend on the context. In an employment environment the Health and Safety Executive describe demands, change, role, control and relationships as the main sources of stress (Martin, Kilfedder, & Powers, 2003). More broadly, Handler and Coghlan (2007) have described career, social, family, relationship and financial pressures as primary stressors. Left unchecked, chronic stress is associated with coronary conditions including strokes (Pandian et al., 2005) and immune system dysfunction (Glaser & Kiecolt-Glaser, 2005). While the precise pathway for this relationship is not well understood, Pickering (2001) has suggested that a perceived loss of control appears to be an important, common component in the experience of stress.

One model that has been used in the UK for treating stress using an LICBT approach is the STEPS model, developed by Jim White. Jim is a consultant psychologist in Glasgow where he and his team (http://glasgowsteps.com/) have popularised psycho-education programmes for common stress problems. This model of service delivery has become one of the most popular available. The programmes are offered as preventive, targetting a range of clinical presentations (such as GAD; White, Keenan, & Brooks, 1992). Van Daele, Hermans, Van Audenhove and Van den Bergh (2011) reviewed the published literature and reported a medium effect size for stress classes with shorter duration and those provided for women offered the best outcomes. Common treatment components include psycho-education, problem solving and relaxation skills (Van Daele et al., 2011).

The evidence for LICBT for anxiety

Although the literature on guided self-help is still emerging and there are few robustly designed outcome trials, the evidence so far is encouraging. The only practical limit on which conditions can be treated with a low intensity intervention seems to be the level of their severity and the availability of suitable materials or treatment programs. In most instances, where mild to moderate anxiety is the presenting problem in primary care settings, some common treatments would seem appropriate. These generic interventions may include treatments that focus on areas that present themselves across conditions, including programmes targeting sleep hygiene (Vincent & Holmqvist, 2010), relaxation (Hoyer, Beesdo, Gloster, Runge, Höfler, & Becker, 2009), exercise (Smits, Berry, Rosenfield, Powers, Behar, & Otto, 2008) and general stress management (White, 2010). These interventions appear to be at least as effective as their high intensity counterparts, when given to the right people at the right time (Cuijpers et al., 2010).

When deciding if LICBT is an appropriate option, it is important to factor in the collaboratively developed understanding of the problem and the range of suitable treatment options. Within LICBT there are materials designed to treat most anxiety presentations (for instance, the *Overcoming* series from Constable and Robinson has volumes on 10 different anxiety conditions). Despite the wide range of options, the evidence for LICBT is less well established than it is for HICBT. The NICE guidance, which is available for a limited range of common anxiety disorders, only promotes LICBT for panic, GAD and mild OCD. Beyond this you are operating on less firm ground, although there is weaker evidence of its effectiveness with other anxiety disorders within the NICE guidance. Instead of trying to treat whole diagnoses, it may make more sense to negotiate with your client which specific symptoms (such as poor sleep or avoidance) it would be most helpful to treat.

Once you have collaboratively developed an understanding of the problem, whether it is a prioritised list of specific complaints or a more traditional understanding using a diagnostic label, we can start to plan the treatment. With such a wide range of forms, anxiety disorders might seem a daunting challenge to treat. However remember, all of the common anxiety disorders have common features. In each case there is a relationship that the person has to a situation, object or feeling, that is either unhelpful or excessive. In skilfully selecting suitable elements, mild to moderate anxiety problems can successfully be treated. The challenge is to match the features of the presentation (or, if it is more helpful, the diagnostic category) with the treatment components that would offer the greatest benefit.

Maintaining anxiety: nothing changes if nothing changes

A few years ago a client gave me a gift at the end of her treatment. She was very talented at needlework and had made a wall hanging with 'Nothing Changes if Nothing Changes' embroidered onto it. With it, she captured the essence of both the maintenance of anxiety and the key to resolving it. As we have seen above, each anxiety disorder manifests in a distinct form with some common and some unique features. In every instance, however, a common mechanism is present that results in the maintenance (or worsening) of the condition. The anxiety is able to be maintained as long as nothing changes in the way that the person relates to their anxiety. Similarly, once we start adjusting the relationship that we have to our anxiety we can introduce new information, new skills and new ability to manage uncomfortable experiences.

As we have discussed above (and as illustrated in the problem-specific models), chronic anxiety occurs when two conditions are met. The first is that anxiety appears at times when it is not helpful, lasts for longer than it should or is more intense than seems manageable. The second is when our reactions to it prevent us from learning corrective information or make the situation worse. It can become entrenched by cognitive, emotional and behavioural responses that are designed to promote safety but ultimately either make the situation worse or prevent the person from discovering more helpful information. Escape, avoidance and safety behaviours are intended to control the perception of risk, danger or threat. By removing the sense of threat and fear, it is likely that the person will continue to use these strategies. The more often they are used and the better they work at controlling the fear, the more entrenched the strategy becomes.

Who is most at risk of developing an anxiety problem?

When we think about a person's vulnerability to developing anxiety, it is helpful to think about it as lying on a continuum, with normal experiences and more severe expressions of anxiety at opposite ends of the spectrum. That said, there are some factors that do appear to make people more vulnerable. These include sex, age, socio-economic status and environment.

Women tend to experience greater rates of anxiety (including anxiety disorders) than men, in particular, panic, GAD, phobias and agoraphobia (Kessler, Anthony, Blazer, Bromet, Eaton, Kendler, Swartz, Wittchen, & Zhao, 1999). Social phobia has a similar representation (Yonkers, Dyck, & Keller, 2001) between the sexes. There are a number of theories that enable us to understand this, including men being less inclined to report anxiety (Pierce & Kirkpatrick, 1992) or the sexes having differing specific physiological responses to stressors (Stoyanova & Hope, 2012; Masataka & Shibasaki, 2012).

As with many mental health problems, anxiety disorders are more common among people with a lower socio-economic position (Horwath & Weissman, 1995). Stansfeld et al. (2008) report that socio-economic position in childhood is a predictor of a range of mental health conditions in adulthood, although this is said to be moderated by their adult socio-economic position (Stansfeld, Clark, Rodgers, Caldwell, & Power, 2008). Socio-economic position also appears to influence outcomes in psychiatric treatment, with lower socio-economic position linked to poorer outcomes, premature mortality and poorer physical health (Roy-Byrne, Joesch, Wang, & Kessler, 2009).

Across the lifespan, anxiety is more common in childhood than in adulthood (Merikangas & Pine, 2002) and its symptoms may present differently in younger populations. For example, after traumatic experiences children and adolescents are more likely to engage in recreating the trauma than adults (for example, acting out their trauma in play; Meiser-Stedman, 2002). There is a further complication that children may have a greater vulnerability to the long-term effects of exposure to high levels of stress hormones, including neurological sensitisation that may make the child more reactive to anxiety (Perry, 1994). At the other end of the age range, older adults may have higher rates of both certain health anxieties and death anxiety (Wink & Scott, 2005).

Finally, there is some evidence that some people may be more likely to develop anxiety because of genetic factors – in particular panic and phobias (Smoller, Gardner-Schuster, & Covino, 2008), PTSD (Koenen, 2007), OCD (Pauls, 2008) and GAD (Koenen, Nugent, & Amstadter, 2008). The issue of psychiatric vulnerabilities is a complex one, with many of the constructs thematically overlapping with each other and other factors influencing each other.

Relapse in anxiety

In CBT we think of problems and difficulties as a coming together of a number of symptom domains including thoughts, feelings, physical sensations and behaviours, in a very specific form. The presence of some of these does not mean that the problem has necessarily returned any more than the presence of eggs, flour and sugar means that you have a cake. If we think of relapse as occurring only when a person returns to health services, we may be missing important information. Most people who have had frontal lobotomies never go back to have more of their brain removed, but this does not necessarily mean that they are well or happy with the treatment they have received.

Exercise 9.5   Understanding relapse

Relapse can be thought of as:

- Presence/absence of symptoms?
- Increase in severity/frequency?
- Proportion of clients who remain in/out of services?
- What factors do you think are important in understanding recovery versus relapse?
- What factors do you think your clients consider to be the most important?
- How does your service measure recovery or relapse?

One of the reasons that anxiety is such a common mental health problem is that it has a habit of coming back with regular episodes of remission and relapse (Yonkers, Bruce, Dyck, & Keller, 2003). In follow-up studies looking at five years post-treatment, between 30 and 60 per cent of people who had received treatment for anxiety were found to remain symptom free (Yonkers, Zlotnick, Allsworth, Warshaw, Shea, & Keller, 1998; Yonkers, Dyck, Warshaw, & Keller, 2000; Yonkers, Dyck, & Keller, 2001). In the next chapter we will look at managing relapse in anxiety.

Conclusion

Chronic anxiety is an experience characterised by feelings, thoughts, physical symptoms and behavioural responses to perceived risk, danger or threat. The most typical features of anxiety include processes of over-estimating danger and under-estimating a capacity to cope, coupled with unhelpful, avoidant behaviours. While anxiety is completely normal (and often helpful), when our responses to anxiety prevent us from either managing the demands of our environments or learning accurate information, or take up too much of our time and attention, treatment may be helpful.

CBT offers a flexible and adaptive way of understanding, describing and treating a range of anxiety disorders that is particularly suited to low intensity treatments. The treatment components will be discussed in the next chapter.

Summary

- Most reactions and responses to anxiety are entirely normal, appropriate and necessary for us to function safely.
- Anxiety becomes a problem when it is not helpful, lasts for longer than it should or is more intense than is proportionate to the situation.
- Safety behaviours stop us from learning objectively accurate, adaptive information and from generating valid conclusions about our experiences.
- Clients should be encouraged to engage in a long-term, balanced approach to managing their anxiety for the best chances at sustained improvements.

Further reading and activities

Like with all new knowledge and skill sets, much of this information and advice will only make clear sense when you start to practise it. Bennett-Levy, Turner, Beaty, Smith, Paterson, & Farmer (2001) suggest that self-practice and self-reflection is a good method for enhancing skills and confidence, while increasing the practitioner's knowledge about themselves.

As discussed above, Salkovskis (1991) provides a clear description of the role of behaviour in anxiety and panic that is particularly helpful for LICBT practitioners.

Cognitive models of anxiety disorders are well established and provide an excellent resource to aid the delivery of typically delivered HICBT. While we are able to generalise some of the features from these models, not all problems translate equally well to LICBT (such as PTSD). The most immediate need in LICBT is for a specific literature examining the common anxiety disorders with specific materials and a standardised treatment protocol. Practitioners and services that have developed or evaluated standardised treatment should consider submitting their work to peer-reviewed journals (for example, *Behavioural and Cognitive Psychotherapy* and the *Journal of Mental Health Training, Education and Practice* have both published LICBT-related material), or less academic publications (such as *CBT Today*).

10

Treatment of Anxiety

Brad Martin

Learning outcomes

- Consider the evidence and rationale for treating anxiety with LICBT.
- Understand the common components of treating anxiety.
- Introduce specific treatment components for treating anxiety with LICBT.

Introduction

There are many anxiety disorders that have a wide range of manifestations. I will, therefore, start by considering the general principles of treating anxiety, before focusing on the applications for specific conditions. However, before I consider how to treat anxiety, let us first consider a personal example of where you experienced intense anxiety and how you coped.

Exercise 10.1   Coping with anxiety

Remember the exercise in the last chapter where you considered a time that you felt high levels of anxiety (Exercise 9.1)? Thinking of that experience again, try to recall how you managed your anxiety. Was there anything that you did that helped you to cope, changed the perceived danger, reduced the anxiety or enhanced your capacity? If you could do it again, is there anything you would do differently? What advice would you give someone in a similar situation? Are the things that help in the moment the same as what is helpful in the long term?

In LICBT we try to utilise many of the same types of strategies that we all use in our everyday lives and use them to help with this sort of common mental problem.

As we have discussed in the previous chapter, anxiety is based on a perception that a situation seems more dangerous than it really is. All that treatment needs to do is provide an opportunity for the client to find better ways of responding to the anxiety and managing the symptoms. This chapter will start with a review of the evidence for LICBT and consider some of the anxiety problems that LICBT may be particularly suited for. In LICBT, treatments may address a particular aspect of the problem (such as offering relaxation or exercise to address the physical parts of the problem) or they could attempt to address the whole range of the anxiety experience, including the emotional, cognitive, physical and behavioural aspects. Although treatments differ according to client need, most comprehensive programs will include some form of:

- Assessment of the anxiety and an agreement on the goals to be worked on.
- Psycho-educational approach to provide information about anxiety.
- Skills development to better enable the client to reduce the occurrence of anxiety or to better manage the distress caused by anxiety.
- Some form of exposure to the situation or object that causes the anxiety.
- Relapse management.

Table 10.1 suggests which treatment components may be most suited to particular types of anxiety. In practice, much of this will come down to the materials used, and

Table 10.1   Problems and treatment options

	LICBT treatment component						
Condition	Psycho-education	Goal setting	Relaxation	Skills development	Thought challenging	Problem solving	Exposure	Relapse prevention
Panic	Yes	Yes	Yes	Yes	Yes	No	Yes	Yes
PTSD	LICBT is not currently indicated							
OCD	Yes	Yes	Yes	Yes	Yes	No	Yes	Yes
Social anxiety	Yes	Yes	Yes	Yes	Yes	No	Yes	Yes
GAD	Yes	Yes	Yes	Yes	No	Yes	No	Yes
Phobias	Yes	Yes	Yes	Yes	Yes	No	Yes	Yes

the collaborative decisions made by the client and practitioner. As you will notice, there is a lot of overlap between the different conditions, which is how LICBT is able to make such efficient use of standardised interventions.

The evidence for LICBT in treating anxiety

Because anxiety has so many forms, it is not possible to make a single statement about whether LICBT works for anxiety (see Chapter 2 for a wide-ranging review regarding the evidence base for the various LICBT vehicles). Some conditions, like PTSD and acute stress disorder, are thought to be sufficiently different from other anxiety disorders that they should be considered separately to the anxiety disorders (Mayo-Wilson & Montgomery, 2007). Even for these conditions, LICBT approaches have some emerging support in the literature (see Knaevelsrud & Maercker, 2007). However, stepped care is not yet recommended for PTSD (NICE, 2008).

LICBT is a relatively new development as a specialist form of intervention unto itself and so the literature that looks at this explicitly is not yet well developed. In some cases we must look at generalising from the high intensity CBT literature and adapt the applications to a low intensity model of service delivery. Some of the clearest evidence for LICBT with anxiety appears to be for social anxiety and panic. Both Furmark et al. (2009) and Abramowitz, Moore, Braddock and Harrington (2009) report significant results for a range of LICBT interventions for *social anxiety* (entirely self-administered written material – bibliotherapy – enhanced with facilitated group sessions, internet-based treatments as well as those with 'minimal therapist involvement'). Equally strong results have been identified for panic (see Robinson, Titov, Andrews, McIntyre, Schwencke, & Solley, 2010; Power, Sharp, Swanson, & Simpson, 2000). There is a clear indication that CBT (including exposure and response prevention) for OCD can be delivered effectively in lower intensities (Tolin, Diefenbach, & Gilliam, 2011). The UK's NICE guidance for GAD suggests that LICBT should be offered as a first line of treatment and this matches the clinical guidance from Wilkinson et al. (2011).

In their excellent review of controlled trials, Coull and Morris (2011) concluded that, while there is some evidence supporting LICBT, the outcomes vary and there continues to be a lack of long-term follow-up reported within studies. It is worth recognising that Coull and Morris excluded studies that considered sub-clinical presentations or participants whose diagnosis had not been confidently established. A result of these exclusion criteria is that many of the clients most likely to be receiving LICBT at an acute stage in the community – including those with mild to moderate symptoms, were not considered. Newman, Erickson, Przeworski, & Dzus (2003: 89) suggest that LICBT is 'most effective for motivated clients', while Gellatly et al. (2007)

emphasise the added benefit of regular support to ensure that clients are getting the greatest benefit from the LICBT. Cavanagh (2010) provides an excellent summary of some of the factors affecting engagement and outcomes in computer-assisted CBT. For a review of the efficacy and cost-effectiveness of LICBT with anxiety disorders, see Lewis et al. (2012).

Overview of treatment

Just as the way that we understand problems depends on where in the stepped care system the client is being seen (see Chapter 3, Figure 3.2), the treatment for most forms of anxiety in the mild to moderate range will depend on their place in the stepped care system. At step one, treatment may consist of the provision of information (including materials such as leaflets available from the client's general practitioner) or 'watchful waiting' to monitor whether the condition will self-resolve. At step two, the treatment options become more tailored to the problem and so the skills necessary to deliver them become more specific. At step three and above, the treatments become longer and increasingly individualised (and, as a result, more expensive to deliver).

LICBT for anxiety will typically start with an assessment of the current difficulties, which will formulate an understanding of the areas that may be suitable for treatment. The initial interview structure is described in Chapter 5 and service-specific decision trees describing the treatments available locally can help match presentations to treatment options (for a LICBT service-based example see Figure 10.1; Cave & Dunwoodie, 2012). Once it is known that the problem corresponds to a particular type of anxiety, problem-specific information sheets (see www.getselfhelp.co.uk) can both give the client an understanding of their condition and allow them to determine the treatment options that might be helpful. If the anxiety does not match one of the common anxiety constellations of symptoms (such as a specific diagnostic category or if it is a subclinical presentation), treatment options can be considered for the specific symptoms that have been identified. An example of this is the popular stress control classes that White et al. (1992) developed in Glasgow.

Psycho-education

Psycho-educational information can be conveyed through printed material (Lucock, Kirby, & Wainwright, 2011), onscreen/online information (Marks, Cavanagh, & Gega, 2007), through classes or on an individual basis (Houghton & Saxon, 2007). The aim is to educate the client about their condition or symptoms, to promote

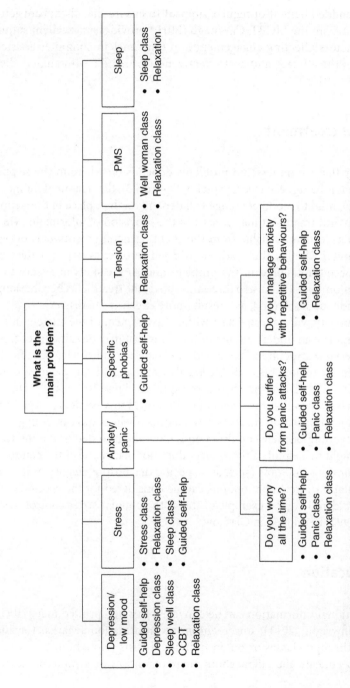

Figure 10.1 Decision tree (© 2012 Cave and Dunwoodie, 2012. Reproduced with permission)

motivation to engage with treatment, and finally provide realistic expectations of what treatment is likely to consist of and what the client might gain from it. I describe these aspects in turn below.

Exercise 10.2   The nature and value of self-help materials

Assuming that you are not already a photocopy machine repair technician, imagine that your photocopier develops a paper jam and you decide to try fixing it yourself. Because you are not trained in how to do this, it might seem like a daunting challenge.

- How would you go about starting this task?
- Would you know where the paper jams might occur or how to fix them?

Fortunately, most photocopiers come with user instructions. These booklets offer a breakdown of all of the user-serviceable components, how they work, advice on finding the fault and what is involved in fixing the problem.

- What difference would having a user guide make in your willingness to try fixing your photocopier?
- What qualities would the guide need to have to be the most use to you?
- Are there problems (or people) that the booklet would be more likely to help with?
- What help could be available for those for whom the user guide would not be suitable?

What does this example say about the value of psycho-educational material for common mental health problems?

The educational role of psycho-education

Psycho-education relates to any information or materials that are designed to provide the client with knowledge about their condition. This often includes descriptions about the problem, for example in the form of diagnostic categories, common symptoms/features or case vignettes that illustrate the phenomena. The main point of this is to offer the client an opportunity to identify that the selected materials are appropriate for them. However, there is the added benefit of offering clients an experience of normalisation when they find out that others have a shared experience and that they are not alone.

With anxiety disorders, because of the nature of these conditions, it is quite common for people to have a strong aversion to openly discussing their experiences. People often report thinking that they are the only ones who experience their problems and fear that others would judge them harshly if they knew. Many aspects of anxiety (for example, intrusive thoughts) may seem quite disturbing if you do not know why they are happening and they may be misinterpreted by the client as a symptom of a more serious condition. Learning that problems are common can be enormously reassuring for some clients.

The motivational role of psycho-education

Prolonged or repeated experiences of anxiety can be exhausting. By the time someone attends for treatment, even in primary care, we can expect that they may have experienced problems for weeks, months or even years. These delays can be due to personal choice, but also sometimes because professionals have failed to recognise problems (Christiana et al., 2000). Before seeing a mental health practitioner, the client may have taken some time to recognise their own need, then negotiated a sometimes tricky referral pathway, and finally may have been placed on a waiting list before being seen (Goldberg & Huxley, 1992). In asking people to engage in treatment, we are not only asking them to approach something they find distressing, but often to do it for a while before they notice any benefits from treatment.

Very closely linked to the importance of the descriptive function of psycho-educational material is the development and enhancement of *motivation* to engage in treatment. Part of the experience of offering someone a sense that their condition is understood is also making them aware that it can be treated. This is important because the treatments for anxiety can be difficult and require a lot of effort.

Prochaska and Diclemente (1983) provide a helpful way of thinking about a person's preparedness for change that has been used in contexts as wide ranging as HIV, dental hygiene, exercise and smoking. They describe people as falling into five different stages of change. These are *pre-contemplation* (not yet begun to consider a need for change), *contemplation* (considering change but not quite ready), *preparation* (ready to change and getting things ready for it to happen), *action* (actually engaging in change) and *maintenance* (keeping the outcomes going). In particular, with clients who are in the pre-contemplation or contemplation stages, psycho-educational materials offer them a chance to consider possible options available to them, potentially opening up new ideas and moving them forward in this cycle of change.

Exercise 10.3   The cycle of change

Consider each of Prochaska and Diclemente's stages described above. For each one, try to identify something in your own life that fits in that category. What things do you think would help a person move from the earlier stages of the cycle towards the later ones?

Managing expectations with psycho-education

Each of the different stages of the change cycle described above has its own need to manage expectations. For clients earlier in the cycle it may be necessary to introduce the idea that change is possible, as well as providing enough specific information about treatment to enable them to make an informed opinion regarding the demands of treatment and the probability of a successful outcome. As a client moves through the cycle, the focus of their expectations may shift towards providing realistic targets for what can be achieved. After change has been completed, the focus of managing their expectations may move towards developing a realistic prediction for the reoccurrence of the problem, along with strategies for managing the risk of relapse.

In the case of some forms of purely self-administered self-help (as is the case for services that offer unsupported information leaflets) and non-interactive classes, psycho-education may be offered as a standalone treatment.

Exposure

In chronic anxiety, as we have discussed in the previous chapter, two of the strategies that people routinely use to prevent their feared outcome or to manage the intensity of their anxiety are avoidance and withdrawal. Usually this works extremely well at regulating the immediate symptoms of anxiety. For some problems, avoidance is a perfectly legitimate strategy – it keeps you out of harm's way and does not cause too much disruption to your life (such as an avoidance of parachute jumping). For some people, an overdependence upon avoidance can cause a great deal of disruption and can leave them feeling out of control of their lives.

Exercise 10.4   The experience of fear

Think back to when you were little. For all children, there are things that make them nervous. Maybe for yourself this might have been barking dogs or strangers. If you cannot remember, consider the young people that you know now.

- What made you (or them) frightened?
- What did you (or they) need to do to get over the fear?
- Were you able to do this alone or did someone help you?
- What would your situation be like now if you had remained afraid or had never come into contact with what made you afraid?

By failing to come into contact with the object (or situation) that provokes their anxiety, a person's beliefs and strategies related to the source of their anxiety are unlikely to be modified. One of the most significant elements of most anxiety treatment plans involves *exposure* to the anxiety-provoking situation or object, and so also to the anxiety itself.

The general principles associated with exposure are that a person must come into contact with the object or situation that they fear in order to (a) challenge irrational cognitions associated with threat, (b) learn how to manage the feelings that they get when in contact with their fear without using strategies to allow them to avoid the experience and (c) get used to the anxiety that is experienced, allowing the intensity of the anxiety to reduce (this is known as *habituation*).

There is a well-documented relationship between arousal and performance which we can easily apply to learning and habituation. When arousal is too high, the person experiencing the arousal will not be able to attend to the situation and new learning about the relative safety of the situation cannot take place (Yerkes & Dodson, 1908). Thus, the goal is normally to have enough arousal that the person is paying attention and is being exposed to the sensation of fear, but not so much that they are overwhelmed (see Figure 10.2). There are several different forms of exposure. To help determine the right type of exposure to use, I describe two of the most common types (graded exposure and prolonged exposure) along with examples of where they may be helpful.

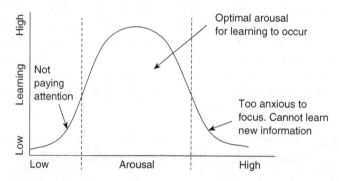

Figure 10.2   Optimal arousal

Graded exposure

Graded exposure is the most common form of exposure work done in CBT. For many people, the anxiety that they avoid is only unbearable when experienced in its more intense forms. In lesser amounts it may be tolerated more easily, albeit with some measure of discomfort. Graded exposure uses bearable levels of anxiety which the person systematically habituates to in order to enhance their capacity to cope. When each dosage becomes manageable, the intensity is increased in small amounts until a high, previously unbearable, level becomes tolerable.

Grading the exposure requires the generation of a *hierarchy* of anxiety-provoking situations (see Figure 10.3; alternative materials can be found in Richards & Whyte, 2009). The hierarchy can consist of as many steps as are required by the person to gradually increase the intensity of their anxiety without feeling overwhelmed. This often means moving closer in proximity to the feared object or changing the characteristics of the object to evoke a stronger fear response.

One common method of measuring the client's level of anxiety is to use subjective units of distress (SUDs). These are generated by the client using a simple scale (for example, a 0–10 point visual analogue scale). This indicates the intensity of the anxiety. By measuring the SUDs at different points in the exposure process, we can establish whether the exposure has resulted in the necessary anxiety and if the level has decreased before the exposure ends. SUDs can be used to help grade the intensity of exposure to ensure that the steps are in the correct order and the increases in intensity are manageable.

A hierarchy should be based on the features of the situation that evoke the anxiety rather than the situation itself. For example, for someone who is afraid of going into a park for fear that a dog may attack her, it would be better to design a graded exposure programme focusing upon the dog rather than the park. Free LICBT materials for graded exposure are available at: www.cci.health.wa.gov.au/docs/SHY-10-Exposureplan.pdf (along with the follow-up guide at: www.cci.health.wa.gov.au/docs/SHY-11-Exposure.pdf).

The purpose of this exercise is to give you a chance to experience your anxiety in a series of graded intensities, with the easiest levels first and then building up to the harder levels when you are ready. You should base your levels on the specific things that make your anxiety increase, rather than the situations that you normally experience them in.

What is the situation that makes you anxious or that you avoid?

_____

_____

What is the key thing in this situation that makes you fearful?

_____

_____

Plan: The task is to expose yourself to the situation that you are afraid of.

- In the order that the items appear on the list, starting with the least threatening, put yourself in the situations.
- How long do you expect it will take (will you have enough time to stay with the feeling until the fear dissipates)?

(Continued)

Figure 10.3   *(Continued)*

- In each situation rate the SUDs while you are experiencing it and stay with it until the SUDs reduce by at least 50 per cent (so if your fear starts at 8/10, stay with it until it is only 4/10).
- Once you are able to engage in the first task comfortably and easily, proceed to the next task and continue through the whole list.
- Expect to practise this several times a day, allowing yourself time in between trials to feel calm and relaxed. The more effort you put into this, the more you get out of it.

In the space below, create a list of situations with the easiest first and then going on to increasingly difficult and anxiety-provoking situations. It may be helpful to start with a situation that can easily be accomplished. For each item rate the predicted SUD on the scale. If there are large gaps in the predicted SUD scores, consider adding an additional level between the two. Try for at least four different levels of intensity.

Easiest situation:

1	2	3	4	5	6	7	8	9	10

Second easiest situation:

1	2	3	4	5	6	7	8	9	10

Middle difficulty situation:

1	2	3	4	5	6	7	8	9	10

Second hardest situation:

1	2	3	4	5	6	7	8	9	10

Hardest situation:

1	2	3	4	5	6	7	8	9	10

Figure 10.3   Graded exposure worksheet

Case example

Karen is terrified of dogs. Even the idea of a dog sends shivers down her spine and seeing one leaves her in tears, usually causing her to flee from the situation. After doing some work aimed at helping her to understand what she was feeling and providing her with information regarding the actual threats posed by normal dogs, Karen was ready to start an exposure programme. Although she 'knew' in her head that the dogs in question would not harm her, her fear of them did not reduce. Karen was able to draw up a hierarchy of situations, starting with those that would cause the least amount of fear/threat and building up from there. In the least feared scenario Karen looked at a series of cartoon pictures of dogs downloaded from an internet search engine. Once she was comfortable with the pictures and could comfortably look at them without much effort (her fear having habituated to them), she moved on down the hierarchy to more challenging items. After several tests at each level, Karen was able to spend time with dogs without feeling overwhelmed. Here is her hierarchy:

1 Easiest – looking at cartoon pictures of dogs (SUDs = 2/10).
2 Second easiest – watching a video of a normal dog on www.youtube.com (SUDs = 4/10 or 5/10).
3 Second hardest – visit a friend who has a dog that you know is safe and controlled (SUDs = 7/10).
4 Hardest – visit the park where there are dogs on leads and under the control of their owners (SUDs = 9/10).

Exercise 10.5   Developing a graded hierarchy

Identify a fear that you have and generate a graded exposure hierarchy. It may be helpful to consider how gradual to make the steps so that you are able to benefit from the exposure without becoming overwhelmed. If you cannot think of a fear you have presently, consider one that you have faced in the past (such as those involved in learning to swim).

Clinical tips

Start acquiring a range of commonly feared items and keep these on hand for your clinical work. A sample jar with a few dead spiders will last for years and will spare you having to try to figure out where to find exposure stimuli every time a new client comes along. Additionally, some insects are impossible to collect at certain points in the year and so a 'library' of items can be essential. Try putting together treatment packs, complete with pictures of the object (these can further be graded into increasingly real models) and toy versions, as well as the actual objects themselves (if this is safe and hygienic).

The exposure must be to the anxiety, not only the thing that causes it. People have a remarkable capacity to block distressing things out of their mind. If they are not becoming anxious the process will not work. Help the client to capture their anxiety by explicitly determining within the assessment what causes the anxiety and use *this* to generate a fear hierarchy.

Prolonged exposure

When you ask people about the things that they fear, you rarely hear about small challenges or minor inconveniences. Instead, people often report fantastic impressions of impossible obstacles and dire consequences. It seems that the nature of anxious expectations is that we 'expect the worst'.

One of the most frequently reported responses to situations that provoke extreme anxiety is to withdraw. After all, if something is dangerous most people will try to get away from it. What is described typically is that arousal increases in the presence of the feared object or situation (or in expectation of it) up to a threshold point where the person thinks that they are about to lose control (see Figure 10.4, line 1). When the person withdraws from the perceived threat the anxiety, predictably, lessens (see Figure 10.4, line 2) and so the avoidance behaviour is reinforced by a reduction of the anxiety (see Chapter 9). Despite the prediction that individuals make regarding the feared situation of an ever-increasing anxiety or an unbearable outcome, what normally occurs (in situations that are objectively safe) is that arousal increases to a maximum level and then plateaus (see Figure 10.4, line 3). How long this takes varies according to the person and the situation. When we fail to habituate it is often because we have ended the exposure prematurely.

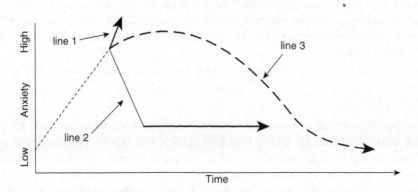

Figure 10.4   Anxiety: expected and experienced

Goal setting

As we have considered in Chapter 9, anxiety is often a complicated set of disorders with different manifestations and treatment approaches that may require the client to encounter some unpleasant experiences in the course of facing their fears. With avoidance being such a common means of trying to cope with anxiety disorders, you may find that a more active approach to resolving problems, including goal setting, is missing from your client's coping skills repertoire. Because of the nature of LICBT, the ability for the materials to sensitively adapt to a shifting target is limited. As such, it is important for the focus to be carefully considered and agreed prior to the selection of the LICBT materials or programme. In some cases there is an explicit invitation to use only the elements of the materials that are likely to target the parts of the anxiety that are important to the client (Williams, 2010).

When we prioritise goals, some factors to consider include:

- Are there risk issues that should be prioritised?
- Which problem is primary, for example, if the client is presenting with both depression and anxiety, which needs addressing first (see Chapter 7)?
- Which is the most disruptive or distressing problem? Is there a rationale for focusing on this first if it would interfere with a client's ability to otherwise engage in treatment?
- Which problem is easiest to address and will result in the quickest gains for the client? In targeting this we can hope to benefit from enhanced motivation, which is likely to have a beneficial effect over the remainder of contact.

In their CBT competencies framework, Roth and Pilling (2007) established a set of standards for goal setting that can be applied to LICBT for anxiety. These include translating vague/abstract goals into concrete goals; identifying goals that will be subjectively and objectively observable and potentially measurable; working with the client to ensure that goals reflect the issues/problems with which they present; and ensuring that goals are realistic and achievable. The development of these in practice is discussed in Chapter 5, and should encompass the generation of a problem statement, reframing problem areas in terms of goals, and then measuring and reviewing the goals.

Box 10.1   The problem statement and goals

Example problem statement from Tom (see Appendix): I have been very anxious when I'm at work. As soon as I get there I worry that I am going to have a panic attack and stop breathing. My hands start to shake and I get all sweaty so I avoid the office and even thinking about my job.

Tom's goals is: I would like to stop having panic attacks at work and get my attendance back to normal, hopefully within the next month or so.

Measuring goals

It is important to agree with the client how they are going to gauge the success of the treatment (see Chapter 3). This should be tailored to the problem. The materials that you are using may also have some measurement techniques built into them, which may include estimates of levels of distress, typical responses to anxiety and situations that are avoided.

As we have already seen, exposure in treating anxiety may require that a certain level of anxiety is experienced in order for the treatment to be effective. A high level of anxiety that does not habituate appears to be linked to more severe forms of anxiety (Eckman & Shean, 1997), suggesting that the client should be stepped up to for HICBT.

Here is Tom's graph of his SUDs that he used to record the experience of fear when going into his office, with additional comments that he added during the exposure task (see Figure 10.5).

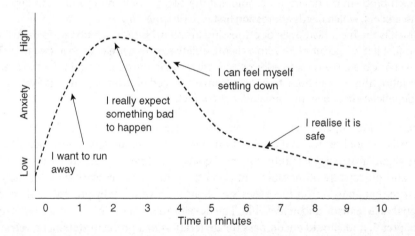

Figure 10.5 **Tom's anxiety associated with an exposure task involving him attending work**

Relaxation

Most of us know what it feels like to be relaxed, even if it is hard to describe. In some ways, it is easier to think about the opposite state, tension. Tension is felt in many parts of our body and our mental experiences. Indeed, Schwartz, Davidson and Goleman (1978) recognised that there are different interventions that can selectively benefit different types of anxiety (such as exercise, which may be effective at managing physical anxiety, while meditation may be better at managing the cognitive features). Physically, tension is characterised by tightness in muscles (often the neck, shoulders and stomach) headaches and agitation that is often episodic and unstable (Pfaltz, Grossman, Michael, Margraf, & Wilhelm, 2010). Mentally, tension is often experienced as distractibility, poor concentration and a tendency to interpret things negatively or expect bad outcomes (Castaneda, Tuulio-Henriksson, Marttunen, Suvisaari, & Lonnqvist, 2008). Emotionally, tension can include feelings like worry, fear, and a sense of upset (Amstadter, 2008). Relaxation, as the absence of the signs of tension, can be described as a state of balance, calm and peace.

Relaxation can be used to promote many desired effects. It can give a break from tension/arousal and can end stressful situations; many people describe it providing an opportunity for pleasure and it is often reported to improve sleep (Alidina & Cooper, 2012). Like so many other aspects of treating anxiety, the right treatment components vary between people, and users should be encouraged to try different forms and/or use several strategies together to achieve the best results (Manzoni, Pagnini, Castelnuovo, & Molinari, 2008).

Meditation

Although there is no universally agreed definition and exact details vary between practices, broadly, meditation is the practice of syncing thoughts, attention and body in a way that results in a greater state of harmony (Walsh & Shapiro, 2006). It is traditionally divided into passive and active forms (Stevens, 2010), although in common practice these distinctions are less obvious. Historically, meditation has been the domain of religious practitioners (most typically with Islamic Sufis, Christian mystics, Buddhists and Hindus), although it is not necessarily a religious or spiritual exercise. In the last 40 years there has been increasing interest in the practice.

Evidence for the benefits of meditation-based relaxation is considerable, with both physical health (Carlson, Ursuliak, Goodey, Angen, & Speca, 2001), stress-related autonomic and endocrine measures (Rubia, 2009), and a wealth of mental health benefits being demonstrated (Dakwar & Levin, 2009).

Progressive muscle relaxation

It may seem counter-intuitive, but for those who struggle with relaxing their bodies, it may be best to start with exaggerating the tension. Progressive muscle relaxation (PMR) was developed by Edmund Jacobson back in 1934 and is still in use today. In a review of the literature on PMR for people with psychophysiological and stress-related disorders, Carlson and Hoyle (1993) found it to have a moderate effect. PMR involves the user tuning into the sensations of tension in their bodies through a series of deliberate and intense tightenings of muscle groups. This can then be followed by the same degree of attention to loosening the tension. By exaggerating the degree of tension that might naturally occur, the user is taught to recognise the signs of tension and to gain the skills necessary to release the tension, leaving the person more relaxed than when they started. The result is an improvement in early recognition and a more rapid de-escalation of tension, in addition to regulating the parasympathetic response to anxiety-provoking conditions (Green, 2011).

PMR can be enhanced with an accompanying script (for example, on an audio recording; Salcedo, 2007) that offers the client both instruction on what to do and strategies for maximising the benefit. With practice, the client may be able to develop an internalised 'script' and may report no longer needing the audio instruction. Further practice can allow the user to activate the relaxation strategies on their own, without using the contrasting tension part of the exercise.

Guided imagery

We have established that cognitions can be triggers for anxiety. For example, people with panic may imagine catastrophic actions or outcomes (Speckens, Hackmann, Ehlers, & Cuthbert, 2007), and in social anxiety there may be a mental image of a scene where the client can 'see' themselves being watched or judged, or 'see' themselves doing something wrong (McNeil, Vrana, Melamed, & Cuthbert, 2007). Holmes, Geddes, Colom and Goodwin (2008) have identified an enhancing role that imagery can exert on emotion, with images acting as powerful and often unquestioned forms of thoughts. Guided imagery exercises can exploit this characteristic of image-based cognitions. Guided imagery exercises are based on the same capacity for vivid and emotive imagery, but are used to generate a more adaptive mental response to situations or to produce a sense of calm.

Common examples of guided imagery relaxation exercises include images of a peaceful place (like a rolling pasture), a good experience (for example, being surrounded by friends) or simple objects to focus your attention on (maybe a candle flame or a simple coloured shape). As with many examples of LICBT materials, the internet is full of excellent resources (samples can be found at www.stress-relief-tools.com/guided-imagery-exercises.html). The exercise often appeals to all of the senses, asking the person to imagine the sights, sounds, touch, smells and emotional responses that would match being in the situation. This 'all encompassing' quality of imagery-based exercises may not appeal to all clients as some people report feeling a loss of control. This is worth exploring with your client as part of your review of suitable options.

Exercise 10.6   The use of imagery for relaxation

Imagine an object or a colour that represents stress to you. For example, you can imagine colour red, or a rope with knots, or a loud startling noise. When you have your image say to yourself: 'I release tension'. Imagine your image slowly transforming into something calming. The colour red can slowly fade into a nice soft and gentle colour pink. The rope with knots can slowly transform into a smooth and soft silk or velvet fabric. And the loud noise can gradually transform into a soothing sound of ocean waves. When you are done with the transformation, say to yourself: 'I am relaxed'.

When you are ready, gently open your eyes and come back to the present moment.

www.stress-relief-tools.com, Simona Sebastian. Reproduced with permission.

A difficulty with offering any guided exercise through low intensity methods is associated with how to achieve the actual delivery. Many supported self-help materials require the user to pay attention to them (for example, to read from a book). This is incompatible with an exercise that requires them to direct their attention on another task. The simplest way around this is to provide a recorded guide to the exercise (see Mayo-Wilson & Montgomery, 2007).

Breathing exercises

As we have discussed, distressed breathing is a commonly reported feature of many types of anxiety. Some people report rapid shallow breathing; others struggle to catch their breath (Wollburg, Roth, & Kim, 2010). Distressed breathing has an anxiogenic effect, provoking a sense of panic or fear. In regulating breathing we can accomplish two things. First, it can help to stabilise the distressed breathing and ensure the right balance of blood gases (Meuret, Wilhelm, Ritz, & Roth, 2008), preventing or resolving a panic response caused by too little carbon dioxide in the blood. Secondly, we can offer the person an alternative focus for their attention, instead of ruminating on their anxiety.

Breathing exercises vary in complexity and detail from simply counting breaths (a meditation exercise; Sessa, 2007) to more technical and deliberate routines like diaphragmatic breathing (this is a form of deep breathing that focuses attention on the diaphragm/belly). Instructions for this are in Herrick and Ainsworth (2000). Although the specifics vary between practices, the objective of a breathing exercise is to gain a sense of control over the breath, to be more deliberate with the actions and more focused in the attention. Sample scripts and instructions can be found online (www.mind-and-body-yoga.com/deep-centre-breathing.html). There is no single right way to practice or enhance breathing. The best strategy is to work with your client to identify a system that best meets their needs, using LI materials to support their goals.

It may well be worth primary care mental health services developing tailored materials to complement the services that are delivered locally. The primary care mental health service in Sunderland, UK recently developed a relaxation CD. The service worked with a local yoga instructor and a recording studio to produce a 1-hour CD with six different guided relaxation exercises. The expense of the final CD (including all production costs) worked out to about 50 pence each – which represents considerable cost savings against the purchase of commercially available materials. These materials can be developed across a range of formats and languages, making this a low intensity intervention that is well suited to working with diverse populations.

Skills development

Problem solving

One anxiety disorder that is associated with a lack of effective problem solving is GAD. Dugas, Letarte, Rhéaume, Freeston and Ladouceur (1995) report that those who worry more do not show deficits in problem solving skills, rather they have difficulties in the area of problem orientation. This suggests that GAD clients may know what to do to solve their problems but have difficulty attending to problem solving. It is thought that this is related to difficulties in tolerating both uncertainty and emotional arousal, which leads to avoidance of thinking about the problem (Dugas, Freeston, & Ladouceur, 1997). A simple problem orientation exercise like the one found at www.getselfhelp.co.uk/docs/worrytree.pdf can be quite helpful. For some other people with anxiety problems, it may be difficult to tell the difference between situations where active problem solving may be helpful and where it is unlikely to make a difference. Table 10.2 offers a sample exercise for distinguishing different responses to problems. Problem solving is discussed in detail in Chapter 8 and this same approach can be applied with anxiety disorders; worry time is discussed later in the chapter.

Table 10.2   Mapping forms of worry and associated intervention strategies

	Can do something about it	Can't do anything about it
Here and now real event worries	• Need to get the kids ready for school. • Haven't opened the bills yet. • My essay hasn't been started. Possible strategy: Problem solving	• Volcanic activity in Iceland causing disruption to the aeroplanes. • Getting old. Possible strategies: Worry time Relaxation Distraction
Future hypothetical event worries	• Might not have enough money when I retire. • I could fail on my exam. Possible strategies: Problem solving Consider timing of your attention. Is it helpful to focus on this now?	• There could be an outbreak of bubonic plague. • The Conservatives could be elected to a majority government. Possible strategies: Worry time Relaxation

Physical exercise

Strangely, one of the simplest and lowest intensity treatments for anxiety (at least on the part of the practitioner) rarely shows up as a treatment option in mental health services. Although the evidence is limited, exercise has been demonstrated as an effective intervention for mild to moderate anxiety (Larun, Nordheim, Ekeland, Hagen, & Heian, 2009), both as a preventive intervention (Beaulac, Carlson, & Boyd, 2011) and as treatment (Herring, Jacob, Suveg, Dishman, & O'Connor, 2011a, 2012).

Prescribed exercise has been used to manage GAD (Herring, Jacob, Suveg, Dishman, & O'Connor, 2011b), OCD (Abrantes et al., 2009) and panic (Broocks et al., 1998). It has been shown to be effective with groups as diverse as children/adolescents (Newman & Motta, 2007), working age adults (Knapen et al., 2009) and older adults (Chodzko-Zajko et al., 2009). It can be delivered individually or in groups, with the latter having the added benefits of increased social contact and normalisation of the client's condition. For an excellent review of exercise as a treatment for anxiety see Wolff, Gaudlitz, von Lindenberger, Plag, Heinz and Strohle (2011).

There is no reason to think that the intensity of the exercise programme has an impact on the results (Roth & Holmes, 1987), so it is best to work collaboratively with the client to develop a treatment plan that suits their interests, capacity and resources (Beaulac et al., 2011). Beaulac et al. offer a helpful system for supporting this treatment, using a helpful 5-As mnemonic: assess, advise, agree, assist and arrange.

Exercise is thought to work through both cognitive and behavioural pathways, offering the client a chance to get used to (habituate) heightened levels of physical arousal (such as a rapid heartbeat), while providing important information that enables the client to understand the experience without resorting to a threat-based explanation (Sabourin, Stewart, Sherry, Watt, Wald, & Grant, 2008).

Exercise 10.7   Devising an exercise programme task

When Tom was at work he experienced a range of physical symptoms including a pounding heart, sweating and hotness. When these happened, he immediately thought they meant that he was having a heart attack. After providing Tom with some information about panic, he agrees to try exercise as a way of being exposed to his symptoms.

- Can you think of an exercise that would be expected to recreate his symptoms safely?
- How would you monitor Tom's response to the exercise to help him learn about these reactions?
- What would a suitable homework assignment be for this, using goals that are SMART (specific, measurable, attainable, relevant and timely)?

In addition to learning new information and decatastrophising symptoms there also appears to be the benefit of increased mastery with exercise. Clients experience an 'increased self-efficacy, a sense of mastery, distraction and changes of self-concept' (Ströhle, 2008: 781). Like with any LICBT intervention, treatment compliance can be an issue. Petrella and Lattanzio (2002) recommend regular brief practitioner support to improve compliance and outcomes.

Applied tension

In most cases clinical anxiety is a disproportionate fear of an undesired outcome. For some people who experience a needle or blood phobia, the feared result (passing out) may be quite realistic. Fainting (sometimes referred to as *syncope*) is usually the result of a sudden drop in blood pressure, so people who are very anxious have little chance of this happening (because of the intramuscular tension caused by the anxiety keeping the blood pressure heightened). In the case of blood phobia or when there is a needle stick injury, the conditions may be present for a sudden decrease of blood pressure (Civera, Granell, Cabedo, & Escorihuela, 2007).

Developed by Öst and Sterner (1987), *applied tension* is a treatment for people with a fear of (or actual experience of) fainting because of a blood phobia. It is easy to offer as a low intensity intervention as it is highly manualised and is largely based on the cumulative benefits of practice (rather than learning new material each week).

Applied tension teaches a client to regulate their blood pressure by deliberately increasing their muscle tension and practising the skills through in vivo exposure (trying it out in real life). While there are no known risks associated with applied tension, common sense suggests this should be negotiated with the client's PCP, in particular when there are physical vulnerabilities (such as cardiac histories, pregnancy or uncontrolled epilepsy). Clients can be given practice sheets with instructions (see Antony & Watling, 2006: 107–9) and the in vivo exposure can be completed almost anywhere (hospital dramas on TV provide a wonderful exposure condition).

Cognitive aspects of treating anxiety

With thoughts about danger and threat being central to many people's experience of anxiety it is sometimes important to consider the cognitive aspects of anxiety carefully. Although the core LICBT treatments will focus on engaging in behavioural change (such as with exposure), cognitive interventions can raise awareness of typical anxious thoughts (for example, with thought records) or use thought challenging (also called cognitive restructuring) to provide a rationale for the behavioural exposure.

Thought records

As with many of our routine experiences, people with problematic anxiety may experience anxiety-related cognitions without being completely aware of the frequency or intensity of them, or having ever taken the time to consider their content. Likewise, some of the reactions to anxiety can be cognitive (for example, worry in GAD), which can occur without the person being deliberately aware of them. As we discussed in the last chapter, the presence of an anxiety-related cognition can act as a trigger for anxiety, so there is a clear rationale for becoming more aware of them. A thought record provides an opportunity to capture some of the anxious cognitions as they are occurring, recording different types of information that may be helpful (the content of the thought, how much the person believes the thought, triggers for the thought; see Figure 8.2).

When used in higher intensity treatments, thought records can be used to monitor specific responses to a range of situations (see Westbrook et al., 2007: 107), and may provide both the clinician and client with a range of material to review in session.

In LICBT, where clients are typically more able to independently engage in their own treatment, this role may be less obviously necessary. Instead, and being particularly relevant in LICBT, self-monitoring may result in spontaneous reactive changes in the cognitions (Nelson & Hayes, 1981), including a reduction and change in thought content. Olson and Winchester (2008) caution that monitoring the frequency of a thought may increase the occurrence of the thought, as is observed in classic cognitive priming exercises; however, this appears to be more likely with thought suppression exercises rather than monitoring alone (Clark, Ball, & Pape, 1991).

Thought challenging

Boden, John, Goldin, Werner, Heimberg and Gross (2012: 287) state that 'beliefs that are negatively biased, inaccurate, and rigid are thought to play a key role in the mood and anxiety disorders'. As we described in the previous chapter, according to the CBT model, typical cognitions relate to a tendency to over-estimate both the danger that a situation presents and the likelihood of the feared outcome occurring, often endorsing distorted or irrational beliefs (Muran & Motta, 1993). These thoughts often prevent a person from approaching the source of their anxiety and gaining the necessary experience to generate reliable evidence. A classic treatment component in CBT is cognitive restructuring. Cognitive restructuring is a name used to describe a range of strategies aimed at helping a client recognise, explore, challenge and adapt the cognitions involved in anxiety. It does not impose new thoughts on a person, but rather provides an opportunity for the client to modify their thoughts and beliefs based on the best available information, using examined logic to form more accurate/balanced conclusions.

Challenging thoughts in CBT is often a matter of setting up a fairly sophisticated analysis of the different evidences for and against, generating and evaluating evidence, considering the outcomes and developing new theories, thoughts and understandings. This can be a challenging task, in particular for clients who become anxious when they focus on their thought content. It is further complicated by the very elusive nature of anxious thoughts – as soon as one has been addressed another one often pops up to take its place. In LICBT for anxiety, cognitive restructuring is best used to establish the basis and focus of exposure-based exercises. In doing so, the client can be supported to change their relationship to anxiety, so reducing their need to neutralise the anxiety.

Fundamentally, chronic anxiety is maintained by treating something as if it is more dangerous than it objectively is. Thus, the treatment needs to ultimately be anchored in exposure to the anxiety-provoking condition, rather than only challenging the related thoughts. This is supported in the literature, where helping people engage in behavioural change has been found to have advantages over purely cognitive treatments (McManus, van Doorn, & Yiend, 2012).

Exercise 10.8   Evaluating thoughts

Imagine that you are travelling down the motorway in a snow storm. As you are driving, the wheels lose traction for a moment and the car starts sliding. What kinds of thoughts might be going through your mind – 'We're going to crash', 'This is going to hurt', 'I am going to die', 'I should have stayed home tonight'?

Now imagine that your passenger in the car said to you:

- 'We'll be fine'.
- 'That was fun'.
- 'Isn't it great that we're doing this right now!'

You would think they were an idiot, right? What sort of information would it take to convince you that your sense of danger and the related thoughts were invalid or disproportionate? Would you think of your thoughts as 'just your opinion', or would they seem pretty accurate? Is there anything that your passenger could offer to shift your perspective?

The four steps involved with working with unhelpful thoughts are discussed in detail in Chapter 8 on treating depression, and I would refer the reader there for a step-by-step guide to working with unhelpful thoughts. Table 10.3 records some typical thoughts that are common in the different forms of anxiety disorder.

Themes include an over-estimation of danger and risk, and of the probability that a feared outcome will occur. There is often a tendency to under-estimate the person's ability to manage, with the person having a belief that they need others to help them cope. Careful attention to the problem description and statements offered by clients during assessment and treatment will offer good information about the beliefs that they hold.

In addition to looking at specific thought content typical of anxious cognitions, some materials are designed to identify and address common thinking errors that may be present. *Unhelpful Thinking Styles* (www.cci.health.wa.gov.au/docs/BB-5-Unhelpful%20 Thinking%20Styles.pdf) and *Unhelpful Thinking Habits* (www.getselfhelp.co.uk/ unhelpful.htm) are two easy to use online resources. For clients who prefer graphical representations or have a low reading age, consider using *Unhelpful Thinking Styles* (www.psychologytools.org/assets/files/Worksheets/Unhelpful_Thinking_Styles.pdf). As we saw in depression, clients may experience specific types of information processing or *cognitive bias*. In anxiety, the most common biases are catastrophising (expecting a worse than probable negative outcome), over-generalising (believing that what happens in one situation is relevant to other situations), personalising (thinking that an event is caused by the person) and selective abstraction (paying attention to certain aspects of an experience while ignoring others; Watts & Weems, 2006).

Table 10.3 Cognitive content in anxiety disorders

Disorder	Cognitive content
Panic	These physical symptoms are dangerous and will cause me harm (such as 'I'm going to die/choke/pass out/go mad/make a fool of myself').
	These are never going to end.
	Having these symptoms means that I cannot do what I want.
	If I monitor my health and recognise early signs I can prevent a worse outcome.[a]
Specific phobia	Thoughts will be specific to the object of their phobia.
	The beliefs will be disproportionate to objective risk.
GAD	Worry can prevent a bad outcome.
	Worry can decrease the likelihood of an event.
	By worrying about small concerns I can distract myself from worse troubles.
	Worrying can help me prepare for the worst.
	Worrying is an effective problem solving strategy.[b]
OCD	In OCD thoughts can be obscure, but common themes include:
	• overestimated responsibility;
	• if I do this x times it will stop x [something bad] from happening;
	• the belief that the content of thoughts has meaning (that something has happened or will happen, or that it reflects your true wishes);
	• a belief that the danger can be controlled with certain safety-related actions.[c]
Social phobia	Other people will notice the things that I do that are wrong.
	I'm boring/inadequate/socially inept.
	I'll make a fool of myself.
	Other people will judge me.
	I am not as good as other people.
	I regularly make significant mistakes.
	If I do x, people will look past my shortcomings.[d]
PTSD	The memories of a past trauma are experienced as if they were current.
	The 'meaning' of the trauma on their sense of self, relationships and the future.
	A retrospective allocation of responsibility, thinking what happened was their fault or could have been avoided.[e]

[a] Wenzel et al. (2006); [b] Borkovec et al. (1999); [c] McLean et al. (2001); [d] Clark and Wells (1995); [e] Ali et al. (2002).

Working empathically with clients while using thought-challenging techniques can be difficult. Firstly, this is because the thoughts can be intense and strongly held, evoking powerful emotions when they are reported. Secondly, because it can feel very out of step with the core CBT principles of both collaborative working and Socratic dialogue to question what a person is saying. Despite this, it may be a skill that you already have developed in other areas of your life and may already be very good at. Even if this is not the case, by being both aware of the challenges and alert to how difficult the work may be, you can sensitively support clients focusing on these problem areas.

Exercise 10.9   Challenging thoughts

Consider the following statement. As you read it, imagine hearing a close friend or a sibling saying this to you. What would your immediate reaction be to them?

> I went to get on the subway and as soon as I stepped on I could tell that every single person was staring at me and they were all thinking: 'What a jerk – he looks like he just dragged himself out of bed. He doesn't belong here with civilised people. He probably doesn't even have a girlfriend'. I could see it in their eyes, they hated me.

Would you want to know if they had any evidence for the accuracy of their thoughts? How would you ask them to explain this to you? What was it about the statement that would have piqued your curiosity? What would you want to watch out for when looking for these sorts of thoughts with clients?

A strategy that can help in highlighting which thoughts are potential problems is to empathically listen to the descriptions, imagining the situations and explanations that are offered, and monitor your own response to these. If you are unable to vividly follow the story, it may be worth asking more questions to focus your understanding further. Often just asking for further information (as we saw with thought records) can cause clients to spontaneously consider the accuracy of their beliefs and generate alternative ideas.

Worry time

For clients with GAD or excessive unhelpful worry, the idea of trying to stop worrying may seem unimaginable. In fact, it is often the disruption to functioning that exceedingly frequent and intense worry causes that leads people to seek support, rather than the desire to get rid of worry outright. Commonly reported positive ideas about worry that clients possess include the notion that it makes you more prepared and so is therefore useful (Prados, 2011). Given the perceived usefulness of worry, it is hardly surprising that clients may be reluctant to try to stop worrying outright. Instead, a graded approach to gradually decreasing the use of worry to regulate anxiety through use of dedicated *worry time* can be considered. The relationship between anxiety and worry in clients with GAD is often characterised by spontaneous worry as an acute response to anxiety.

Worry time offers a client an opportunity to defer worry until a scheduled and time-restricted period. The advantage of this is that it breaks the immediate negative reinforcement (the removal of an unwelcome condition – anxiety – that makes the mental behaviour – worry – more likely to occur again) while offering a chance to generate evidence related to the belief that worry is effective at controlling outcomes. In the spirit of graded exposure, it may be suitable to start with very minor restrictions (perhaps delaying worrying by 10 or 20 minutes when the urge rises) and build up, ultimately reducing the overall time spent worrying or the frequency of dedicated worry periods (Wilkinson, Meares, & Freeston, 2011). Depending on the goal of the client, once the worrying is sufficiently disrupted, the client's goal may be achieved or there may then be enough new information for them to reconsider the usefulness of their worry in its entirety. For LICBT materials on worry consider 'What? Me worry!?!' (from www.cci. health.wa.gov.au/resources/infopax.cfm?Info_ID=46) or the relevant section in Chris Williams's *Overcoming anxiety: a five areas approach* (2010).

Behavioural experiments

As we saw above, sometimes the expectations and understandings that we have are either inaccurate or based on inadequate information. Where thought challenging asks the person to consider other options, behavioural experiments provide the opportunity to actually test out ideas and generate new evidence to inform our thoughts and expectations. A behavioural experiment is essentially an exposure exercise with a question/testable hypothesis added to it. Some LICBT materials have been designed specifically for this purpose, including www.psychologytools.org/assets/files/Worksheets/Behavioural_Experiment.pdf and www.getselfhelp.co.uk/docs/BehaviouralExperimentWorksheet.pdf, as well as the exercises found in printed sources such as 'Mind over mood' (Padesky & Greenberger, 1995).

Broadly, the evidence we use to inform our understanding of our experiences falls into four categories. These include *historical* (what the person already knows or has already encountered), *observational* (what the person is able to generalise from things they have seen or heard about from others), *expert* (the evidence that we can draw from recognised authorities that might not normally be available to us because of costs, risks or uniqueness of opportunity) and *experimental* (things that we can find out by testing and gathering new data and information). These sources of evidence are revisited below in the case study (Tom).

The cognitive treatment components that we have considered so far have largely used 'logical analysis and empirical hypothesis-testing which leads individuals to realign their thinking with reality' (Clark, 1995: 115). These 'tests' can use any of the above sources of information. When the tests are purely cognitive, they are often based on information already available, albeit subject to a more robust analysis. In anxicty, where avoidance may have limited the quality or range of evidence, the best evidence already available may be biased or invalid. In these instances, it may be more helpful to base some of the new tests on new information that has been generated in a more transparent manner.

When the information available (for example, existing knowledge and expertise) is insufficient to generate more adaptive strategies, it may be necessary to generate new evidence and information using behavioural experiments. Bennett-Levy, Westbrook, Fennell, Cooper, Rouf and Hackmann (2004: 8) state that:

> Behavioural experiments are planned experiential activities, based on experimentation or observation, which are undertaken by clients in or between therapy sessions. Their design is derived directly from a cognitive formulation of the problem, and their primary purpose is to obtain new information which may help to test the validity of the client's existing beliefs about themselves, others, and the world; construct new/or test new, more adaptive, beliefs; and contribute to the development and verification of the cognitive formulation.

Like any scientific experiment, behavioural experiments must include a few key components in order to be effective. All behavioural experiments must include:

- a question, theory, or expectation to evaluate or generate evidence for;
- a prediction of the results, along with an agreed means of recording and reviewing the results;
- observations about what actually happened;
- reflection/consideration of the results – in other words, what are the implications and next steps?

Holly, Boughton and Roberts (2010: 239) add that 'behavioural experiments are a particularly powerful method for bringing about enduring change in unhelpful thinking and related unhelpful behaviours because they include an active as well as a reflective component'. Despite the name ('*behavioural*'), behavioural experiments are most certainly a cognitive treatment component, generating new information with which thoughts can be challenged and newer, more adaptive cognitions formed.

To help understand the application of behavioural experiments, we will return to the case of Tom (see the Appendix). When he first came into the service, Tom had distressing automatic thoughts triggered by his physical symptoms. The thought was that the symptoms meant that he was having a heart attack. We started by considering the evidence that Tom would already have access to from his previous (*historical*) experiences. Tom understood that heart attacks were serious problems that would require medical attention. He had gone to the hospital twice, but they had sent him home untreated. Tom recognised that he had had many episodes of what he thought were heart attacks, but he had never been treated for one and was still alive and able to do most things. In reviewing the implications of this observation, Tom thought that we (myself being his practitioner) should seek some specialist advice.

Obviously a heart attack is a very serious condition and I would want to make sure Tom was safe, so we checked with Tom's primary care physician (*expert*). Tom predicted that his PCP would find evidence of a heart attack or at least a cardiac condition, and agreed that his PCP was qualified to make this diagnosis. Tom's PCP, after completing some health examinations, confirmed that Tom was in perfect health and had not previously had a heart attack, nor was he at increased risk of having a heart attack.

After reviewing the information from the PCP with Tom, he agreed that he had not already suffered a heart attack, but still had concerns about the symptoms that he experienced. If they were not caused by a heart attack, what were they? We agreed for Tom to conduct a survey of his friends to see if they had had any similar experiences and, if so, investigate the cause of their symptoms. Between sessions, Tom generated four questions and asked them to his friends through a group email (*observational*). The questions included:

- Have you ever had an episode of feeling hot and sweaty with tightness in your chest?
- What do you think those symptoms mean?
- What would you do if this happened to you?
- Other than having a heart attack, can you think of any reasons for these problems?

The results of the survey surprised Tom. Not only were the symptoms more common than he predicted, but people identified the symptoms as sounding like a possible panic attack (which is also what the PCP had originally said it could be).

Doing some follow-up reading on panic using the psycho-educational materials available in the service, Tom recognised that many of the symptoms of panic matched his own. Tom decided that there was now enough evidence pointing to a non-heart attack explanation that he was willing to put it to a direct test (*experimental*). Following the exercises in his workbook, Tom decided to test out the hypothesis that he had been experiencing panic rather than a heart attack, and that he had been misinterpreting these symptoms. Tom read that symptoms similar to the ones he had experienced could be triggered by hyperventilation. Tom completed the behavioural experiment record sheet provided by his clinician (Westbrook et al., 2007: 138). He predicted that the 'panic' symptoms would feel different to the ones he experienced during his episodes. Tom had a friend come along for the experiment in case something catastrophic happened and also to record the outcome. Just as his self-help materials suggested, Tom's experience while hyperventilating was almost identical to his previous episodes. He got hot and was sweating and felt tightness in his chest.

As in the case of a traditional experiment, it is necessary to review the results of the experiment once it is completed. The evidence generated should be considered in the context of the original hypothesis or question that it was meant to evaluate. It may be helpful to structure this process using a learning cycle (see Kolb, 1984), which offers a model for generating, reflecting on, conceptualising and implementing new knowledge (see Figure 10.6).

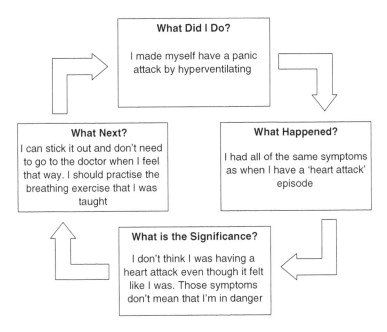

Figure 10.6   Tom's learning cycle

Medication compliance

A complete discussion of medications that are used in treating anxiety is beyond the scope of this book. However, there are three issues that will frequently appear in the low intensity treatment of anxiety that are related to medications: (a) addressing beliefs about medications (including reasons to not start medications and reasons to stop taking them; (b) enhancing medication compliance; and (c) the difficulty of using sedatives during exposure or behavioural experiments. These are discussed in turn.

Beliefs about medication

Bystritsky et al. (2005) explored people's beliefs about medications and identified six factors that predicted medication compliance:

- Does medication help a person cope better?
- Should someone with anxiety take medication?
- Is medication important in the treatment of anxiety?

- Can medication help improve problems with anxiety?
- Do medications for anxiety make you feel better physically?
- Are medications for anxiety addictive?

Beck (2001) suggests that clinicians should ask specific, targeted questions related to medication beliefs in order to obtain relevant information, including details about specific fears regarding medication and the impact that medication decisions will have on the client's relationships. With clients where medication compliance is an issue, where unhelpful beliefs are identified, these can be reviewed, evaluated and updated in the same way as other beliefs using the cognitive restructuring techniques described above and in Chapter 8.

Enhancing medication compliance

Medication non-compliance can include not taking the medication at the prescribed dosage, at the prescribed interval or simply not taking it at all. Nearly half of individuals will stop taking their prescription when they start feeling better (Evans & Spelman, 1983). Some of the characteristics of an anxious population including biases towards expecting a negative outcome, over-estimating risk and a hypersensitivity to monitoring for (and expecting) side effects. These could all impact upon medication compliance.

One means of enhancing compliance with pharmacological treatments is through the use of psycho-education. Topics to consider include:

- the rationale for treatment;
- the delay of onset;
- the time course of treatment;
- possible side effects;
- problems with relapse if the medications are withdrawn too quickly;
- concerns about addiction and cravings.

Mitchell and Selmes (2007; see Box 10.2) offer an easy to use set of tips to explore when working with a client where medication compliance is one of the agreed goals.

Box 10.2   Strategies for improving medication adherence

Basic communication

- Establish a therapeutic relationship and trust.
- Identify the patient's concerns.
- Take into account the patient's preferences.
- Explain the benefits and hazards of treatment options.

Strategy-specific interventions

- Adjusting medication timing and dosage for least intrusion.
- Minimise adverse effects.
- Maximise effectiveness.
- Provide support, encouragement and follow-up.

Reminders

- Consider adherence aids such as medication boxes and alarms.
- Consider reminders via mail, email or telephone.
- Home visits, family support, counselling.

Evaluating adherence

- Ask about problems with medication.
- Ask specifically about missed doses.
- Ask about thoughts of discontinuation.
- With the patient's consent, consider direct methods: pill counting, measuring serum or urine drug levels.
- Liaise with general practitioners and pharmacists regarding prescriptions.

Source: Mitchell and Selmes (2007: 342); © 2007 Royal College of Psychiatrists. Reproduced with permission.

Sedatives and exposure/experiments

Sedatives are often prescribed for people presenting with anxiety disorders to help manage the intensity of the symptoms (NICE, 2011b). However, during exposure or behavioural experiments, they may prevent the client from fully experiencing their anxiety and so may reduce the effects of treatment. While medication in these instances can be helpful initially in allowing the client to feel sufficiently safe or calm to be able to gather additional information, as a general principle its use is not recommended (Salkovskis, 2007). When the anxiety is restricted, several unhelpful things happen. First, the client is provided with an alternative understanding of how they managed the situation, attributing their success to the medication rather than their own efforts or to a lack of actual danger. Second, they may not have generated evidence regarding the actual facts of the situation (such as whether it is dangerous, or if they are able to manage). Finally, in reflecting on what they have learnt from the exposure, there is less evidence of self-efficacy and mastery. As such, sedatives may be used cautiously at the beginning of treatment, but limited once the client has the minimal necessary information to enable them to tolerate the condition without them.

Relapse prevention

There is a very strong argument in favour of making relapse prevention an important part of treating anxiety. In follow-up studies, relapse rates among anxiety disordered clients receiving treatment vary significantly from 6.9 per cent (Shapiro, Rees, Barkham, Hardy, Reynolds, & Startup, 1995) to about two-thirds of all anxiety disorder clients who receive treatment (Yonkers et al., 2003).

Exercise 10.10   Working with relapse

- Consider the reasons why you think relapse occurs.
- What do you think are the 'risk factors'?
- What does this suggest about preventing/managing relapse?

The first thing to remember about maintaining change in LICBT for anxiety disorders is that *the treatment is what the client does*, rather than the clinician, the support sessions or the books. As such, for change to occur the client must be doing things differently in their lives (this includes their actions and their thoughts). Likewise, for the benefits of treatment to be maintained, change must be maintained.

The goals for relapse prevention are three-fold:

- preventing relapse;
- increasing wellness; and
- developing skills to promote and sustain well-being.

Collaboration in relapse prevention

As discussed in Chapter 3, a guiding principle in LICBT is that people should be collaboratively involved in the planning and implementation of their care. This includes clients being involved in developing the focus and goals within their treatment, being active throughout treatment (and aware of their responsibility for change) and in maintaining the helpful strategies that they have learnt.

There are many different LI instruments available to support relapse prevention (a useful downloadable one is found at: anxietyuk.org.uk/wp-content/uploads/2010/07/Relapse-prevention-kit-final.pdf). One less structured system is the development of 'psychological first aid' boxes (see Box 10.3). These can take any form that may be helpful, like a shoebox or a notebook, and can include material that the person would find helpful during periods of challenge, but also any individualised items that they may benefit from, including books/worksheets, phone numbers of friends or helplines, and even simple comforts like a favourite tea.

> ## Box 10.3   Psychological first aid kit
>
> - New learning that has been helpful:
>   - Copies of psycho-education materials;
>   - Letters to self.
> - Strategies that maintain well-being:
>   - routine, necessary and pleasurable activities;
>   - time to relax and reflect;
>   - exercises to promote helpful thinking styles.
> - Strategies that reverse undesired symptoms:
>   - promoting activity;
>   - promoting comfort;
>   - promoting support.
> - Materials, resources and tips that will be useful:
>   - completed worksheets with helpful results;
>   - cue cards with reminders and prompts of what worked.
> - Early warning signs:
>   - avoidance of things or situations that cause fear and anxiety;
>   - critical or negative self-talk;
>   - use of safety behaviours.
> - What to do if …
>   - Contact details for GP, Mental Health Service self-referral line and Samaritans or local Crisis Services.

Summary

- Anxiety is a normal experience that can become a problem when it becomes so powerful that our normal ability to manage becomes restricted.
- Treating anxiety is about understanding the specific details well enough to know which thoughts and which behaviours are maintaining the problem, and then finding more helpful ways of coping.
- LICBT for anxiety can be delivered in a range of styles, including over the telephone, face to face, individually or in groups, and using computer-based interventions.

- Understanding what sort of anxiety (through diagnostic categories) can help focus your work considerably.
- Ultimately, interventions must introduce actual changes to the client's behaviours in order for the problem to get resolved.
- This can include psycho-education and relaxation as preparation, and some form of exposure to learn new information, develop new skills or habituate to the anxiety.
- Cognitive restructuring may be helpful, but only if it accompanies behavioural change, including exposure to the feared conditions.
- LICBT can include a range of supportive roles, including supporting medication compliance, promoting healthy lifestyles and planning for the long-term maintenance of gains and relapse prevention.

Further reading and activities

If you are going to treat anxiety using LICBT, this will mean supporting people to engage with what they see as the fearful or dangerous things in their lives. Unsurprisingly, this will lead to you having some clients who 'just won't change' no matter how clearly they understand the problem or how obvious the rationale for treatment is. The very best thing that you can do to prepare yourself for this clinical inevitability is to go through the process yourself. Start by recognising your own anxieties and areas where your thoughts, feelings, physical symptoms and behaviours overlap to prevent you from functioning as well as you might wish. Hopefully this is all in a sub-clinical form, but look back over the models of anxiety that we have considered here. Are there elements that look familiar or help you to recognise the patterns in your own experiences? Follow the advice in this chapter and use the available materials (such as those at: www.cci.health.wa.gov.au/resources/mhp.cfm) to make a plan for bringing about change in one of your own anxiety areas. Finally, implement your plan. It may be helpful if you keep a record of what you are doing. Work through this with a friend/colleague or take it to your own skills supervision (if this is available). Be kind to yourself; this is hard work. By the end of this, you will have a much clearer idea of the sort of challenge that treatment for anxiety disorders brings to people, and also insight into how to identify and work through these challenges. You will almost certainly be better able to empathise after this experience.

For readers interested in learning more about the treating anxiety with CBT I would recommend Meares and Freeston (2008) and Wells (1997). While both of these are undeniably aimed at a high intensity reader, the clarity of the problem and treatment descriptions more than make up for the need to 'translate' the material into LICBT applications.

11

Adapting LICBT for Use with Individuals from Minority Groups

Mark Papworth

Learning objectives

- To understand the need to accommodate clients' diversity.
- To be aware of the multi-layered influences on distress.
- To be able to consider how diversity might impact upon the individual via these influences.
- To be able to adapt therapeutic contact to take account of these factors.

Introduction

All practitioners will have contact with individuals from diverse backgrounds. These clients will be members of a minority group. Practitioners are directed by their professional bodies to make adjustments to minimise barriers into, and maximise the effectiveness of, treatment for these individuals. For example, the British Association for Counselling and Psychotherapy states that: 'The practitioner is responsible for learning about and taking account of the different protocols, conventions and customs that can pertain to different working contexts and cultures' (British Association for Counselling and Psychotherapy, 2007: 8).

Within this chapter I guide the reader in making these necessary adaptations by introducing a novel model that brings together a number of established concepts. I will firstly consider the different influences upon distress that are common for all. Then, using this model the chapter considers how these can particularly impact upon those with diverse backgrounds. Finally, I describe how to use this understanding to successfully work with diversity.

Where does distress come from?

What is the source of people's mental distress? This will vary from person to person. One common trigger is 'life events'. Life events are significant changes to an individual's lifestyle that are beyond the norm. Examples of these include bereavement, separation, a child leaving home or retirement (Holmes & Rahe, 1967). It has long been established that life events can be involved in triggering a variety of mental health problems (Myers et al., 1972). What in turn influences life events? One possible answer to this question (there are many others) is debt. There is also evidence to suggest that debt has an impact upon mental health (Fitch, Hamilton, Bassett, & Davey, 2011). It is reasonable to assume that, if individuals are more affluent, this can serve as a buffer against larger magnitude life events such as a job loss (as they can self-finance their living expenses while they are looking for a new job). Conversely, bills can become significant events if people do not have the capacity to pay them, perhaps eventually resulting in court action (thus, because of debt, a minor event can become a major one). Notice that the relationship between these two factors can be *bi-directional*: each can influence the other. Thus, life events (such as a job loss) can result in debt. Debt can result in an increase in negative life events.

Exercise 11.1   Life events

Holmes and Rahe (1967) developed a scale that allows you to measure the likely impact of life events upon your health. This is commonly available on the internet (www.mindtools.com/pages/article/newTCS_82.htm, www.stresstips.com/lifeevents.htm or www.actsweb.org/stress_test.php). Complete the scale and see whether life events are likely to contribute to you developing a stress-related illness.

What in turn then influences debt? An obvious influence here is the availability of opportunities to earn money within the community. Levels of employment are influenced by

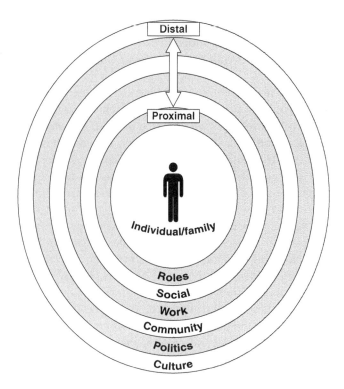

Figure 11.1   Contexts for living that influence distress

local and national government policy. Government policy is, in turn, influenced by the country's economic situation, and so forth. In this way, an individual exists within a multi-layered 'eco-system' consisting of 'contexts for living' that surround them like the layers of an onion, the individual being at the core (see Figure 11.1; Bronfenbrenner, 1979; Smail, 1990). These layers are hugely powerful and can influence each other in a bi-directional way, ultimately impacting upon the individual's well-being. I next examine the layers of this eco-system in more detail.

The layers of influence

Community psychologists and sociologists have taken a great deal of interest in the factors that affect well-being, and that are located at a 'systemic' level beyond the individual and their family (the layers of the onion that surround the core in Figure 11.1).

Smail (1990) categorises the levels closer to the individual as 'proximal' influences and those that are more distant as 'distal'. Individuals are less aware of distal factors because they do not have direct contact with them. However, these are nevertheless extremely influential.

The most distal layer is the *culture* that we live in. Culture is rather like air in that it surrounds us. It is vital but, for the most part, we remain unaware of it. The classic definition of culture is 'that complex whole which includes knowledge, belief, art, morals, law, custom, and any other capabilities and habits acquired by man as a member of society' (Tylor, 1871: 1). Understanding the impact of culture can be facilitated through considering some examples. In Eastern culture (such as Japanese and Chinese), there is more of an emphasis upon a 'holistic' philosophy to life, whereas in the west matters tend to be understood in a more isolated fashion (Leung & Sung-Chan, 2002). This is reflected in the Eastern approach to medicine where the major organs are seen as being connected to each other in a balanced system. So, Eastern treatment has an emphasis on 'adjusting' or 'supplementing' the body rather than treating it, to re-establish a healthy balance (Norwood, 2002). Likewise, the family unit has generally a greater priority in Eastern culture. Family bonds are seen as being paramount and the family has a hierarchal structure with the father/husband at the head (Leung & Sung-Chan, 2002). As such, he influences or determines the decisions of the children into adulthood, for instance traditionally arranging their marriage and choosing their spouse. These examples illustrate how culture has a direct influence upon both society and individuals' lives.

The next layer in the onion is the *political* system. The policies that governments construct have a large bearing upon public health. For instance, in Scandinavian countries where incomes have been distributed more equally and means-tested benefits have been more generous (in comparison to the UK), better health outcomes have consistently been found (Marmot, 2005). The precise mechanisms behind this relationship are revealed in some of the more proximal factors discussed below, but include the 'stigmatising' effects of being poor, which result in individuals seeing themselves of being of less value within society; those in less well paying jobs having less control over their working environment, which results in increased stress; and finally, larger discrepancies between wages creating competition rather than support within societies (Wilkinson & Marmot, 2003).

Exercise 11.2   Relative deprivation

This exercise illustrates the impact of relative deprivation. Imagine that you are working in a new team of LICBT practitioners. You are in the first month of this new job and all of the team are performing the same role. You are on a journey together. You are all excited about the new venture. By using your imagination and, if possible, by drawing upon similar experiences that you have had in the past, place yourself into this scenario. Next, write down the answers to the following questions before you read on: How do you feel about your new role? How do you feel about your colleagues?

Now consider a new piece of information. You discover that two of your colleagues have negotiated a significantly higher salary than both your own and the rest of the team's. Write down the answers to the following questions: How do you feel about this situation? Does that influence the emotions that you have about these colleagues? How does this information affect how you feel about your role and the service? What have you lost in learning this new information? What have you learned from this exercise?

Well-established research also highlights the effects of occupational status upon health. Studies that involved UK civil servants found a three-fold increase in mortality (the number of deaths occurring over time) in those working in lower status roles (Marmot, Shipley, & Rose, 1984). More recently, Wilkinson and Marmot's (2003) review described a difference in life expectancy of almost eight years between professional men and those working in unskilled manual jobs. They also found that unemployed individuals are over twice as likely to have mental health difficulties as those employed in secure jobs, with those in insecure roles also being vulnerable to distress. Finally, those who suffered the highest levels of deprivation had a greater dependency upon alcohol, nicotine and drugs.

The third layer is *community*. The physical environment (for example, our houses, parks, recreation centres, shops and churches) has an impact upon well-being. Hannay (1981) investigated the effects of housing upon mental distress and found higher levels of psychiatric symptoms amongst people living on the fifth floor or above in high-rise accommodation. However, a community consists of much more than bricks and mortar. Robert Putnam (1941–) popularised the idea of 'social capital', which describes a number of positive social characteristics of a community. One characteristic is the level of trust between citizens, another is their willingness to support each other. It is clear that higher levels of such characteristics result in an increased connectedness between people. Unsurprisingly, studies have found such communities to be healthier in terms of better mental and physical health in comparison to those with less social capital (Baum, 1999; Kawachi, Kennedy, & Glass, 1999; McCulloch, 2001).

Many of us also exist within another community: our places of *work*. These are situated within larger local communities and are therefore the next, more proximal layer of the onion. Management researchers have found that each work organisation has its own culture. This determines how it tackles issues and organises itself (Schein, 2010). The values of the organisation are a part of this wider culture, influencing the actions of the staff and defining organisational character. Dysfunctional values can compromise performance and impact upon employee well-being, making some organisations toxic places in which to work. A UK hospital trust received a great deal of negative attention when its high rate of a bacterial infection (*Clostridium difficile*) resulted in approximately 90 deaths (Healthcare Commission, 2007). The official investigation concluded that the organisation's values (which were associated with meeting performance targets such as waiting times) were contributory to the outbreak. The pressure for higher bed occupancy led to less time for thorough cleaning of the beds in between patients' use of them. Beds were placed too close together to allow proper cleaning around them and patients were placed in unsuitable areas where bathroom facilities were inadequate. Additionally, because of under-staffing, patients were told to defecate into their bed sheets because this was less time-consuming for staff, staff not having the time to keep themselves or the ward equipment hygienically clean. This example illustrates how an organisation's values can lead to disastrous consequences. The official report did not describe the morale of the staff, but with the working conditions and inadequate staffing levels, it is likely to have been poor. Organisational psychologists such as Cary Cooper (1940–) have determined that under- or over-demand, as well as a lack of control within the workplace, can result in stress-related symptoms. In this way, depending on the organisational culture, work can have a negative impact upon mental health.

Most individuals have a 'natural' support network of family and friends that they come into contact with away from their work environment. This is the next layer of the model. *Social* support has been shown to be a pivotal in terms of giving individuals resistance against the development of mental health problems. Kessler and McLeod (1985: 215) refer to 'compelling evidence that support is significantly associated with well-being and the absence of psychological distress in normal population samples'. For example, studies have noted benefits in terms of lower rates of hospitalisation, more regular attendance at outpatient clinics, as well as both improved social functioning and recovery for those suffering with enduring mental health problems (Boath, Bradley, & Anthony, 2004; Green, Hayes, Dickinson, Whittaker, & Gilheany, 2002).

The final and most proximal layer in the model consists of the *roles* that individuals hold within the community. The roles that we hold are crucial to the value that individuals place upon themselves. They place us within networks of social relationships and define our status within society (Jackoway, Rogers, & Snow, 1987; Moen, Dempster-McClain, & Erickson, 2000). Roles are held by the individual but are positioned within the community. We can think of roles as occurring on differing, overlapping levels. For instance, one can be a citizen, husband, father, concert pianist and community volunteer, all at the same time. Additionally, part of the role of being a citizen will involve expectations associated with work, which then encompasses another role, that of concert pianist.

Sarbin (1970) presents a framework for making sense of the influence that these roles can have upon an individual's value within society. He proposes that roles can be understood across three dimensions: status, value and involvement. At one end of the *status* continuum is the *ascribed* role. Ascribed roles are generally linked to biological (for example, being of working age and a heterosexual male) and social characteristics (such as being a citizen and a father). At the other end of this dimension is the *achieved* role. Achieved roles are characterised by attainment. Thus, while we can choose to be a concert pianist, we cannot choose which gender we are born with. Additionally, we may have trained for perhaps 20 years before attaining the role of concert pianist, whereas being born male involves no personal effort. Thus, the former lies towards the achieved end of the spectrum, the latter the ascribed.

The next, linked dimension is associated with the status of these roles. While some ascribed roles may be of great personal value, communities rarely give them the *value* that is allocated to achieved roles. For example, it is unusual for people to be given money or a medal for being a good citizen. However, a person could earn a lot of money or win a prize for being a good concert pianist. In this way, little status is usually given to ascribed roles, but a great deal of status can be earned through achieved ones.

The last dimension is *involvement*. With ascribed roles, the level of involvement is usually high in that we spend a lot of time and energy undertaking these roles. However, for achieved roles, much less investment is required. One can step out of the role of being a concert pianist when attending a funeral or visiting friends, but it would not usually be possible to step out of the role of being either a citizen (for instance, by disobeying the law) or a male. In this way, Sarbin demonstrates the superiority of achieved roles in that they involve less investment yet contribute more positively to an individual's identity.

Exercise 11.3   Achieved and ascribed roles

Consider your life and think about all the roles that you inhabit. While 'ascribed' and 'achieved' represent two ends of a continuum, for the sake of the exercise, try to allocate each of these roles to one of these categories. Examples of ascribed roles are: relative, sister, wife, step-mother, woman and citizen. Examples of achieved roles are: trainee practitioner, volunteer shop assistant, member of a horse-riding team, graduate and union representative. Make a list of your roles in the first two columns of a four-column table (column one for ascribed roles and column two for achieved roles).

Now complete the same exercise either for a client you know well from a deprived community or a retired member of your family. Put their information in the last two columns of the table.

What do you notice about the different role profile you have observed between yourself and your relative or client (it is not unusual for practitioners to report having more achieved roles as well as a greater general variety of roles)? What do you think might be the consequences of this? Do you have any preliminary thoughts regarding what you might do if it would be helpful to rectify this?

All six layers of the model have now been reviewed. I next use this framework to consider both the personal challenges that may be experienced because of belonging to a diverse group, and the adjustments that the practitioner can make to accommodate this.

Diversity, disadvantage and the therapeutic context

Diversity is a term used to highlight differences between groups of individuals. Several authors have presented frameworks for scoping the areas of difference that are linked to diversity. Hays's (2001) ADDRESSING framework does so by considering the following areas: *a*ge and generational influences; *d*evelopmental or acquired *d*isabilities; *r*eligion and spiritual orientation; *e*thnicity; *s*ocio-economic status; *s*exual orientation; *i*ndigenous heritage; *n*ational origin; and *g*ender. Hays states that therapists should build up a profile of their client based upon this framework. This is illustrated with a case example.

Nina is an asylum seeker from Bosnia. She was born in 1933 and so, at the time of writing, is 78 years old. In terms of her *age and generational influences*, she is now an 'older person' but was a teenager/young adult during the events of World War Two. She came to Britain during the Bosnian war (1992–1995), which followed her country's independence from the Yugoslav federation. With regard to her *developmental or acquired disabilities*, Nina suffered a left hemispheric stroke 20 years ago, which left her with difficulty in movement in the right side of her body, as well as with reduced fluency in her speech. However, she is able to walk short distances with a stick and can communicate verbally.

Like many Bosnians, Nina is a practising Muslim. Her family all share this *religion and spiritual orientation*. Her *ethnic group* is Bosniak; she speaks Bosnian as her first language and she can also communicate effectively in English. In terms of her *socio-economic status*, Nina worked as an architect in Bosnia. In the UK, she worked as a teaching assistant before being forced to retire at age 65. As such, Nina might previously have been considered to be a member of the middle class prior to her immigration, but in financial terms became a member of the lower class following her settlement in the UK. Nina would describe her *sexual orientation* as being heterosexual. Indigenous people share a common cultural identity and are native to a land or region. Thus, in regard to Nina's *indigenous heritage*, her parents and grandparents were Bosniak. Nina's *national identity* is Bosnian, although she was born at a time when the national Bosnian identity was subsumed into Yugoslavia. More latterly, after the break-up of Yugoslavia in the 1990s, the Bosnian War resulted in war crimes (including genocide) against the Bosniaks. In regard to *gender*, Nina is female and she has no children.

Hays instructs the practitioner to explore the client's ADDRESSING profile and determine, for each of these factors, whether or not the client is a member of a minority group for each particular domain. Note that an individual can be in a minority group over several of these domains. These will be areas for particular consideration for the practitioner in terms of accommodating diversity. However, the practitioner also needs to consider their own ADDRESSING profile with a view to highlighting the differences between themselves and the client. This is likely to have particular significance where the client is part of a minority group and the practitioner is a member of the majority or dominant group (see below).

Exercise 11.4   Your ADDRESSING profile

Complete the nine domains of the profile with yourself as the focus. Next, highlight the domains where you believe that you are in the dominant or majority group. Those that you have highlighted should, depending on the nature of your service and its catchment area, be areas for you to consider because you will be less aware of the experience of disadvantage within this domain. You are in the majority group; what is the experience of being in the minority group for this category?

Which of Nina's domains are in the minority group? What implication does this have for your work with Nina? What areas do you feel you need to research before you meet her?

Exercise 11.5   The experience of disadvantage

Think of your day so far. Picture it as if you are watching a film. List all the activities that you have engaged in (for example, turning off the alarm clock, getting washed and dressed, watching breakfast-time television, choosing and making breakfast, as well as getting to the bus stop and catching the bus into town). Now think about one or two of these activities in more detail (such as catching the bus). What has this involved? For example, it may have involved seeing if it was the right bus by the number on the front, getting up a step into the bus and paying the driver, finding your way around the bus to select a seat, being aware of when you were approaching your stop, ringing the bell to notify the driver and then leaving the bus at the right stop.

Now consider these activities again and imagine carrying them out as if you were a member of a diverse group (such as an older person, a person with a mild learning

(Continued)

(Continued)

difficulty or someone with a physical disability). Firstly, specify the nature of the diversity. For example, is the physical disability associated with blindness or a lack of mobility? Now consider the implications of this diversity in terms of the person's ability to perform the activities you have detailed. A blind person will not be able to see the number of the bus, the bus timetable, the layout of the bus and may not know when they are at their destination. From this exercise, consider the nature of society: who it is designed for and by whom? What is the possible impact upon the individual's ability to carry out everyday activities and access services?

The following videos produced by the Disability Rights Commission also illustrate this point:

- www.youtube.com/watch?v=FZfOVNwjFU0
- www.youtube.com/watch?v=A9a2ZqLhuAwVNwjFU0

Working with diversity through the consideration of culture

We have explored how to use the ADDRESSING framework to map out the rich tapestry of diversity for the client and practitioner. I now introduce how the 'contexts for living' (that constitute the model described earlier) for those from diverse backgrounds can influence their mental health presentations and inform the adjustments required by the practitioner. I start with culture, which was the first layer of the model.

Those from diverse backgrounds have been shaped by a culture that is often alien to the practitioner's. This can have a large impact upon a client's understanding of mental health, as well as the development and meaning of their psychological difficulties. For example, in China depression is rarely diagnosed. This is, in part, because of the concept of 'madness' in Chinese culture having a greater emphasis upon the presence of bizarre or anti-social behaviours (which are not an aspect of depression). Additionally, the Chinese have been reported to display a reluctance to discuss feelings, particularly with those outside of the family (Lin, 1983). Distinct mental health difficulties that are not observed in the West arise from other cultures. One example of these is *Taijin Kyofusho*. This is included in the Japanese mental health diagnostic system and is an intense fear of offending others by the body or its functions (for instance, by emitting offensive odours). The focus of the disorder is associated with avoiding distress in others rather than oneself. It is clear from the nature of the disorder that it is more likely to develop within cultures where the functioning of the collective (or groups of individuals) is given a greater emphasis.

A final point to make about culture and distress is that it is the dominant culture that usually defines what is 'normal'. This can lead to a process where those who deviate from the norm are labelled as 'mad' and are offered treatments that are designed to either change their behaviour or remove them from society at large. In this way, the status quo is maintained, and there is a risk of mental health professions acting as agents of society by way of a form of 'normality police'. A historical example here is the case of 'homosexuality', which was previously classified as a mental illness. With increasing gay activism over the 1960s and 1970s, this eventually ceased to be classified as a mental illness by the American Psychiatric Association in 1973.

With these factors in mind, how should the LICBT practitioner incorporate this understanding into their clinical practice? Firstly, Hays (2001) suggests that they actively research the culture in question. While, inevitably, the practitioner learns about a client's culture through conversations that take place in the clinic room, it is clear from Hays's method and relevant codes of practice that this is not in itself sufficient. For example, she suggests that the practitioner critically engages with books, films and other media, history and political science texts as well as groups that represent individuals with diversity (such as religious institutions, support groups and recreational centres). When engaging with such information, factors should be borne in mind such as the affiliations of the authors or groups, and whether materials or resources in use were created by the people from minority groups in question. To illustrate the importance of author affiliation, a book about hunting will obviously have a very different emphasis depending upon whether it is written by a marksman or an animal rights activist!

It is important to remember that it is not just individuals who are from abroad or who hold different religious faiths that have experienced a different culture. For example, Mona, Romesser-Scehnet, Cameron and Cardenas (2006) describe how those with a disability have a shared culture arising from commonalities in their background in terms of an experience of disadvantage. This consists of a number of core values including, for instance, a particular form of disability humour together with an increased tolerance for living with uncertainty or less-than-desired outcomes. In this way, culture is relevant to all forms of diversity.

The results of this personal research and experience will then mean that the LICBT practitioner can make informed adjustments to their practice in terms of: (a) therapeutic goals; (b) the interpersonal relationship; and (c) other practical accommodations. These are next considered in turn.

Therapeutic goals

In considering the possible adjustments to therapeutic goals, the practitioner must take into account the limits imposed by an individual's culture. Leung and Sung-Chan (2002) report a case study where they modified therapy for a Chinese client. This lady was referred for lower back pain (without a known physical cause) following a miscarriage where, subsequently, marital issues became evident. Here, a Western therapeutic approach might have involved individual-focused goals (for example, associated with self-esteem). However, in this cultural context, these might have destabilised the marital relationship. Consequently, Leung and Sung-Chan incorporated goals to facilitate family harmony and included sacrificial tasks to facilitate personal atonement (associated with a culturally unacceptable past sexual relationship), which produced a reduction of feelings of shame. In this way, the therapist was utilising cultural values to direct the methods and goals of therapy: compensatory sacrifices to atone for past wrongdoings and virtue associated with continuing the family lineage.

Exercise 11.6   Cultural values and therapeutic goals

You receive the following referral: Ghazala is a 30-year-old lady who lives in the UK but her parents are from Pakistan. She is married to Malik who owns a local corner convenience store. They both work long hours and have little time for pleasurable activities. Prior to the marriage, Ghazala used to socialise with her family and friends (who now live 150 miles away) while she attended university. She was previously a happy individual but over the last few years she has become increasingly depressed, having little opportunity to socialise because the shop is open over long hours for seven days a week. She is now struggling and has found herself becoming tearful when alone. What therapeutic goals do you think might help in lifting Ghazala's mood? Consider this question before you read on.

   According to Ghazala's cultural values, she must support her husband as he is head of the household. Marital failure would result in great shame and stigma for her in her local cultural community. Additionally, it is not considered to be acceptable for her to socialise outside of the family and the women from her cultural group. Has this information affected the goals you constructed earlier?

The interpersonal relationship

The effective practitioner must pay careful attention to the interpersonal relationship that they have with their client. Non-specific factors (such as the warmth, empathy and genuineness displayed by the practitioner) can account for a significant amount of client improvement (Lambert & Barley, 2002). Further, to maximise therapeutic effect, practitioners consciously alter their behaviour to beneficially influence the relationship. For example, Young (1999) recommends using the relationship as a tool to help counter maladaptive earlier experience (for instance, emotional deprivation by increasing the practitioner's nurturing- and caring-related behaviours). Returning to the LICBT approach and Nina, when we meet her for the first time, how might we consider changing our practice, given her cultural background?

To consider this, we first need to be aware of factors that fuel the power differential between the practitioner and Nina. Proctor (2002) notes that there are several elements to power within therapy. These are associated with:

1 the practitioner's role;
2 the individuals' histories (practitioner and client); and
3 their positions within society.

In terms of the *practitioner's role*, the specialist knowledge that Nina's practitioner holds, which is broadly associated with her psychological condition and the appropriate therapeutic options, is a form of power via expertise ('expert power'). Additionally, as stated earlier, the practitioner can exert a form of power through the therapeutic relationship ('referent power') through use of non-specific factors such as warmth and empathy, but also through other factors such as positive feedback. A further source of power for the practitioner is the research evidence or best practice information that can be relayed to the client ('legitimate power' which is related to a client's expectation that the practitioner can help them). With regard to *individual histories*, Nina's LICBT practitioner is from a white, British, middle class background. As such, a comparison of the two ADDRESSING profiles highlights several domains that suggest a need to be mindful that Nina's is characterised by oppression. In terms of *societal positions*, through the authority that society places in the practitioner, he or she also has the ability to directly influence the situation of the client ('ecological power'; for example, through writing letters of support to housing or welfare agencies).

Exercise 11.7   Power and relationships

Consider a situation where you are dependent on someone else who is in a position of power (for example, a lawyer or plumber). What is the form of this power? What is the impact of this power upon your relationship and your interactions with this person (place yourself back in the situation and bring to mind your thoughts, feelings, behaviours, bodily sensations and beliefs)? How would you behave differently in comparison to your interactions within a non-professional relationship (such as a friend or a shop assistant) or one where you held more power? What have you learned from this exercise that is relevant to LICBT?

The LICBT practitioner should consciously choose to use these forms of power to a greater or lesser extent across the course of contact. For example, practitioner behaviours associated with expert power should reduce over contact as the client is socialised to the LICBT approach and can direct more of the agenda themselves. On the other hand, referent power is likely to be maintained over the course of the therapy. The practitioner should consider possible means of increasing Nina's power from the outset to reduce the larger differential which exists as a consequence of her cultural background. This might involve being particularly mindful and taking more time to give Nina the rationale behind the LICBT approach/techniques and explore a greater range of options with her than is usual to enhance her ability to make an informed choice (for instance, in regard to homework tasks). This should include giving her the option of rejecting or modifying the choices that emerge through the discussion. The latter is particularly important as some cultures (such as Indian) are less likely to give negative responses even if they disagree with a statement, this being considered impolite. Likewise, the practitioner might reduce or temper 'power behaviours' such as interruptions.

The practitioner should also be mindful of the interpersonal relationship when utilising their ecological power (see below). Many individuals who are in Nina's position require letters of support to aid them in asylum seeking, welfare benefits or housing application processes. In this situation, the practitioner can reduce the power differential by carefully discussing the content of letters, showing the client a draft prior to sending, perhaps even giving the client the finished letter to take away to post themselves once they have understood and are satisfied with it.

Exercise 11.8   Use of power behaviours

With your colleagues, form triad groups where you take turns in adopting the roles of practitioner, client and observer. The observer provides feedback at the end of the role-play segment for those in the role of practitioner and client. For the role play, use a case from the Appendix or choose one of your own.

Within appropriate limits, those playing the role of the practitioner should try within the exercise to act in keeping with the two extreme ends of the continua below. Pick one or, at most, two of the continua to experiment within the role play at any one time:

- Directing ↔ non-directive
  When *directing*, you are telling the client which tasks need to be completed for them to become better. You are both negotiating less with the client and checking out their reactions to your comments to a lesser extent. In the non-directive mode you are leaving the client with the responsibility to make suggestions and decisions.
- Interrupting ↔ speak only in long pauses
  In *interrupting* you are speaking over the client's speech as thoughts come into your mind.

- Judging ↔ non-judgemental
  In *judging* you are offering frequent comments about what is helpful and unhelpful about the client's past behaviour and their contributions to the sessions.
- Instruct ↔ do not offer definite advice
  In the *instruct* mode you are offering more advice and background rationale.
- Reinforce ↔ do not offer positive feedback
  In the *reinforce* mode you are offering positive feedback wherever possible for client suggestions, achievements and past behaviour.

Practical accommodations

When taking into account the client's ADDRESSING profile, certain practical accommodations also are likely to be required. The purpose of these adjustments is to minimise any barriers that the client experiences in accessing help. In Nina's case, this might include the use of a ground floor clinic room or the provision of lift access to counter her physical health limitations. Depending on Nina's proficiency in reading English, it may be helpful to include the use of translated materials. The timing of sessions might also be important, for example, working around or avoiding booking sessions during Muslim festivals such as Eid-al-Adha. Additionally, to minimise cultural differences, a female therapist may be consciously more conservative in their dress on days that they are due to meet Nina, Muslim women being expected to dress more modestly than is normal for Western cultural standards. Nina may also benefit from telephonic contact if she does not have access to convenient public transport routes or in icy weather.

Box 11.1   Examples of other practical accommodations

- Providing self-help materials in an audio format for an individual with dyslexia.
- Providing large print versions of materials and more verbal summaries within sessions for an older person with poorer eyesight and short-term memory.
- Adding colourful images to self-help materials and record sheets to help a client who experiences attention deficit disorder focus upon them.
- Altering the layout of the furniture in the therapy room to accommodate a wheelchair user.
- Learning how to 'sign' some key phrases (such as greetings as well as the practitioner's and interpreter's names) in preparation for contact with a deaf client.
- Fitting the timing of sessions around daily prayers for a Muslim client.

We have explored how being mindfully aware of the client's culture can allow the LICBT practitioner to make informed adjustments to clinical contact. As one might expect, this is a rich and complex area to consider when working with diversity. I now consider the other layers of our model (political, community, occupational, social and roles) to determine the impact of diversity upon these and, consequentially, what additional practical considerations might be helpful.

Working with diversity through the consideration of other contexts for living

Throughout history, individuals from minority groups have faced discrimination and persecution. Perhaps the most infamous example of this is the persecution that Jewish people faced at the hands of the German Nazi movement. Life remains unfair for those from minority groups. Despite such discriminative practices usually being illegal, individuals face inequality in terms of disproportionate difficulty in accessing employment, housing or educational opportunities. Examples of this are reported regularly in the media, and in the UK this ranges from councils evicting or refusing to house asylum seekers (BBC, 2010; Kemp, 2010), gay individuals being denied holiday accommodation (Minchin, 2011), to claims that the health service is institutionally ageist (Evans, 2009). Prejudice is endemic within society and can also be observed in more routine matters such as being unable to find a sticking plaster to match a non-white skin type or being unable to buy dolls that represent a particular ethnicity (McIntosh, 1998).

Interventions to help influence political sources of distress often involve the practitioner making use of his or her ecological power (for instance, by writing letters and attending meetings on behalf of patients). Additionally, Smail (1990) highlights that a client's sense of personal power and levels of social support can be enhanced through their attendance at relevant support groups. In Nina's case, her LICBT practitioner was able to locate a local Bosnia Herzegovina club for her which offered a drop-in centre and an advice forum as well as a programme of social activities.

When Nina came to the UK, she was placed in poor housing stock in a large city. Sarbin (1970) noted that individuals from minority groups are often 'ghettoed' together within deprived areas of communities (which have a more limited repertoire of opportunities for achieved roles). This means that clients experience community issues that are associated with the effects of low levels of social capital (such as increased crime). This had a large impact upon Nina given her historical background and age, both of which heightened her sense of vulnerability. Additionally, at times asylum seekers who have been antagonistic towards each other in their home country have been housed in close proximity to each other. This may impact upon clients. In such circumstances, as well as offering support for clients to be re-housed, the practitioner should also be mindful that the environment they create in the clinic does not mirror the stressful realities that can exist in the local community. Consideration of the client running order in LICBT clinics can avoid clients feeling threatened by others in the waiting room (such as those from rival ethnic factions). Thought should also be given to the ethnic background of interpreters and opportunities must be created for the client to veto their interpreter in preference for a fresh start with another one. Waiting room materials should be scrutinised so that clients do not feel any discomfort caused by them. For instance, posters advertising the British Legion (an organisation for retired army personnel) may make Forces veterans feel more comfortable, but at the expense of being off-putting to those who have had negative experiences associated with the military (typically some refugees and asylum seekers). Further, the membership of therapeutic groups may need to be considered so that they do not replicate oppressive conditions in the larger society by including, say, one individual from a minority group among a remainder who have an ADDRESSING profile more in keeping with the dominant culture (although this is less of a factor in psycho-educational groups because of the minimal interactivity between clients with this format). In contrast, it should also be borne in mind that, because of the close-knit nature of some minority groups, confidentiality can be undermined by a group approach.

When Nina first came to the UK, she did not have a right to work; rather she needed to apply for this from the government. This meant that she was unable to offer financial support to her family who remained in Bosnia. In considering the work domain of our model, levels of discrimination here are common in respect of age, sex, disability and culture (BBC, 2005, 2007). Methods of increasing access into work and/or meaningful activity is considered in detail in Chapter 12. In Nina's case, when she first came to the UK her level of English was quite low and the refugee service helped her to enrol in a local college to improve her language skills. She then took up their invitation to volunteer at the refugee service by offering talks on asylum issues to local groups and schools. In this way, the refugee service increased her employability by widening her repertoire of skills and experience. From the contacts that she made through this activity, she eventually achieved a goal of working as a teaching assistant in a local school (she has since retired). This helped Nina to integrate into the local community, develop an additional support network and also acquire an achieved role that was extremely valuable to her. In Nina's case, the contacts at the refugee service facilitated these positive changes to her life. However, in similar instances, the LICBT practitioner might also support such progression to increased meaningful activity through referral to employment and educational advisors.

Nina's story illustrates the usefulness of forming networks with other agencies. It is worth noting that the means of increasing achieved roles, levels of social support and rewarding activity do not lie solely in the domain of paid employment. For example, the goals that Nina achieved during her contact with her LICBT practitioner included an increased attendance at events in the local community (such as Bingo) as well as attending some daytime adult education classes to increase her feelings of 'belonging'.

Conclusion

In regard to accommodating diversity, the practitioner is on a voyage of professional discovery that occurs in tandem with the help that he or she is providing to individuals from diverse groups. However, while much of the clients' relevant development will occur over the six to eight weeks of LICBT contact, the practitioner's will be spanning their career. Practitioners are viewing their clients through the lens of their own contexts for living. As such, the therapeutic contact must be informed by their own background which will, in turn, inform a process of ongoing personal research and exploration (illustrated by Figure 11.2). It is by this process that they will be better able to meet the needs of their clients through conscious adjustments to the therapeutic relationship, the goals of contact and also the practical arrangements associated with the delivery of psychological help.

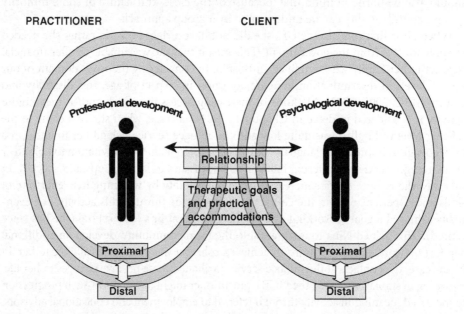

Figure 11.2   Practitioner's and client's contexts for living and considerations for therapeutic adjustment

Summary

- Professional codes of conduct state that practitioners are required to make adjustments to accommodate the differences that are commonplace in those from minority groups.
- There are various influences upon the individual's distress that operate above and beyond the level of individual or family unit. These arise from culture, political factors, features of the community and workplace, social networks and the roles that individuals possess.
- An understanding of these influences allows the practitioner to consider and accommodate the issues that are likely to be relevant to individuals from minority groups.
- In helping clients, practitioners also need to consider their own background and use this to inform their foci for continuing professional development. This is because the adjustments required will be partly dependent on the practitioner's own experience.
- Hays's (2001) ADDRESSING framework is a means of profiling both the client's and the practitioner's backgrounds.

Further reading and activities

- Hays's (2001) text provides a detailed description of the ADDRESSING framework, with useful illustrative case examples and self-development exercises.
- Hays and Iwamasa (2006) provide useful background information and case examples associated with delivering CBT to individuals from a variety of minority groups.
- Proctor (2002) overviews the influence of power in psychotherapy, both more generally and then more specifically in regard to selected therapeutic approaches (CBT, person-centred therapy and psychodynamic psychotherapy).

Use census data to find out what ethnic and religious minority groups are represented in your service's catchment area (for England see: www.ons.gov.uk/ons/rel/peeg/population-estimates-by-ethnic-group--experimental-/current-estimates/population-estimates-by-ethnic-group-mid-2009-for-primary-care-organisations--experimental-.xls). Then undertake personal research associated with these groups. Engage with any groups representing diversity in your local area. What information is available about them? Can you arrange to visit them to find out about its members? Use this visit as an opportunity to promote your service – minority groups are usually poorly represented in mental health services.

(Continued)

(Continued)

If you are a practitioner who is already seeing clients, does the material in this chapter relate to some of the clients that you have been seeing? If so, consider the following questions:

- What adjustments have you made to your contact with them, either consciously or unconsciously (explore this with your supervisor)?
- What additional adjustments could you now make that you were unaware of prior to reading this chapter?
- How might these affect your contact with the client?
- Are there any other ways in which you might personally develop to help you in your work with individuals from diverse backgrounds (for instance, volunteering for an organisation representing diversity)?

If you are not yet seeing clients but working in a service, form a small group and each person develop a fictional case study arising from differing minority groups. Find out information about the minority group's culture and their understanding of mental health (through the internet, books, magazines, newspapers, films, theatre, workshops and culture specific community events). Share the information and, in your group, consider how assessment and treatment might be altered to meet that group's needs. Here are some prompts for consideration in this exercise (see Hays, 2001, if you need more information on these areas):

- practical arrangements (such as time, venue, seating arrangements, use of interpreters and the physical environment);
- materials (large font and translated information);
- techniques (for example, pacing and the use of appropriate clinical examples);
- verbal communication (appropriate client name – surname or forename, practitioner self-disclosure and changes to language/communication);
- non-verbal communication (for instance, handshake and personal space);
- power and the relationship;
- procedural adjustments to the assessment (such as total allotted time);
- adjustments to the formulation and treatment goals; and
- the cultural meanings of symptoms.

With your supervisor or peers, view a video of yourself with a client from a minority group. Consider the appropriateness of your 'power behaviours' (see Exercise 11.8). What sort of factors can influence your power behaviours (for example, time pressures or client characteristics)? With your supervisor or through self-reflection, consider how you can adjust these to best facilitate client engagement.

Finally, make contact with your local interpreting service. Find out what information they have about the adjustments that need to be made in order to incorporate the translator into therapeutic contact (for example, www.eastlondon.nhs.uk/uploads/documents/best_practice_guide.pdf).

12

Employment and Mental Health

Theresa Marrinan

Learning objectives

- To have an awareness of the links between work and mental health.
- To gain an appreciation of the difficulties encountered by those in employment who experience mental ill health.
- To understand how work-related stress can contribute to or exacerbate existing mental health problems.
- To be able to recognise the obstacles faced by those who have been out of work because of mental ill health, to re-entering the job market.
- To understand the role of the LICBT practitioner in helping those with employment issues who present to mental health services.
- To understand the role of other professionals and the range of resources available, in helping people with mental health problems either retain their job role or return to work following a period of ill health.

Introduction

This chapter will consider the impact of unemployment on mental health and the benefits to the individual of engaging in work-related activities. There will be an exploration of ways to help clients manage employment issues while experiencing poor mental health, as well as a consideration of the impact of work-related stress. There will also be a focus on how to enable people with mental health problems to return to work following a period of unemployment. Case examples will be used throughout to illustrate how LICBT practitioners can link up with other professionals and services, to help people with mild to moderate mental health problems to manage employment difficulties or return to work following a period of unemployment.

Work and well-being

Work is thought to play a central role in the well-being of individuals. As well as having a positive impact on physical and mental health, the benefits of being employed include having sufficient economic resources, feeling included in a society where working is considered the norm and having a sense of identity, social role and status (Waddell & Burton, 2006). There is good evidence that people who are unemployed are more likely to have poorer mental and physical health, use health services more and have higher rates of mortality (Waddell & Burton, 2006). How these factors may impact upon each other is difficult to tease out – for example, does unemployment lead to poorer physical health or are those with poorer physical health less likely to look for work? However, longitudinal studies of individuals moving in and out of work provide some evidence that becoming unemployed leads to a decline in psychological well-being, whereas returning to work results in an improvement (McKee-Ryan, Song, Wanberg, & Kinicki, 2005). For this reason work is an important consideration, and surveys of people with mental health problems indicate that they themselves view having a job as a key life goal (Secker, Grove, & Seebohm, 2001). Despite this, there is often a lack of attention paid to the employment needs of clients and the obstacles they face in re-entering the job market. This is reflected perhaps most starkly for those with serious mental illnesses, for whom the unemployment rate has been found to be as high as 85 per cent (Evans & Repper, 2000).

Definitions

While the term *work* is often used to signify paid employment, it actually refers to a much broader concept. Waddell and Burton (2006) provide a useful definition in which they describe work as denoting any activity that involves physical or mental effort, and requires the application of skills, knowledge or other personal resources. As well as paid work this can include 'unpaid work or voluntary work, education and training, family responsibilities and caring' (Waddell & Burton, 2006: 4). Work can be differentiated from *employment*, which typically implies a contractual relationship between an employer and employee, and involves financial remuneration. *Worklessness* is a fairly recent term and its exact definition may vary. However, in general it refers to those who are not engaged in any form of paid work, so may include those who are officially classified as *unemployed* (those who are actively seeking work, and in receipt of unemployment benefits), as well as those who are not currently looking for work for reasons such as illness and family responsibilities.

When exploring the benefits of work, we are using the term in its broadest sense. From this perspective, it is possible to see how unpaid work can deliver many of the same benefits as being employed. For example, volunteering in a supportive environment may provide a sense of routine, add purpose and meaning, increase social contact and help the person to develop skills. On the other hand being employed in a poor working environment, for instance where there is a lack of safety or high levels of stress, may prove less beneficial or even harmful to a person's health (Dodu, 2005). Furthermore, we cannot always assume that being unemployed is detrimental to a person's health and well-being. Some people may choose to take on family responsibilities or may be in position to take a break from paid employment. Others may be unable to work because of serious or long-term illness, or other reasons. Thus, when considering the impact of unemployment we need to take all of these factors into account.

Exercise 12.1   Work and well-being

Let us consider why working may be beneficial to a person's well-being. Think about your own situation. If you are working or studying, consider the benefits you may gain as a result of doing this. If you are not currently employed, perhaps you do some voluntary work. If none of these apply, think back to a time when you were engaged in some type of work or study. Make a list of all the benefits that you experienced as a result of engaging in such activities.

Benefits of work

One of the most obvious advantages of having paid work is the financial reward. Most fundamentally, a certain level of income is required in order to satisfy our basic needs for food, clothing and housing. Lack of money may limit our ability to fulfil such basic functions. In countries without a welfare system, paid work may be the only means of securing an income. In those countries with a welfare system, payments or unemployment benefits may be provided to help individuals with their basic requirements. However, sometimes these may be temporary and are usually only sufficient to cover essential needs. There are often conditions attached to receiving these benefits, such as providing regular evidence of looking for work. Depending on the fulfilment or not of these conditions, the benefits can be removed. All of these factors can result in the person feeling vulnerable and under financial strain, leading to high levels of anxiety and placing family relationships under pressure. Having a steady or comfortable income, on the other hand, enables a person to feel more financially secure, have increased choice over many aspects of their life, and plan for the future.

Financial stability, however, is not the only benefit of being employed. In the industrialised world, the job we do plays a vital role in defining our identity and social status, and consequently is integral to how we view ourselves. Indeed it may be one of the first facts we find out when we meet someone new. This has significant implications for self-esteem and well-being (Dodu, 2005). As others have pointed out, the right to paid employment is considered so fundamental that it is enshrined in Article 23 of the United Nations Declaration of Human Rights (Dodu, 2005; Lelliott, Tullock, Boardman, Harvey, Henderson, & Knapp, 2008). Work can also be important for giving meaning and a sense of purpose to our lives, providing structure and routine, and engaging us in activities that may be experienced as rewarding or that contribute to a sense of personal achievement. Furthermore, it offers an important source of social interaction beyond the family (Dodu, 2005; Lelliott et al., 2008). As mentioned earlier, both paid and unpaid work can offer these benefits.

Exercise 12.2   The impact of becoming unemployed

Consider Andrew, a 28-year-old, single man who lost his job 18 months ago. He worked as a sales assistant for a property development company. He had to move out of his flat a year ago, after it was repossessed when he fell behind with his mortgage payments. He has been applying for jobs but has not had much response. Reflect on all the possible disadvantages to Andrew of being unemployed, considering all areas of his life.

Disadvantages of being unemployed

Having explored the beneficial impact of work, it is now important to consider the disadvantages of not working. Unemployment will be principally focused upon, as having a paid job is often the main way in which people gain the rewards attached to work. There are also wider societal aspects to being unemployed which deserve further consideration.

Losing one's job or being out of work for significant periods of time can result in a number of negative effects. As mentioned above, there are some clear rewards to being employed that go beyond financial security and are likely to impact upon our sense of well-being. Thus, while the loss of income can have a major impact, this is not the only significant change likely to be encountered (see Figure 12.1). There may be a loss of routine or structure, as well as reduced opportunities for engaging in rewarding or purposeful activities. Being out of work can also be very isolating, since work often provides an important source of social contact and support. More fundamentally, the person may experience a loss of identity or status.

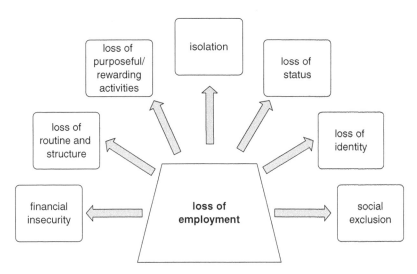

Figure 12.1   Impact of loss of employment

In addition there may be deeper societal effects. Being unemployed can lead a person to feel as though they are living on the margins of society. This is known as *social exclusion*, a process by which a person's situation may prevent them from fully participating in the normal activities of the society in which they live. This may include not having equal access to decent housing, education and healthcare, or refer more generally to engagement with the democratic processes. It has been described by the Social Exclusion Unit (2001: 10) as: 'a shorthand term for what can happen when people or areas suffer from a combination of linked problems such as unemployment, poor skills, low incomes, poor housing, high crime, bad health and family breakdown'.

Andrew's experience can help to illustrate how loss of employment can lead to social exclusion. When he lost his flat he managed to secure accommodation with a housing association. However, he now lives in an area with a high level of crime and feels nervous about walking around in his neighbourhood. He also had to sell his car and now uses public transport but cannot afford to spend much on travel, which limits where he can go. His local shops are more expensive and do not provide the same level of choice that he had available previously when he was able to drive to large out-of-town supermarkets.

Andrew is desperate to find a job and in the first couple of months of being unemployed he submitted countless job applications. Over time he has become disheartened with the lack of response and rejection letters. The longer he is unemployed, the harder he finds it to promote himself as a valuable asset. This has reduced his motivation. However, he feels increasingly pressured by his Job Centre advisor to find work. When he first started attending the Job Centre he was shocked to see there were security guards present. Initially he wondered if the Job Centre might be a dangerous place. However, at a recent meeting with his advisor, he became frustrated and angry as he thought she was accusing him of not trying hard enough to find work. As a result, the advisor called the security guard over and he now perceives that he is seen as a 'trouble maker'. He has considered retraining but is unsure what to do and is worried about being able to afford the associated fees.

Andrew's friends are concerned about him and have made efforts to keep him involved in their social group. One friend recently invited him to a social gathering, offering to collect him and pay his taxi fare home. Although Andrew wanted to go, he felt embarrassed that his friend was offering to pay and worried about being unable to afford to buy drinks once there. He was also reluctant to meet new people, as he did not want to admit to being unemployed. As a result, he made an excuse and avoided going. This is happening more and more, with the result that he feels increasingly lonely and isolated.

The case example above illustrates how being unemployed can lead a person to feel socially excluded in many ways. Certainly a large part of this may be financial, but there are many other factors involved, which may impact more generally on a person's life. Andrew does not have mental health problems but it is possible to imagine that he might become depressed or anxious as a result of these circumstances. Imagine how much more difficult it may be for a person in a similar situation who also has mental health problems.

Employment issues to consider

Having explored the links between work and well-being, the following section will now detail particular employment issues with which the LICBT practitioner might be presented:

- clients who are currently in paid employment, who develop mental health difficulties owing to factors unrelated to their job;
- clients in paid employment, who are experiencing mental health difficulties as a result of work-related stress;
- clients who are unemployed and recovering from depression or anxiety, who wish to re-enter the job market.

Experiencing mental health difficulties while in employment

> ### Box 12.1   Case study 1: experiencing mental health difficulties while in employment
>
> Louise is a 22-year-old woman who works in a call centre. She started experiencing low mood five months ago following the death of her father. She has been finding it difficult to concentrate at work and has made a number of small errors. She has also been late on two occasions, which has resulted in her receiving a verbal warning from her manager. Louise went off on sick leave two weeks ago. She spends most of her days being inactive and she is experiencing high levels of anxiety. Louise was referred to the LICBT service and attended her first appointment a week ago.

Estimates suggest that as many as one in six of the workforce may have a mental health disorder at any one time, yet this tends to be poorly recognised by employers (Sainsbury Centre for Mental Health, 2007a). In the UK, stress, depression and anxiety have been found to comprise the second most common cause of work-related illness and may result in as many as 12.8 million working days being lost each year (Jones, Huxtable, & Hodgson, 2005). Experiencing mental health difficulties can lead to *absenteeism* – taking time off because of ill health, or *presenteeism* – where the person continues to work despite feeling unwell.

It is thought that presenteeism may actually be more costly to employers than absenteeism, because of the impact of reduced productivity (Sainsbury Centre for Mental Health, 2007a). Presenteeism is particularly important to consider for people with mental health problems as they may be reluctant to admit to having difficulties for fear of being stigmatised (Sainsbury Centre for Mental Health, 2007b). Evidence suggests that workers who have been off sick with mental health problems are more likely to be demoted, placed under supervision or dismissed (Lelliott et al., 2008). In order to avoid this, many people may continue to work despite experiencing depression or anxiety. This can result in them becoming more ill and in addition, they may experience significant impairments in their work performance. People experiencing depression, for example, report particular difficulties in time management, mental tasks and interpersonal activities, such as team working (Adler, McLaughlin, Rogers, Chang, Lapitsky, & Lerner, 2006; Burton, Pransky, Conti, Chen, & Edington, 2004). This is unhelpful both for the person trying to recover from mental health difficulties, and for the employer, who loses out through reduced productivity. In addition, where the mental health problem goes unrecognised, there is a danger that poor performance may lead a manager to make negative judgements about the person's capacity to work. This, in turn, could lead to damaging consequences such as lack of opportunities for promotion or even disciplinary action being taken against the employee.

However, while it is important that people take time from work to recover from ill health, long-term absences can be problematic, and the longer a person is off work because of sickness, the lower their chances of returning. Indeed, some studies indicate that those off work for six months or more as the result of illness have a significantly reduced chance of ever getting back to work (see Waddell & Burton, 2006). Furthermore, a long-term absence may contribute to or exacerbate symptoms. In particular, it may lead to a loss of structure and routine, reduce opportunities to engage in purposeful or rewarding activities, increase social isolation and allow more time to dwell on negative thoughts. All of these factors may contribute to a downward cycle where the person loses confidence in their capacity to cope with the demands of work, which may have the effect of prolonging their symptoms of anxiety or depression. Consequently, they may be even less likely to return to work. As the cycle continues they may feel increasingly worried that returning to work will only exacerbate their mental health difficulties (see Figure 12.2).

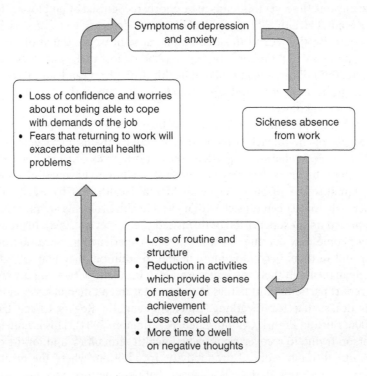

Figure 12.2   Negative impact of long-term sickness absence

Managing a person's return to work, therefore, needs careful consideration. Presenteeism is not helpful to the employer or employee. However, prolonged absences may also be detrimental to the person's mental health. When a person has been off work with depression or anxiety it is important that they are not left feeling isolated. A coordinated approach between the mental health service and the employer needs to take place, in order to ensure that the person is supported to return to work as soon as they feel able. A plan should be put in place, which is tailored to the individual's needs and capabilities, and which fits in with any treatment they may be receiving from the LICBT service. On the employer's side this might include a risk assessment of their working environment, temporary changes to their roles and responsibilities, flexible working and the provision of extra support. The task of the LICBT practitioner will be to identify any employment issues, liaise with relevant professionals who have expertise in this area, and link this in with any treatment the person is receiving. The practitioner will need to give particular consideration to the client's mental health needs, paying close attention to what they can manage in terms of increasing their activity levels. The behavioural activation approach discussed in Chapter 8 will be helpful here in guiding the client to take a graded approach to reintroducing activities, including a return to work. If goals are too ambitious, the person may become overwhelmed and end up doing nothing. At worst this may play into fears about failing and increase their levels of hopelessness. In addition, if the person returns to work before they are ready this is likely to result in poor performance, which may be interpreted by their manager as a lack of motivation or competence, which in turn can result in adverse consequences (Lelliott et al., 2008).

Work-related stress

Box 12.2   Case study 2: work-related stress

Judith is a 53-year-old primary school teacher. Over the past few years she has experienced significant changes in her job. She has found this increasingly stressful and has had four periods of sickness absence in two years. Her school has been subject to a number of external reviews because of failing performance and she has felt personally criticised within this process. As a result she has been devoting increasing amounts of time to preparing her classes and estimates that she works an average of 60 hours a week. However, she says that she never feels on top of her work demands. Her sleep has been affected and she has lost a great deal of confidence in herself generally. She worries about the future and reports that she feels anxious much of the time. She has been referred to the LICBT service.

Surveys show that around one in seven employees in the UK rate their job as very or extremely stressful (Health and Safety Executive, 2007). In practice it can be difficult to distinguish between 'stress' and depression or anxiety, as symptoms of stress tend to be very similar to those of mild to moderate anxiety or depression. In addition, experiencing stress at work may impact on all aspects of a person's functioning, not solely their work performance. *Work-related stress* is said to occur when there are excessive pressures or demands placed upon the employee (Health and Safety Executive, 2007). While pressure at work is not in itself problematic, and indeed may be positive or motivating, it is the capacity to cope with this that is crucial. Difficulties coping with pressure may occur when there is a lack of resources provided to help the employee deal with such demands, for example not being given sufficient time, support or training. Other sources of stress include lack of control over the pace of work, poorly defined job roles, bullying or interpersonal conflict, and poor management of organisational change (Health and Safety Executive, 2007). In the UK, employers have a duty to protect their employees from undue stress under the Management of Health and Safety at Work Regulations (1999).

It is important that the LICBT practitioner is aware of whether the client's workplace is the main source of their mental health difficulties, in order to gain an accurate picture of the factors that may be maintaining their symptoms. Planning a return to work needs to involve a careful assessment of the workplace, with sufficient consideration given to the possible causes of stress, allowing for necessary adjustments to be made. This might include a reduction in workload, the provision of extra training or support and the management of interpersonal conflicts. Such an assessment is best carried out by those with the relevant expertise, such as the occupational health service or workplace health and safety representatives, who would work closely with the person's employer and the human resources department. The LICBT practitioner's role is likely to involve liaising with such professionals as is discussed later in the chapter.

Returning to work after a period of unemployment

Box 12.3   Case study 3: returning to work after a period of unemployment

Jim is a 23-year-old man who was employed as an apprentice joiner in the furniture industry. Three years ago he started to experience panic attacks, the first of which occurred while he was at work. At the time he attributed his symptoms to choking on dust generated from the machinery he was operating. Following this he had numerous periods of sickness absence and found it increasingly difficult to go to work. He was eventually retired from his job two years ago, on the grounds of ill health. Subsequently, he began to experience panic attacks whenever he was in crowded situations, such as town centres, and found it increasingly difficult to go out. He was recently referred to the LICBT service where he was assessed and diagnosed as having panic disorder with agoraphobia.

Surveys of people with mental health problems who are currently unemployed, demonstrate that many wish to return to some form of work (Secker et al., 2001). Furthermore, as described earlier, evidence suggests that returning to work after a period of unemployment is associated with improvements in both physical and mental health, self-esteem and general well-being (McKee-Ryan et al., 2005; Waddell & Burton, 2006). However, significant obstacles may be encountered in this process, which can act as barriers to getting back into work. These include:

- general factors associated with being out of work for a considerable period of time;
- the effects of stigmatisation;
- financial disincentives.

These will be explored further below.

General factors

Being out of work for any period of time may impact upon a person's confidence and beliefs in their capacity to manage the demands of work, responsibility and pressure. This is likely be even more accentuated in people who have experienced mental ill health, who may have concerns about their capacity to cope with life in general. In addition, people who have been unemployed for long periods of time may be unused to structure and routine, and may not have up-to-date skills or knowledge. This can make the process of applying for jobs and attending job interviews extremely anxiety-provoking, and indeed may affect performance during interviews.

Stigmatisation

A particular barrier facing people with mental health difficulties when re-entering the job market is the stigma associated with their condition (Lelliott et al., 2008). Surveys show that people with mental health disorders often feel discriminated against when applying for work (Read & Baker, 1996). This perception appears to be justified, as studies suggest that many employers hold negative attitudes toward those with mental health problems (Manning & White, 1995; Scheid, 2005). This is despite the existence of laws that prohibit disability discrimination, such as the UK Equality Act, 2010. As a result, many applicants struggle with the dilemma of whether or not to disclose mental health problems to their prospective employer (Stuart, 2006). Unfortunately, non-disclosure can also place the person at a disadvantage since they may need to be open about their condition if they require necessary adjustments or extra support (Lelliott et al., 2008).

Financial disincentives

Returning to work, particularly low-paid work, can result in some people becoming worse off financially. This can happen because they lose welfare payments such as housing benefit, or because they need to find extra money for childcare and other costs such as those involved in travelling to work. Not surprisingly, this can prove a major disincentive to looking for a job. In addition, when individuals or families are dependent on welfare benefits, any change of circumstances that might result in these being withdrawn, even temporarily, can be experienced as highly anxiety-provoking. For example, taking a job may mean that there is a significant gap between benefits being stopped and receipt of the first month's salary. Some people fear that even looking for work could lead to benefits being withdrawn (Department for Work and Pensions, 2002). In addition, it can be difficult to navigate the benefits system and individuals may be unaware of potential payments they might be entitled to receive despite working, such as housing benefit and disability payments.

Supporting clients with employment issues

LICBT practitioners have an important role to play in identifying and managing employment issues with their clients. During the assessment process, the practitioner will gather information around all aspects of the client's presenting problem (see Chapter 5). A particular area to explore is the client's level of functioning, including employment status and involvement in other vocational activities. Issues such as sickness absence, stress and worklessness need to be considered within this. When looking at treatment options, the practitioner can help the client to make decisions about whether there are significant work issues to consider, and whether these need to be prioritised or focused on at a later point.

Exercise 12.3 Prioritising employment issues in treatment

Consider the case examples provided earlier – Louise, Judith and Jim. For each case, list all of the possible factors that may be important to consider in determining whether employment issues should be a priority during treatment.

There are a number of questions to consider when determining whether to prioritise employment or work issues. These include:

- Is this a goal or priority for the client?
- Are work issues causing distress for the client and contributing to their poor mental health?
- Is the client ready to address work issues or do they need to focus on other goals first?

Alongside the LICBT practitioner there are a range of other professionals and support services that can be essential in supporting the client with work issues. Thus, liaising with other professionals who may have expertise and experience these areas, within both the mental health service and the client's workplace, is vital. The roles and functions of the employment advisor (EA), and the occupational health service deserve particular consideration, as they are likely to be the first port of call for the LICBT practitioner. These respective roles will be discussed further below.

The role of the EA

EAs have been a fairly recent addition to primary mental healthcare services in England, and were introduced as part of an ongoing recognition of the need to help people with mental health problems either to retain their job role or make a return to work in cases where they have been unemployed for some time (IAPT, 2011a). Their role is to work together with mental health practitioners offering guidance and practical support for clients with work issues. The exact remit of the EA may vary according to local practice (IAPT, 2011b). Thus, they may work either within or in conjunction with services, and have shared or independent referral pathways. They may also have an overarching role of liaising with job centres or employment support providers to ensure integration or coordination of services. EAs will usually take referrals for people who are currently employed but on sickness absence, or experiencing difficulties in their work, including those who may be facing redundancy. They can also provide support and guidance to people who are currently out of work but who wish to make a return.

Referrals to EAs may happen in a variety of ways:

- EAs may routinely attend team meetings in the mental health service to discuss all new referrals to the service;
- all clients who are off sick from work, or currently unemployed, may be asked at their initial appointment if they would like an assessment appointment with the EA;
- during the course of treatment, or as a result of discussions in supervision, clients with employment issues may be referred to the EA.

When a client has been on sick leave from their job, the EA can perform a number of tasks. These include:

- carrying out a detailed assessment of the individual's employment situation, including a review of whether returning to work is realistic or achievable;
- identifying potential sources of stress and possible barriers to returning to work;
- helping the client to consider reasonable adjustments that could be made to enable them to return to work, for example phased return to work, changes in shift patterns, adaptations to the physical environment, flexible working and time off for appointments;
- liaising with other agencies, for example, occupational health or voluntary services organisations;
- providing follow-up once the person is back at work.

A return to work plan and necessary adjustments need to be agreed with the employer. This may involve the EA working directly with the employer and all others concerned, such as occupational health services and trade union representatives. The human resources department (HR) is also likely to be included in this process. The role of HR within a workplace involves having an overarching strategy for how employees are managed. This may include anything from recruitment and selection, through to training, performance appraisal and safety.

For individuals who are unemployed the EA may help them to look at:

- tackling barriers to getting a job, including lack of confidence, skills or opportunities;
- increasing employability skills by carrying out a skills audit, identifying needs for training and considering means of gaining skills, for example, through doing voluntary work;
- referral to external agencies, who may be able to provide advice, training or work placements.

LICBT practitioners will need to work closely with the EA to decide when referrals are appropriate and whether they need to co-work with a client. For some clients it may make sense to work alongside the EA, providing ongoing treatment for the client and ensuring that a return to work ties in with their treatment plan. In other cases the LICBT practitioner may offer treatment initially, until the client's symptoms have subsided sufficiently for the person to feel ready to consider a return to work. At this point, it may then be helpful to involve the EA. Where work-related stress is the main focus, the LICBT practitioner may take a step back, allowing the EA to take the lead in helping the client to resolve these issues. This is on the understanding that reducing the stress caused by the work situation is likely to be the key to reducing the client's distress. Unfortunately, funding for EAs has been withdrawn in some areas of England and so the availability of such services may vary from region to region. Where no such service exists, the LICBT practitioner may need to take on more of this role with their clients.

Occupational health services

Occupational health services can be critical in helping employees with mental health problems manage work issues. The World Health Organization states that all workers should have access to occupational health services (WHO, 1994). Indeed there are compelling reasons for employers to invest in such schemes both for the health of their employees and to reduce the cost of sickness absence (Black, 2008). Despite this, best estimates suggest that only 15 per cent of UK employers provide basic access to occupational health, and just three per cent have a comprehensive occupational health service (Pilkington et al., 2002). This is mainly limited to larger employers, who are more likely to have in-house occupational health services, while smaller companies tend to use external or private agencies. In order to address this situation, the UK government commissioned a joint report by the Department for Work and Pensions, the Department of Health and the Health and Safety Executive, which recommended an increase in the number of workplaces with access to occupational health services (Department for Work and Pensions, Department of Health, & Health and Safety Executive, 2004).

The role of occupational health services is to protect the health of employees at both an organisational and an individual level. Typically a variety of professionals are employed within occupational health services to help achieve this aim, including doctors, nurses, physiotherapists, psychological therapists, and health and safety specialists. At an organisational level, occupational health professionals are involved in the assessment and monitoring of workplace practices, as well as the work environment, in order to minimise risk to workers and prevent work-related ill health. They may also lead on health promotion initiatives to improve the overall well-being of the workforce.

When an employee is experiencing mental health problems, the role of the occupational health service is to provide the necessary support to enable the person to recover and to facilitate a safe return to work. This may involve a number of functions, including:

- carrying out assessments following a prolonged period of sickness absence;
- maintaining contact with employees who are on sickness absence to prevent a sense of isolation and unnecessarily long absences;
- acting as a link between the treating physician, line manager and HR department;
- identifying sources of work-related stress and barriers to returning to work;
- negotiating adjustments needed for the person to manage their job and make a return to work;
- providing guidance to managers on dealing with employee work-related stress and interpersonal conflicts;
- providing counselling or support;
- acting as a referral pathway to other services.

LICBT practitioners or EAs may advise clients to make contact with their occupational health service or link up themselves with such services with the client's consent. This is important in ensuring that employment issues are carefully managed. As described earlier, negotiation of changes to a person's job role or conditions of employment requires close cooperation between the mental health service, the occupational health service, the employer, HR and often trade union representatives.

Other sources of support

As well as EAs and occupational health services there are a range of other services that may be helpful to direct the client towards, including:

- welfare rights organisations to discuss which benefit payments a person might be able to claim if unable to work, or if they are in the process of returning to work;
- student support services, where a person is in full-time education and experiencing difficulties with study;
- Job Centre advisors for help with a job search, filling in applications and confidence building programs, as well as 'in-work benefit calculations', which can predict take home pay rates and benefits available to support someone who moves into paid work;
- voluntary work organisations;
- debt counselling services for help with managing financial problems;
- organisations that provide free legal aid and advice.

Exercise 12.4   Liaising with others

Let us return to the case examples provided earlier (Louise, Judith and Jim). Consider each case in turn. If you were assessing these cases, which other services or professionals might you refer to, or liaise with, in order to help them to manage their employment issues?

Each of the case examples will now be described further below in order to illustrate the processes that may be involved in helping clients with employment issues.

Case example 1 – Louise

Louise had an initial assessment session with the LICBT practitioner who identified that she was experiencing moderate levels of depression, with some accompanying symptoms of anxiety arising from her employment situation. The agreed treatment plan was to have six to eight sessions of guided self-help. She was also offered an appointment with the EA. At that appointment, it was agreed that it would be useful for Louise to contact the occupational health department at her workplace to inform them of her difficulties and approach her trade union representative for some advice regarding the disciplinary action. Louise saw the occupational health nurse, who discussed various options with her to help manage the situation. The occupational health nurse liaised with Louise's manager, the HR department and her trade union representative, and it was agreed that Louise could work reduced hours, which would be reviewed after a month. She was also given permission to take time off to attend her appointments with the LICBT service and her manager agreed to lift the disciplinary action. Louise was pleased with the outcome and reported feeling much less anxious about work as a result. She completed her sessions of LICBT and was able to return to full-time work, six weeks after the meeting with her manager. The LICBT practitioner also provided some information about bereavement counselling agencies. However, once the work issues had been resolved Louise felt more able to manage the grieving process.

Case example 2 – Judith

Following Judith's initial appointment with the LICBT practitioner, she was referred on to the EA because her difficulties appeared to originate from work-related stress. With the help of the EA, Judith was able to recognise the key sources of stress in her job and identify some possible changes to improve the situation, including reducing her hours and responsibilities. Judith gave consent for the EA to contact her manager and a meeting was set up between Judith, the EA, a representative from HR and her manager. At that meeting, Judith was able to express the difficulties she had been experiencing and request a number of changes. As a result, her manager agreed to temporarily reduce her hours and responsibilities. Her manager also expressed regret that Judith had been feeling so under-valued, and expressed her appreciation about how supportive Judith had been to the other staff while they had all been under pressure. She suggested that Judith ask her general practitioner to sign her off work temporarily because of her stress levels, with a plan to return gradually over the following month. A review was arranged with the EA six weeks after the meeting with her manager, at which point Judith informed the EA that she was back at work and her stress levels had significantly reduced. At her request, her manager had also agreed to a permanent reduction in her hours.

Case example 3 – Jim

Jim identified that getting back to work was a priority. However, it became clear in the assessment session that he needed to overcome his panic attacks and agoraphobia in order to realise this goal. He was offered eight sessions of guided self-help with the LICBT practitioner. As a result of the treatment, he experienced a significant reduction in the frequency of his panic attacks and was able to go out on a more regular basis. Following this, an appointment was arranged with the EA at which Jim described his concerns about starting a job, in particular his fear of having a panic attack while at work. The EA suggested that it might be useful initially for Jim to do some voluntary work in order to build up his confidence. The EA was also able to help Jim to identify some possible areas for retraining. Jim mentioned that he was interested in a career as a plumber and the EA was able to provide him with some information on a training course in plumbing at a local college which he could attend at a concessionary rate. The EA also set up an appointment with an advisor at a voluntary services agency, who was able to help him find work with a housing association that required volunteers to do gardening and odd jobs for older residents. A follow-up appointment was arranged for a month later, with both the LICBT practitioner and the EA, to review Jim's progress. At that appointment, Jim reported that he was enjoying the voluntary work and, despite feeling anxious on his first day, had settled in without experiencing any panic attacks. He had also applied for the plumbing course and was due to start two months later.

The case examples provided above illustrate the close liaison that is needed between LICBT practitioners, EAs and other services to enable people with mental health problems to manage the difficulties they may experience in relation to employment. This underlines the importance for the LICBT practitioner of becoming knowledgeable about the roles of other such professionals involved in this area, as well as the need to become familiar with the various services and agencies that can play a part in helping clients back to work. The exact nature and remit of these will vary across localities, and this chapter can only provide a general outline of what may be available. Thus, a key task for the practitioner is to build up their knowledge and develop close working relationships, in order to promote an integrated approach when helping clients remain in, or return to work.

Conclusion

Work is central to most people's lives. As well as providing financial resources, it enables us to engage in meaningful activities, gives purpose and structure, offers opportunities for social interaction, allows us to develop skills, and helps us to feel part of society. Indeed, it can shape our very identity and is thought to play an important role in our well-being. On the other hand lack of employment appears to increase the risk of mental and physical ill health. Thus, helping people with common mental health problems to manage employment issues is likely to be a key issue for the LICBT practitioner. This may involve supporting clients to remain at work or return to work following a period of illness and requires knowledge of, and usually close liaison with, the relevant organisations and professionals who are part of this process.

Summary

- Work plays a key role in well-being.
- Lack of employment is associated with a range of negative effects, including poorer mental health and social exclusion.
- For those in employment who experience mental health problems, careful planning is needed in order to ensure that mental health problems are not exacerbated either by returning to work too soon or by extended absences.
- Where people have been unemployed for a significant period of time following mental ill health, they may face significant barriers to getting back into work.
- LICBT practitioners have a significant role to play in identifying employment issues and helping clients to manage these. This requires knowledge of, and liaison with, a range of other relevant professionals and services who may be key to this process.

Further reading and activities

If you are currently working as a LICBT practitioner, find out if there is an employment advisor attached to your service and arrange to meet with them to discuss their role. Discuss how you would link up when working with clients with employment difficulties – it may be useful to present some of the case studies from this chapter to see how the process would work in your service. If there is not an EA available locally, explore other possible sources of support that clients can access, such as the local job centre/employment office. Find out about the role of the occupational health service in your organisation. Begin to build up a resource pack of services, and arrange to visit two or three of those that might be most relevant to link in with, for example, voluntary services, local colleges, welfare rights agencies and debt counselling services.

(Continued)

(Continued)

In order to consolidate your learning from this chapter some key references are recommended for further reading. Dodu (2005), Lelliott et al. (2008) and Waddell and Burton (2006) all provide excellent overviews of the impact of work on well-being. Guidance is available from the IAPT website (IAPT, 2011b) regarding the role of employment advisors. The following UK websites may also be useful:

- The Society of Occupational Medicine (www.som.org.uk) for information about occupational health;
- Health and Safety Executive website (www.hse.gov.uk/stress) for information about work-related stress;
- Directgov (www.direct.gov.uk), which provides access to a range of useful services such as debt counselling, job search and benefits claims;
- Citizen's Advice Bureau (www.citizensadvice.org.uk), which offers free legal and financial advice;
- Do it – Volunteering made easy (www.do-it.org.uk), for information about opportunities to volunteer.

13

Supervision

Dominique Keegan

Learning outcomes

- To understand the importance of supervision for LICBT practitioners.
- To understand the distinctive features of LICBT supervision versus traditional forms of clinical supervision.
- To understand the nature and role of case management and skills development within LICBT supervision.
- To know how to make best use of case management supervision and skills development supervision in LICBT.
- To be aware of the issues that may arise in LICBT supervision.

Introduction

The aim of this chapter is to give the reader a clear understanding of the forms of clinical supervision which support LICBT. The chapter will start with a review of why supervision is important for clinical practice. It will then consider the definition and role of LICBT supervision, in contrast to traditional forms of clinical supervision and given the particular nature of the LICBT practitioner role. Two forms of supervision are used in LICBT: case management and skills development supervision. Case management supervision is considered in relation to what is required to ensure that it is effective, namely the clear and structured presentation of clinical information. The section on skills development supervision considers the need for a contract, the models, methods and modalities that may be used, and the factors that may influence the decision to provide supervision in an individual versus group format. Guidance will be offered on how to make the most of LICBT supervision, through a collaborative supervisory relationship, clear goals, a review of learning styles and the ways in which competence can be developed. The chapter concludes with a summary of complex issues that can arise within supervision and how these can be managed. These issues include confidentiality, professional standards, limits to staff disclosure and uncertainties associated with clinical competence. Exercises and case studies are provided, to illustrate some of the themes that are discussed.

What is clinical supervision and why is it important?

Clinical supervision is an activity that is key to the effective delivery of psychological therapies. LICBT is no exception to this (Richards & Suckling, 2009). While much is written about it, clinical supervision nonetheless lacks a clear, formal definition (Milne, 2009). One that is frequently cited broadly describes it as a formal but collaborative relationship involving a supervisor, typically a more senior clinician with greater clinical knowledge, skills and experience, and a supervisee, who may be more junior and seeking the development of such knowledge, skills and experience (Bernard & Goodyear, 2004). One key task in clinical supervision, therefore, is for the supervisor to use their knowledge, skills and experience to help the supervisee to develop as a clinician. It is also important, however, to consider the other functions that supervision may serve.

Exercise 13.1   Functions of supervision

To consider the other functions that supervision may serve, imagine that you have recently started to work in a LICBT service and have built up a caseload of 10 clients. You are due to meet with your supervisor first thing tomorrow. What kinds of issues do you think you will want to discuss? Consider the following examples and decide which you might bring:

- a client who has risk issues;
- a client who has not attended the past two appointments;
- a client who is making good progress;
- a client who told you about a traumatic incident that has disturbed you;
- concerns about where to refer a client unsuitable for your service;

- questions about building your caseload;
- how to access further therapy training;
- difficulties that you have experienced with practitioners in your team.

Think about which of these examples may or may not be appropriate to bring to supervision. Think of other issues that may be suitable to discuss in supervision and why.

The functions of clinical supervision

Inskipp and Proctor (1993) provide a way of understanding the different roles that clinical supervision can play by highlighting how it can be normative, formative and restorative. For example, an issue that is classically brought to supervision is one in which the supervisee seeks advice about difficulties in their clinical work with a client. Where this issue is explored and the supervisee develops the requisite knowledge and skills to address it, supervision can be said to have played a *formative* role. This is not the only function that supervision serves. Supervision also ensures that the supervisee performs certain organisational responsibilities and procedures. These tasks can include regular monitoring of risky clients, adhering to the correct referral processes, keeping accurate clinical records or completing administration in a timely fashion. In this way, supervision may perform a *normative* role. Supervision also, however, helps practitioners to manage some of the difficulties that may result from working with distressed clients. A supervisee may, for example, wish to discuss particular issues that have been upsetting or challenging for them. Supervision thus performs a *restorative* function, as it provides supervisees with the opportunity to reflect on such cases.

This way of understanding the functions of supervision can be useful for clarifying the respective roles of the two forms of supervision that have been developed for LICBT working. These are case management and skills development supervision. Richards (2010b, citing Turpin & Wheeler, 2008) describes how case management supervision seeks an overview of clinical activity, to help ensure that cases are managed competently and that clinical practice remains faithful to the evidence base ('treatment fidelity'), to most effectively benefit clients. It also serves to ensure that clinical practice is conducted in a way that is safe and effectively manages risk. This is in line with UK National Health Service principles of Clinical Governance (Richards & Suckling, 2009), which require high and transparent standards of clinical care for which the provider is accountable.

Skills development supervision, by contrast, primarily focuses on the needs of the practitioner and provides the means to develop their skills through detailed discussion of a smaller number of cases, in order that this learning can be generalised. This form of supervision provides support to the supervisee, may lead to the identification of further training needs and helps prevent staff burnout.

It can be argued that case management and skills development supervision both perform formative, normative and restorative functions, but the extent to which they do this varies significantly. Case management supervision appears to prioritise the normative and formative functions of supervision, but there may be some restorative effects to regularly reviewing a large caseload. Skills development supervision performs the restorative and formative functions of supervision more typically emphasised in the clinical supervision literature. Where it highlights the need to continue to monitor a case, it may nonetheless also perform a normative function. In combination, both forms of supervision address several priorities that are important to the service context and the LICBT practitioner as well as the client.

It is important that LICBT practitioners receive both types of supervision, as these fuel as well as complement each other. Case management supervision, while reviewing high volumes of clients, may generate topics for discussion within skills development supervision which, when addressed, may develop the supervisee's capacity to deliver LICBT. This would become evident in case management supervision, where the LICBT practitioner could apply learning to other cases. In this way, these two forms of supervision facilitate each other, to perform the functions classically associated with this activity.

What is different about LICBT supervision?

Having considered the broader functions of supervision and the relevance of this to LICBT supervision, it is important to consider the particular challenges that the LICBT practitioner faces. This will then lead to consideration of case management and skills development supervision in detail.

Firstly, LICBT work is characterised by a high volume caseload. The caseload for the LICBT practitioner tends to be much higher than for high intensity therapists or counsellors, as the sessions are shorter. Indeed LICBT practitioners may, at any one time, be carrying as many as 45 active cases and complete treatment for between 175 and 250 clients per year (Richards & Whyte, 2009).

Secondly, CBT practitioners largely work by enabling clients to help themselves and so they manage cases rather than acting as therapists *per se*. This distinction is important. The LICBT practitioner is akin to a coach or trainer, who acts as educator and supporter, helping to motivate their clients to define and deliver the work themselves (Richards, 2010b). They are, nonetheless, trained to be able to develop and maintain therapeutic relationships with clients and to be aware of the range of factors that may contribute to these.

The clinical supervision literature, however, operates on various assumptions which may appear at odds with LICBT supervision. Often written from the point of view of the supervisor, the literature presumes that supervisees are working as therapists with clients. This may shape the expectations of supervision that some prospective LICBT supervisees hold. As Richards (2010b) highlights, however, if traditional supervision practices were to be employed in LICBT, many cases would be omitted from supervision with implications for the extent to which service, LICBT practitioner or client priorities could be met.

The work of the LICBT practitioner thus differs from traditional therapy, in the approach used and the numbers of clients seen. LICBT supervision also, therefore, has to be organised differently. The evidence suggests that LICBT practitioner client outcomes can be improved by regular, structured supervision (Bower, Gilbody, Richards, Fletcher, & Sutton, 2006, cited in Richards, 2010b) and some key principles that shape this are common to all supervision models. In contrast to traditional definitions of supervision, however, the two functions of case management and skills development have been separated out and may be provided by different supervisors. These are now described in detail below.

Case management supervision

Case management supervision is a tightly structured form of supervision, which allows regular and comprehensive review of a practitioner's caseload. Best practice suggests that LICBT practitioners should receive one hour of case management supervision fortnightly (Richards & Whyte, 2009), in an individual rather than group format. This ensures that all cases are discussed at agreed intervals in accordance with specific criteria, to provide support for those carrying a high volume of clients and prevent cases from 'slipping through the net'.

This also enables the supervisor to more readily identify those LICBT practitioners who may lack experience or struggle to detect important information. This may be especially important where clients present with risk issues that require identification, monitoring and management. There are other reasons why this is important, for example when the supervisee is working with cases that do not conform to the typical profile of LI clients, when a supervisee lacks confidence in particular approaches or when there are difficult decisions to be made about supporting or discharging clients.

Given the high volume caseloads that practitioners often carry within LICBT services, it is not feasible or necessary to discuss every patient each week. The cases are, therefore, presented in a systematic way that prioritises those most in need of discussion while ensuring that all patients are nonetheless regularly reviewed (Richards & Whyte, 2009).

Exercise 13.2   Devising a system for case management supervision

Imagine you are carrying a caseload of 30–40 cases and you have an hour's case management supervision each week, which might allow you time to discuss 10 or so cases at each session. How would you prioritise which cases to bring for advice (for example, those cases where there is significant levels of risk)?

A structured format

The IAPT system of case management supervision recommends the use of several criteria to identify those cases for case management supervision (Richards & Whyte, 2009). These criteria are described as:

- all new clients;
- clients where there are significant risk issues;
- clients with high scores on their outcome measures;
- clients who have not attended their scheduled appointment or who have not been contacted recently by the practitioner;
- clients who have not been discussed recently (all clients on the practitioner's caseload should be discussed regularly – at least every four weeks); and
- clients with whom the practitioner would like further support.

The LICBT practitioner starts supervision by identifying the number of clients they hold, to enable the supervisor to assess their ability to manage their caseload. The supervisee then states how many cases he or she would like to discuss, in each of the categories given above.

Once the practitioner has decided which cases to bring to supervision, they need to present enough information about each case to enable supervisor and supervisee to make decisions about treatment and management. Discussions about cases may be wide-ranging and involve anything from making decisions about the suitability of LICBT and the way in which it is delivered to managing risk issues, referral on to other services, housing and debt issues, the presence of complicating physical health problems or handling non-attendance. Given the high volume of clients to be discussed, this information needs to be presented in a way that is succinct yet sufficiently detailed to enable the supervisor and supervisee to identify how to proceed.

Exercise 13.3   Key features of a case

Imagine you have only five minutes to present a case, what key features would you choose to present?

Presenting case information

The supervisor needs a minimum amount of information to be sufficiently informed about every case to be discussed. The framework for presenting case information used here is based on the English Low Intensity IAPT model mentioned above (Richards & Whyte, 2009). Firstly, the LICBT practitioner presents identifying information, such as age and gender. It is also helpful for the supervisee to provide a summary of the presenting problem (the problem statement; see Chapter 3). It is important to present information about risk early on, as discussion of this will take precedence over other issues.

The supervisee will then present background information about the client, including when their problem started, its duration, previous episodes and past treatment. This can be useful in determining whether the LICBT model is likely to help. Current scores on the outcome measures are reviewed as these indicate the level of symptomatology. Related to this is the issue of co-morbidity, since clients presenting with more than one difficulty may be more complex and require adjustments to treatment (see Chapters 8 and 10). Other important contextual information includes culture, language, disability (see Chapter 11), and employment status (see Chapter 12). It is helpful to know about any treatment that the client may be receiving from elsewhere, including medication. Once this information has been presented for new clients, the practitioner details the plan of treatment. This may include work that they have already started, for example reviewing psycho-educational materials, or referring the client to other services such as an employment advisor.

Where the client is to be reviewed, risk is a concern or scores on outcome measures merit discussion, further information is required. The supervisee will also state the number of times the client has been seen and the length of these contacts. This indicates the extent of treatment so far as well as its content. It is also important to inform the supervisor about the way in which the client has engaged with treatment. This may indicate the suitability of the LICBT approach, its mode of delivery and the patient's willingness to try it. The supervisor and supervisee will also consider the extent that the client has been helped by treatment. It may be, for example, that the client has engaged well but LICBT has not been helpful. There may be various explanations for this. The approach may, for example, have been inappropriate or appropriate but poorly implemented.

Where clients have not attended or have missed a scheduled appointment, the practitioner needs to summarise the nature and frequency of their actual and attempted contact with the client. Such difficulties may be harder to monitor with forms of client contact such as telephone consultation, CCBT or group work, than when contact is face to face. The format of case management supervision not only guards against such difficulties but encourages practitioners to be proactive in their efforts to engage clients. Supervisees may be encouraged, for example, to telephone clients at different times of the day or to check with primary care physicians about other means of contacting them.

The supervisee then outlines an action plan for each client, to be discussed with the supervisor. This may identify a course of action different to that initially recommended,

Table 13.1 Case management supervision information (based on Richards & Whyte, 2009)

Information to present in case management supervision	
Number of clients on caseload Number of clients requiring supervision	
For all clients	Gender, age
	Main problem statement
	Level of risk
	Onset and duration of current problem
	Previous episodes and past treatment
	Current scores on clinical measures
	Co-morbidity issues
	Cultural, language or disability considerations
	Employment status
	Treatment from referring doctor or other workers
	LICBT treatment plan
	Action already initiated
Additional information for any clients: • Due a scheduled review • With high scores • At risk • Supervisee wishes to discuss	Reason for supervision
	Intervention summary
	Number and duration of contacts
	Engagement with low-intensity treatment
	Response to low-intensity treatment
	Outcome measures for all sessions
	Alternative treatment plan
Additional information for clients who have missed their appointment or 'dropped out'	Reason for supervision
	Summary of progress before non-contact
	Number of attempts made to contact the client, including methods of contact and times of any telephone calls

including adjustments or adaptations to current treatment, stepping the client up to a different treatment approach, contacting agencies to help manage risk or discharging a client who has made sufficient recovery. The supervisor guides the supervisee in these decisions in a collaborative way. Table 13.1 summarises the information that the supervisee presents. Supervisor and supervisee conclude supervision by agreeing and formally signing the supervision record, and recording any decisions or actions to be taken in the client's notes.

Importance of preparation

A key task for the LICBT practitioner, therefore, is to present clinical information in supervision clearly, quickly, accurately and efficiently. This is essential to cover the number of clients in the time available. This can prove difficult for the novice practitioner or for those schooled in a different method of supervision. It requires a disciplined approach, using a highly structured format. It also requires the supervisee to prepare carefully, with a clear understanding of the information to be presented. The supervisee will, as part of their routine management of cases, have to keep and retrieve accurate records of their clinical contacts and the routine outcome measures. The supervisee will then need to review such material for case management supervision. Automated IT-based management systems can facilitate this process by allowing efficient retrieval of notes, outcome measures, details of risk and clinical activity.

Skills development supervision

Case management supervision thus allows close monitoring of all cases and ensures that practitioners are delivering appropriate treatment. Skills development supervision, by contrast, allows the supervisor to assess the extent to which the supervisee's use of LICBT processes and techniques is effective and conforms to their training. Furthermore, this form of supervision permits the supervisee to continue to develop their abilities through teaching, discussion and forms of experiential learning such as role plays. The LICBT role is continuously expanding and this type of supervision provides a crucial forum for the development of skills to meet these demands. Best practice suggests that the LICBT practitioner receives skills development supervision for one hour every fortnight (Richards & Whyte, 2009). This may be on an individual or group basis. It is important that, as a first step to setting up supervision, supervisors carefully assess supervisees' needs, particularly when supervisees are in training.

Agreeing a supervision contract

The first task in skills development supervision, therefore, is for the supervisor and supervisee to discuss and agree a supervision contract. This is to clarify various aspects of supervision, including practicalities such as the frequency, duration and location of sessions. The contract also serves to clarify the goals for supervision, its boundaries and the respective responsibilities of supervisor and supervisee for, for example, confidentiality. The goals represent what the supervisee would hope to achieve over the course of skills development supervision.

It may be important to consider how these goals may change over time, as the LICBT practitioner becomes more experienced and develops their skills. Early on, for example, the supervisee may focus on discriminating between different presentations of anxiety and successfully managing the constraints of case management supervision. Subsequently, the same supervisee may focus on developing their skills in engaging clients or on improving their use of particular treatment strategies. It would be important to include a date to review supervision and its goals, to accommodate this development.

Just as supervisor and supervisee will need to develop a shared understanding of the focus of supervision, it is also important to clarify its scope, in other words, what it will and will not cover, and its boundaries. In LICBT skills development supervision, the focus is on the work rather than the worker. While some therapy-based models of supervision may use the supervisees' personal reflections as source material when understanding clients' difficulties, skills development supervision is primarily educational and is much less focused on this. It is important that, as in case management supervision, a shared record is kept of the decisions made and, where appropriate, added to the client's notes. This record is also useful for continuity between supervisors as both case management and skills development supervisors may refer to such notes. This may be to review the extent to which a practitioner has implemented agreed actions, any difficulties that the supervisee may have experienced with this and the outcome of these actions.

Part of the supervision contract is to clarify the confidentiality of information shared in supervision and the conditions under which confidentiality may be broken. Both supervisor and supervisee have a responsibility to maintain the confidentiality of client information, including personal details and notes relating to clinical contacts. This duty is one that is discussed and agreed with the client and, for many, is a precondition of engagement with the service. When client information is shared in supervision, there are several ways in which this can be anonymised, for example through the use of serial numbers allocated to clients through the electronic system used.

Any personal information pertaining to the supervisee that is disclosed should also remain confidential. A supervisee may, for example, have experienced a difficulty similar to that raised by a client, which may hinder their capacity to engage in helping this individual.

A supervisor may also, however, be obligated to break confidentiality when a supervisee discloses something that indicates that a client or colleague may be at risk of harm. The need to share information that indicates risk applies as much to supervision as to therapy. A supervisor may, for example, have to intervene where supervision indicates that a supervisee has taken insufficient steps to ensure client safety. While this needs to be managed carefully and in a way that optimises supervisee learning, the supervisor's primary duty is to the client and this will govern their actions. Figure 13.1 gives an example of a supervision contract.

SUPERVISION CONTRACT – Skills development supervision

Where will skills development supervision take place?	The Cambridge Centre, Fox Bridge
Time, duration, frequency	Session frequency and duration is a minimum of one hour per fortnight.
	Jenny (supervisee) is responsible for booking the venue in the first instance, and both Jenny and Trevor (supervisor) are responsible for confirming the arrangements.
	Cancellation arrangements: the canceller is responsible for making alternative arrangements.
Purpose and goals	Aim of supervision: the primary focus of supervision is the treatment of the client through the supervisee's supervisory process.
	Goals for supervision:
	• Development of clinical skills, knowledge, conceptualisation and confidence within a cognitive behavioural therapy model.
	• In particular, Jenny has identified an initial focus to be her therapeutic interpersonal skills - for instance, her use of questions.
	• Development of reflective practice.
	These goals will be reviewed on a fortnightly basis.
	Time spent on each of the above will be negotiated by both Jenny and Trevor.
Summary of issues and associated solutions	Confidentiality:
	• All professional and clinical issues discussed are confidential and not to be discussed outside of the supervision session. The exception to this is where professional malpractice may be evident.
	• Where the tape recording of sessions takes place, this must be agreed with and have the informed consent of the service user. Jenny is responsible for wiping these recordings directly after use.

(Continued)

Figure 13.1 *(Continued)*

	Governance: Practice will follow the policy of North Bridge Trust and the requirements of Newcastle University postgraduate certificate in low intensity psychological therapies.
	Steps in the event of a breakdown in the arrangements for clinical supervision: this should be discussed initially together. If this is not possible to resolve then the service manager should appropriately be involved.
Range of activities	Supervision methods and content are to include: • Discussion of therapeutic relationship and engagement issues. • Case conceptualisation/formulation. • Rehearsal of therapeutic techniques through role play. • Discussion of therapeutic strategies. • Case presentation. • Review of audio and video tapes. • Direct observation of case-work. • Identification and reflection upon supervisee thoughts, attitudes and beliefs where these impact upon therapeutic and/or professional behaviour. • Other strategies as agreed.
Who will keep a record of supervision?	Jenny will keep minutes of the sessions which will be dated and signed at the end of the session. Both Jenny and Trevor will keep a copy of minutes.

Student's signature: *Jenny Jones*   Date: *14/8/12*

Clinical supervisor's name (please print): *TREVOR TAYLOR*

Clinical supervisor's signature: *Trevor Taylor*   Date: *14/8/12*

Figure 13.1   Example of supervision contract format

Models of supervision

There are various models of supervision that may shape the process and understanding of this activity. While it is beyond the scope of this chapter to consider these models in detail, it may be useful to have an orientation towards them here. Briefly, there are therapy-based, developmental, social role and systemic models of supervision (Beinart, 2004). Each of these differs in terms of structure, focus and function of supervision, as suggested in Table 13.2.

As CBT is the theoretical underpinning of LICBT, it seems appropriate that a therapy-based model grounded in CBT should provide a broad framework for skills development

Table 13.2   Models of supervision

Model of supervision	Key features
Therapy-based	Models particular therapy approaches (such as CBT or psychodynamic psychotherapy)
Developmental (for example, Hawkins & Shohet, 2004)	Focuses on how supervisees' goals change as they move from beginner to intermediate to advanced practitioner
Social role	Considers the various roles that supervisor performs (for instance, teacher or manager)
Systemic	Reflects on the context or system within which supervision is delivered

supervision. Developmental models may also have something to offer as the LICBT supervisee moves from dependent to independent clinical decision-making and the process and understanding of supervision as well as the needs of the supervisee evolve. Social role models highlight how the supervisor may inhabit different positions, for example of teacher or manager, in relation to the supervisee. This may lead them to engage in different tasks, with different outcomes in mind. The supervisor's use of techniques, such as interviewing, may usefully mirror those used with clients while the task of conceptualising problems may position the supervisor as educator. A systemic model of supervision provides a different perspective again. This allows reflection on the broader context to supervision, which may be important when considering the impact of political changes, service developments or when working with the wider system.

Developing competence

Having set up the supervision contract and being aware of the different forms that skills development supervision may take, supervisees may also reflect on what is entailed in developing competence. The 'Four Stages of Competence' cycle (Inskipp & Proctor, 1993) may help this, as it describes the psychological states that may be involved in progressing from incompetence to competence when acquiring a particular skill. The diagram that illustrates this process is reproduced at: www.pincltd.com/2011/06/three-questions-for-achieving-a-successful-change/or http://speakwellpartners.com/blog/2012/02/28/dont-sit-on-your-assets/.

This model suggests that the learner passes through several stages. At the first stage, prior to developing the skill, the learner may be unaware of what they do not know – in other words 'they don't know what they don't know'. In the second stage, they begin to become aware of all that they have to learn – in other words, they become conscious of their lack of competence. In the third stage, the learner may have developed some competence in the skill, but it takes a conscious effort to apply this. Finally, once they have mastered the skill and can apply it without thinking they can be said to be 'unconsciously competent'.

The 'unconsciously incompetent' supervisee may, therefore, be unaware that they do not know something important, but as they become more aware ('consciously incompetent'), they may seek to address this. The supervisee may then realise that they do something well in practice, but that they consciously have to work at this ('consciously competent'). They may then move to a position in which they can apply their skill without too much effort and may be unaware that they are doing something well ('unconsciously competent'). This descriptive framework thus helps to define the supervisee's stage of development. It also helps to highlight what may facilitate their learning. The 'unconsciously incompetent' trainee may, for example, start to record their sessions, to become more aware of how their practice impacts on patients.

Exercise 13.4   Stages of competence

A common skill that many people have is the ability to drive. If you can drive, think back to how you felt when you first started learning to do this. Can you remember moving through the stages of competence? Think about a current hobby or skill and try to identify where you are in the stages of competence. Now think about this in relation to your current level of skill in LICBT. Which stage would you identify now and what might help you to move to the next stage of competence? For example, if you are at the first stage of 'unconscious incompetence' would it be helpful for your supervisor to observe your work to help identify where you need to focus? If you are beginning to become aware of your gaps in knowledge, can you pinpoint which areas it would be useful to concentrate on? This can be helpful at the contracting stage of skills development supervision, in defining goals for this activity. The contract can then be reviewed regularly, to consider how goals have changed.

Methods of supervision

A range of methods can be used within skills development supervision to facilitate supervisees' development. These methods will reflect the task or question that the supervisee seeks to address in skills development supervision. Initially, the new supervisee may struggle with the very task of defining this question or the broader goals for this supervision as a whole. The supervisor may employ methods such as Socratic questioning to help elicit and develop the supervisee's thinking about this. These questions, which are at the heart of CBT (Padesky, 1993), will help the supervisee to systematically work this through.

According to the focus for both the specific sessions and course of skills development supervision, it may be helpful for supervisees to have supervision in vivo. Alternatively, they may show sessions that they have taped in order to be observed with clients. A review of in vivo or taped sessions allows the supervisor to more accurately gauge supervisee competences in depth and may be particularly useful where practitioners have limited experience and are less aware of skills deficits. Such supervision approaches may be time-consuming and limit the number of clients that can be discussed but they often provide valuable opportunities to scrutinise and develop practice.

Case discussion, based on self-report, conversely allows greater breadth of coverage of clients but less attention to specific skills, and may be shaped and potentially limited by what the supervisee chooses to present. Role play can be a useful way of practising new techniques and allows the supervisor to both demonstrate proper application of a skill and observe the practitioner's level of ability or understanding with different skills and techniques. For optimal skills development, it is likely that a mixture of in vivo or live approaches and case discussion will be used.

There may be work between supervision sessions, akin to the homework set for LICBT clients, which supervisees are encouraged to complete and review. This work may include the use of self-help techniques to help supervisees familiarise themselves with resources and materials. This can be particularly helpful if supervisees use materials for relevant and appropriate personal goals, for example, a graded hierarchy for a personal phobia or thought records for negative thinking. Supervisors may also encourage supervisees to refer to recent publications or research in order to address gaps in their knowledge. Supervisors may teach novel techniques or models and share materials such as references that may help with this work.

Supervision in different modalities

Skills development supervision may also help the supervisee to think about the issues that arise from working within different modalities. Supervision may, for example, include a session that focuses on the particular skills required for engaging clients in a telephone consultation. Some services provide live supervision for practitioners new to delivering LICBT by telephone. The supervisor may listen in to the session, offering guidance to the supervisee either during or after the contact. Practitioners need to explain this process to clients – for instance, specifying that there may be pauses in the telephone conversation while they receive live supervision – and should seek their permission for supervisory input in this way. Supervision itself may, therefore, be conducted using the very modality through which LICBT is delivered. In this way it may model some of the difficulties that occur as well as the solutions that may help to address these difficulties.

Supervision in groups

Skills development supervision may be conducted one to one, in pairs or groups. There may be service advantages and economies of scale, in terms of time, money and expertise, from conducting supervision in this way.

Exercise 13.5 Advantages and disadvantages of the different forms of supervision

Consider whether you would prefer to have skills based supervision one to one or in a group. Think about the advantages and disadvantages of each of these, in order to help clarify your view.

There may be various benefits for supervisees from receiving supervision in groups (Hawkins & Shohet, 2004). Supervisees may find this a very supportive experience. They may learn from observing discussion of their colleagues' cases as well as from receiving additional input into their own clinical work. There may be increased opportunities for experiential learning through activities such as role plays. Supervisees nonetheless report anxiety within group supervision, for example, when reviewing taped observations of their clinical practice. Supervisees' fears of reviewing tapes of clinical work nonetheless provide an extremely useful learning opportunity, not only for the reflections they permit on clinical practice. Such activities represent an opportunity for supervisees to engage in some of the work they may ask their patients to complete. Supervisees can, therefore, report and test out their own anxious predictions about the impact of watching such tapes ('I'll be shown to be rubbish at my job'). They may then repeatedly engage in this activity to gain a different perspective and consolidate this learning ('I may not always get it right but I do a good job').

Group supervision nonetheless requires careful consideration. There are important decisions to be made, for example, about the size of the group. Clinical experience suggests that supervision groups with more than three members are unlikely to be effective, as the time required to supervise all members can lead to an overly long session that may lose momentum. Supervisees may need to be encouraged to consider the distribution of time across the group and to give balanced feedback rather than proscriptive advice to fellow members. Some supervisees may nonetheless feel more exposed in this form of supervision, for their perceived lack of knowledge or because of particular difficulties that they have experienced.

The supervisor is likely, therefore, to consider the composition of the group and the individuals within it, to try and establish collaborative working. It may be helpful for a supervisor to have experience of working with groups and of attending to group processes, to ensure that they can manage dynamics where supervisees may become dominant, competitive or passive.

The negotiation of the group supervision contract, with its attention to questions of confidentiality, boundaries and responsibilities, may help to address some of these questions. It may help to clarify the boundaries of the group in relation, for example, to the circumstances under which a supervisee may seek a one-to-one meeting with a supervisor to discuss a personal matter. The working relationship between group members and the way in which group information is managed within the broader professional context may also need to be considered.

As practitioners develop their knowledge, skills and experience, they may move to a different model of supervision, where for example they meet with an equally experienced colleague for co-supervision or with colleagues for peer group supervision.

Exercise 13.6   Differences between case management and skills development supervision

Reflecting on what you have read so far, describe what you think are the key differences between case management and skills development supervision.

How to make the most of supervision

Both supervisees and supervisors are responsible for the success of supervision. There are several ways in which both parties may optimise this arrangement.

Exercise 13.7   Effective supervision

List what you think are the most important ingredients for effective supervision. Give your reasons for this.

A collaborative working relationship

It is very important that the supervisee feels as though they can relate to their supervisor, as a strong alliance is seen to be one of the key factors in determining how well the supervision process works. Indeed, a strong supervisory alliance will be valued by both parties and is likely to increase the effectiveness of the work done. Clear definitions of the professional framework and boundaries for supervision, which can be clarified through work done on preparing the supervision contract, will both build and be aided by collaboration.

Feeling safe

A successful supervisory alliance rests on what supervisees may describe as feeling safe within supervision. Indeed, Scaife (2009) has described supervision as a 'safe base' for supervisees. The supervision literature suggests that supervisors can contribute to this in various ways, for example, by maintaining confidentiality, being consistent and respectful, engaging in only moderate levels of self-disclosure, demonstrating specific approaches before asking a supervisee to undertake a task, sharing their own work and taking responsibility when difficult issues arise. Furthermore, supervisees also report that there are specific things that they find helpful (see Cushway & Knibbs, 2010). These include good rapport, receiving appropriate positive and critical feedback, feeling supported by the supervisor and having clear boundaries. On rare occasions, the supervisory relationship may nonetheless break down. The supervisor and supervisee should agree a process to manage this event, should it arise. This may usefully include identifying a named professional within the service to help manage such a difficulty. These details are recorded in the supervision contract when this is initially negotiated.

Clear goals for skills development supervision

As has already been noted elsewhere in this chapter, there is a need for clarity about the goals for skills development supervision. These will be discussed at the point that the contract is negotiated and the supervision is set up. These goals will then guide the form that this supervision will take.

Openness to feedback

There are ways in which a supervisee can enhance what can be gained from supervision. Effective supervision requires that the supervisee provide an honest and open account of their clinical work. The supervisee needs to be open to receiving feedback from their supervisor and to acting on this. Much of this may depend on the way in which feedback is given. Hawkins and Shohet (2004) provide some helpful guidance for supervisors regarding how to give accurate and constructive feedback. They suggest it should be:

- clear;
- detailed and specific;
- given regularly or as close to events as possible;
- balanced; and
- based on observations rather than inferences.

They also advise that the giver of feedback should be clear that this is their own view rather than the only perspective to be taken. The supervisor, by collaborating with the supervisee, may facilitate the task of finding solutions where particular difficulties emerge in supervision.

Identifying learning styles

Given the educative function of supervision, a clear understanding of what will help supervisee learning may be useful. Kolb's (1984) experiential learning theory provides a framework to understand this. The figure that illustrates this process can be found at: http://serc.carleton.edu/introgeo/enviroprojects/what.html or www.faculty.londondeanery.ac.uk/e-learning/facilitating-learning-in-the-workplace/theoretical-perspectives-on-workplace-based-learning/.

This process is described in Chapter 5. Kolb suggests that learners engage in different modes when learning to implement a new skill. The act of doing ('concrete experience') is differentiated from thinking about the experience of doing this ('reflection'). Making sense of experience may, furthermore, involve integrating theories and abstract ideas into these reflections (a process of 'abstract conceptualisation'). The learner may subsequently develop their practice by acting on the learning generated by going through these modes ('active experimentation').

Kolb's experiential learning theory suggests that individuals favour particular modes of learning. Some, for example, may tend to spend more time reflecting while others are experimenters and prefer to learn through doing. An overemphasis on one preferred mode, however, may inhibit further learning. This can be helpful to consider within supervision. Those supervisees who are keen reflectors and spend a lot of time understanding or conceptualising the problem at the expense of action may, for example, need to engage in more active experimentation and to focus on concrete experience. Supervisees who are keen to problem solve or try new things without spending much time reflecting may likewise need to observe, think and learn more about their practice to develop a more reflective learning style.

Issues within supervision

There are various issues that can arise within supervision, which may need to be addressed. Some of these are generic issues, which relate to ethical and professional practice and are common to supervision for all forms of psychological intervention. Some issues are, however, particular to LICBT supervision. Ethical and professional issues relating to the practitioner's role are discussed in Chapter 2. Some of these issues are nonetheless pertinent to the practice of supervision and so are also briefly considered here.

Confidentiality

Where supervisees do not take necessary and sufficient care to protect client confidentiality, this is an issue to be raised in supervision. Should a breach of confidentiality arise, this will be formally raised, documented and investigated by the service. In this event, the client has a right to be informed of what has occurred and its potential implications. Depending on the gravity of the breach and the extent to which this infringes the employer's definitions of appropriate behaviour, this may lead to disciplinary action.

Professional standards

Both supervisor and supervisee have a duty to conduct themselves in accordance with professional standards. This may be within the code of conduct outlined by the organisation with which the individual is registered as a practitioner or supervisor, for example the British Association of Behavioural and Cognitive Psychotherapies, or with which the individual is registered through their professional training, for example, the British Psychological Society. Employers may also provide definitions of behaviours that constitute disciplinary offences. The initiation of intimate relationships by clinicians with clients, for example, would clearly fall within this area.

Dual relationships between supervisors and supervisees, where a supervisor is in an intimate relationship with their supervisee, would be equally inappropriate, given the potential for the relationship to disrupt professional conduct. It would be the supervisor's responsibility to address this issue by recognising the conflict of interest posed by the dual role and by seeking an alternative supervisor for this supervisee. The supervisee also has a responsibility to avoid such relationships and to report them should they occur. This would be either directly to a supervisor or, if this was judged inappropriate or difficult, to another professional. This individual should have been identified within the supervision contract as a possible point of contact, in the event of such difficulties.

Limits to self-report

Supervisees may find it difficult to be open in supervision and to discuss cases where they are struggling. The supervision literature suggests that this may occur because supervisees fear that such disclosures will reflect poorly on their own competence and performance (Ladany, Hill, Corbett, & Nutt, 1996; Ladany, 2004). Less experienced workers may overlook information that is important to a case. High volume caseloads and the pressure of work in some services increase the likelihood that there may be limits to information shared by supervisees in supervision. The format of case management supervision should, however, protect against clients 'slipping through the net'.

Supervisees may nonetheless need to anticipate the conditions in which they may limit their reports and to consider what the consequences of this could be. This may enable both supervisor and supervisee to put mechanisms in place to help prevent this. A strong supervisory alliance will help to address this. The supervision contract also provides the means to be explicit about gaps in learning and to prompt the supervisee to discuss rather than conceal these.

Competence

A range of factors can lead the LICBT practitioner to feel deskilled. One example is where services permit the referral of inappropriate clients to LICBT. Some LICBT workers may struggle with their work because of lack of knowledge and experience. Supervision may thus become a forum to explore 'unconscious' and 'conscious incompetence'. Where this exploration indicates that clients are at risk because of a lack of practitioner competence, the supervisor will discuss this with the supervisee and devise a plan to address this. As the LICBT supervisor carries clinical responsibility for client safety, they may become more active and directive when clients present with risk. The immediate priority, as noted earlier, will be effective risk management. The supervisor may then identify ways in which the supervisee should develop their practice following this work.

Moving beyond competence

LICBT practitioners move beyond the boundaries of their training where they attempt to deliver treatments that are not supported by the evidence. This may happen when workers, with prior training as counsellors or different types of therapist, revert to former ways of working when confronted with certain types of client. This may also happen where LICBT practitioners seek to integrate former approaches within their current practice in an attempt to develop this further. LICBT practitioners may try to engage clients who are not suitable for LICBT and need a more intensive approach. This phenomenon, known as 'medium intensity drift' (Richards & Whyte, 2009), may occur where LICBT practitioners aspire to high intensity working and may reflect their ambitions to perform this role.

Table 13.3   What LICBT practitioners do not do

Ethical LICBT practitioners do not:

1   Carry out high intensity CBT

2   Carry out 'medium intensity, pseudo-therapy' (drift away from using evidence-based low intensity principles)

3   Support non-evidence-based interventions

4   Work in isolation from other colleagues outside of a stepped care system or a supervisory framework

5   Work with clients who have complex, serious, enduring problems such as psychosis and bipolar disorder (or other clients who are not on the appropriate 'step' of the healthcare system)

'Medium intensity drift' is an important issue. The English IAPT programme stresses the need for LICBT practitioners to be clear about those things they do not do (see Table 13.3). LICBT practitioners are not trained to deliver high intensity CBT and to attempt to practise in this way would be unethical. It would, furthermore, diminish treatment fidelity, lead to poorer client outcomes and undermine the contribution that LICBT can make to the management of mental health difficulties. The NHS Clinical Governance agenda highlights how the supervisor has an ethical responsibility to ensure that clients receive treatments that practitioners have been trained to deliver, as they have been trained to deliver them. Concerns about 'medium intensity drift' would need to be raised in skills development supervision.

It is also worth considering that, if 'medium intensity drift' were tolerated, LICBT caseloads, time and resources would render such practice unsustainable and lead to staff burnout. This practice could, furthermore, lead to difficulties both within and between services as it could raise professional tensions between LICBT and high intensity workers as well as create confusion amongst referrers (such as primary care physicians) about the LICBT role.

Service conditions may contribute to LICBT practitioners going 'off piste'. Service managers may, for example, remain unclear about the LICBT remit, allow an elastic definition of LICBT working and encourage such practitioners to see cases that are inappropriate for LICBT. Supervisors may have limited understanding of the particular features of LICBT and unwittingly encourage LICBT practitioners to move beyond their competence. Long waiting lists, limited access to alternative provision and the need to establish LICBT services within existing mental health provision are some of the other factors that can lead to such 'drift'.

In such circumstances, both case management and skills supervision play a critical role. A supervisee may, for example, raise a question about how to work with a client in skills development supervision. This may highlight how the practitioner is moving beyond their competence and training, and that this client needs a different form of psychological input. The supervisor will raise this concern, the discussion will be documented and this information fed into case management supervision to alert this supervisor to the need to review this case. The LICBT practitioner is then encouraged to reflect on the boundaries to their work and when it is necessary to seek further advice.

Reluctance to step up

A related difficulty may be when LICBT practitioners retain clients on their caseload and do not step them up for more appropriate treatment. Again, various factors may contribute to this. These may reflect the LICBT practitioner's belief that stepping up a client will cause distress, their ambitions to develop their skills further or difficulties accessing other services. Once again, it is important for supervision to highlight the LICBT remit and the NHS Clinical Governance issues that would arise if clients' needs were not appropriately met. It may be important for LICBT supervisors to have a forum in which these broader issues can be raised and considered at a service level.

Securing appropriate supervision

Precisely because of the particular character of LICBT and the supervision demands that follow from this, it is clear that those providing LICBT supervision need to have a good understanding and some experience of working in the LICBT role. This will enable them to integrate the broad overview of cases with the fine-grained understanding of supervisees' clinical work permitted by case management and skills development supervision in combination.

Roth and Pilling (2008) have mapped out competences judged to be important to CBT supervision and identify a specific set of requirements for those supervising LICBT workers. These requirements include those generic skills required for the effective supervision of anyone working within psychological therapies. It is also likely, however, that some aspects of LICBT supervision will require supervisors to develop their own knowledge, skills and experience of LICBT working further, for example, medication or telephone working.

Finally, where case management and skills development supervision are provided by different supervisors, good communication between these supervisors is essential. It will be important, therefore, that services are set up to allow this particular need to be met.

Conclusion

LICBT practitioners face many challenges when managing high volume caseloads of distressed patients, in pressured environments focused on social and clinical outcome targets. These practitioners need to be keenly aware of the relationship between their clinical practice and their competence, and of the boundaries between their role and those of adjacent services. Case management and skills development are the two, complementary forms of supervision that may help them to meet these challenges effectively.

Summary

- Supervision is an essential requirement for LICBT working.
- It takes two forms: case management and skills development.
- Case management supervision is highly structured and ensures that all patients are regularly reviewed.
- Skills development supervision focuses on the needs, skills, knowledge and experience of the LICBT practitioner.
- Skills development supervision requires a contract and clearly defined goals and may use a range of methods and modalities. This form of supervision can be optimised in various ways for example by working collaboratively and identifying learning styles.
- Several issues may emerge in LICBT working, such as 'medium intensity drift', which need to be managed through both case management and skills development supervision.

Further reading and activities

Consider what you have learnt from this chapter. Are there any particular points that stand out for you? If you are already working within an LICBT service, is there anything that you need to do to improve your supervision arrangements? Could you discuss this further in supervision? In this chapter you have already been guided to some resources that may be helpful. I also recommend IAPT (n.d.) and Richards (2010b) for further reading. The IAPT website (2012) also holds DVDs which illustrate the way in which case management supervision is conducted, see: www.iapt.nhs.uk/workforce/low-intensity/reach-out-clinical-case-management-supervision-dvd

Appendix

The use of case studies

Mark Papworth

In the final section of the book I outline three case studies. These serve several functions. Firstly, two of them describe the presentations of the individuals we have used as examples within the book. In particular, details of Tom and Judy have been used in Chapters 3, 5, 6 and 10. The case studies provide you with a brief overall summary of these clients' cases. This negates the need for you to attempt to piece together the cases from the fragments described within the chapters to obtain an overview of the individuals' presentations. These summaries also illustrate how the elements of the client's difficulties make up a problem presentation.

Secondly, at various points in the book, we have suggested that you practise specific skills within a role play exercise format. These examples can form the basis of the case to be played by the individual who is in the client role. However, it is also recommended that the 'actor' gets 'into role' by revising the symptoms associated with the client's condition (see Chapters 7 and 9), and also by attempting to access these symptoms experientially. This can be done by attempting (as far as is possible) to get into a similar frame of mind to the client. For example, with depression, this might involve vividly imagining a time when you experienced a loss (for instance, the break-up of a relationship), then starting the exercise at a point when you are able to feel some of the emotions associated with that experience. You might then find that you more naturally slump in the chair, become 'flatter' in mood and less animated in response to questions. You might also hold less eye contact with the practitioner, perhaps tending to look down at the floor. This will give the individual who is playing the role of the practitioner a more realistic experience.

The first two case studies provide information that is useful for an assessment interview role play exercise (Exercise 5.2). The final case study provides the necessary information and homework materials to complete a treatment interview role play exercise (Exercise 5.3).

Case 1 – Judy

The referral letter

Dear colleague

Re: Judy Jenkins   Date of birth: 1/3/66
4 Front Street, Greenside, Newcastle-Upon-Tyne

I would be grateful if you could see this lady who works at a local garage. She has told me that she has been struggling at work. She is experiencing symptoms of depression and she has not been able to attend at her work over the last four weeks.

I have started her on Fluoxetine, 20 mg.

I would be most grateful for your help.

Yours sincerely
Dr F. Jones

Overview of difficulties

Judy is experiencing a major depression. This has developed after difficulties emerged at work following her taking on additional duties. Some errors occurred in her organising rotas and also in arranging some customer appointments. As a result, the garage manager reviewed her performance within a formal meeting with her. This activated patterns of cognition associated with failure and she felt humiliated by the meeting. She felt unable to face work following this meeting, which occurred one month ago. Additionally, there are stresses at home in that her husband has received a promotion. He is now undertaking a training role that involves the preparation of materials in the evenings and also travelling around the country. Consequently, he is less available for Judy at home. She feels down and is at times tearful. She reports being tired, and having difficulty sleeping and concentrating. She is unable to cope with household activities and is avoiding socialising with others. She experiences some suicidal thoughts but has no intention to act on them.

These symptoms are maintained for Judy by at least three cycles:

1   The problems at work have triggered a depressed mood and have activated patterns of negative self-perceptions (for example, 'I am a failure'). These involve negative thinking biases which confirm dysfunctional views of herself, and also fuel pessimism associated with her life and her future. Consequently, she is less inclined to engage in activities and this reduces the level of stimulation and reinforcement in her lifestyle. This in turn impacts upon mood.

2   Negative cognition and also physical symptoms such as a loss of energy and motivation undermine coping and problem-solving skills for Judy. Consequently, she is unable to develop possible solutions for the issues in her life. As a result, problems remain and nothing improves for her. This fuels hopelessness which, in turn, also impacts upon her mood.

3   Her confidence has been undermined and, as a result, Judy feels unable to go to work anymore. This avoidance of work means that she does not have any opportunities to experience success. These experiences would counter her beliefs associated with failure and challenge her negative patterns of cognition.

Role playing Judy

Here are some possible topics/responses that you can offer in response to the practitioner's questions. This information is also further background detail for her case. This cannot be a comprehensive set of answers and some ad-libbing will be required within a role play exercise.

4 'Ws'

What is the problem?

> Depression (for example, low mood, loss of appetite, difficulty sleeping, lack of energy, perceptions of failure and worthlessness as well as difficulty concentrating).

Where does the problem occur?

> Judy is at home much of the time where she is experiencing symptoms. She avoids going out on her own other than to the corner shop to get essential supplies in. She appreciates this change of scenery. She does not feel motivated to leave the house on other occasions.

With whom is the problem better or worse?

> Her parents and step-parents call to see her, they are concerned. They provide practical support with her household tasks. She appreciates the break in the monotony of the day. They do not understand her difficulties (they gently suggest that she needs to 'pull herself together'). She feels guilty about the distress that she is causing them and she sees her difficulties as being an imposition on them.

When does the problem happen?

> Her mood tends to be worse in the morning and she finds it particularly difficult to 'get started' in the day. Her mood does lift a little when John is able to spend time with her.

Five areas

Emotional aspects of the problem

> Low mood and tearfulness, also guilt associated with the impact of her difficulties upon others. Some anger focused towards the garage manager.

Autonomic (physiological) aspects of the problem

> Tiredness, loss of energy, difficulty sleeping and problems with concentration.

Behavioural aspects of the problem

> Lack of activity, and avoidance of social and work situations.

Cognitive aspects of the problem

> Thoughts of being a failure and of being a burden on others.

Triggers (current)

> She feels worse when her workplace contacts her or if reminded about her work situation (for instance, via news events associated with employment or health). Rumination about the work events fuels low mood.

Triggers (historical)

> She experienced a prior relationship break-up 10 years ago. This resulted in mood-related symptoms. She had some counselling input at this point.

Impact (consequence) of the problem

She is away from work, has stopped social and leisure activities (for example, meeting friends at a cafe and at a book club, as well as mixing with other couples with her husband).

Assessment of risk

Hopelessness

Mild level is present.

Intent: suicidal thoughts

Occasional and fleeting.

Plans: specific action plans

None.

Actions: current/past; access to the means

Prior episode of mood-related difficulties, occasional ideation and no prior acts.

Prevention: social network, services

Reduction in social contacts, parents and step-parents actively supportive. Husband is also supportive.

Risk to others

None.

Neglect of self or others

Sometimes not getting out of bed until mid-morning; is getting washed and dressed every day though.

Routine outcome measures (see Chapter 3)

PHQ-9

Q1 = 2, Q2 = 3, Q3 = 2, Q4 = 2, Q5 = 1, Q6 = 3, Q7 = 2, Q8 = 0, Q9 = 1; total = 16.

GAD-7

> Q1 = 1, Q2 = 2, Q3 = 3, Q4 = 1, Q5 = 0, Q6 = 2, Q7 = 1; total = 10.

WSAS

> Q1 = 8, Q2 = 6, Q3 = 6, Q4 = 4, Q5 = 5; total = 29.

Other important issues

Onset and maintenance

> Work and relationship issues, see cycles above.

Modifying factors

> Contact with husband lifts mood, practical support from others worsens mood (triggering cognitions associated with imposing on others).

Why does the patient want help now?

> Recent onset of difficulties.

Patient expectations and goals

> She wishes to be back to her 'old self', and would like to return to her previous levels of activity and lifestyle.

Past episodes and treatments

> A prior episode 10 years ago.

Drugs, alcohol and caffeine

> Increase in alcohol intake; approximately two-thirds of a bottle of wine, three or four times per week. Two cups of tea per day.

Current medication and attitude to this

> Fluoxetine, 20 mg; is comfortable taking medication.

Other treatment being provided

> Nil.

Case 2 – Tom

The referral letter

Dear colleague

Re: Tom Smith   Date of birth: 26/5/82
**   8 High Street, Greenside, Newcastle-Upon-Tyne**

I would be grateful if you could see this man who has been having anxiety difficulties which have led to him taking sickness absence from work.

I have been prescribing him: Seroxat, 40 mg, and he appears a little more settled although remains with significant difficulties.

I would be most grateful for your help.

Yours sincerely
Dr F. Jones

Overview of difficulties

Tom is experiencing panic disorder with agoraphobia. He developed this following some work-related stress. The symptoms undermined his attendance at work. He misinterprets his symptoms of panic as life-threatening (he believes that he is having cardiac difficulties). There is a history of cardiac problems on his father's side of the family. These difficulties are resulting in some low mood and hopelessness for him, although he is not at all suicidal.

These symptoms are maintained for Tom by a number of cycles:

1 Cycle one was initially triggered by work-related stress. Tom's role at work was changed in that he was required to train a number of individuals. This involved a doubling of his work-load and it also involved him standing up and presenting material to a group of trainees – a situation that Tom found to be very challenging. He began to notice symptoms of anxiety (heart pounding, chest pain, sweating, dizziness and hotness), but misinterpreted these as the beginnings of a problem with his heart. This worsened his stress and symptoms still further, resulting in panic at times (he witnessed his father having a heart attack shortly before he died). Finally, after a particularly bad episode, Tom left work feeling unable to cope, saw his doctor and subsequently received a sick note. Some medical tests were completed (including blood tests and heart monitoring), but nothing abnormal was found.

2 Tom then found that he tended to experience these symptoms in busy, crowded situations. These included shops (particularly the checkout queue), shopping centres, the theatre or cinema, as well as busy pubs and restaurants. Additionally, if Tom entertained thoughts about a return to work, these also produced these symptoms. Consequently, he began to avoid these situations or went shopping late at night when the supermarket was empty. Tom has a partner and he can face some situations only if accompanied by her. Because Tom avoids these situations, it leaves some underlying beliefs unchallenged: that his symptoms are life-threatening and that the medical tests have missed an important cardiac problem.

3 Tom is now on sickness absence away from work and is pre-occupied with the state of his heart. He sometimes takes his own pulse and, as he does so, he notices that his heart rate is elevated. This information is taken by him to confirm that there is something wrong with his health. He is also acutely aware of any pain experienced in his chest and arms. If this is present, this similarly confirms his fears. In reality, Tom is now focusing on and misinterpreting normal sensations and phenomena. For example, when taking his pulse he experiences a level of anticipatory anxiety that results in it being elevated.

4 A final cycle involves Tom attempting to keep himself safe by adopting certain dysfunctional strategies. He asks his partner to accompany him when he goes out. This is because, if he does have a heart attack, his partner will be on-hand to call for help. He also takes herbal Kalms tablets to 'relax his heart'. Additionally, if it is necessary for him to leave the house while unaccompanied, he makes sure that he has his mobile phone 'topped-up' and close to hand. In reality, these 'safety behaviours' mean that Tom deprives himself of an opportunity to learn that he can cope/survive in these situations unaided and that the symptoms are harmless.

Role playing Tom

Here are some possible topics/responses that you can offer in response to the practitioner's questions. This information is also further background detail for his case. This cannot be a comprehensive set of answers and some ad-libbing will be required within a role play exercise.

4 'Ws'

What is the problem?

> Anxiety symptoms (for example, heart racing, sweating, hotness, dizziness, discomfort in his chest and abdomen). Tom is unconvinced that they are linked to anxiety, although his doctor has said that this is the case.

Where does the problem occur?

> Initially at work, with increasing demands and when placed in a pressure situation; then it started to occur in crowded situations.

With whom is the problem better or worse?

> Tom can do more if accompanied.

When does the problem happen?

> See 'where', but he is usually okay in the morning when he is at home and distracted while watching day-time TV.

Five areas

Emotional aspects of the problem

> A fear of dying; he also experiences some low mood and hopelessness associated with his predicament.

Autonomic (physiological) aspects of the problem

> See anxiety symptoms (above).

Behavioural aspects of the problem

> Avoidance, escape and safety behaviours (see above).

Cognitive aspects of the problem

> Misinterpretation of anxiety symptoms and normal bodily sensations.

Triggers

> Crowds and busy areas, when he perceives himself to be boxed in and escape to be more difficult. When he was at work, symptoms were triggered by a situation where he was the focus of attention.

Triggers (historical)

> No specific problems were experienced previously, although Tom remembers being an anxious child. He was unwilling to put his hand up in class and hated reading aloud to the rest of the class.

Impact (consequence) of the problem

> He is away from work and has stopped his leisure activities (for instance, meeting a friend in a local pub for a game of darts and also to watch football). His partner is supportive, although this is causing a strain on the relationship.

Assessment of risk

Intent: suicidal thoughts

> Occasional and fleeting: 'my partner would be better off without me'.

Plans: specific action plans

> None.

Actions: current/past; access to the means

> None.

Prevention: social network, services

> There is a reduction in his social contacts.

Risk to others

> None.

Neglect of self or others

> Sometimes he is not getting out of bed until mid-day. He is getting washed and dressed every day.

Routine outcome measures (see Chapter 3)

PHQ-9

> Q1 = 1, Q2 = 1, Q3 = 1, Q4 = 0, Q5 = 0, Q6 = 2, Q7 = 1, Q8 = 0, Q9 = 1; total = 7.

GAD-7

> Q1 = 3, Q2 = 3, Q3 = 2, Q4 = 2, Q5 = 2, Q6 = 1, Q7 = 3; total = 16.

WSAS

Q1 = 8, Q2 = 0, Q3 = 6, Q4 = 0, Q5 = 3; total = 17.

Other important issues

Onset and maintenance

Onset triggered by work (three months ago) and also see the maintenance cycles described above.

Modifying factors

Approaching situations away from the house is easier if he is accompanied by his partner.

Why does the patient want help now?

He believes that there is a risk of losing his job in due course if he is unable to return.

Patient expectations and goals

Desires a return to work. He remains uncertain whether difficulties are linked to anxiety or cardiac problems.

Past episodes and treatments

Nil.

Drugs and alcohol

Nil of note.

Current medication and attitude to this

Seroxat, 40 mg; is comfortable taking medication.

Other treatment being provided

Nil.

Case 3 – Julian

Here are the details of a case study that can be used to practise the treatment interview, as detailed in Exercise 5.3.

General instructions

For this task you will need to use 'Rethink: A recovery programme for depression' (Lovell & Richards, 2008). This is available from: www.mentalhealthshop.org/products/ rethink_publications/recovery_booklet.html. If it is not possible for you to obtain this manual, the task can be adapted for use with other guided self-help materials that cover the same topics.

Instructions for the practitioner role

You are focusing on the following situation in the role play. You have completed your initial interview with Julian and he attends the meeting (your third session) having read and completed step two of the programme (pp. 15–21; information about depression, vicious cycle of depression, diary record of thoughts, behaviours and physical aspects, and setting goals) and stage one of step three (p. 29; behavioural activation diary sheet). Your task is, depending on the time available to you, to review this work and introduce behavioural activation to him in a manner that is in keeping with the LICBT role. You will introduce the client to these parts of the manual. You will help him to think about a limited number of examples for page 31 to get him started (routine, necessary and pleasurable activities). He will need to complete this for homework in addition to page 33 (difficult, medium and easy activities). You will guide Julian in how to produce a new behavioural activation diary to be discussed at your next meeting (complete stages two to four of step three; identifying activities, organising the activities and then scheduling the activities).

Client presentation

A summary page is presented in Figure A.1. If information relevant to the role play is not detailed, the practitioner and client should 'ad-lib' rather than allow the focus to move back to the assessment process.

Instructions for the client

You are to play a client (Julian Roberts, date of birth 3/4/79) who is suffering with depression. He developed difficulties after losing his job. The therapist's task is to

Client: **Julian Roberts (date of birth: 3/4/79)**

Historical trigger: Loss of job, made redundant

Past trigger: Reacted badly to previous relationship break-up some 2 years ago (was
prescribed some medication at this point, no long-term relationship since)

Emotional: Sadness, hopelessness, shame

Autonomic: Lethargy, loss of motivation, difficulty sleeping, loss of appetite

Behavioural: Avoidance of going out, social isolation (he is single but has some friends),
poverty of activity, napping in day time, reduced self-care (for example, not
getting dressed and not shaving)

Cognitive: I am a failure, I'm on the scrapheap
Others will look down on me, they will find me boring
My life will never improve
Self-criticism, poor concentration, indecisiveness

Problem statement: My main problem is the lack of interest and hopelessness which I experience
every day. Since I was made redundant, I avoid activities that I used to enjoy and I experience:
tiredness, difficulty sleeping, loss of appetite, lethargy, tearfulness, reduced activity and thoughts
of being a failure. As a result, I find it difficult to socialise, look for work and look after myself.

Situation: Is single, no immediate financial worries, has supportive/concerned parents
who live in the same town; previously worked as a car salesman.
Risk: Occasional suicidal thoughts, no intention to act on them.
Latest PHQ-9:   3, 3, 1, 2, 1, 2, 2, 0, 1; total = 15.
Latest GAD-7:   0, 2, 1, 1, 0, 2, 2; total = 8.
Latest WSAS: N/A, 7, 7, 7, 6; total = 27.
Medication: Seroxat, 20 mg, is comfortable taking this.

Figure A.1   Case study summary sheet for Julian

help you to change your behaviour with a view to this impacting beneficially on
your mood through use of the behavioural activation technique. 'Behavioural activation is a technique where we focus on re-establishing our daily routines, increase
our pleasurable activities and do the things that are necessary for us. Basically,
behavioural activation is about "acting our way out of depression"' (Lovell &
Richards, 2008: 27).

You are likely to be less talkative, sad, might find the conversation difficult at times
because of a lack energy and concentration, and may provide more limited eye contact.

However, avoid a monosyllabic style as this will make the interview overly difficult for the practitioner. See the description of the depressive condition given in Chapter 7 which should help you in playing this role.

Client homework

Below and in Table A.1 are the materials that Julian has completed over the last week (you can write these into a print-out of the self-help materials to increase the realism of the exercise).

Impact (the information relates to Lovell & Richards, 2008: 13, 'Impact sheet'):

- Home – 'Cleaning, cooking for myself, vacuuming, making the bed, tidying up'.
- Work – 'I am not working; I do not have anyone to care for'.
- Relationships – 'I avoid seeing my friends. I don't do anything and so have nothing to talk about. I don't feel I have anything in common with them now. I think people feel sorry for me and I don't like this'.
- Social – 'I can't make conversation; I have nothing to talk about to others. I worry that the conversation will dry-up, that they'll find me boring and dread seeing me or see me as a charity case'.
- Personal – 'I don't have the concentration I used to and so find reading difficult. Also, I can't seem to follow TV programmes. I seem to find things boring now that I used to be interested in'.

Three areas (the information relates to Lovell & Richards, 2008: 18, 'Your own personal feelings, behaviours and thoughts'):

- Physical feelings – 'I am tired all the time, I have no energy, but I can't sleep! I haven't got the energy to do anything'.
- Behaviours – 'I don't go out. I don't bother with anything or anyone (what's the point!). I don't bother looking for anything else (work or new things to do)'.
- Thoughts – 'I am on the scrapheap. I am useless. Who is going to want to employ me? I could not hold down a job if I wanted to. I'm finished!'

Goals (the information relates to Lovell & Richards, 2008: 21, 'My goals'):

- Goal 1 – 'To start looking for and applying for work'; rating: 0/10.
- Goal 2 – 'To be able to enjoy seeing my friends'; rating: 1/10.
- Goal 3 – 'To start to look after myself (for instance, to eat healthily)'; rating: 2/10.

Table A.1 Julian's pre-intervention diary

	Monday	Tuesday	Wednesday	Thursday	Friday	Saturday	Sunday
Morning	In bed, home, to 11, alone	In bed, home, 11.30, alone	In bed, home, to 11, alone	In bed, home, to 12.30, alone	In bed, home, to 12, alone	In bed, home, to 11, alone	In bed, home, to 4, alone
	TV, home, 11–1.30, alone	TV/tea, home, 11.30–2, alone	Tea, home, 11–1.30, with mother	See LICBT practitioner, Surgery, 1–2.30, with mother	PC game, home, 12–1.30, alone	TV, home 11–1.30, alone	
Afternoon	Shopping, Asda, 2–4, with mother	TV, home, 2–6, alone	Cat to vet, shops, 1.30–3, with mother	Snacks, home, 3–4, alone	Lunch, home, 2–2.30, alone	Shopping, Asda, 2–4, with mother	Lunch, home, 5–5.30, alone
	Bed, home, 4–6, alone	Snacks, home, 6–8, alone	Washing, home, 3–5, alone	See doctor, surgery, 4–5, with mother	Snacks, home, 4–5, alone	PC game, home, 4–6, alone	Washing, home, 6–7, alone
Evening	Supper, home, 6–8, alone	PC game, home, 8–1.30, alone	Supper, home, 6–8, alone	PC game, home, 7–8, alone	Friend phoned, home, 7–7.15, alone	Bath, home, 8–9, alone	PC game, home, 7–9, alone
	TV, home, 8–2, alone		Bath, home, 8–9, alone	TV, home, 8–11, alone	Visiting parents, 8–10	TV, home, 11–1.30, alone	

Source: The information relates to Lovell & Richards, 2008: 29, 'Behavioural activation diary'.

References

Abramowitz, J.S., Moore, E.L., Braddock, A.E., & Harrington, D.L. (2009). Self-help cognitive behavioral therapy with minimal therapist contact for social phobia: a controlled trial. *Journal of Behavior Therapy and Experimental Psychiatry, 40*, 98–105.

Abrantes, A.M., Strong, D.R., Cohn, A., Cameron, A.Y., Greenberg, B.D., Mancebo, M.C., & Brown, R.A. (2009). Acute changes in obsessions and compulsions following moderate-intensity aerobic exercise among patients with obsessive–compulsive disorder. *Journal of Anxiety Disorders, 23*, 923–7.

Adler, D.A., McLaughlin, T.J., Rogers, W.H., Chang, H., Lapitsky, L., & Lerner, D. (2006). Job performance deficits due to depression. *American Journal of Psychiatry, 163*, 1569–76.

Ali, T., Dunmore, E., Clark, D., & Ehlers, A. (2002). The role of negative beliefs in posttraumatic stress disorder: A comparison of assault victims and non victims. *Behavioural and Cognitive Psychotherapy, 30*, 249–57.

Alidina, S., & Cooper, C.L. (2012). *Relaxation for dummies*. Chichester: John Wiley & Sons.

Allgulander, C., Florea, I., & Huusom, A.K.T. (2006). Prevention of relapse in generalized anxiety disorder by escitalopram treatment. *International Journal of Neuro-Psychopharmacology, 9*, 495–506.

Amstadter, A. (2008). Emotion regulation and anxiety disorders. *Journal of Anxiety Disorders, 22*, 211–21.

Anderson, D.N. (2001). Treating depression in old age: the reasons to be positive. *Age and Ageing, 30*, 13–17.

Anderson, L., Lewis, G., Araya, R., Elgie, R., Harrison, G., Proudfoot, J., Scmidt, U., Sharp, D., Weightman, A., & Williams, C. (2005). Self-help books for depression: how can practitioners and clients make the right choice? *British Journal of General Practice, 55*, 387–92.

Antony, M.M., & Watling, M.A. (2006). *Overcoming medical phobias: how to conquer fear of blood, needles, doctors, and dentists*. Oakland, CA: New Harbinger.

APA (2000). *Diagnostic and statistical manual of mental disorders* (4th ed., text rev.) (*DSM-IV-TR*). Washington, DC: American Psychological Association.

APA (2003). *Practice guideline for the assessment and treatment of patients with suicidal behaviors*. Washington, DC: American Psychological Association.

Apodaca, T.R., & Miller, R.W. (2003). A meta-analysis of the effectiveness of bibliotherapy for alcohol problems. *Journal of Clinical Psychology, 59*, 289–304.

Atkinson, R.L., Atkinson, R.C., Smith, E.E., Bem, D.L., & Hilgard, E.R. (1990). *Introduction to psychology* (10th ed.). San Diego, CA: Harcourt Brace Jonanovich.

Ballenger, J.C., Davidson, J.R., Lecrubier, Y., Nutt, D.J., Borkovec, T.D, Rickels, K., Stein, D.J., & Wittchen, H.U. (2001). Consensus statement on generalized anxiety disorder from the international consensus group on depression and anxiety. *Journal of Clinical Psychiatry, 62* (Suppl. 11), 53–8.

Balta, G., & Paparrigopoulos, T. (2010). Comorbid anxiety and depression: diagnostic issues and treatment management. *Psychiatrike, 21*, 107–14.

Bandura, A. (1973). *Aggression: a social learning analysis*. Englewood Cliffs, NJ: Prentice-Hall.

Barkham, M., Evans, C., Margison, F., Mcgrath, G., Mellor-Clark, J., Milne, D., & Connell, J. (1998). The rationale for developing and implementing core outcome batteries for routine use in service settings and psychotherapy outcome research. *Journal of Mental Health, 7*, 35–47.

Barrera, M., Rosen, G.M., & Glasgow, R.E. (1981). Rights, risks, and responsibilities in the use of self-help psychotherapy. In G.T. Hannah, W.P. Christian & H.P. Clark (Eds.) *Preservation of client rights* (pp. 204–20). New York: Free Press.

Bassett, H., & Lloyd, C. (2001). Occupational therapy in mental health: managing stress and burnout. *British Journal of Occupational Therapy, 64*, 406–11.

Baum, F. (1999). Social capital: is it good for your health? *Journal of Epidemiological and Community Health, 53*, 185–6.

BBC (2005). French Muslims face job discrimination. British Broadcasting Company. Retrieved 19 May 2011 from http://news.bbc.co.uk/1/hi/world/europe/4399748.stm

BBC (2007). Mothers 'face job discrimination'. British Broadcasting Company. Retrieved 19 May 2011 from http://news.bbc.co.uk/1/hi/uk/6402933.stm

BBC (2010). Birmingham City Council to stop housing asylum seekers. British Broadcasting Company. Retrieved 17 May 2011 from www.bbc.co.uk/news/uk-england-birmingham-11501640

Beauchamp, T.L., & Childress, J.F. (1994). *Principles of biomedical ethics* (4th ed.). Oxford: Oxford University Press.

Beaulac, J., Carlson, A., & Boyd, R.J. (2011). Counseling on physical activity to promote mental health: practical guidelines for family physicians. *Canadian Family Physician, 57*, 399–401.

Beck, A.T. (1967). *Depression: clinical, experimental and theoretical aspects*. New York: Harper & Row.

Beck, A.T. (1976). *Cognitive therapy and the emotional disorders*. London: Penguin Books.

Beck, A.T., Kovacs, M., & Weissman, A. (1975). Hopelessness and suicidal behavior. An overview. *The Journal of the American Medical Association, 234,* 1146–9.

Beck, A.T., Rush, A.J., Shaw, B.F., & Emery, G. (1979). *Cognitive therapy of depression.* New York: Guilford Press.

Beck, A.T., Steer, R.A., & Brown, G.K. (1996). *Manual for the Beck Depression Inventory–II.* San Antonio, TX: Psychological Corporation.

Beck, A.T., Steer, R.A., Kovacs, M., & Garrison, B.A. (1985). Hopelessness and eventual suicide: a 10-year prospective study of patients hospitalized with suicidal ideation. *American Journal of Psychiatry, 142,* 559–63.

Beck, J. (1995). *Cognitive therapy: basics and beyond.* New York: Guilford Press.

Beck, J.S. (2001). A cognitive therapy approach to medication compliance. In J. Kay (Ed.) *Review of psychiatry: Vol. 20. Integrated treatment of psychiatric disorders* (pp. 113–41). Washington, DC: American Psychiatric Press.

Bee, P.E., Bower, P., Lovell, K., Gilbody, S., Richards, D., Gask, L., & Roach, R. (2008). Psychotherapy mediated by remote communication technologies: a meta-analytic review. *BMC Psychiatry, 8,* 60–73.

Beinart, H. (2004). Models of supervision and the supervisory relationship and their evidence base. In I. Fleming & L. Steen (Eds.) *Supervision and clinical psychology. Theory, practice and perspectives* (pp. 36–50). Hove: Routledge.

Beitman, B., Goldfried, M., & Norcross, J. (1989). The movement towards integrating the psychotherapies: an overview. *American Journal of Psychiatry, 146,* 136–47.

Bell, A.C., & D'Zurilla, T.J. (2009). Problem-solving therapy for depression: a meta-analysis. *Clinical Psychology Review, 29,* 348–53.

Belle, D., & Doucet, J. (2003). Poverty, inequality and discrimination as sources of depression among US women. *Psychology of Women Quarterly, 27,* 101–13.

Belzer, K., & Schneier, F.R. (2004). Comorbidity of anxiety and depressive disorders: issues in conceptualization, assessment, and treatment. *Journal of Psychiatric Practice, 10,* 296–306.

Bennett-Levy, J., & Farrand, P. (2010). Low intensity CBT models and conceptual underpinnings: overview. In J. Bennett-Levy, D.A. Richards, P. Farrand, H. Christensen, K.M. Griffiths, D.J. Kavanagh, B. Klein, M.A. Lau, J. Proudfoot, L. Ritterband, J. White, & C. Williams (Eds.) *Oxford guide to low intensity CBT interventions* (pp. 1–2). Oxford: Oxford University Press.

Bennett-Levy, J., Lee, N., Travers, K., Pohlman, S., & Hamernik, E. (2003). Cognitive therapy from the inside: enhancing therapist skills through practicing what we preach. *Behavioural and Cognitive Psychotherapy, 31,* 143–58.

Bennett-Levy, J., Richards, D., & Farrand, P. (2010a). Low intensity CBT interventions: a revolution in mental health care. In J. Bennett-Levy, D.A. Richards, P. Farrand, H. Christensen, K.M. Griffiths, D.J. Kavanagh, B. Klein, M.A. Lau, J. Proudfoot, L. Ritterband, J. White, & C. Williams (Eds.) *Oxford guide to low intensity CBT interventions* (pp. 3–18). Oxford: Oxford University Press.

Bennett-Levy, J., Richards, D.A., Farrand, P., Christensen, H., Griffiths, K.M., Kavanagh, D., Klein, J.B., Lau, M.A., Proudfoot, J., Ritterband, L., White, J., & Williams, C. (Eds.) (2010b). *Oxford guide to low intensity CBT interventions*. Oxford: Oxford University Press.

Bennett-Levy, J., Thwaites, R., Chaddock, A., & Davis, M. (2009) Reflective practice in cognitive behaviour therapy: the engine of lifelong learning. In J. Stedmon & R. Dallos (Eds.) *Reflective practice in psychotherapy & counselling* (pp. 115–35). Maidenhead: Open University Press.

Bennett-Levy, J., Turner, F., Beaty, T., Smith, M., Paterson, B., & Farmer, S. (2001). The value of self-practice of cognitive therapy techniques and self-reflection in the training of cognitive therapists. *Behavioural and Cognitive Psychotherapy, 29,* 203–20.

Bennett-Levy, J., Westbrook, D., Fennell, M., Cooper, M., Rouf, K., & Hackmann, A. (2004). Behavioural experiments: historical and conceptual underpinnings. In J. Bennett-Levy, G. Butler, M. Fennell, A. Hackmann, M. Mueller & D. Westbrook (Eds.) *Oxford guide to behavioural experiments in cognitive therapy* (pp. 1–20). Oxford: Oxford University Press.

Bernard, J.M., & Goodyear, R.K. (2004). *Fundamentals of clinical supervision* (3rd ed.). London: Pearson.

Bhui, K., Bhugra, D., Goldberg, D., Sauer, J., & Tylee, A. (2004). Assessing the prevalence of depression in Punjabi and English primary care attenders: the role of culture, physical illness and somatic symptoms. *Transcultural Psychiatry, 41,* 307–22.

Bieling, P.J., McCabe, R.E., & Antony, M.M. (2006). *Cognitive-behavioral therapy in groups*. New York: Guilford Press.

Black, C. (2008). *Working for a healthier tomorrow*. London: The Stationery Office.

Blackburn, I., & Davidson, K. (1996). *Cognitive therapy for depression and anxiety*. Oxford: Blackwell Science Ltd.

Blackburn, I., & Twaddle, V. (1996). *Cognitive therapy in action*. London: Souvenir Press.

Blenkiron, P. (1999). Who is suitable for cognitive behavioural therapy? *Journal of the Royal Society of Medicine, 92,* 222–9.

Blenkiron, P. (2010). *Stories and analogies in cognitive behaviour therapy*. Chichester: Wiley-Blackwell.

Boath, E., Bradley, E., & Anthony, P. (2004). Users' views of two alternative approaches to the treatment of postnatal depression. *Journal of Reproductive and Infant Psychology, 22,* 13–24.

Boden, M.T., John, O.P., Goldin, P.R., Werner, K., Heimberg, R.G., & Gross, J.J. (2012). The role of maladaptive beliefs in cognitive-behavioral therapy: evidence from social anxiety disorder. *Behaviour Research and Therapy, 50,* 287–91.

Bohart, A.C., Elliott, R., Greenberg, L.S., & Watson, J.C. (2002). Empathy. In J.C. Norcross (Ed.) *Psychotherapy relationships that work* (pp. 89–108). New York: Oxford University Press.

Borkovec, T.D., Hazlett-Stevens, H., & Diaz, M.L. (1999). The role of positive beliefs about worry in generalized anxiety disorder and its treatment. *Clinical Psychology & Psychotherapy, 6*, 126–38.

Bower, P., & Gilbody, S. (2005). Stepped care in psychological therapies: access, effectiveness and efficiency. *British Journal of Psychiatry, 186*, 11–17.

Bower, P., Gilbody, S., Richards, D.A., Fletcher, J., & Sutton, A. (2006). Collaborative care for depression in primary care. Making sense of complex interventions: systematic review and meta-regression. *British Journal of Psychiatry, 189*, 484–93.

British Association of Behavioural and Cognitive Psychotherapy (n.d.). *Guidelines for good practice of behavioural and cognitive psychotherapy.* BABCP.

British Association for Counselling and Psychotherapy (2007). *Ethical framework for good practice in counselling and psychotherapy.* Lutterworth: BACP.

Bronfenbrenner, U. (1979). *The ecology of human development: experiments by nature and design,* Cambridge, MA: Harvard University Press.

Broocks, A., Bandelow, B., Pekrun, G., George, A., Meyer, T., Bartmann, U., Hillmer-Vogel, U., & Ruther, E. (1998). Comparison of aerobic exercise, clomipramine, and placebo in the treatment of panic disorder. *American Journal of Psychiatry, 155*, 603–9.

Brosan, L., & Hogan, B. (2007). *An introduction to coping with depression.* Robinson: London.

Brown, G.K., Have, T.T., Henriques, G.R., Xie, S.X., Hollander, J.E., & Beck, A.T. (2005). Cognitive therapy for the prevention of suicide attempts: a randomized controlled trial. *Journal of the American Medical Association, 294*, 563–70.

Brown, G.W., & Harris, T.O. (1978). *Social origins of depression: a study of psychiatric disorder in women.* London: Tavistock.

Brown, R.A., & Lewinsohn, P.M. (1984). A psycheducational approach to the treatment of depression: comparison of group, individual, and minimal contact procedures. *Journal of Consulting and Clinical Psychology, 52*, 774–83.

Brown, T.A., Campbell, L.A., Lehman, C.L., Grisham, J., & Mancill, R.A. (2001). Current and lifetime comorbidity of the DSM-IV anxiety and mood disorders in a large clinical sample. *Journal of Abnormal Psychology, 110*, 585–99.

Bryan, C.J. (2007). Empirically-based outpatient treatment for a patient at risk for suicide: the case of 'John'. *Pragmatic Case Studies in Psychotherapy, 3*, 1–40.

Bryan, C.J., Corso, K.A., Neal-Walden, T.A., & Rudd, M.D. (2009). Managing suicide risk in primary care: practice recommendations for behavioral health consultants. *Professional Psychology: Research and Practice, 40*, 148–55.

Bryan, C.J., & Rudd, M.D. (2006). Advances in the assessment of suicide risk. *Journal of Clinical Psychology: In Session, 62*, 185–200.

Burns, D.D., & Auerbach, A. (1996). Therapeutic empathy in cognitive-behavioural therapy: does it make a difference? In P.M. Salkovskis (Ed.) *Frontiers in Cognitive Therapy* (pp. 135–64). London: Guilford Press.

Burton, W.N., Pransky, G., Conti, D.J., Chen, C.Y., & Edington, D.W. (2004). The association of medical conditions and presenteeism. *Journal of Occupational and Environmental Medicine, 46*, 38–45.

Bystritsky, A., Wagner, A.W., Russo, J.E., Stein, M.B., Sherbourne, C.D., Craske, M.G., & Roy-Byrne, P.P. (2005). Assessment of beliefs about psychotropic medication and psychotherapy: development of a measure for patients with anxiety disorders. *General Hospital Psychiatry, 27*, 313–18.

Cape, J., Whittington, C., Buszewicz, M., Wallace, P., & Underwood, L. (2010). Brief psychological therapies for anxiety and depression in primary care: meta-analysis and meta-regression. *BMC Medicine, 8*, 1–13.

Carlat, D.J. (2005). *The psychiatric interview* (2nd ed.). Philadelphia, PA: Lippincott, Williams & Williams.

Carlson, C.R., & Hoyle, R.H. (1993). Efficacy of abbreviated progressive muscle relaxation training: a quantitative review of behavioral medicine research. *Journal of Consulting and Clinical Psychology, 61*, 1059–67.

Carlson, L.E., Ursuliak, Z., Goodey, E., Angen, M., & Speca, M. (2001). The effects of a mindfulness meditation-based stress reduction program on mood and symptoms of stress in cancer outpatients: 6-month follow up. *Supportive Care in Cancer, 9*, 112–23.

Castaneda, A.E., Tuulio-Henriksson, A., Marttunen, M., Suvisaari, J., & Lonnqvist, J. (2008). A review on cognitive impairments in depressive and anxiety disorders with a focus on young adults. *Journal of Affective Disorders, 106*, 1–27.

Castonguay, L.G. (1993). 'Common factors' and 'non-specific variables': clarifications of the two concepts and recommendations for research. *Journal of Psychotherapy Integration, 3*, 267–86.

Castonguay, L.G. (2000). A common factors approach to psychotherapy training. *Journal of Psychotherapy Integration, 10*, 263–82.

Castonguay, L.G., & Holtforth, M.G. (2005). Change in psychotherapy: a plea for no more 'non-specific' and false dichotomies. *Clinical Psychology: Science and Practice, 12*, 198–201.

Cavanagh, K. (2010). Turn on, tune in and (don't) drop out: engagement, adherence, attrition, and alliance with internet-based interventions. In J. Bennett-Levy, D. Richards, P. Farrand, H. Christensen, K.M. Griffiths, D.J. Kavanagh, B. Klein, M. Lau, J. Proudfoot, L. Ritterband, J. White, & C. Williams (Eds.) *Oxford guide to low intensity CBT interventions* (pp. 227–34). Oxford: Oxford University Press.

Cavanagh, K., Seccombe, N., Lidbetter, N., & Bunnell, D. (2011). Supported, service-user led, computerised cognitive behavioural therapy (CCBT) self-help clinics scale. *Journal of Public Mental Health, 10*, 225–33.

Cave, A., & Dunwoodie, A. (2012). *Services available: Sunderland Primary Care and Psychological Wellbeing Services.* Unpublished report, Northumberland, Tyne and Wear NHS Foundation Trust.

Chodzko-Zajko, W.J., Proctor, D.N., Fiatarone Singh, M.A., Minson, C.T., Nigg, C.R., Salem, G.J., Skinner, J.S. (2009). American College of Sports Medicine position stand. Exercise and physical activity for older adults. *Medicine and Science in Sports and Exercise, 41*, 1510–30.

Christiana, J.M., Gilman, S.E., Guardino, M., Mickelson, K., Morselli, P.L., Olfson, M., & Kessler, R.C. (2000). Duration between onset and time of obtaining initial treatment among people with anxiety and mood disorders: an international survey of members of mental health patient advocate groups. *Psychological Medicine, 30*, 693–703.

Civera, R.G., Granell, R.R., Cabedo, S.M., & Escorihuela, A.L. (2007). Typical vasovagal syncope (blood/injury phobia). In R. García-Civera, G. Barón-Esquivias, J.J. Blanc, M. Brignole, A.M. i Mitjans, R. Ruiz-Granell, & W. Wieling (Eds.) *Syncope cases* (pp. 8–9). Malden, MA: Blackwell.

Clark, D.A. (1995). Perceived limitations of standard cognitive therapy: a reconsideration of efforts to revise Beck's theory and therapy. *Journal of Cognitive Psychotherapy, 9*, 153–72.

Clark, D.M. (1986). A cognitive approach to panic. *Behaviour Research and Therapy, 5*, 27–50.

Clark, D.M., Ball, S., & Pape, D. (1991). An experimental investigation of thought suppression. *Behaviour Research and Therapy, 29*, 253–7.

Clark, D.M., Fonagy, P., Turpin, G., Pilling, S., Adams, M., Burke, M., Cape, J., Cate, T., Ehlers, A., Garety, P., Holland, R., Liebowitz, J., MacDonald, K., Roth, T., & Shafran, R. (2009a). Speaking up for IAPT. *The Psychologist, 22*, 446–7.

Clark, D.M., Layard, R., Smithies, R., Richards, D.A., Suckling, R., & Wright, B. (2009b). Improving access to psychological therapy: initial evaluation of two UK demonstration sites. *Behaviour Research and Therapy, 47*, 910–20.

Clark, D.M., & Wells, A. (1995). A cognitive model of social phobia. *Social phobia: Diagnosis, assessment, and treatment, 41*, 68.

Connor, K., Davidson, J.R.T., Churchill, L.E., Sherwood, A., Weisler, R.H., & Foa, E. (2000). Psychometric properties of the Social Phobia Inventory (SPIN): new self-rating scale. *The British Journal of Psychiatry, 176*, 379–86.

Cottam, J. (2012) Personal communication, 9 April 2012.

Coull, G., & Morris, P.G. (2011). The clinical effectiveness of CBT-based guided self-help interventions for anxiety and depressive disorders: a systematic review. *Psychological Medicine, 41*, 2239–52.

Cox, B.J., Parker, J.D.A., & Swinson, R.P. (1996). Confirmatory factor analysis of the Fear Questionnaire with social phobia patients. *British Journal of Psychiatry, 168*, 497–9.

Coyne, J.C., Thombs, B.D., & Mitchell, A.J. (2009). Letter to the editor: PHQ-9 and PHQ-2 in Western Kenya. *Journal of General Internal Medicine, 24*, 890.

Creamer, M., Bell, R., & Failla, S. (2003). Psychometric properties of the Impact of Event Scale – Revised. *Behaviour Research and Therapy, 41*, 1489–96.

Cuijpers, P., Donker, T., Van Straten, A., Li, J., & Andersson, G. (2010). Is guided self-help as effective as face-to-face psychotherapy for depression and anxiety disorders? A systematic review and meta-analysis of comparative outcome studies. *Psychological Medicine*, 40, 1943–57.

Cuijpers, P., Muñoz, R., Clarke, G., & Lewinsohn, P.M. (2009). Psychoeducational treatment and prevention of depression: the 'Coping with Depression' course thirty years later. *Clinical Psychology Review*, 29, 449–58.

Cuijpers, P., van Straten, A., & Warmerdam, L. (2007a). Behavioral activation treatments of depression: a meta-analysis. *Clinical Psychology Review*, 27, 318–26.

Cuijpers, P., van Straten, A., & Warmerdam, L. (2007b). Problem solving therapies for depression: a meta-analysis. *European Psychiatry*, 22, 9–15.

Cushway, D., & Knibbs, J. (2010). Trainees' and supervisors' perceptions of supervision. In Fleming, I., & Steen, L. (Eds.) *Supervision and clinical psychology. Theory, practice and perspectives* (pp. 162–85). Hove: Routledge.

Dakwar, E., & Levin, F.R. (2009). The emerging role of meditation in addressing psychiatric illness, with a focus on substance abuse disorders. *Harvard Review of Psychiatry*, 17, 254–67.

Dalgard, O.S. (2006). A randomized controlled trial of a psychoeducational group program for unipolar depression in adults in Norway. *Clinical Practice and Epidemiology in Mental Health*, 2, 2–15.

Deffenbacher, J.L. (1999). Cognitive-behavioral conceptualisation and treatment of anger. *Psychotherapy in Practice*, 55, 295–309.

Department of Health (1999). *National service frameworks: mental health*. London: HMSO.

Department of Health (2002). *National suicide prevention strategy for England*. London: HMSO.

Department of Health (2007). *Best practice in managing risk*. London: HMSO.

Department for Work and Pensions (2002). *Pathways to work: helping people into employment* (Cm 5690). London: Department for Work and Pensions.

Department for Work and Pensions, Department of Health & Health and Safety Executive (2004). *Health, work and well-being – caring for our future*. London: HM Government.

Dimsdale, J.E. (2008). Psychological stress and cardiovascular disease. *Journal of American College of Cardiology*, 51, 1237–46.

Dingfelder, S.F. (2008). An insidious enemy. *Monitor on Psychology*, 39, 22.

Dodu, N. (2005). Is employment good for well-being? A literature review. *Journal of Occupational Psychology, Employment and Disability*, 7, 17–33.

Donker, T., Griffith, K.M., Cuijpers, P., & Christensen, H. (2009). Psychoeducation for depression, anxiety and psychological distress: a meta-analysis. *BMC Medicine*, 7, 79–88.

Dowrick, C., Dunn, G., Ayuso-Mateos, J.L., Dalgard, O.S., Page, H., Lehtinen, V., Casey, P., Wilkinson, C., Vazquez-Barquero, J.L., Wilkinson, G., & the Outcomes of Depression International Network (ODIN) Group (2000). Problem solving treatment and group psychoeducation for depression: multicentre randomised controlled trial. *British Medical Journal, 321*, 1450–4.

Driscoll, J. (2000). *Practising clinical supervision: a reflective approach*. London: Ballière Tindall.

Driver, H.S., & Taylor, S.R. (2000). Exercise and sleep. *Sleep Medicine Reviews, 4*, 387–402.

Dugas, M.J., Letarte, H., Rhéaume, J., Freeston, M.H., & Ladouceur, R. (1995). Worry and problem solving: Evidence of a specific relationship. *Cognitive Therapy and Research, 19*, 109–20.

Dugas, M.J., Freeston, M.H., & Ladouceur, R. (1997). Intolerance of uncertainty and problem orientation in worry. *Cognitive therapy and research, 21*, 593–606.

Eckman, P.S., & Shean, G.D. (1997). Habituation of cognitive and physiological arousal and social anxiety. *Behavior Research and Therapy, 35*, 1113–21.

Ekers, D., Richards, D., & Gilbody, S. (2008). A meta analysis of randomized trials of behavioural treatment of depression. *Psychological Medicine, 38*, 611–23.

Espie, C. (2006). *Overcoming insomnia and sleep problems*. London: Robinson.

Evans, J., & Repper, J. (2000). Employment, social inclusion and mental health. *Journal of Psychiatric and Mental Health Nursing, 7*, 15–24.

Evans, L., & Spelman, M. (1983). The problem of noncompliance with drug therapy. *Drugs, 25*, 63–76.

Evans, R. (2009). *Specialist doctors say NHS is institutionally ageist*. Retrieved 17 May 2011 from www.hsj.co.uk/news/specialist-doctors-say-nhs-is-institutionally-ageist/1975073 article.

Eysenck, H.J. (1947). *Dimensions of personality*. London: Routledge and Kegan Paul.

Farrand, P., Perry, J., & Linsley, S. (2010). Enhancing self-practice/self-reflection (SP/SR) approach to cognitive behaviour training through the use of reflective blogs. *Behavioural & Cognitive Psychotherapy, 38*, 473–7.

Farrand, P., & Williams, C. (2010). Low Intensity CBT assessment: in person or by phone. In J. Bennett-Levy, D.A. Richards, P. Farrand, H. Christensen, K.M. Griffiths, D.J. Kavanagh, B. Klein, M.A. Lau, J. Proudfoot, L. Ritterband, J. White, & C. Williams (Eds.) *Oxford guide to low intensity CBT interventions* (pp. 89–98). Oxford: Oxford University Press.

Fava, M., & Kendler, K. (2000). Major depressive disorder. *Neuron, 28*, 335–41.

First, M.B., Spitzer, R.L., Gibbon, M., & Williams, J.B.W. (2002). *Structured clinical interview for DSM-IV-TR axis I disorders, research version, non-patient edition (SCID-I/NP)*. New York: Biometrics Research, New York State Psychiatric Institute.

Fitch, C., Hamilton, S., Bassett, P., & Davey, R. (2011). The relationship between personal debt and mental health: a systematic review. *Mental Health Review Journal, 16*, 153–66.

Foa, E.B., Kozak, M.J., Salkovskis, P.M., Coles, M.E., & Amir, N. (1998). The validation of a new obsessive–compulsive disorder scale: the Obsessive–Compulsive Inventory. *Psychological Assessment, 10*, 206–14.

Ford, D., & Kamerow, D. (1989). Epidemiologic study of sleep disturbances and psychiatric disorders. *Journal of the American Medical Association, 262*, 1479–84.

Foroushani, P.S., Schneider, J., & Assareh, N. (2011). Meta-review of the effectiveness of computerised CBT in treatment depression. *BMC Psychiatry, 11*, 131–7.

France, R., & Robson, M. (1997). *Cognitive behavioural therapy in primary care: a practical guide*. London: Jessica Kingsley.

Franzen, P.L., & Buysse, D.J. (2008). Sleep disturbances and depression: risk relationships for subsequent depression and therapeutic implications. *Dialogues in Clinical Neuroscience, 10*, 473–81.

Free, M.L. (2007). *Cognitive therapy in groups* (2nd ed.). Chichester: John Wiley & Sons.

Fries, J., Koop, C., & Beadle, C. (1993). Reducing health care costs by reducing the need and demand for medical services. *New England Journal of Medicine, 329*, 321–5.

Furmark, T., Carlbring, P., Hedman, E., Sonnenstein, A., Clevberger, P., Bohman, B., Eriksson, A., Hallen, A., Frykman, M., Holmstrom, A., Spathan, E., Tilfors, M., Ihrfelt, E.N., Spak, M., Erikson, A., Ekselius, L., & Andersson, G. (2009). Guided and unguided self-help for social anxiety disorder: randomised controlled trial. *British Journal of Psychiatry, 195*, 440–7.

Gallo, J.J., Anthony, J.C., & Bengt, O.M. (1994). Age differences in the symptoms of depression: a latent trait analysis. *Journal of Gerontology, 49*, 251–64.

Gellatly, J., Bower, P., Hennessy, S., Richards, D., Gilbody, S., & Lovell, K. (2007). What makes self-help interventions effective in the management of depressive symptoms? Meta-analysis and meta-regression. *Psychological Medicine, 37*, 1217–28.

Gilbert, P. (2007). Evolved minds and compassion in the therapeutic relationship. In P. Gilbert & R.L. Leahy (Eds.) *The therapeutic relationship in the cognitive-behavioural therapies* (pp. 106–42). London: Routledge.

Gilbert, P. (2009). *Overcoming depression. A self help guide using cognitive behavioral techniques* (3rd ed.). London: Constable Robinson.

Gilbert, P., & Leahy, R.L. (2007). *The therapeutic relationship in the cognitive-behavioural therapies*. London: Routledge.

Gilbody, S., Richards, D., Brealey, S., & Hewitt, C. (2007). Screening for depression in medical settings with the Patient Health Questionnaire (PHQ): a diagnostic meta-analysis. *Journal of General Internal Medicine, 22*, 1596–602.

Glaser, R., & Kiecolt-Glaser, J.K. (2005). Stress-induced immune dysfunction: implications for health. *Nature Reviews Immunology, 5*, 243–51.

Glasgow, R.E., & Rosen, G.M. (1978). Behavioral bibliotherapy: a review of self-help behavior therapy manuals. *Psychological Bulletin, 85*, 1–23.

Gloaguen, V., Cottraux, J., & Cucherat, M. (1998). A meta-analysis of the effects of cognitive therapy. *Journal of Affective Disorders, 49*, 59–72.

Goldberg, D.P., & Huxley, P.J. (1992). *Common mental disorders: a biosocial model.* Routledge: London.

Grant, A., Townend, M., Mills, J., & Cockx, A. (2008). *Assessment and case formulation in cognitive behavioural therapy.* London: Sage.

Green, G., Hayes, C., Dickinson, D., Whittaker, A., & Gilheany, B. (2002). The role and impact of social relationships upon wellbeing reported by mental health service users: a qualitative study. *Journal of Mental Health, 11,* 565–79.

Green, S.M. (2011). *I am not stressed! How about you? A look at the impact of progressive muscle relaxation on the autonomic nervous system.* Unpublished doctoral dissertation, Howard University, Washington, DC.

Greenberger, D., & Padesky, C.A. (1995). *Mind over mood.* New York: Guilford Press.

Griffith, K.M., Farrer, L., & Christensen, H. (2010). The efficacy of internet interventions for depression and anxiety: a review of randomised controlled trials. *Medical Journal of Australia, 192,* S4–S11.

Gyani, A., Shafran, R., Layard, R., & Clark, D. (2011). *Enhancing recovery rates in IAPT Services: lessons from analysis of the Year One data.* Retrieved 13 March 2012 from www.iapt.nhs.uk/silo/files/enhancing-recovery-rates--iapt-year-one-report.pdf

Hackmann, A., Day, S.J., & Holmes, E.A. (2009). Agoraphobia: imagery and the threatened self. In L. Stopa (Ed.) *Imagery and the threatened self: perspectives on mental imagery and the self in cognitive therapy* (pp. 112–36). Hove: Routledge.

Hagan, T., & Donnison, J. (1999). Social power: some implications for the theory and practice of cognitive behaviour therapy. *Journal of Community and Applied Social Psychology, 9,* 119–35.

Hamilton, M. (1960). A rating scale for depression. *Journal of Neurology, Neurosurgery and Psychiatry, 23,* 56–62.

Handler, C., & Coghlan, G. (2007). *Living with coronary disease.* London: Springer.

Hannay, D.R. (1981). Mental health and high flats. *Journal of Chronic Diseases, 34,* 431–2.

Hawkins, P., & Shohet, R. (2004*). Supervising in the helping professions* (2nd ed.). Maidenhead: Open University Press.

Hays, P. (2001). *Addressing cultural complexities in practice: a framework for clinicians and counsellors.* Washington, DC: American Psychological Association.

Hays, P., & Iwamasa, G.Y. (2006). *Culturally responsive cognitive-behavioural therapy: assessment, practice and supervision.* Washington, DC: American Psychological Association.

Health and Safety Executive (2007). *Managing the causes of work-related stress: a step-by-step approach using the Management Standards HSG218* (2nd ed.). Suffolk: HSE Books.

Healthcare Commission (2007). *Investigation into outbreaks of Clostridium difficile at Maidstone and Tunbridge Wells NHS Trust.* London: Healthcare Commission.

Healy, D. (2009). *Psychiatric drugs explained* (5th ed.). Edinburgh: Churchill Livingston.

Healy, A.F., & Bourne, L.E., Jr. (2005). *Training to minimize the decay of knowledge and skills.* Final Report to the National Science Foundation, REC-0335674.

Herrick, C.M., & Ainsworth, A.D. (2000). Invest in yourself. Yoga as a self-care strategy. *Nursing Forum, 35*, 32–6.

Herring, M.P., Jacob, M.L., Suveg, C., Dishman, R., & O'Connor, P.J. (2011a). Short-term exercise training for treatment of generalized anxiety disorder: a randomized controlled trial. *Medicine & Science in Sports & Exercise, 43*, 21–2.

Herring, M.P., Jacob, M.L., Suveg, C., & O'Connor, P.J. (2011b). Effects of short-term exercise training on signs and symptoms of generalized anxiety disorder. *Mental Health and Physical Activity, 4*, 71–7.

Herring, M.P., Jacob, M.L., Suveg, C., Dishman, R.K., & O'Connor, P.J. (2012). Feasibility of exercise training for the short-term treatment of generalized anxiety disorder: a randomized controlled trial. *Psychotherapy and Psychosomatics, 81*, 21–8.

Hoffart, A., Versland, S., & Sexton, H. (2002). Self-understanding, empathy, guided discovery, and schema belief in schema-focused cognitive therapy of personality problems: a process-outcome study. *Cognitive Therapy & Research, 26*, 199–219.

Holly, P., Boughton, N., & Roberts, J. (2010). CBT with inpatients in mental health settings. In M. Mueller, H. Kennerley, F. McManus, & D. Westbrook (Eds.) *Oxford guide to surviving as a CBT therapist* (pp. 233–52). Oxford: Oxford University Press.

Holmes, E.A., Geddes, J.R., Colom, F., & Goodwin, G.M. (2008). Mental imagery as an emotional amplifier: application to bipolar disorder. *Behaviour Research and Therapy, 46*, 1251–8.

Holmes, T.H. & Rahe, R.H. (1967). The Social Readjustment Rating Scale. *Journal of Psychosomatic Research, 11*, 213–18.

Holt, C.A., & Laury, S.K. (2002). Risk aversion and incentive effects. *American Economic Review, 92*, 1644–55.

Hopko, D.R., Lejuez, C.W., LePage, J.P., Hopko, S.D., & McNeil, D.W. (2003). A brief behavioral activation treatment for depression. *Behavior Modification, 27*, 458–69.

Horwath, E., & Weissman, M.M. (1995). *Epidemiology of depression and anxiety disorders*. In M.T. Tsuang, M. Tohen, & G.E.P. Zahner (Eds.). *Textbook in psychiatric epidemiology* (pp. 317–44). New York: Wiley-Liss.

Houghton, S., & Saxon, D. (2007). An evaluation of large group CBT psycho-education for anxiety disorders delivered in routine practice. *Patient Education and Counselling, 68*, 107–10.

Hoyer, J., Beesdo, K., Gloster, A.T., Runge, J., Höfler, M., & Becker, E.S. (2009). Worry exposure versus applied relaxation in the treatment of generalized anxiety disorder. *Psychotherapy and psychosomatics, 78*, 106–15.

IAPT (n.d.). *Psychological wellbeing practitioners: playing a key role in maintaining the nation's wellbeing: best practice guide. National IAPT Programme.* Improving Access to Psychological Therapies. Retrieved 12 January 2012 from www.iapt.nhs.uk/silo/files/psychological-wellbeing-practitioners--best-practice-guide.pdf

IAPT (2008). *Improving Access to Psychological Therapies (IAPT) outcomes toolkit 2008/9.* Improving Access to Psychological Therapies. Retrieved 12 January 2012 from www.eoe.nhs.uk/

IAPT (2010). *Good practice guidance on the use of self-help materials within IAPT services.* Improving Access to Psychological Therapies. Retrieved 12 January 2012 from www.iapt.nhs.uk/silo/files/good-practice-guidance-on-the-use-of-selfhelp-materials-within-iapt-services.pdf

IAPT (2011a). *Building a business case for employment advice and support in IAPT.* Improving Access to Psychological Therapies. Retrieved 24 June 2012 from www.iapt.nhs.uk/silo/files/building-a-business-case-for-employment-advice-and-support-in-iapt.pdf

IAPT (2011b). *Employment advice and employment support co-ordination in IAPT service design principles.* Improving Access to Psychological Therapies. Retrieved 24 June 2012 from www.iapt.nhs.uk/silo/files/employment-advice-and-employment-support-coordination-in-iapt-service-design-principles.pdf

Inskipp, F., & Proctor, B. (1993). *The art, craft and tasks of counselling supervision. Part 1: making the most of supervision.* Twickenham: Cascade.

Jackoway, I., Rogers, J., & Snow, T. (1987). The role change assessment: an interview tool for evaluating older adults. *Occupational Therapy in Mental Health, 7,* 17–37.

Jacobson, E. (1934). *You must relax.* Oxford: Whittlesey House.

Jacobson, N.S., Dobson, K.S., Truax, P.A., Addis, M.E., Koerner, K., Gollan, J.K., Gortner, E., & Prince, S.E. (1996). A component analysis of cognitive-behavioral treatment for depression. *Journal of Consulting and Clinical Psychology, 64,* 295–304.

Jacobson, N.S., Martell, C.R., & Dimidjian, S. (2001). Behavioral activation treatment for depression: returning to contextual roots. *Clinical Psychology: Science and Practice, 8,* 255–70.

Johnstone, M. (2007). *I had a black dog.* London: Robinson.

Johnston, M., Pollard, B., & Hennessey, P. (2000). Construct validation of the Hospital Anxiety and Depression scale with clinical populations. *Journal of Psychosomatic Research, 48,* 579–84.

Joiner, T.E. (2005). *Why people die by suicide.* Cambridge, MA: Harvard University Press.

Jones, J., Huxtable, C., & Hodgson, J. (2005). *Self-reported work-related illness in 2004/2005: results from the Labour Force Survey.* London: Health & Safety Executive.

Josefowitz, N., & Myran, D. (2005). Towards a person-centred cognitive behaviour therapy. *Counselling Psychology Quarterly, 18,* 329–36.

Kaltenthaler, E., Braziet, J., De Nigris, E., Tumur, I., Ferriter, M., Beverley, C., Parry, G., Rooney, G., & Sutcliffe, P. (2006). Computerised cognitive behaviour therapy for depression and anxiety update: a systematic review and economic evaluation. *Health Technology Assessment, 10,* 33.

Katon, W., Von Korff, M., Lin, E., Simon, G., Walker, E., Unützer, J., Bush, T., Russo, J., & Ludman, E. (1999). Stepped collaborative care for primary care patients with persistent symptoms of depression: a: randomized trial. *Archives of General Psychiatry, 56*, 1109–15. Copyright 1999 American Medical Association. All Rights Reserved. Applicable FARS/DFARS Restrictions Apply to Government Use.*More Author Information*

Katzow, A.W., & Safran, J.D. (2007). Recognizing and resolving ruptures in the therapeutic alliance. In P. Gilbert & R.L. Leahy (Eds.) *The therapeutic relationship in the cognitive-behavioural therapies*. London: Routledge.

Kaufman, J., & Charney, D. (2000). Comorbidity of mood and anxiety disorders. *Depression and Anxiety, 12*, 69–76.

Kawachi, I., Kennedy, P., & Glass, R. (1999). Social capital and self rated health: a contextual analysis. *American Journal of Public Health, 89*, 1187–93.

Kemp, J. (2010). *Asylum seekers in Glasgow face eviction*. Retrieved 17 May 2011 from www.guardian.co.uk/society/2010/nov/24/asylum-seekers-glasgow-face-eviction

Kendal, S., Callery, P., & Keeley, P. (2011). The feasibility and acceptability of an approach to emotional wellbeing support for high school students. *Child and Adolescent Mental Health, 16*, 193–200.

Kendrick, T., Dowrick, C., McBride, A., Howe, A., Clarke, P., Maisey, Moore, M., & Smith, P.W. (2009). Management of depression in UK general practice in relation to scores on depression severity questionnaires: analysis of medical record data. *British Medical Journal, 338*, b750.

Kessler, D., Lloyd, K., Lewis, G., & Gray, D.P. (1999). Cross sectional study of symptom attribution and recognition of depression and anxiety in primary care. *British Medical Journal, 318*, 436–40.

Kessler, R.C. (1997). The prevalence of psychiatric comorbidity. In S. Wetzler & W.C. Sanderson (Eds.) *Treatment strategies for patients with psychiatric comorbidity* (pp. 23–48). New York: John Wiley & Sons.

Kessler, R.C., Anthony, J.C., Blazer, D.G., Bromet, E., Eaton, W.W., Kendler, K., Swartz, M., Wittchen, H.U., & Zhao, S. (1997). The US National Comorbidity Survey: Overview and future directions. *Epidemiology and Psychiatric Sciences, 6* (1), 4–16.

Kessler, R.C., & McLeod, J.D. (1985). Social support and mental health in community samples. In S. Cohen & S.L. Syme (Eds.) *Social support and health.* (pp. 219–40). New York: Academic.

Kinsella, P., & Garland, A. (2008). *Cognitive behaviour therapy for mental health workers. A beginners guide*. Hove: Routledge.

Knaevelsrud, C., & Maercker, A. (2007). Internet-based treatment for PTSD reduces distress and facilitates the development of a strong therapeutic alliance: a randomized controlled clinical trial. *BMC Psychiatry, 7*, 13.

Knapen, J., Sommerijns, E., Vancampfort, D., Sienaert, P., Pieters, G., Haake, P., Probst, P., & Peuskens, J. (2009). State anxiety and subjective well-being responses to acute bouts of aerobic exercise in patients with depressive and anxiety disorders. *British Journal of Sports Medicine, 43,* 756–9.

Knight, B.G., & Poon, C.Y.M. (2008). Contextual adult life span theory for adapting psychotherapy with older adults. *Journal of Rational-emotive and Cognitive-behavioural Therapy, 26,* 232–49.

Koenen, K.C. (2007). Genetics of posttraumatic stress disorder: review and recommendations for future studies. *Journal of Traumatic Stress, 20,* 737–50.

Koenen, K.C., Nugent, N.R., & Amstadter, A.B. (2008). Gene–environment interaction in posttraumatic stress disorder. *European archives of psychiatry and clinical neuroscience, 258,* 82–96.

Kolb, D. (1984). *Experiential learning: experience as the source of learning and development.* Englewood Cliffs, NJ: Prentice Hall.

Kroenke, K., Spitzer, R.L., & Williams, J.B. (2001). The PHQ-9: validity of a brief depression severity measure. *Journal of General Internal Medicine, 16,* 606–13.

Kroenke, K., Spitzer, R.L., Williams, J.B., Monahan, P.O., & Löwe, B. (2007). Anxiety disorders in primary care: prevalence, impairment, comorbidity, and detection. *Annals of Internal Medicine, 146,* 317–25.

Kropp, P.R., & Hart, S.D. (1997). Assessing risk of violence in wide assaulters. In C.D. Webster & M.A. Jackson (Eds.) *Impulsivity: theory, assessment and treatment* (pp. 302–25). New York: Guilford Press.

Kupfer, D.J. (1991). Long-term treatment of depression. *Journal of Clinical Psychiatry, 52* (Suppl. 5), 28–34.

Kuyken, W., Padesky, C.A., & Dudley, R. (2009). *Collaborative Case Conceptualization: Working Effectively with Clients in Cognitive-behavioural Therapy.* New York: Guilford.

Ladany, N. (2004). Psychotherapy supervision: what lies beneath. *Psychotherapy Research, 14,* 1–19.

Ladany, N., Hill, C.E., Corbett, M., & Nutt, L. (1996). Nature, extent, and importance of what therapy trainees do not disclose to their supervisors. *Journal of Counseling Psychology, 43,* 10–24.

Lambert, M.J., & Barley, D.E. (2002). Research summary on the therapeutic relationship and psychotherapy outcome. In J. Norcross (Ed.) *Psychotherapy relationships that work: therapist contribution and psychotherapeutic outcome* (pp. 17–32). Oxford: Oxford University Press.

Lang, P.J. (1968). Fear reduction and fear behaviour: problems in treating a construct. In J.M. Shilen (Ed.) *Research in Psychotherapy* (vol. 3, pp. 90–102). Washington, DC: American Psychological Association.

Larun, L., Nordheim, L.V., Ekeland, E., Hagen, K.B., & Heian, F. (2009). *Exercise in prevention and treatment of anxiety and depression among children and young people.* The Cochrane Library. New York: John Wiley & Sons.

Layard, R., Bell, S., Clark, D.M., Knapp, M., Meacher, M., Priebe, S., & Wright, B. (2006). *The depression report: a new deal for depression and anxiety disorders*. London: London School of Economics.

Lelliott, P., Tullock, S., Boardman, J., Harvey, S., Henderson, M., & Knapp, M. (2008). *Mental health and work*. London: Royal College of Psychiatrists.

Lenkowsky, B., & Lenkowsky, R.S. (1978). Bibliotherapy for the learning disabled adolescent. *Academic Therapy, 14*, 179–85.

Leung, P.W.L., & Sung-Chan, P.P.L. (2002). Cultural values and choice of strategic move in therapy. *Clinical Case Studies, 1*, 342–52.

Lewinsohn, P.M., Antonuccio, D.O., Brechenridge, J.S., & Teri, L. (1984). *The 'Coping with Depression' course*. Eugene, OR: Castalia.

Lewis, G., Anderson, L., Araya, R., Harrison, G., Proudfoot, J., Schmidt, U., Sharp, D., Weightman, A., & Williams, C. (2003). *Self-help interventions for mental health problems*. London: Department of Health.

Lewis, C., Pearce, J., & Bisson, J.I. (2012). Efficacy, cost-effectiveness and acceptability of self-help interventions for anxiety disorders: a systematic review. *British Journal of Psychiatry, 200*, 15–21.

Lilienfeld, S.O. (2007). Psychological treatments that cause harm. *Perspectives on Psychological Science, 2*, 53–70.

Lin, T. (1983). Psychiatry and Chinese culture. *Western Journal of Medicine, 139*, 862–7.

Lipton, R.B., Stewart, W.F., Stone, A.M., Lainez, M.J.A., & Sawyer, J.P.C. (2000). Stratified care vs. stepped care strategies for migraine. *Journal of the American Medical Association, 284*, 2599–605.

Lopez, J.F., Akil, H., & Watson, S.J. (1999). Neural circuits mediating stress. *Biological Psychiatry, 46*, 1461–71.

Lovell, K. (2010). Supporting low intensity interventions using the telephone. In J. Bennett-Levy, D. Richards, P. Farrand, H. Christensen, K.M. Griffiths, D.J. Kavanagh, B. Klein, M. Lau, J. Proudfoot, L. Ritterband, J. White, & C. Williams (Eds.) *Oxford guide to low intensity CBT interventions* (pp. 275–80). Oxford: Oxford University Press.

Lovell, K., & Richards, D. (2008). *A recovery programme for depression*. London: Rethink.

Löwe, B., Decker, O., Müller, S., Brähler, E., Schellberg, D., Herzog, W., & Herzberg, P. (2008). Validation and standardization of the generalized anxiety disorder screener (GAD-7) in the general population. *Medical Care, 46*, 266–74.

Lucock, M., Kirby, R., & Wainwright, N. (2011). A pragmatic randomized controlled trial of a guided self-help intervention versus a waiting list control in a routine primary care mental health service. *British Journal of Clinical Psychology, 50*, 298–309.

Luoma, J.B., Martin, C.E., & Pearson, J.L. (2002). Contact with mental health and primary care providers before suicide: a review of the evidence. *American Journal of Psychiatry, 159*, 909–16.

Manning, C., & White, P.D. (1995). Attitudes of employers to the mentally ill. *The Psychiatrist, 19*, 541–3.

Manzoni, G.M., Pagnini, F., Castelnuovo, G., & Molinari, E. (2008). Relaxation training for anxiety: a ten-years systematic review with meta-analysis. *BMC Psychiatry, 8*, 41.

Marks, I.M., Cavanagh, K., & Gega, L. (2007). Computer-aided psychotherapy: revolution or bubble? *British Journal of Psychiatry, 191*, 471–3.

Marks, I., & Nesse, R.M. (1994). Fears and fitness: an evolutionary analysis of anxiety disorders. *Ethology and Sociobiology, 15*, 247–1.

Marmot, M. (2005). Social determinants of health inequalities. *Lancet, 365*, 1099–104.

Marmot, M.G., Shipley, M.J., & Rose, G. (1984). Inequalities in death – specific explanations of a general pattern? *Lancet, 323*, 1003–6.

Martell, C.R., Addis, M.E., & Jacobson, N.S. (2001). *Depression in context: strategies for guided action*. New York: Norton.

Martin, B., Kilfedder, C., & Powers, K. (2003). Occupational stress in NHS staff. *Occupational Health Review*, July/August, 37–9.

Martinez, R., & Williams, C. (2010). Matching clients to CBT self-help resources. In J. Bennett-Levy, D. Richards, P. Farrand, H. Christensen, K.M. Griffiths, D.J. Kavanagh, B. Klein, M. Lau, J. Proudfoot, L. Ritterband, J. White, & C. Williams (Eds.) *Oxford guide to low intensity CBT interventions* (pp. 113–20). Oxford: Oxford University Press.

Masataka, N., & Shibasaki, M. (2012). Premenstrual enhancement of snake detection in visual search in healthy women. *Scientific Reports, 2*.

Mataix-Cols, D., & Marks, I.M. (2006). Self-help with minimal therapist contact for obsessive–compulsive disorder: a review. *European Psychiatry, 21*, 75–80.

Mataix-Cols, D., Cowley, A.J., Hankins, M., Schneider, A., Bachofen, M., Kenwright, M., & Marks, I.M. (2003). Reliability and validity of the Work and Social Adjustment Scale in phobic disorders. *Comprehensive Psychiatry, 46*, 223–8.

Mathews, A., & Mackintosh, B. (2000). Induced emotional interpretation bias and anxiety. *Journal of Abnormal Psychology, 109*, 602–15.

Maunder, L., & Cameron, L. (2010). *Sleeping problems. A self help guide*. Northumberland, Tyne and Wear NHS Foundation Trust. Available at www.ntw.nhs.uk/pic

Maynard, C.K. (2003). Differentiate depression from dementia. *The Nurse Practitioner, 28*, 18–27.

Mayo-Wilson, E., & Montgomery, P. (2007). *Media-delivered cognitive behavioural therapy and behavioural therapy (self-help) for anxiety disorders in adults*. London: Cochrane Database of Systematic Reviews.

McCarthy, P., & Hatcher, C. (2002). *Presentation skills: the essential guide for students*. London: Sage.

McCormack, B., & Farrell, M. (2009). Translating quality of life into service action: use of personal outcome measures in the Republic of Ireland. *British Journal of Learning Disabilities, 37*, 300–7.

McCulloch, A. (2001). Social environments and health: a cross sectional survey. *British Medical Journal, 323,* 208–9.

McGuire, M.T., Marks, I., Nesse, R.M., & Troisi, A. (1992). Evolutionary biology: a basic science for psychiatry? *Acta Psychiatrica Scandinavica, 86,* 89–96.

McIntosh, P. (1998). White privilege: unpacking the invisible knapsack. In M. McGoldrick (Ed.) *Revisioning family therapy* (pp. 147–52). London: Guilford.

McKee-Ryan, F.M., Song, Z., Wanberg, C.R., & Kinicki, A.J. (2005). Psychological and physical well-being during unemployment: a meta-analytic study. *Journal of Applied Psychology, 90,* 53–76.

McLean, P.D., Whittal, M.L., Thordarson, D.S., Taylor, S., Söchting, I., Koch, W.J., Patterson, R., & Anderson, K.W. (2001). Cognitive versus behavior therapy in the group treatment of obsessive-compulsive disorder. *Journal of Consulting and Clinical Psychology, 69,* 205.

McLeod, H.J., Deane, F.P., & Hogbin, B. (2002). Changing staff attitudes and empathy for working with people with psychosis. *Behavioural and Cognitive Psychotherapy, 30,* 459–70.

McManus, S., Meltzer, H., Brugha, T., Bebbington, P., & Jenkins, R. (Eds.) (2009). *Adult Psychiatric Morbidity in England: Results of a Household Survey.* Leeds: The NHS Information Centre. (available at www.ic.nhs.uk/pubs/psychiatricmorbidity07).

McManus, F., van Doorn, K., & Yiend, J. (2012). Examining the effects of thought records and behavioural experiments in instigating belief change. *Journal of Behavior Therapy and Experimental Psychiatry, 43,* 540–7.

McMullen, J.D., O'Callaghan, P.S., Richards, J.A., Eakin, J.G., & Rafferty, H. (2011). Screening for traumatic exposure and psychological distress among war-affected adolescents in post-conflict northern Uganda. *Social Psychiatry and Psychiatric Epidemiology, 47,* 1489–98.

McNeil, D.W., Vrana, S.R., Melamed, B.G., Cuthbert, B.N., & Lang, P.J. (1993). Emotional imagery in simple and social phobia: fear versus anxiety. *Journal of Abnormal Psychology, 102,* 212–25.

Meares, K., & Freeston, M. (2008). *Overcoming worry.* London: Robinson.

Meiser-Stedman, R. (2002). Towards a cognitive-behavioral model of PTSD in children and adolescents. *Clinical Child and Family Psychology Review, 5,* 217–32.

Meltzer, H., Bebbington, P., Brugha, T., Farrell, M., Jenkins, R., & Lewis, G. (2000). The reluctance to seek treatment for neurotic disorders. *Journal of Mental Health, 9,* 319–27.

Merikangas, K.R., & Pine, D. (2002). Genetic and other vulnerability factors for anxiety and stress disorders. In K.L. Davis, D. Charney, J.T. Coyle, & C. Nemeroff (Eds.) *Neuropsychopharmacology: The Fifth Generation of Progress* (pp. 867–82). Philadelphia: Lippincott, Williams & Wilkins.

Meuret, A.E., Wilhelm, F.H., Ritz, T., & Roth, W.T. (2008). Feedback of end-tidal pCO_2 as a therapeutic approach for panic disorder. *Journal of Psychiatric Research, 42,* 560–8.

Meyer, T.J., Miller, M.L., Metzger, R.L., & Borkovec, T.D. (1990). Development and validation of the Penn State Worry Questionnaire. *Behaviour Research and Therapy*, *28*, 487–95.

Michael, T., Zetsche, U., & Margraf, J. (2007). Epidemiology of anxiety disorders. *Psychiatry*, *6*, 136–42.

Miller, S., Hubble, M., & Duncan, B.L. (2008). Supershrinks. Who are they? What is the secret of their success? *Psychotherapy in Australia*, *14*, 14–22.

Milne, D. (2009). *Evidence-based clinical supervision*. Malden, MA: BPS Blackwell.

Minchin, R. (2011). *Gay couple win bed and breakfast snub case*. Retrieved 17 May 2011 from www.independent.co.uk/news/uk/home-news/gay-couple-win-bed-and-breakfast-snub-case-2187347.html

Mitchell, A.J., & Selmes, T. (2007). Why don't patients take their medicine? Reasons and solutions in psychiatry. *Advances in Psychiatric Treatment*, *13*, 336–46.

Moen, P., Dempster-McClain, D., & Erickson, M.A. (2000). *Role transitions, project 2015: the future of aging in New York State*. New York: New York State Office for the Aging.

Mona, L.R., Romesser-Scehnet, J.M., Cameron, R.P., & Cardenas, V. (2006). Cognitive–behavioral therapy and people with disabilities. In P.A. Hays & G.Y. Iwamasa (Eds.) *Culturally responsive cognitive-behavioral therapy: assessment, practice, and supervision* (pp. 199–222). Washington, DC: American Psychological Association.

Morrey, S. (1995). Cognitive therapy. In W. Dryden (Ed.) *Individual therapy: a handbook* (pp. 226–51). Buckingham: Open University.

Mowrer, O.H. (1947). On the dual nature of learning – a reinterpretation of 'conditioning' and 'problem solving'. *Harvard Educational Review*, *17*, 102–48.

Mullican, C. (Ed.) (2011). *A national agenda for research in collaborative care*. Rockville, MD: Agency for Healthcare Research and Quality.

Mundt, J.C., Marks, I.M., Shear, K., & Griest, J.H. (2002). The work and social adjustment scale: a simple measure of impairment in functioning. *British Journal of Psychiatry*, *180*, 461–4.

Muran, E.M., & Motta, R.W. (1993). Cognitive distortions and irrational beliefs in post traumatic stress, anxiety, and depressive disorders. *Journal of Clinical Psychology*, *49*, 166–76.

Myers, J.K., Lindenthal, J.J., Pepper, M.P., & Ostrander, D.R. (1972). Life events and mental status: a Longitudinal Study. *Journal of Health and Social Behavior*, *13*, 398–406.

Myles, P., & Rushford, D. (Eds.) (2007). *A complete guide to primary care mental health*. London: Constable & Robinson.

Mynors-Wallis, L.M., Gath, D.H., Lloyd-Thomas, A.R., & Tomlinson, D. (1995). Randomised controlled trial comparing problem solving treatment with amitriptyline and placebo for major depression in primary care. *British Medical Journal*, *310*, 441–5.

Mynors-Wallis, L.M., & Lau, M.A. (2010). Problem solving as a low intensity intervention. In J. Bennett-Levy, D. Richards, P. Farrand, H. Christensen, K.M. Griffiths, D.J. Kavanagh, B. Klein, M. Lau, J. Proudfoot, L. Ritterband, J. White & C. Williams (Eds.) *Oxford guide to low intensity CBT interventions* (pp. 151–8). Oxford: Oxford University Press.

Nelson, R.O., & Hayes, S.C. (1981). Theoretical explanations for reactivity in self-monitoring. *Behavior Modification, 5,* 3–14.

Newman, M.G., Erickson, T., Przeworski, A., & Dzus, E. (2003). Self-help and minimal-contact therapies for anxiety disorders: Is human contact necessary for therapeutic efficacy? *Journal of Clinical Psychology, 59,* 251–74.

Newman, C.L., & Motta, R.W. (2007). The effects of aerobic exercise on childhood PTSD, anxiety, and depression. *International Journal of Emergency Mental Health, 9,* 133–58.

Newman, M.G., Szkodny, L.E., Llera, S.J., & Przeworski, A. (2011). A review of technology-assisted self-help and minimal contact therapies for anxiety and depression: is human contact necessary for therapeutic efficacy. *Clinical Psychology Review, 31,* 89–103.

NICE (2005). *Obsessive–compulsive disorder: core interventions in the treatment of obsessive–compulsive disorder and body dysmorphic disorder.* London: National Institute of Clinical Excellence.

NICE (2006). *Computerised cognitive behaviour therapy for depression and anxiety.* London: National Institute of Clinical Excellence.

NICE (2007). *Anxiety: management of anxiety (panic disorder, with or without agoraphobia, and generalised anxiety disorder) in adults in primary, secondary and community care.* London: National Institute of Clinical Excellence.

NICE (2008). *Cognitive behavioural therapy for the management of common mental health problems: commissioning guide.* National Institute of Clinical Excellence. Retrieved 8 April 2012 from www.nice.org.uk/media/878/F7/CBTCommissioningGuide.pdf

NICE (2009a). *Common mental health disorders: identification and pathways to care.* London: National Institute of Clinical Excellence.

NICE (2009b). *The treatment and management of depression in adults.* London: National Institute of Clinical Excellence.

NICE (2011a). *Commissioning stepped care for people with common mental health disorders.* London: National Institute of Clinical Excellence.

NICE (2011b). *Generalised anxiety disorder and panic disorder (with or without agoraphobia) in adults.* London: National Institute of Clinical Excellence.

Nolen-Hoeksema, S. (1991). Responses to depression and their effects on the duration of depressive episodes. *Journal of Abnormal Psychology, 100,* 569–82.

Norwood, M. (2002). *Eastern versus Western medicine.* Retrieved 10 April 2012 from: www.stresssolutions.info/vrs.htm

O'Carroll, P.W., Berman, A., Maris, R.W., & Moscicki, E.K. (1996). Beyond the Tower of Babel: a nomenclature for suicidology. *Suicide and Life-Threatening Behavior, 26,* 237–52.

Olson, R., & Winchester, J. (2008). Behavioral self-monitoring of safety and productivity in the workplace: a methodological primer and quantitative literature review. *Journal of Organizational Behavior Management, 28,* 9–75.

Öst, L.G., & Sterner, U. (1987). Applied tension. A specific behavioral method for treatment of blood phobia. *Behaviour Research and Therapy, 25,* 25–9.

Overholser, J.C., & Silverman, E.J. (1998). Cognitive-behavioral treatment of depression, part VIII. Developing and utilising the therapeutic relationship. *Journal of Contemporary Psychotherapy, 28,* 199–214.

Padesky, C.A. (1993). Socratic questioning: changing minds or guiding discovery? *European Congress of Behavioural & Cognitive Therapies,* 24-9-93, London.

Padesky, C., & Greenberger, D. (1995). *Clinicians' guide to mind over mood.* New York: Guilford Press.

Padesky, C.A., & Mooney, K.A. (1990). Clinical tip: presenting the cognitive model to clients. *International Cognitive Therapy Newsletter, 6,* 13–14.

Pandian, J.D., Jaison, A., Deepak, S.S., Kalra, G., Shamsher, S., Lincoln, D.J., & Abraham, G. (2005). Public awareness of warning symptoms, risk factors, and treatment of stroke in northwest India. *Stroke, 36,* 644–8.

Papworth, M.A. (2006). Issues and outcomes associated with adult mental health self-help materials: a 'second order' review or 'qualitative meta-review'. *Journal of Mental Health, 15,* 387–409.

Pardeck, J. (1998). *Using books in clinical social work practice.* New York: Haworth Press.

Pauls, D.L. (2008). The genetics of obsessive compulsive disorder: A review of the evidence. *American Journal of Medical Genetics Part C: Seminars in Medical Genetics, 148,* 133–9.

Perry, B.D. (1994). Neurobiological sequelae of childhood trauma: PTSD in children. In M.M. Murburg (Ed.) *Catecholamine Function in Posttraumatic Stress Disorder: Emerging Concepts* (pp. 173–89). Washington, DC: American Psychiatric Press.

Perry, G., Barkham, M., Brazier, J., Dent-Brown, K., Hardy, G., Kendrick, T., Rick, J., Chambers, E., Luisgnan, S., Mukuria, C., Saxon, D., Bower, P., & Lovell, K. (2011). *An evaluation of a new service model: improving access to psychological therapies demonstration sites 2006–2009.* NIHR Service Delivery and Organization Programme.

Petrella, R.J., & Lattanzio, C.N. (2002). Does counseling help patients get active? Systematic review of the literature. *Canadian Family Physician, 48,* 72–80.

Pfaltz, M.C., Grossman, P., Michael, T., Margraf, J., & Wilhelm, F.H. (2010). Physical activity and respiratory behavior in daily life of patients with panic disorder and healthy controls. *International Journal of Psychophysiology, 78,* 42–9.

Pickering, T.G. (2001). Mental stress as a causal factor in the development of hypertension and cardiovascular disease. *Current Hypertension Reports, 3,* 249–54.

Pierce, K.A., & Kirkpatrick, D.R. (1992). Do men lie on fear surveys? *Behaviour Research and Therapy, 30*, 415–18.

Pilkington, A., Graham, M.K., Cowie, H.A., Mulholland, R.E., Dempsey, S., Melrose, A.S., & Hutchinson, P.A. (2002). *Survey of use of occupational health support. Contract Research Report 445/2002.* Norwich: HSE Books.

Pirkis, J., & Burgess, P. (1998). Suicide and recency of health care contacts: a systematic review. *British Journal of Psychiatry, 173*, 462–74.

Plutchik, R. (1994). *The psychology and biology of emotion.* New York: HarperCollins.

Power, K.G., Sharp, D.M., Swanson, V., & Simpson, R.J. (2000). Therapist contact in cognitive behavior therapy for panic disorder and agoraphobia in primary care. *Clinical Psychology and Psychotherapy, 7*, 37–46.

Prados, J.M. (2011). Do beliefs about the utility of worry facilitate worry? *Journal of Anxiety Disorders, 25*, 217–23.

Prochaska, J.O., & Diclemente, C.C. (1983). States and processes of self-change in smoking: toward an integrative model of change. *Journal of Consulting and Clinical Psychiatry, 51*, 390–5.

Proctor, G. (2002). *The dynamics of power in counselling and psychotherapy.* Ross-on-Wye: PCCS.

Proudfoot, J., & Nicholas, J. (2010). Monitoring and Evaluation in low intensity CBT interventions. In J. Bennett-Levy, D. Richards, P. Farrand, H. Christensen, K.M. Griffiths, D.J. Kavanagh, B. Klein, M. Lau, J. Proudfoot, L. Ritterband, J. White, & C. Williams (Eds.) *Oxford guide to low intensity CBT interventions* (pp. 97–104). Oxford: Oxford University Press.

Read, J., & Baker, S. (1996). *Not just sticks and stones. A survey of the stigma, taboos and the discrimination experienced by people with mental health problems.* London: Mind Publications.

Reis, B.F., & Brown, L.G. (1999). Reducing psychotherapy dropouts: maximising perspective convergence in the psychotherapy dyad. *Psychotherapy: Theory, Research, Practice, Training, 36*, 123–36.

Richards, D.A. (2010a). Behavioural activation. In J. Bennett-Levy, D. Richards, P. Farrand, H. Christensen, K.M. Griffiths, D.J. Kavanagh, B. Klein, M. Lau, J. Proudfoot, L. Ritterband, J. White, & C. Williams (Eds.) *Oxford guide to low intensity CBT interventions* (pp. 141–50). Oxford: Oxford University Press.

Richards, D.A. (2010b). Supervising low intensity workers in high volume clinical environments. In J. Bennett-Levy, D. Richards, P. Farrand, H. Christensen, K.M. Griffiths, D.J. Kavanagh, B. Klein, M. Lau, J. Proudfoot, L. Ritterband, J. White, & C. Williams (Eds.) *Oxford guide to low intensity CBT interventions* (pp. 129–36). Oxford: Oxford University Press.

Richards, D.A. (2010c). Training low intensity workers. In J. Bennett-Levy, D. Richards, P. Farrand, H. Christensen, K.M. Griffiths, D.J. Kavanagh, B. Klein, M. Lau,

J. Proudfoot, L. Ritterband, J. White, & C. Williams (Eds.) *Oxford guide to low intensity CBT interventions* (pp. 419–26). Oxford: Oxford University Press.

Richards, D.A., & Farrand, P. (2010). Choosing self-help books wisely: sorting the wheat from the chaff. In J. Bennett-Levy, D. Richards, P. Farrand, H. Christensen, K.M. Griffiths, D.J. Kavanagh, B. Klein, M. Lau, J. Proudfoot, L. Ritterband, J. White, & C. Williams (Eds.) *Oxford guide to low intensity CBT interventions* (pp. 201–8). Oxford: Oxford University Press.

Richards, D.A., & Suckling, R. (2009). Improving Access to Psychological Therapies (IAPT): phase IV prospective cohort study. *British Journal of Clinical Psychology, 48*, 377–96.

Richards, D., & Whyte, M. (2009). *Reach out: national programme educator materials to support the delivery of training for practitioners delivering low intensity interventions* (2nd ed.). London: Rethink.

Richardson, R., & Richards, D. (2006). Self-help: towards the new generation. *Behavioural and Cognitive Psychotherapy, 34*, 13–23.

Richardson, R., Richards, D., & Barkham, M. (2010). Self-help books for people with depression: the role of the therapeutic relationship. *Behavioural and Cognitive Psychotherapy, 38*, 67–81.

Riemann, D., & Voderholzer, U. (2003). Primary insomnia: a risk factor to develop depression? *Journal of Affective Disorders, 76*, 255–9.

Rippere, V. (1977). Commonsense beliefs about depression and antidepressive behaviour. A study of social consensus. *Behaviour Research and Therapy, 17*, 465–73.

Rizq, R. (2012). The perversion of care: psychological therapies in a time of IAPT. *Psychodynamic Practice, 18*, 7–24.

Robb, C., Haley, W.E., Becker, M.A., Polivka, L.A., & Chwa, H.J. (2003). Attitudes towards mental health care in younger and older adults: similarities and differences. *Aging and Mental Health, 7*, 142–52.

Robinson, E., Titov, N., Andrews, G., McIntyre, K., Schwencke, G., & Solley, K. (2010). Internet treatment for generalized anxiety disorder: a randomized controlled trial comparing clinician vs. technician assistance. *PloS One, 5*, e10942.

Roth, M., & Argyle, N. (1988). Anxiety, panic and phobic disorders: an overview. *Journal of Psychiatric Research, 22* (suppl. 1), 35–54.

Roth, A., & Fonagy, P. (2005). *What works for whom? A critical review of psychotherapy research* (2nd ed.). New York: Guilford Press.

Roth, D.L., & Holmes, D.S. (1987). Influence of aerobic exercise training and relaxation training on physical and psychological health following stressful life events. *Psychosomatic Medicine, 49*, 355–65.

Roth, A.D., & Pilling, S. (2007). *The competences required to deliver effective cognitive and behavioural therapy for people with depression and with anxiety disorders.* London: Department of Health.

Roth, A.D., & Pilling, S. (2008). *A competence framework for the supervision of psychological therapies.* Available at: www.ucl.ac.uk/CORE

Roy-Byrne, P., Joesch, J., Wang, P., & Kessler, R. (2009). Low socioeconomic status and mental health care use among respondents with anxiety and depression in the NCS-R. *Psychiatric Services, 60* (9), 1190–7.

Rubia, K. (2009). The neurobiology of meditation and its clinical effectiveness in psychiatric disorders. *Biological Psychology, 82* (1), 1–11.

Sabourin, B.C., Stewart, S.H., Sherry, S.B., Watt, M.C., Wald, J., & Grant, V.V. (2008). Physical exercise as interoceptive exposure within a brief cognitive-behavioral treatment for anxiety-sensitive women. *Journal of Cognitive Psychotherapy, 22,* 303–20.

Sainsbury Centre for Mental Health (2007a). *Mental health at work: developing the business case. Policy paper 8.* London: Sainsbury Centre for Mental Health.

Sainsbury Centre for Mental Health (2007b). *Mental health and employment. Briefing No. 33.* London: Sainsbury Centre for Mental Health.

Salcado, B. (2007). *Progressive muscle relaxation* [CD].

Salkovskis, P.M. (1991). The importance of behaviour in the maintenance of anxiety and panic: a cognitive account. *Behavioural Psychotherapy, 19,* 6–19.

Salkovskis, P.M. (2007). Cognitive behavioural treatment for panic disorder. *Journal of Psychiatry, 6,* 193–7.

Salkovskis, P.M., Rimes, K.A., Warwick, H.M.C., & Clark, D.M. (2002). The Health Anxiety Inventory: development and validation of scales for the measurement of health anxiety and hypochondriasis. *Psychological Medicine, 32,* 843–53.

Sarbin, T.R. (1970). The culture of poverty, social identity, and cognitive outcomes. In V.L. Allen (Ed.) *Psychological factors in poverty* (pp. 29–46). Chicago, IL: Markham.

Scaife, J. (2009). *Supervision in clinical practice* (2nd ed.). London: Routledge.

Scheid, T.L. (2005). Stigma as a barrier to employment. Mental disability and the Americans with Disabilities Act. *International Journal of Law and Psychiatry, 28,* 670–90.

Schein, E.H. (2010). *Organizational culture and leadership* (4th ed.). San Francisco, CA: Jossey-Bass.

Schneck, J.M. (1944). Studies in bibliotherapy in a neuropsychiatric hospital. *American Journal of Physical Medicine, 8,* 316–23.

Schofield, W. (1964). *Psychotherapy: the purchase of friendship.* Englewood Cliffs, NJ: Prentice-Hall.

Schwartz, G.E., Davidson, R.J., & Goleman, D.J. (1978). Patterning of cognitive and somatic processes in the self-regulation of anxiety: Effects of meditation versus exercise. *Psychosomatic Medicine, 40* (4), 321–8.

Secker, J., Grove, B., & Seebohm, P. (2001). Challenging barriers to employment, training and education for mental health service users: the service user's perspective. *Journal of Mental Health, 10,* 395–404.

Segal, D.L., Coolidge, F.L., Mincic, M.S., & O'Riley, A. (2005). Beliefs about mental illness and willingness to seek help: a cross-sectional study. *Aging and Mental Health*, *9*, 363–7.

Segal, Z.V., Swallow, S.R., Bizzini, L., & Rouget, B.W. (1996). How we assess for short-term cognitive behaviour therapy. In C. Mace (Eds.) *The art and science of assessment in psychotherapy* (pp. 102–16). London: Routledge.

Seligman, M.E.P. (1973). Fall into helplessness. *Psychology Today*, *7*, 43–8.

Sessa, S.A. (2007). Meditation, breath work, and focus training for teachers and students – the five minutes a day that can really make a difference. *Journal of College Teaching and Learning*, *4*, 57–62.

Shapiro, D.A., Rees, A., Barkham, M., Hardy, G., Reynolds, S., & Startup, M. (1995). Effects of treatment duration and severity of depression on the maintenance of gains after cognitive-behavioral and psychodynamic-interpersonal psychotherapy. *Journal of Consulting and Clinical Psychology*, *63*, 378–87.

Singleton, N., Bumpstead, R., O'Brien, M., Lee, A., & Meltzer, H. (2001). *Psychiatric morbidity among adults living in private households 2000*. London: The Stationery Office.

Sloan, G. (1999). The therapeutic relationship in cognitive behaviour therapy. *British Journal of Community Nursing*, *4*, 58–65.

Smail, D. (1990). Design for a post-behaviourist clinical psychology. *Clinical Psychology Forum*, *28*, 2–10.

Smith, D.L. (1995). Psychodynamic therapy: the Freudian approach. In W. Dryden (Ed.) *Individual therapy: a handbook* (pp. 18–38). Buckingham: Open University Press.

Smits, J.A., Berry, A.C., Rosenfield, D., Powers, M.B., Behar, E., & Otto, M.W. (2008). Reducing anxiety sensitivity with exercise. *Depression and Anxiety*, *25*, 689–9.

Smoller, J.W., Gardner-Schuster, E., & Covino, J. (2008). The genetic basis of panic and phobic anxiety disorders. *American Journal of Medical Genetics Part C: Seminars in Medical Genetics*, *148*, 118–26.

Social Exclusion Unit (2001). *Preventing social exclusion*. London: Social Exclusion Unit.

Speckens, A.E.M., Hackmann, A., Ehlers, A., & Cuthbert, B. (2007). Intrusive images and memories of earlier adverse events in patients with obsessive compulsive disorder. *Journal of Behavior Therapy and Experimental Psychiatry*, *38*, 411–22.

Spitzer, R.L., Kroenke, K., & Williams, J.B. (1999). Validation and utility of a self-report version of PRIME-MD: the PHQ primary care study. *Journal of the American Medical Association*, *282*, 1737–44.

Spitzer, R.L., Kroenke, K., Williams, J.B., & Löwe, B. (2006). A brief measure for assessing generalized anxiety disorder: the GAD-7. *Archives of Internal Medicine*, *166*, 1092–7.

Staner, L. (2010). Comorbidity of insomnia and depression. *Sleep Medicine Reviews*, *14*, 35–46.

Stansfeld, S.A., Clark, C., Rodgers, B., Caldwell, T., & Power, C. (2008). Childhood and adulthood socio-economic position and midlife depressive and anxiety disorders, *British Journal of Psychiatry, 192,* 152–3.

Stevens, P. (2010). What is meditation? *Journal of Yoga: Ontogenetic and Therapeutic Investigation, 2,* 16.

Stiles, W.B., Agnew-Davis, R., Hardy, G., Barkham, M., & Shapiro, D. (1998). Relations of alliance with psychotherapy outcome: findings in the second Sheffield Psychotherapy Project. *Journal of Consulting and Clinical Psychology, 66,* 791–802.

Stott, R., Mansell, W., Salkovskis, P., Lavender, A., & Cartwright-Hatton, S. (2010). *Oxford guide to metaphors in CBT.* Oxford: Oxford University Press.

Stoyanova, M., & Hope, D. (2012). Gender, gender roles, and anxiety: Perceived confirmability of self report, behavioral avoidance, and physiological reactivity. *Journal of Anxiety Disorders, 26,* 206–14.

Ströhle, A. (2009). Physical activity, exercise, depression and anxiety disorders. *Journal of Neural Transmission, 116,* 777–84.

Stuart, H. (2006). Mental illness and employment discrimination. *Current Opinion in Psychiatry, 19,* 522–6.

Summerfield, D. (2001). The invention of post-traumatic stress disorder and the social usefulness of a psychiatric category. *British Medical Journal, 322,* 95–8.

Tausig, M., & Fenwick, R. (2012). *Work and mental health in context.* New York: Springer.

Tavabie, J. (2007). *How can a mental health questionnaire influence GPs in managing depression?* Retrieved 1 April 12 from http://cms.rcgp.org.uk/conference/pdf/SP2.5%20Jackie%20Tavabie.pdf

Taylor, F., & Bryant, R.A. (2007). The tendency to suppress, inhibiting thoughts, and dream rebound. *Behaviour Research and Therapy, 45,* 163–8.

Tews, R.M. (1970). Progress in bibliotherapy. In M.J. Voight (Ed.) *Advances in librarianship* (vol. 1, pp. 57–62). New York: Academic Press.

Thomas, M., Bruton, A., Moffatt, M., & Cleland, J. (2011). Asthma and psychological dysfunction. *Primary Care Respiratory Journal, 20,* 250–6.

Thwaites, R., & Bennett-Levy, J. (2007). Conceptualising empathy in cognitive behaviour therapy: making the implicit explicit. *Behavioural and Cognitive Psychotherapy, 35,* 591–612.

Thwaites, R., Bennett-Levy, J., Davis, M., & Chaddock, A.V. (in press). Using self-practice and self-reflection to develop as a therapist (and as an individual …). In A. Whittington & N. Grey (Eds.) *The cognitive behavioural therapist: from theory to clinical practice.* Chichester: John Wiley & Sons.

Tolin, D., Diefenbach, G., & Gilliam, C. (2011). Stepped care versus standard cognitive-behavioral therapy for obsessive–compulsive disorder: a preliminary study of efficacy and costs. *Depression and Anxiety, 28,* 314–23.

Turpin, G. (Ed.) (2010). *Good practice guidance on the use of self-help materials within IAPT services*. London: IAPT.

Turpin, G., & Wheeler, S. (2008). *Improving access to psychological therapies (IAPT), supervision guidance, December, 2008*. London: Department of Health/IAPT Programme.

Tylor, E.B. (1871). *Primitive culture*. New York: Harper.

Van Daele, T., Hermans, D., Van Audenhove, C., & Van den Bergh, O. (2011). Stress reduction through psychoeducation: a meta-analytic review. *Health Education & Behavior, 10*, 1–12.

Van Emden, J., & Becker, L. (2004). *Presentation skills for students*. Basingstoke: Palgrave Macmillan.

Verhaak, P.F.M. (1995). Determinants of the help seeking process. Goldberg and Huxley's first level and first filter. *Psychological Medicine, 25*, 95–104.

Vincent, N., & Holmqvist, M. (2010). Low intensity CBT interventions for chronic insomnia. In J. Bennett-Levy, D. Richards, P. Farrand, H. Christensen, K.M. Griffiths, D.J. Kavanagh, B. Klein, M. Lau, J. Proudfoot, L. Ritterband, J. White, & C. Williams (Eds.) *Oxford guide to low intensity CBT interventions* (pp. 187–96). Oxford: Oxford University Press.

Waddell, G., & Burton, A.K. (2006). *Is work good for your health and well-being?* Norwich: The Stationery Office.

Walsh, R., & Shapiro, S.L. (2006). The meeting of meditative disciplines and western psychology: a mutually enriching dialogue. *American Psychologist, 61*, 227–39.

Waraich, P., Goldner, E.M., Somers, J.M., & Hsu, L. (2004). Prevalence and incidence studies of mood disorders: a systematic review of the literature. *Canadian Journal of Psychiatry, 49*, 124–38.

Warner, C.M., Reigada, L.C., Fisher, P.H., Saborsky, A.L., & Benkov, K.J. (2009). CBT for anxiety and associated somatic complaints in pediatric medical settings: an open pilot study. *Journal of Clinical Psychology in Medical Settings, 16*, 169–77.

Watkins, P.C., Mathews, A., Williamson, D.A., & Fuller, R.D. (1992). Mood-congruent memory in depression: emotional priming or elaboration? *Journal of Abnormal Psychology, 101*, 581–6.

Watts, S.E., & Weems, C.F. (2006). Associations among selective attention, memory bias, cognitive errors and symptoms of anxiety in youth. *Journal of Abnormal Child Psychology, 34*, 838–49.

Webster, C.D., Douglas, D.S., Eaves, D., & Hart, S.D. (1997). Assessing risk of violence to others. In C.D. Webster & M.A. Jackson (Eds.) *Impulsivity: theory, assessment and treatment* (pp. 251–77). New York: Guilford Press.

Weerasekera, P. (1996). *Multi-perspective case formulation: A step towards treatment integration*. Malabar, FL: Krieger.

Weimerskirsh, P. (1965). Benjamin Rush and John Milton Galt II. Pioneers of bibliotherapy in America. *Bulletin of the Medical Library Association, 53*, 510–13.

Wells, A. (1997). *Cognitive therapy of anxiety disorders: a practice manual and conceptual guide*. London: Wiley-Blackwell.

Wenzel, A., Sharp, I.R., Brown, G.K., Greenberg, R.L., & Beck, A.T. (2006). Dysfunctional beliefs in panic disorder: The Panic Belief Inventory. *Behaviour Research and Therapy, 44*, 819–33.

Westbrook, D., Kennerley, H., & Kirk, J. (2007). *An introduction to cognitive behaviour therapy: skills and applications*. London: Sage.

Westbrook, D., Kennerley, H., & Kirk, J. (2011). *An introduction to cognitive behavioural therapy: skills and applications* (2nd ed.). Los Angeles, CA: Sage.

White, J. (2000). *Treating anxiety and stress: a group psychoeducational approach using brief CBT*. Chichester: John Wiley & Sons.

White, J. (2010). Large group didactic CBT classes for common mental health problems. In J. Bennett-Levy, D. Richards, P. Farrand, H. Christensen, K.M. Griffiths, D.J. Kavanagh, B. Klein, M. Lau, J. Proudfoot, L. Ritterband, J. White, & C. Williams (Eds.) *Oxford guide to low intensity CBT interventions* (pp. 313–22). Oxford: Oxford University Press.

White, J., & Richards, D. (n.d.). *STEPS Services* [leaflet].

White, J., Joice, A., Petrie, S., Johnston, S., Gilroy, D., Hutton, P., & Hynes, N. (2008). STEPS: going beyond the tip of the iceberg. A multi-level, multipurpose approach to common mental health problems. *Journal of Public Mental Health, 7*, 42–50.

White, J., Keenan, M., & Brooks, N. (1992). Stress control: a controlled comparative investigation of large group therapy for generalized anxiety disorder. *Behavioural Psychotherapy, 20*, 97–114.

WHO (1994). *Declaration on occupational health for all*. Geneva: World Health Organization.

WHO (2000) Cross-national comparisons of the prevalences and correlates of mental disorders. WHO International Consortium in Psychiatric Epidemiology. *Bulletin of the World Health Organization, 78*, 413–26.

WHO (2008a). *ICD-10: international statistical classification of diseases and related health problems* (10th rev. ed.). New York: World Health Organization.

WHO (2008b). *The global burden of disease 2004 update*. Geneva: World Health Organization.

Wilkin, D., Hallam, L., & Doggett, M. (1992). *Measures of need and outcome for primary health care*. Oxford: Oxford Medical Publications.

Wilkinson, A., Meares, K., & Freeston, M. (2011). *CBT for worry and generalised anxiety disorder*. London: Sage.

Wilkinson, R., & Marmot, M. (2003). *Social determinants of health: the solid facts* (2nd ed.). Copenhagen: World Health Organization.

Wilkinson, A., Meares, K., & Freeston, M.H. (2011). *CBT for worry and generalised anxiety disorder*. London: Sage.

Williams, C. (2003). *Overcoming anxiety: a five areas approach.* London: Hodder Arnold.

Williams, C. (2009). *Overcoming depression and low mood: a five areas approach* (3rd ed.). London: Hodder Arnold.

Williams, C. (2010). *Overcoming anxiety, stress and panic: a five areas approach* (2nd ed.). London: Hodder Arnold.

Williams, C., & Chellingsworth, M. (2010). *CBT. A clinicians' guide to using the five areas approach.* London: Hodder Arnold.

Williams, C., & Garland, A. (2002). A cognitive-behavioural therapy assessment model for use in everyday clinical practice. *Advances in Psychiatric Treatment, 8,* 172–9.

Williams, C., & Morrison, J. (2010). A new language for CBT: new ways of working require new thinking, as well as new words. In J. Bennett-Levy, D. Richards, P. Farrand, H. Christensen, K.M. Griffiths, D.J. Kavanagh, B. Klein, M. Lau, J. Proudfoot, L. Ritterband, J. White, & C. Williams (Eds.) *Oxford guide to low intensity CBT interventions* (pp. 69–86). Oxford: Oxford University Press.

Wink, P., & Scott, J. (2005). Does religiousness buffer against the fear of death and dying in late adulthood? Findings from a longitudinal study. *Journal of Gerontology: Psychological Sciences, 60,* 207–14.

Wolff, E., Gaudlitz, K., von Lindenberger, B.L., Plag, J., Heinz, A., & Strohle, A. (2011). Exercise and physical activity in mental disorders. *European Archives of Psychiatry and Clinical Neuroscience, 261* (Suppl. 2), 186–91.

Wollburg, E., Roth, W.T., & Kim, S. (2011). Effects of breathing training on voluntary hypo- and hyperventilation in patients with panic disorder and episodic anxiety. *Applied Psychophysiology and Biofeedback, 36,* 81–91.

Wolpe, J. (1969). *The practice of behavioural therapy.* New York: Pergamon Press.

Wright, B., Williams, C., & Garland, A. (2002). Using the five areas cognitive-behavioural model with psychiatric patients. *Advances in Psychiatric Treatment, 8,* 307–15.

Wright, S.L., & Persad, C. (2007). Distinguishing between depression and dementia in older persons: neuropsychological and neuropathological correlates. *Journal of Geriatric Psychiatry and Neurology, 20,* 189–98.

Yalom, I.D. (1995). *The theory and practice of group psychotherapy* (4th ed.). New York: Basic Books.

Yerkes, R.M., & Dodson, J.D. (1908). The relation of strength of stimulus to rapidity of habit-formation. *Journal of Comparative Neurology and Psychology, 18,* 459–82.

Yonkers, K.A., Bruce, S.E., Dyck, I.R., & Keller, M.B. (2003). Chronicity, relapse, and illness-course of panic disorder, social phobia, and generalized anxiety disorder: findings in men and women from 8 years of follow-up. *Depression and Anxiety, 17,* 173–9.

Yonkers, K.A., Dyck, I.R., & Keller, M.B. (2001). An 8-year longitudinal comparison of clinical course and characteristics of social phobia among men and women. *Psychiatric Services, 52,* 637–43.

Yonkers, K.A., Dyck, I.R., Warshaw, M., & Keller, M.B. (2000). Factors predicting the clinical course of generalised anxiety disorders. *British Journal of Psychiatry, 176,* 544–50.

Yonkers, K.A., Zlotnick, C., Allsworth, J., Warshaw, M., Shea, T., & Keller, M.B. (1998). Is the course of panic disorder the same in women and men? *American Journal of Psychiatry, 155,* 596–602.

Young, J.D., & Taylor, E. (1998). Meditation as a voluntary hypometabolic state of biological activation. *News in Physiological Sciences, 13,* 149–53.

Young, J.E. (1999). *Schema therapy for personality disorders: a schema-focussed approach.* Sarasota, FL: Professional Resource Press.

Younger, A., Schneider, B., & Guirguis-Younger, M. (2008). How children describe their shy/withdrawn peers. *Infant & Child Development, 17,* 447–56.

Index